LYING

IN STATE

ALSO BY ERIC ALTERMAN

LYING

IN STATE

WHY PRESIDENTS LIE—
AND WHY TRUMP IS WORSE

ERIC ALTERMAN

BASIC BOOKS
New York

Basic Books
Hachette Book Group
1290 Avenue of the Americas, New York, NY 10104
www.basicbooks.com

Printed in the United States of America

First Edition: August 2020

Published by Basic Books, an imprint of Perseus Books, LLC, a subsidiary of Hachette Book Group, Inc. The Basic Books name and logo is a trademark of the Hachette Book Group.

The Hachette Speakers Bureau provides a wide range of authors for speaking events. To find out more, go to www.hachettespeakersbureau.com or call (866) 376-6591.

The publisher is not responsible for websites (or their content) that are not owned by the publisher.

Library of Congress Cataloging-in-Publication Data
Names: Alterman, Eric, author.
Title: Lying in state: why presidents lie—and why Trump is worse / Eric Alterman.
Other titles: Why presidents lie—and why Trump is worse
Description: First edition. | New York, NY: Basic Books, 2020. | Includes bibliographical
    references and index.
Identifiers: LCCN 2020008737 | ISBN 9781541616820 (hardcover) |
    ISBN 9781541616813 (ebook)
Subjects: LCSH: Presidents—United States—History. | Truthfulness and falsehood—
    Political aspects—United States—History. | United States—Politics and
    government. | Political ethics—United States.
Classification: LCC E176.1 .A628 2020 | DDC 177/.30973—dc23
LC record available at https://lccn.loc.gov/2020008737

ISBNs: 978-1-5416-1682-0 (hardcover), 978-1-5416-1681-3 (e-book)

LSC-C

10 9 8 7 6 5 4 3 2 1

To Laura Hercher,
my "shelter from the storm,"
with love, gratitude and admiration.
(And most of all, alas...amazement.)

That's the thing about lies, right? Individually, they don't amount to much. But you never know how many others you'll need to tell to protect that first one. And damned if they don't add up. Over time they all get tangled up, until one day you realize it isn't even the lies themselves that matter, it's that somehow lying has become your default mode and the person you lie to most is yourself.

—RICHARD RUSSO, *Chances Are* (2019)

CONTENTS

Contents

A NOTE ON DEFINITIONS

My understanding of the meaning of the word "lie" begins with the Augustinian argument that "a lie consists in speaking a falsehood with the intention of deceiving."[1] But because a president is more than just an individual, our definition must be considerably more expansive. A presidential lie takes place when the president or someone with the authority to speak for the president seeks to purposely mislead the country about a matter of political significance. The president can remain silent while his subordinates lie for him. He can censor the truth or impede the means to discover it. In my judgment, the only significant criterion is whether the deception itself, however operationally undertaken, is purposeful. If it was accidental or based on ignorance or a misunderstanding, it can be corrected and therefore should be.

One reason journalists often offer for eschewing the word "lie" when writing or talking about presidential lies is their inability to discern the speaker's intent. In this book, however, I am less interested in intent than responsibility. If it was the president's professional responsibility to know the truth about something and he did not bother to learn it, or he and his subordinates purposely avoided sharing information in order to establish "plausible deniability," I still call it a lie.

In the pages that follow, I reject the excuses often offered for the kinds of deceptions I've just described, such as that the president was "disengaged," "confused," or "distracted"; that "God told him"; or that "he's just an unbelievable narcissist." I also consider censorship, when it is purposely deployed to misinform, to count as a lie. This is not to condemn censorship per se. Societies cannot protect themselves without it. The Constitution, as various Supreme Court justices have observed (albeit for competing arguments), is "not a suicide pact."[2] But the power to prevent speech is awfully easy to abuse for personal and political gain, and when this happens, it functions as a lie. Secrecy is also an a priori necessity of governance, especially in wartime. But it, too, can easily bleed into dishonesty when abused, and abuse tends to its natural path when presidents are given the power to determine what citizens should and should not know. Under certain circumstances, therefore, as we shall see, it is possible for a president or his representative to lie by silencing others, and by saying nothing at all.

Introduction

HOW COULD TRUMP HAPPEN?

I hardly need to make the argument that Donald Trump is a liar. Neither is it news that previous presidents have also lied quite a bit. At the same time, the depth and breadth of Trump's dishonesty is something decidedly new. As the MSNBC host Chris Hayes wrote in a *New York Times* book review just eighteen months after Trump's inauguration: "The president is a liar. He lies about matters of the utmost consequence (nuclear diplomacy) and about the most trivial (his golf game). He lies about things you can see with your own eyes. He lies about things he said just moments ago. He lies the way a woodpecker attacks a tree: compulsively, insistently, instinctively. He lies until your temples throb. He lies until you want to submerge your head in a bucket of ice and pray for release."[1]

President Trump's ability to lie without concern for credibility is both shocking and gruesomely impressive. In one three-day period in

April 2019, Trump managed to make 171 "false or misleading claims," according to the *Washington Post* fact-checking team. During a telephone interview with the Fox News talk-show host Sean Hannity, he uttered 45 falsehoods in 45 minutes.[2] It is fair to call someone who lies that frequently and shamelessly "pathological." So yes, America has a pathological liar for its president, and literally nothing he says can be taken at face value. How did such a thing become possible? How could the world's most powerful nation, and its oldest democratic republic, allow itself to be led by such a person? And what are the implications of allowing this liar to not only set the policies of the United States but also dominate its political culture to a degree that is no less unprecedented than his dishonesty?

For so common a human occurrence, lying can be quite complicated, both morally and practically. We teach our children that lying is always wrong, but we don't really mean it. As a young child in Hebrew school, I was taught to admire Jacob for tricking his father, Isaac, into giving the birthright blessing to him rather than its rightful recipient, his older brother, Esau.[3] My classmates and I were also taught to admire the Egyptian midwives' lie to Pharaoh's men about having murdered the Israelites' firstborn sons, as commanded, including the little fellow who grew up to be Moses.[4]

While few of us would willingly call ourselves "liars," the person who does not lie with some frequency is rare indeed. Sociologists Deborah A. Kashy and Bella M. DePaulo observed that lies are "a fact of social life rather than an extraordinary or unusual event. People tell lies to accomplish the most basic social interaction goals, such as influencing others, managing impressions, and providing reassurance and support."[5]

In certain contexts and cultures, lying is both appreciated and admired. According to a study by another sociologist, J. A. Barnes, "the San Blas Kuna, of northeastern Panama, are said to 'enjoy deceiving each other.'" The Kalapalo, an indigenous people of central Brazil, also allegedly "welcome being tricked," said Barnes. In contemporary culture, however, lies are most often tolerated or ignored, especially when they are not believed anyway. People expect to be told lies when dealing with certain types of businesses, such as, to name just three, real estate, car sales, and public relations. In Hollywood, it is considered foolish to assume anyone is telling the truth without a signed contract, and it is sometimes even considered an insult. The protagonist of Ward Just's 2002 novel *The Weather in Berlin*, a Hollywood-based film director, describes this sort of dishonesty as "a sacrament…the bread and wine of industry communions." Lies in these businesses are often not even considered dishonest. Indeed, the nineteenth-century British statesman Sir Henry Taylor maintained that a "falsehood ceases to be a falsehood when it is understood on all sides that the truth is not expected to be spoken." The business of politics is no different. Hannah Arendt sardonically noted that "no one has ever doubted that truth and politics are on rather bad terms with each other, and no one, as far as I know, has ever counted truthfulness among the political virtues." To the contrary, she went on, "lies have always been regarded as necessary and justifiable tools not only of the politician's or the demagogue's but also of the statesman's trade."[6]

Clearly, politics is not a profession that rewards, much less fetishizes, honesty. Results are what matter. In failing to hold presidents accountable for their lies, the American press has reflected a larger ambivalence about doing so among the American people. Historically, the public has tended to accept presidential lies as the cost of doing business, although some lies are contested and a few are considered shocking and unacceptable. It is no easy task to discern in advance, however, which lies will inspire which reaction, or even to define what constitutes a presidential lie and what does not.

Americans have tended to be willing to indulge presidential lies so long as they get the job done. In 2017, C-Span surveyed ninety-one historians in order to rank presidents for their effectiveness, a measure that included "moral authority." What was striking about the result was that presidents' reputations for lying or truth-telling did not appear to matter. Compulsive liars Ronald Reagan and Lyndon Johnson both made it into the top ten. Relative truth-tellers Barack Obama and Jimmy Carter came in twelfth and twenty-sixth, respectively, the latter just barely above the presidency's most egregious (pre-Trump) liar, Richard Nixon, who was twenty-eighth on the list. In presidential rankings based on public polling, the famous liars do even better, albeit largely as a result of ongoing political arguments and loyalties rather than careful historical consideration and comparisons. In a 2011 Gallup poll, for instance, Reagan was number one and Bill Clinton was number three, with Abraham Lincoln squeaking into second place.[7]

These results are regrettable. A purposeful presidential falsehood on a matter of consequence necessarily sets off a chain reaction that can easily ricochet out of control.[8] Presidential lies—even when spoken by a subordinate—have the power to create their own reality, a fact that often complicates the original problem the lie was intended to address. When this happens, it can become impossible to respond effectively. Rather than admit to the lie and endure the humiliation of being caught in it, presidents usually double, triple, and quadruple down on the lie, inevitably making the problem worse. Lies must be piled atop other lies ad infinitum until the entire edifice collapses beneath the weight of the many falsehoods.

Under such circumstances, democracy cannot properly function. As Arendt observed, "if everybody always lies to you, the consequence is not that you believe the lies, but rather that nobody believes anything any longer....And a people that no longer can believe anything cannot make up its mind. It is deprived not only of its capacity to act but also of its capacity to think and to judge. And with such a people you can then do what you please."[9] Arendt said this in the wake of Nixon's Watergate scandal, but her warning has never felt more prophetic—and more ominous—than under the presidency of Donald J. Trump.

And yet, we cannot simply offer a blanket condemnation of presidential lying, as it is not always wrong. We can celebrate the fact that Franklin Roosevelt possessed the vision to ready the nation for war against Hitler and Hirohito even if he had to lie repeatedly to do it—that is, publicly proclaiming a commitment to keeping America out of foreign wars, while secretly taking steps to prepare for the one he believed to be inevitable. America's readiness to fight the Nazis and the Japanese imperialists when the time came no doubt saved millions of lives and likely prevented Europe from falling to the fascists. Yet Lyndon Johnson's lies during the lead-up to America's direct involvement in the Vietnam War, while almost perfectly analogous to those FDR told a generation earlier, were undertaken in the service of an unnecessary and ultimately failed war. As the senator J. William Fulbright of Arkansas observed during that catastrophe, "FDR's deviousness in a good cause made it easier for LBJ to practice the same kind of deviousness in a bad cause."[10] Presidential lying remains a conundrum we have yet to solve.

Presidents who do not lie to the nation have been the exception, not the rule. But early in American history, presidents lied in most cases without anything like the consequences that have become possible in modern times. The United States was not a terribly powerful nation in its infancy. The federal government was not even all that powerful within the United States. And the presidency held less power within the federal government than it does today. Until the mid-nineteenth century, the decisions of a US president played precious little visible role in the daily lives of most citizens.

Despite its constant expansion across North America, until the twentieth century the United States was not terribly influential beyond its shores. One history of the period quotes a nineteenth-century secretary of state observing, "There are just two rules at the State Department: one, that no business is ever done out of business hours; and the other is, that no business is ever done *in* business hours."[11] Yet the early presidents (and their secretaries of state) set precedents that lay the foundation for future presidential lies. And these lies would assume much greater significance once the presidency grew more powerful within the government, the government grew more powerful within the nation, and the nation grew more powerful in the world.

In 1896 the great American historian Frederick Jackson Turner looked back across three centuries and pronounced the drive for expansion to be the "dominant fact" of the nation's life thus far. But this drive for expansion differed from Europe's, because Americans did not see themselves as colonialists. Early Americans "truly believed," as the historian Walter Nugent observed, "that their providential mission and destiny permitted, even demanded," their commitment to the cause of constant expansion. They felt themselves "exempted from normal rules against theft or invasion of other people's territory," Nugent wrote, and believed that "their own racial superiority exempted them from regarding others as equals." They were bolstered in this belief by their all-but-universal commitment to an ideology of white supremacy, one that expressed itself in the institution of slavery and the near eradication of the Native American population. Soon afterward, these beliefs inspired the conquest of foreign lands in which nonwhite peoples lived and worked.[12]

As a consequence, presidential lying during this time was largely a matter of advancing a narrative designed to justify a series of brutal policies in the service of a strict racial hierarchy—while American citizens continued to flatter themselves that they lived in a land where "all men are created equal."[13] This contradiction haunted the United States as it rose to become the world's wealthiest nation and then its most powerful militarily.

Following the defeat of Nazi Germany and imperial Japan in 1945, Americans came to see their country, in President Harry Truman's words, as "the greatest Republic the world has ever seen, the greatest country that the sun ever shone on."[14] At the same time, as the Cold War dawned, the US government adopted an almost limitless definition of its "national security" needs. Its official strategy was laid out in a top-secret document titled "United States Objectives and Programs for National Security," better known as NSC 68, which argued that "the cold war is in fact a real war in which the survival of the free world is at stake."[15] The combination of the perceived existential challenge posed by the Soviets and the precarious nature of the nuclear standoff meant that Cold War US presidents shouldered greater responsibilities and were accorded greater powers than any previous leaders in history. In this context of saving "the free world" from Soviet domination or preventing the world's destruction by nuclear weapons, the telling of a few presidential lies hardly registered as objectionable.

This awesome responsibility would prove too great for several of the presidents charged with carrying it out. Lyndon Johnson's lies, combined with his mental and emotional instability late in his presidency, led to the catastrophe in Vietnam and could easily have spun even further out of control. Richard Nixon's incessant dishonesty, together with his noxious combination of ambition, racism, and criminality, produced an even more volatile situation, which, thanks to bipartisan efforts in Congress, was brought swiftly to an end without a constitutional crisis. Nevertheless, the policies of these presidents caused over fifty-seven thousand senseless American battle deaths and likely at least three million more deaths among the soldiers and civilians of Vietnam and Cambodia.[16] Jimmy Carter seemed unable to manage America's empire satisfactorily, and his presidency was derailed by it. America on his watch endured humiliations by Iranian militants and Soviet generals because of his refusal to risk provoking widespread war. Ronald Reagan, in the years following Carter, revived and expanded the nation's commitment to aggressively defending and expanding its empire, but he would find himself telling lie after lie in pursuit of illegal wars based on ideological fixations; when explaining his actions, frequently he behaved as if detached from reality. The wars he pursued undermined his own authority as president and played a significant role in the defeat of his successor, George H. W. Bush, in seeking a second term.[17]

We need not minimize the often horrific consequences of past presidential lies in order to observe that they pale in comparison to the depth and breadth of the lies told by Donald Trump. The wars, coups, and assassinations that these presidents lied about resulted in the deaths of millions of innocent people and the displacement of many millions more. Trillions of dollars were wasted in the process, and the good name of the United States of America suffered around the world. These presidents surely lied—but they did not lie about everything. The office of the presidency continued to function with the understanding that although the president would have to lie on occasion for reasons of national security, the office and its occupant should remain more or less tethered to reality. Those days ended on January 20, 2017, the day of Donald Trump's inauguration.

The role of the media has always been crucial to the phenomenon of presidential lying. In theory, the responsibility of the press to hold the government accountable is enshrined in the First Amendment of the Constitution. It's the press's job to tell the truth about what the government is doing, what it means, and why it matters. When a president considers telling a lie—again, at least theoretically—he is forced to consider the likelihood that his mendacity may be exposed to the public by some conscientious journalistic institution working to ferret out the truth in the public interest. These hard-earned truths empower citizens to make informed judgments about their leaders despite any dishonesty or demagoguery those leaders may exhibit. In practice, however, members of the press have historically proven themselves to be decidedly ambivalent about holding presidents to a standard of basic truthfulness. In the century following the American Revolution, journalism was primarily a partisan endeavor, with news-sheets and journals tied explicitly to one of the major political parties or local bosses. News articles at the time, like life itself, were largely nasty and brutish (though not always short). When it comes to scurrilous accusations and paranoid fantasies, the likes of Fox News's Sean Hannity, Laura Ingraham, and Tucker Carlson have nothing on George Washington's scourge, Benjamin Franklin Bache, publisher of the *Philadelphia Aurora*, much less the pamphleteer James Thomson Callender, whose work would malign Alexander Hamilton, Thomas Jefferson, and John Adams, among others.

When it comes to lying, modern political reporters have found it challenging to call presidents out. The reasons are both multifaceted and self-reinforcing. On matters of "national security"—a term that in most cases denotes the expansion or maintenance of the American empire—journalists have repeatedly proven themselves eager to give presidents and their advisers a wide berth, lest they appear unpatriotic, or somehow find themselves responsible for undermining the nation's safety. Another cause for reticence has been the expectation that journalists show respect for the office of the presidency, which they—publicly at least—have been more than happy to fulfill. A third barrier arises from the ideology of journalistic objectivity, which dictates that there are always two sides to any given issue, and that it is wrong to take one over the other, despite the fact that one (or both) might be based on a lie. Even at its most elite level, a majority of political news reporters are satisfied to rely on the typical "he said, she said" formula. Conflict, after all, is what makes a good story. Truth or lies—well, that's a matter for the fact-checkers. This is why, as the pundit Michael Kinsley noted during the second Bush administration, "if some politician declares that two plus two is five, reporters might note that this position is not without controversy. Indeed there are critics, including politicians of the opposite party, who contend that two plus two may actually be four." This tendency can be relatively innocuous so long as politicians hew close enough to the truth. The problem, as the *Washington Post*'s legendary editor Ben Bradlee once explained, is that "even the very best newspapers have never learned how to handle public figures who lie with a straight face."[18]

Prior to Donald Trump's 2016 campaign, politicians' lies were treated in the mainstream media as an everyday occurrence that could

be countered. And they were countered not by calling them "lies"—
which was considered nonobjective, and evidence of liberal bias, since
it was most often Republicans doing the lying—but by quoting "both
sides." In recent decades, this reluctance on the part of mainstream
journalists to make a judgment about falsehoods came to be understood by right-wing Republican politicians as a license to lie. These
lies were repeated and amplified by an enormous and growing web of
conservative media outlets that arose during these same decades. These
institutions operated on the radio, in print, on cable television, and
eventually across almost all social media. Conservative billionaires,
media entrepreneurs, and shamelessly amoral self-promoters joined
together to create an entire media ecosystem in which false assertions
and deliberately distorted reporting held sway. The result is that today lies have been built atop other lies, and these have come to define
reality—or what the columnist and political philosopher Walter Lippmann once termed "the pictures in our heads"—for tens of millions of
Americans, despite the fact that they bear virtually no relation to "the
world outside," or, in other words, actual reality.[19]

Given the influence that this right-wing media ecosystem came to
enjoy among Republican voters, its members were able to demand
the fealty of almost every Republican politician seeking national office. In order to survive in this hothouse of extremist ideology combined with casual, constant dishonesty, the historian Garry Wills
observed, Republicans ended up renouncing virtually the entire Enlightenment, and with it, "reason, facts, science, open-mindedness,
tolerance, secularity, [and] modernity." It was a long time coming,
but by 2011, veteran ex-Republican congressional staffer Mike Lofgren admitted that his former political home was looking "less and
less like a traditional political party in a representative democracy
and becoming more like an apocalyptic cult." Not long after the publication of Lofgren's article containing this cri de coeur, on Sunday,
April 29, 2012, the respected nonpartisan political analysts Thomas
Mann of the centrist Brookings Institution and Norman Ornstein

of the conservative American Enterprise Institute grew so frustrated with Republican recalcitrance that they joined together to author a missive in the *Washington Post* titled "Let's Just Say It: The Republicans Are the Problem." The piece was remarkable owing to the fact that Mann and Ornstein represented the heart of what had been the bipartisan political establishment, offering what had been treated as unbiased political analysis to journalists for over forty years. Now they were warning of "an insurgent outlier in American politics"—a political party that had grown "ideologically extreme; scornful of compromise; unmoved by conventional understanding of facts, evidence and science; and dismissive of the legitimacy of its political opposition." They told journalists that the ideology of objectivity notwithstanding, "a balanced treatment of an unbalanced phenomenon distorts reality."[20] The op-ed proved to be among the most widely read, cited, and retweeted of any published in the paper since the earliest days of the Internet. Many journalists congratulated its authors in private for saying what they could not say publicly.

Yet nothing changed. Editors and producers, Mann explained, were "concerned about their professional standing and vulnerability to charges of partisan bias."[21] So, like the man in the joke whose doctor tells him to give up drinking and instead gives up doctors, reporters simply stopped speaking to Mann and Ornstein—at least without hearing from "both sides." It was the media's willingness to embrace the culture of dishonesty that helped to open a door for a president openly contemptuous of the media—and of the truth itself. How this happened is central to the story of presidential lying and the threat it has come to pose to our democracy and political culture.

The Frankfurt School philosopher Jürgen Habermas offered a distinction between "misinformation" and "disinformation": the former applies to mistaken statements, while the latter denotes purposeful deception. This is a book about both. A president does not have to mean to lie in order to lie. He just needs to stick to the falsehood once he learns the truth. To Habermas's two categories, moreover, we must add two more. The first is the "bald-faced lie." Philosophers, including Thomas Carson, author of *Lying and Deception: Theory and Practice*, define these as lies that are understood by their audience to be lies and hence do not function as lies typically do, with an intention to deceive. The problem with this category is that, in the case of a president, or almost any politician, it is almost impossible to identify such lies, since both the liar and those being lied to have every incentive to refuse to admit that they are purposely embracing a lie and ignoring what they know to true. The second category is "bullshit." According to Princeton University professor emeritus Harry Frankfurt, this refers to statements in which the speaker "does not care whether the things he says describe reality correctly. He just picks them out, or makes them up, to suit his purpose." "Bullshit" enables both misinformation and disinformation to thrive.[22] In spouting his "bullshit," along with his misinformation, disinformation, and bald-faced lies, President Trump has been empowered by decades of increasing Republican radicalism, amplified by a conservative media establishment that not only encourages lies among its members but demands them. These media personalities and institutions act swiftly to punish any politician who deviates from the political and ideological lines they draw, and they do so with no apparent concern for the public good and with a shocking willingness to discount reality itself. Thus, America's political history has somehow arrived at a moment in which, at the highest levels of government and media, the right kinds of lies are casually and consistently prized above truth. For that reason, in the pages that follow, the story I tell becomes as much about the damage wrought by the failure of the media to hold presidents accountable for lying as about the presidential lying itself. Together, the media and the growing trend of presidential dishonesty have laid the groundwork for the otherwise implausible presidency of Donald J. Trump.

1

"The Serpent's Eye That Charms but to Destroy"

Ever since the first slave ship arrived in Jamestown in the Colony of Virginia in 1619, the racist assumptions underlying the ideology of white supremacy have remained, for the most part, just below the surface of American political life. Yet these beliefs have profoundly contradicted Americans' understanding of themselves and their professed belief that "all men are created equal." Rather than confront this contradiction, American presidents have felt it necessary to elide it with lies. George Washington was no exception.

Literally nothing mattered more to America's first president than his honor. Historian Gordon Wood admitted that to modern eyes Washington's concern for his reputation may appear "embarrassing," even "obsessive and egotistical." But it differed only in degree from that of his contemporaries. "All gentlemen tried scrupulously to guard their reputations, which is what they meant by their honor," Wood explained. "To have honor across space and time was to have fame, and fame is what the founders were after, Washington above all."[1]

By the standards of his time, Washington's treatment of his slaves was considered unusually humane, and it contributed to the esteem he enjoyed among his peers. His relationship with his slaves was in many respects patriarchal. He thought of them as children who were incapable of looking after themselves or understanding their own self-interest. He saw to their health and welfare and even included a provision giving them their freedom upon his death. But he was tough as well, and would punish and sometimes sell those slaves deemed guilty of "indolence" or "insubordination."[2] He was capable of demonstrating a shocking callousness toward them on occasion, treating them worse than most would treat a favored pet that failed to obey them. And when it came to matters of commerce, they were property, pure and simple, no different from land or livestock. He traded them with fellow slave owners when it suited his economic interests.[3]

It is fitting that Washington's only discernible lie as president arose from his role as the beneficiary of this barbaric institution. When the nation's capital was moved from New York to Philadelphia in 1790, he faced a Pennsylvania law that freed all slaves residing in the state for six consecutive months. The president and his wife circumvented this inconvenience by shuttling their favorite slaves back and forth to their Virginia home at Mount Vernon. As Washington wrote to his plantation manager, Tobias Lear: "I wish to have it accomplished under pretext that may deceive both them and the Public." He was worried not only about the law and his reputation but also about the fact that "the idea of freedom might be too great a temptation for them to resist."[4]

It could hardly have been otherwise. America's "original sin" could not but stain the character of every white man and woman it touched. Washington's lie about the location of his slaves was decidedly a minor one, given that it was of little consequence outside his immediate household. And yet, as the only identifiable lie he told as president, it changes our understanding of Washington and of the founding of the United States more generally. He was, after all, in historian Joseph Ellis's words, "the Foundingest Father of them all," and yet one is hard-pressed to disagree with fellow historian Eric Foner's 2019 judgment that "when it came to taking action to end slavery, he, like most of the revolutionary generation, must be found wanting."[5]

The conduct of Washington's fellow Virginia planter and slave owner Thomas Jefferson adds a far more problematic dimension to our understanding of the nation's founding. We now know for certain that this revered author of the Declaration of Independence, who served as governor of Virginia and president of the United States and became the founder of the University of Virginia, fathered at least one child with his slave Sally Hemings—and quite possibly all six of her children—during the thirty-eight years she served him.[6]

Jefferson lied about this relationship for almost his entire life. The first person to publicly accuse him was the raffish Scottish journalist James Thomson Callender, who reported, in the *Richmond Recorder* on September 1, 1802, "It is well known that the man, *whom it delighteth the people to honor*, keeps, and for many years has kept, as his concubine, one of his own slaves. Her name is SALLY....By this wench Sally, our president has had several children." Callender was admirably nonpartisan in his choice of targets. Before he exposed the rumors about Jefferson, a Republican, Callender was best known for tormenting Jefferson's political nemesis, the Federalist mastermind Alexander Hamilton, who had been George Washington's treasury secretary and closest adviser. It was Callender who, five years earlier, had revealed the tawdry tale of Hamilton's extramarital affair and his blackmailing by his mistress's husband—a story that, in his day, marred Hamilton's reputation beyond repair. Callender also attacked then president John Adams, calling him a "hideous hermaphroditical character."[7]

The Federalists had jailed and fined Callender in retaliation, but they had also apparently converted him. It was after leaving prison in 1801 that he started after Jefferson. Although his conversion had come after Jefferson had pardoned him as a "martyr" to the Republican cause, Callender was quick to blackmail the new president with the demand that he pay him $200—the cost of his fine—and appoint him postmaster of Richmond in order to keep quiet. Jefferson agreed to pay only $50, which was not enough to quiet his new adversary. Rather than admit the truth of his relationship with Hemings, Jefferson blamed "the Federalists" for "open[ing] all their sluices of calumny." Privately, he claimed that Callender knew "nothing of which I am not willing to declare to the world myself."[8] Alas, as we now know from DNA evidence, that was a lie. Conveniently, however, a drunken Callender soon drowned himself.

Historians long accepted Jefferson's word for his innocence, following on the view expressed by his biographer James Parton, who wrote in 1874 that "if Jefferson was wrong, America is wrong."[9] This was, in fact, true, but in the sense opposite to what Parton intended. Slavery was wrong. Jefferson was wrong. And America was wrong. But in Jefferson's Virginia, such behavior was no cause for concern. General John Hartwell Cocke, who, together with Jefferson, would found the University of Virginia, noted that in their home state "all Batchelors, or a large majority at least, [kept] a substitute for a wife" among their slaves.[10] John Quincy Adams even wrote a humorous poem about the rumor. But his father, John Adams, predicted that "Callender and Sally will be remembered as long as Jefferson has Blotts in his Character," and called the whole episode "a natural and almost unavoidable Consequence of that foul contagion (pox) in the human Character [of] Negro Slavery."[11] And here Jefferson's predecessor in the presidency spoke not for his fellow founders, or for his countrymen, but for posterity. Jefferson lied because he owned slaves and enjoyed what was understood to be the rightful advantages of his position in his own time and place. But from posterity's viewpoint, slavery made liars of anyone who professed to prize their honor, and the stain it left on the character of America's revered founders has remained indelible throughout its subsequent history.

America's founders disagreed on a great deal, both materially and philosophically, but they shared a fundamental sense that they had embarked on a great experiment upon which the future of civilization itself depended. "We have it in our power," declared the American Revolution's great ideologist, Thomas Paine, "to begin the world over again."[12] It was, simultaneously, a boast and a prayer, but it was also an endeavor they were prepared to try to protect at almost any cost.

The founders understood the European system of military competition between states for territory and riches to be the root cause of the continent's deepest problems—endless war, class oppression, and mass impoverishment—and they feared that such a system could undermine their revolution. Armies and navies liked to fight wars. Wars, they knew, tended to enrich the few at the expense of the many and create a class of leaders who loved luxury more than virtue. This sequence of events had, in their eyes, led to the collapse of both Athenian democracy and the Roman republic, and they sought to avoid it all costs.

It was the founders' most profound wish to absent themselves from the kinds of Old World quarrels and rivalries that might result in war and put them on this destructive pathway. Their natural inclination was to try to withdraw themselves entirely from the world of diplomacy. But they simultaneously understood that the success of their grand experiment rested at least in part on the ability of the nation's citizens to participate in unfettered transatlantic trade. And engaging in trade would require a means of protecting US merchant ships from pirates and other countries' navies, as well as keeping trading routes open in the parts of North America where France,

Britain, and Spain continued to hold sway. Hence, they acknowledged the need for an army and a navy and all the associated things that could threaten to undermine a nascent republic.

Washington's famous farewell address of 1796 should be seen in this light. In this letter to "friends and fellow citizens," the departing president proclaimed that America should protect itself and its ships but go no further. It should avoid "permanent alliances." (An earlier draft, prepared four years earlier, had included the warning that the new nation should "never unsheathe the sword except in self-defense.") John Quincy Adams reiterated this warning with even greater force and eloquence in 1821, when he said that "wherever the standard of freedom and Independence has been or shall be unfurled, there will [America's] heart, her benedictions and her prayers be." But the nation must not "[go] abroad, in search of monsters to destroy.... [America's] glory is not *dominion*, but *liberty*."[13]

At the same time, the volatile energies and ensuing population explosion that the American Revolution catalyzed needed somewhere to go. Fortunately, there happened to be an immense, sparsely populated continent just beyond the borders of the original thirteen colonies ready to absorb them. By far the most consequential lies told by early American presidents were those told in the service of this ceaseless expansion, as the continent was not nearly so sparsely populated as Americans had led themselves to believe. This vast expanse offered not only the world's greatest source of untapped natural resources but also a means of avoiding Old World decadence and corruption. America did not need to compete with European nations for access to the materials it needed to grow powerful. Nor was the growing population a problem. Americans just needed to move westward. Almost no one took note of the colonial claims of foreign nations to any of this territory, much less of the tens of millions of Native Americans who were already there. In many respects, as the historian Walter Nugent convincingly argued, American history was "a continuous narrative of territorial acquisition."

Nugent broke down its components as follows: "Military solutions, overlain by rationales and high ideals, have consistently been considered effective and justified. Expansion has also been premised on the conviction that America and Americans are not tainted with evil or self-serving motives. Americans, the ideology says, are exceptions to the moral infirmities that plague the rest of humankind, because our ideals are pure, a 'beacon to humankind,' and, as Lincoln said, 'the last best hope of earth.'"[14]

These beliefs are deeply held convictions at the core of American public life, and yet they are not even remotely consistent with reality. Therefore, US presidents have been forced to lie to the public in the pursuit of their expansionist goals, and history has tended to reward these same presidents for their lies, judging them exclusively on the basis of their effectiveness rather than on their honesty. Each "success" provided a path for the next president, who then built on both the new conquests and the lies his predecessor told to win them. And, as with so many of the consequential turns in the early history of the American presidency, the tradition begins with Thomas Jefferson.

The five years Jefferson spent representing the colonies in France, from 1784 to 1789, had left him haunted by the specter of mass poverty. In the landless peasants he saw there, he had observed a poverty that was passed from generation to generation. American yeoman farmers, he believed, stood in contrast to these peasants. America's farmers, citizens who owned their own plots of land, were "the chosen people of God," the source of "His peculiar deposit for substantial and genuine virtue." Only such farmers, and likewise tradesmen, could uphold the Enlightenment values necessary to sustain the spirit of the Revolution. Were American farmers and tradesmen ever to sink to the level of dependence he witnessed in France, he believed, the dream of liberty and virtue would sink irretrievably with them. America's salvation thus lay westward, beyond the original confines of the new nation. The continent's beautiful, bountiful lands would draw Americans out of the corrupt cities already developing in the east and allow future generations the opportunity to create a nation of virtuous, socially and politically equal yeoman farmers. "By enlarging the empire of liberty," Jefferson wrote, "we multiply its auxiliaries, and provide new sources of renovation, should its principles at any time degenerate in those portions of our country which gave them birth." In a letter to James Monroe shortly after the latter became president, Jefferson admitted to dreaming of a day when the infant nation would "cover the whole Northern, if not the Southern continent with a people speaking in the same language, governing in similar forms and by similar laws."[15]

In pursuit of this dream, Jefferson was willing to set aside his lifelong commitment to limited government. Previously, he had been a fierce opponent of the concentration of power in the new federal government created by the Constitution, and with it, the implied powers that Hamilton and company had insisted it contained. He was no doubt driven by fears that his rival's vision of a powerful, urbanized, commercial nation-state would result in a corrupt, moneyed aristocracy that might undermine the virtue that Jefferson so prized in its citizens.

Jefferson's presidency will always be associated with the 1803 Louisiana Purchase from France, and properly so. The new lands were considered so vast at the time that no one could say exactly where the territory began or ended, or whose sovereignty counted where. Under the Louisiana Purchase Treaty, the United States paid $15 million for roughly 830,000 square miles. The price was significantly more than the entire federal budget at the time, but the deal, signed in May, more than doubled the size of the country. Today, the area stretches across fifteen US states and two Canadian provinces. According to Jefferson's former, literalist interpretation of the president's constitutional powers, he lacked the authority to commit to this purchase on his own. He did it anyway, though, because he believed that the opportunities for expansion into the new territories would likely be the salvation of the nation's virtue for generations to come. America's population was already growing at a remarkable rate, and it was only getting started.[16] But whether he was right about the future—or even about the virtue of yeoman farmers—is beside the point. The point is that this would hardly be the last time a president would claim for himself powers that, before assuming office, he had insisted lay beyond any president's rightful mandate.

Indeed, Jefferson had been plotting to find a way to capture the territory for his country well before France offered to sell it. Moreover, a few months earlier, in February 1803, he had recruited men for an expedition that he disguised as a scientific endeavor when in truth it was a commercial and military one: an exploration of the trans-Mississippi West, which at the time remained in Spain's hands. "The idea that you are going to explore the Mississippi has generally been given out," Jefferson confided to Meriwether Lewis (of Lewis and Clark) in a letter dated April 27. The reason, he continued, was that it "satisfies public curiosity and masks sufficiently the real destination"—which was, in fact, the Pacific.[17] Here Jefferson was admitting to a lie, albeit a small one as he understood it, given what he believed to be at stake.

Jefferson's successor, James Madison, a fellow Virginia planter—and Jefferson's partner in almost all their political and philosophical endeavors—was a clearer thinker and a less impetuous politician. His role in drafting the Constitution and recording the debates that took place over it, together with the essays he penned in *The Federalist Papers* to argue for its ratification, speak to his extraordinary intellect and commitment to the cause of the new nation. But as a practicing politician, Madison was not in Jefferson's league, and as president, he soon found himself overwhelmed and compelled to lie. Less practiced in the art of deception than his mercurial mentor, Madison ultimately set the nation on a path toward a nearly ruinous and unnecessary war.

Like Jefferson, Madison dedicated himself to using his office to strengthen the young nation's commitment to liberty and virtue by means of expansion. Also like his predecessor, he did not much

occupy himself with the intellectual compromises necessary to rec-
oncile that goal with the ideas he had previously espoused about the
limited powers of the presidency. In 1811, Madison asserted US jurisdiction over Spanish West Florida on the basis of an intellectually
indefensible interpretation of the Louisiana Purchase, and pretended
to Congress, without any evidence, that the British were about to
invade the territory. (Jefferson, Madison, Monroe, and their fellow
Republicans insisted against all evidence that Napoleon had sold
Florida to the United States as part of the Louisiana Purchase. But
Florida belonged to Spain, and France never disputed this, so obviously France could not sell it to the United States.) A year later,
in 1812, he sought and received congressional authorization to use
force to prevent a foreign takeover of East Florida, which this time
did lead to war. Ironically, Madison had previously gone to great
lengths to avoid just this outcome. In public, he had taken a tough
line against the British on the issue of the impressment of American
sailors while privately allowing that if the crown would just tone
down its rhetoric a bit, it need not change its actual policy. When the
British laughed at what they considered to be ridiculous demands
from a pipsqueak, nearly navy-less nation, Madison reversed himself and charged England with spilling "American blood" within
US territory via "pretended blockades" and the "plundering" of US
ships. The British were actually seizing fewer US ships than France
was during this period, and a great many of the sailors they grabbed
off them were genuine deserters from the Royal Navy. Most important, however, the British announced before the war began that they
would be suspending these activities. This news did not reach the
public until after hostilities had begun and Madison had gotten his
war—a war that almost cost the country its independence.[18]

Madison's successor and the fourth and final member of the Virginia planters presidential club was James Monroe. To be sure, he
remained committed to the program of continuous expansion established by his predecessors—but, to be fair, most of his administration's

dishonesty in that pursuit proved somewhat circumstantial. Once again, the United States had its sights set on Florida, along with parts of Georgia. Following a series of minor skirmishes there in early 1818, General Andrew Jackson ordered his troops to seize these territories from Spain, in the process engaging in a veritable orgy of murderous violence against the Native Americans living there. Jackson defied Monroe's orders by massacring not only "savages" but also those British citizens he accused of conspiring with them. Monroe was angered less by Jackson's barbaric tactics, however, than by his insubordination, to say nothing of the diplomatic danger it entailed. Spain continued to insist that it was the rightful owner of Florida, but it had grown too weak to defend the territory militarily in the face of the American demands. America's interpretation of where Spanish sovereignty ended and America's began had no basis in reality, save that of the strong taking what they will and the weak suffering what they must.[19]

A crucial component of the nation's commitment to unbroken westward expansion was its denial of the humanity of the Native Americans, and no president better illustrates this characteristic than Andrew Jackson, who defeated incumbent John Quincy Adams in the presidential election of 1828. The westward push was predicated on the belief that what constituted "the West" was essentially unpopulated. This claim was false, of course. Tens of millions of Native Americans lived across the continent, as they had for centuries. But the racial hierarchies to which Americans adhered invited them to ignore the humanity of people they considered mere "savages," just as they justified enslaving African Americans. The US government undeniably took this view during Jackson's presidency, pursuing what we would now judge to be a brutal and dehumanizing policy of "Indian removal" to facilitate the nation's expansion. But we cannot take men and women out of their historical moments, or ignore the beliefs that characterized their time and place. Most of the lies Jackson and his supporters told themselves about Native Americans would not have been judged lies by their contemporaries.

Yet, even given the standards of the day, President Jackson did lie repeatedly about his Indian removal policy. His first State of the Union address, in 1829, promised that the Indian Removal Act he was proposing would achieve its goals by encouraging Indian populations to "voluntarily" relocate from their tribal lands; once they arrived at their new home, they would be under the protection of the US government. The government promised to "forever secure and guarantee to them...the country so exchanged," and to secure their safety from "all interruption or disturbance." These promises would be comical had their violation not brought such tragic consequences. Jackson surely must have known they would be broken at the first moment they ceased to be convenient. As the historian Daniel Walker Howe noted in 2007, "Jackson was personally well experienced in the techniques of bribery, intimidation, and fraud through which treaties were imposed on reluctant peoples, having been active in a series of land cessations by the Civilized Tribes since 1816." Senator John Forsyth of Georgia had provided justification for such policies back in 1802, when he said that native peoples' oaths were meaningless, since they were not Christians, and therefore had no awareness of "future rewards and punishments." And with their oaths rendered meaningless, so were any treaties or other legal documents they signed or testimony they offered.[20]

In this period of the nation's history, Americans understood themselves to be playing a leading role in a Divine drama called "Manifest Destiny." The lies that US presidents told during this period inevitably reflected the influence of this belief. And none of the lies would prove more consequential than those told by the one-term president James K. Polk.

"The Serpent's Eye That Charms but to Destroy"

Manifest Destiny was originally popularized by the *New York Morning News* writer and editor John O'Sullivan, who memorably cited the doctrine while arguing for the annexation of both Texas and the Oregon territories in 1845. O'Sullivan insisted that any attempt by European nations to interfere with this expansion—regardless of who actually owned the territories at the time—would be considered an act of hostility against "the fulfillment of our manifest destiny to overspread the continent allotted by Providence for the free development of your yearly multiplying millions." The fact that much of the continent was filled with nonwhite people might have been considered a barrier to its incorporation into the nation at large, but the racial assumptions behind Manifest Destiny took care of this potential conflict. Those assumptions applied not only to the Native Americans but also to the Mexicans in what is now Texas, California, New Mexico, and so on—all the places where white Americans might have wished to settle. *New York Herald* editor James Gordon Bennett argued that "barbarism" had "receded before the face of civilization" before, and in the same manner, the "imbecile" Mexicans would be "sure to melt away at the approach of Anglo-Saxon energy and enterprise as snow before a southern sun."[21]

This conquest would take a war, but this, too, fit neatly into the collective psyche of Manifest Destiny America. In his massive study of the building of America's empire, the historian A. G. Hopkins observed that American leaders believed that "war...would strengthen national solidarity," and that "empire...would serve as a laboratory of good government." Therefore, "the two together would enhance the role of the executive and return to the president the power he had exercised in the days when the leaders of the Republic were great men."[22] What's more, Americans believed themselves to have God on their side. US Treasury Secretary Robert J. Walker said nothing controversial in 1847 when he maintained, in an official government report, that a force "higher than any earthly power" had guided America's expansion and "still guards and directs our destiny, impels us onward, and has selected our great and happy country as a model and ultimate center of attraction for all the nations of the world."[23] Polk's term in office, from 1845 to 1849, was a nearly perfect demonstration of the power of these beliefs. Not only did Polk's commitment to Manifest Destiny—and the dishonest fashion in which he proved willing to pursue it—catalyze a war of conquest that vastly increased the landmass of the United States, but he also set the nation on the path to civil war and transformed it politically, economically, culturally, and socially—indeed, in almost every way possible.

Polk's early political career gave little indication of the audacity he would demonstrate as president. The darkest of dark-horse candidates, he was chosen by his party as a compromise candidate during the ninth ballot of the 1844 Democratic National Convention. That move followed a mini-rebellion by slaveholding states against New Yorker Martin van Buren over his refusal to support the annexation of (slaveholding) Texas into the union. (Van Buren had served as president from 1837 to 1841, had lost his reelection bid in 1840 to William Henry Harrison, and was now seeking the nomination again.) Polk, a "third-rate politician—who never devised a measure nor said a thing worth remembering," in the estimation of the *New York Tribune*, had not been considered by anyone as a potential president until his name was placed in the running on the eighth ballot. His primary qualification was his advocacy for annexing Texas, which he slyly called "re-annexation," as well as for the "reoccupation" of the Oregon territories, which were then in dispute with Britain, but believed by Polk to be the rightful property of the United States. After the votes were counted in the 1844 election, a Polk banner was placed above a slave market in Washington, DC. A Polk opponent saw it and predicted, "That flag means Texas and Texas means civil war, before we have done with it."[24]

On October 16, 1845, Polk ordered General Zachary Taylor to station his men on the banks of the Rio Grande in an area under dispute between the still-independent state of Texas and Mexico, but which housed only Mexicans at the time. The troops soon made their way to the Mexican town of Matamoros, and in April 1846, a clash finally broke out there between US and Mexican soldiers. Polk would insist that war had arrived only "after a long-continued series of menaces have at last invaded our territory." Mexico, he pretended, had "shed the blood of our fellow-citizens on our own soil." He demanded that Congress declare war immediately. The opposition party in Congress, the Whigs, refused to buy into Polk's transparent scheming, as did the former vice president and South Carolina champion of slavery John C. Calhoun, who worried that dark-skinned Mexicans might one day make a claim to US citizenship. Polk would eventually go so far as to admit that the battle had taken place on "disputed" rather than American soil. This was, of course, long after he got his war and the issue had become exclusively one of semantics.[25]

Congress had no choice but to support its soldiers when the war came to a vote in April 1846. Recalcitrant Whigs nevertheless forced Polk and company to undertake all manner of subterfuge in accounting for the myriad discrepancies between his account of events and the facts on the ground. In the end, just fourteen House members and two senators voted to oppose the war, with the vast majority accepting Polk's assertion that "the act of the Republic of Mexico" was to blame for the "state of war" and authorizing the recruitment of fifty thousand volunteers and an expenditure of $10 million. A century later, when President Harry Truman sent US forces to Korea without first asking Congress for a declaration of war, he would express his admiration for Polk—"because Polk regularly told Congress to go to Hell on foreign policy matters."[26]

Polk's arguments drew a remarkably articulate opponent in Congress, a thirty-seven-year-old first-term Whig representative from

Illinois named Abraham Lincoln. Lincoln condemned Polk's "unconstitutional" demand for war and introduced a series of resolutions demanding that the president specify "the spot on which the blood of our citizens was shed" and poked holes in his claim that the war had broken out on "American soil."

In a speech to the House of Representatives, Lincoln elaborated on Polk's dishonesty. He was "fully convinced" of several points:

> that the President was deeply conscious of being in the wrong in this matter; that he felt the blood of this war, like the blood of Abel, was crying from the ground against him; that originally he must have had some strong motive—what it was he would not now stop to inquire—for involving the two countries in war; that, having that motive, he had trusted to avoid the scrutiny of his own conduct by directing the attention of the nation, by fixing the public eye upon military glory—that rainbow that rises in showers of blood—that serpent's eye that charms but to destroy; and thus calculating, had plunged into this war, until disappointed as to the ease by which Mexico could be subdued, he found himself at last he knew not where.[27]

Lincoln's colleagues in the House largely ignored his "spot resolutions" and refused even to vote on them. One Washington newspaper accused him of taking sides "against his own country" with an "unpatriotic and anti-American speech." His former law partner warned him that he was dooming his reelection chances. Lincoln decided to persist in his quest for honest answers and then retire from Congress. "Allow the President to invade a neighboring nation whenever he shall deem it necessary to repel an invasion," he replied, "and you allow him to make war at pleasure. Study to see if you can fix any limit to his power in this respect."[28]

During the now-famous 1858 debates between Abraham Lincoln and his opponent Stephen Douglas during their campaign for the Illinois Senate, the latter mocked the future president's opposition to the war, calling him "Spotty Lincoln." Douglas ultimately deployed the same tactics that Polk would use against his critics: insisting that Lincoln had "distinguished himself by his opposition to the Mexican war, taking the side of the common enemy, in time of war, against his own country."[29] Douglas won that election, but, of course President Lincoln would have the last laugh, however brief it may have been.

After the Mexican-American War, Polk was occasionally called to account for his deception, but he gave no quarter to his opponents, much less to the truth. Whenever he was questioned or criticized, he took the now all-too-familiar presidential strategy of impugning the honor and patriotism of his critic, including the soon-to-be ex-congressman Lincoln: "A more effective means could not have been devised to encourage the enemy and protract the war than to advocate and adhere to their cause, and thus give them 'aid and comfort.'"[30]

By the time the negotiator Nicholas Trist concluded what would later become known as the "Treaty of Guadalupe Hidalgo" on February 2, 1848, Polk had increased the American landmass by fully 25 percent. The new territories included present-day Arizona, Utah, Nevada, California, much of New Mexico, and significant portions of Wyoming and Colorado—an area even larger than Jefferson's Louisiana Purchase. What's more, as historian Steven Hahn pointed out, Polk's adventure would prove profoundly transformational for the young republic, setting it on a path from which there was no return. The war, Hahn wrote,

> involved the full-scale invasion of a foreign country for offensive purposes. It required a major mobilization of manpower and financial resources. It inflicted depredations and atrocities on the Mexican people, motivated in large measure by bitter racism and anti-Catholicism among American troops. It resulted in an inordinately high rate of American casualties. It raised the prospect of the

conquest and acquisition of territory and subject populations that might occupy a distinctive status in relation to the rest of the United States. It reopened the increasingly acrimonious questions about the future of slavery and cultural tendencies in American life. And it would leave a legacy of tension, confusion, violence and militarism around a newly carved US-Mexican "border." It posed, that is, in the most fundamental ways, the problems of continental empire.[31]

Significantly, Polk's reputation, both during his presidency and afterward, did not suffer for his mendacity. Lying on behalf of a successful war of expansion, however aggressively pursued, came to be viewed as an expression of "leadership." In this young, self-confident nation, results were what counted. Polk had been elected to bring Texas into the union—and as it turned out, it took a few lies to get there. That was considered by almost everyone, save Abraham Lincoln and a few other far-sighted critics, to be a decidedly fair proposition. And at least in pre–Civil War America, the results of Polk's audacious expeditions looked awfully impressive, no matter what manner of subterfuge turned out to be necessary to realize them. "For what," asked historian Richard Shenkman, "was honesty compared with the acquisition of California and the Southwest?"[32]

Polk's lies had succeeded in putting the United States on a path to becoming a great power—and one whose burgeoning empire would, in many respects, give rise to many of the same dangers that George Washington, Thomas Jefferson, and John Quincy Adams had so feared. But becoming such a power would also bring opportunities and dangers they could hardly have imagined, along with new challenges for future American presidents in terms of their ability to be truthful with their citizens. In the meantime, however, the nation would fight a bloody civil war—one that was necessitated by the consequences of those same lies and the imperial conquests that President Polk had set in motion.

2

"Yankeedoodledum"

The ideas embodied in Manifest Destiny continued their conquest of the collective psyche of America's leaders through the close of the nineteenth century and the beginning of the twentieth. These leaders believed that the cause of constant westward expansion necessitated the displacement—and frequently, the extermination—of indigenous peoples throughout North America as well as the subjugation of Spanish-speaking nations on America's western borders. But given their deeply ingrained beliefs about racial hierarchies and Divine guidance, these same leaders understood the process of endless expansion to be less a policy choice than the unavoidable expression of the nation's collective purpose as ordained by God. The poet Walt Whitman meant just that when in 1847 he celebrated "Yankeedoodledum," which he said was "going ahead with the resistless energy of a sixty-five-hundred-thousand-horsepower steam engine." This was Whitman's word for the nation's spirit that was to sweep through "everything before it South and West, and may one day put the Canadas and Russian America [Alaska] in its fob pocket!" He understood that this conquest might not be carried out in a "conventionally 'genteel' style," but he expressed confidence that it would "tenderly regard human life, property and rights, whatever step it takes."[1]

Whitman was a poet, not a pundit, but neither was he entirely wrong. In the late 1890s, America's twenty-fifth president, William McKinley, found himself leading what had become the largest and most dynamic economy in the world.[2] The United States was still building up its nascent military strength, but it enjoyed an abundance of economic energy and an inexhaustible supply of self-confidence.

The military component would come, too. In 1890 Congress had passed a naval appropriations bill that included funding for the construction of a protected cruiser, a torpedo boat, and "three seagoing coast-line battle ships designed to carry the heaviest armor and most powerful ordnance." That same year, Alfred Thayer Mahan, president of the US Naval War College and close friend of Theodore Roosevelt—who would later follow McKinley in the presidency—published his famous opus, *The Influence of Sea Power upon History*. Mahan was a great admirer of the British naval empire and believed that the United States had no choice but to follow in Britain's path, given the younger nation's now far-flung strategic and economic interests. Three years later, the historian Frederick Jackson Turner laid out his no-less-influential thesis in an essay titled "The Significance of the Frontier in American History," which he presented to the American Historical Association in Chicago during the famous World's Columbian Exposition. The frontier, in Turner's view, had many meanings, but, most significantly, it was a place of America's "perennial rebirth." Indeed, American democracy "gained new strength each time it touched a new frontier."[3] According to Turner, the land was now nearly full, and new "frontiers" beyond the boundaries of North America were required to inspire the nation to greater glory.

The obvious answer to the challenges posed by Mahan and Turner was for the nation to finally throw off the warnings that Washington, Adams, and others had issued about foreign wars and turn its expansionist energies to distant lands. The western frontier had been a line, Turner argued, between "savagery and civilization." Now it was imperative that America go abroad to conquer and civilize new nations, spreading capitalism and Christianity in equal measure while at the same time securing access to the markets as well as the raw materials necessary to sustain its wondrous economic machine.

This fusion of the Mahan and Turner theses, together with Americans' belief in their racial superiority, found its most lyrical voice, ironically, in the paean written to the United States by another friend of Theodore Roosevelt's: the supremely jingoistic British novelist and poet Rudyard Kipling. Writing in honor of McKinley and his Philippine war, Kipling bid Americans to

Take up the White Man's burden—
Send forth the best ye breed—
Go bind your sons to exile
To serve your captives' need.[4]

Given both the nation's history of expansion and the intensity of its ideological commitment to conquest, it is difficult to see how any president would have been able to resist the prevailing belief in what the diplomatic historian Walter LaFeber would term the "shadowy underside of American thinking…'Expand or die.'"[5] But given the fact that the nation was expanding into places that contained non-white and sometimes non-Christian populations, an impossible contradiction arose between the national mythos that had governed the American imagination since its founding and the reality of its demand for constant expansion. As a result, someone needed to lie about what was really happening, and that someone, inevitably, was the president.

It's unclear what exactly led President William McKinley to commit to war with Spain over Cuba in 1898, but there's no doubt about the belief system behind the decision. It's hardly evident that McKinley wanted the war, judging by his initial resistance to the jingoistic demands from his own party in Congress and the press. The new "yellow journalism," led by William Randolph Hearst's *New York Journal* and Joseph Pulitzer's *New York World*, produced a steady drumbeat of outrage, including horror stories about the Spanish raping and torturing Cuban citizens—which frequently turned out to be invented. ("Fact-checkers" were unknown to the industry at the time.) The final straw came when a battleship, the USS *Maine*, exploded in Havana Harbor on February 15, 1898, killing 266 of its crew members. There was no evidence at the time—and none has since come to light—that it was anything other than an unfortunate accident.[6] But the slogan "Remember the *Maine*! To hell with Spain!" became a battle cry for McKinley. He found it impossible to resist and ceaselessly repeated it.

Although McKinley caved into the hysteria manufactured by an increasingly irresponsible press, it's hard to locate an obvious lie among his explanations for the need for war in Cuba. This is less true, however, regarding his decision to wage war against Spain in the Philippines in the wake of America's easy victory in Cuba. Upon deciding to invade the Philippines, he insisted that his intent was merely to defend the Oregon and California coasts. But the president offered up a decidedly different reason for that decision according to an account by a military man who interviewed him, General James Rusling. Although some of the details of Rusling's account have been disputed, Rusling reported that McKinley told him the islands had been "a gift from the gods." McKinley further told Rusling that he had "walked the floor of the White House night after night until midnight," and that he "went down on [his] knees and prayed Almighty God for light and guidance more than one night." The Lord apparently instructed the president to "take them all"—meaning the entire archipelago of more than four hundred islands—"and to educate the Filipinos, and uplift and civilize and Christianize them."[7]

It's not easy to disprove a man who claims to be acting on the basis of Divine inspiration, but the available evidence suggests that McKinley wanted to annex Manila Bay from the moment he heard of Admiral George Dewey's naval victory there in May 1898. He feared that any half measure might result in chaos that could easily be exploited by "our commercial rivals in the orient." The naval base at Manila Bay could not be protected without control over all the islands, as one US Army officer testified, because "a cannon shot can be fired from one to another in many instances."[8] More to the point, however, is that McKinley, like Polk, saw Spain's colonial empire crumbling and made up excuses to grab what looked like even more low-hanging fruit. "We want new markets and trade," he explained at the time, adding that "it looks very much as if we are going to have new markets."[9]

Manila Bay fell to Dewey's forces in a single morning with no loss of American life, but this would prove the falsest of false dawns. Indeed, McKinley's disastrous attempt to occupy the archipelago would reverberate for another century to come. The United States never successfully subdued the Filipino nationalists, who continued to wage a guerrilla war for independence, and the Filipino population bore the brunt of the suffering. McKinley instructed the commanding general of the occupation, Elwell S. Otis, to promise the Filipinos that "we come not as invaders or conquerors but as friends," with a mission of what he called "benevolent assimilation." Despite this compassionate rhetoric, the United States had no intention of granting Filipinos independence, and US forces were soon drawn into what would be a brutal four-year battle to subdue the islands. American troops fought local resistance with the same harsh tactics they had previously used on America's native population, only this time with far more sophisticated weaponry. (It was during this war that US forces invented the procedure we now call "waterboarding" that was used to torture prisoners in the aftermath of the 9/11 attacks in 2001 and in the Iraq War starting in 2003 under President George W. Bush, who would also lie about it.) In the end, according to recent historical estimates, between the fighting itself and the disease and economic disruptions it brought, the conflict ended up killing as many as 750,000 Filipinos— a greater number of lives even than were lost in the American Civil War—while the United States lost fewer than 4,200 troops.[10] And even after the war had been won and the rebel leaders captured, the insurrection continued for another fifteen years.

Had the anarchist Leon Czolgosz not fired two shots into President McKinley's abdomen while shaking his hand at the Pan-American Exposition in Buffalo in September 1901, the history of American expansion would likely have been considerably different than it turned out to be. Theodore Roosevelt, McKinley's vice president, became president at the age of forty-two (and to this day he remains the youngest person ever to assume the office). He embodied much about his youthful country at the time. McKinley had agonized about his decision to fight Spain over Cuba, and then apparently believed he was heeding the word of God in taking on the Philippines. Roosevelt, in contrast, rarely evinced doubt of any kind. He had charged up San Juan Hill to fight the Spanish even though the war had already been won, and then he did it a second time for a film crew (making him the star of the world's first battle documentary). But Teddy Roosevelt charged pretty much everywhere he went. Prior to Roosevelt, no assistant secretary of the navy had personally fought in a war, and none has since. But Roosevelt wanted more. "I should welcome almost any war," he announced in 1897, "for I think this country needs one."[11]

Roosevelt had been fretting about the closing of the frontier even before Frederick Jackson Turner offered his famous thesis—and it was therefore no surprise that he was powerfully drawn to the idea of building an overland canal running through Central and South America to connect the Atlantic and Pacific Oceans. The notion had gestated since the early days of European exploration, and the French had tried their hand at the project three times without success. In

1903, Roosevelt believed himself to be on the cusp of striking a deal with Colombia to build such a canal when he signed the Hay-Herrán Treaty, but the Colombian senate rejected its terms. America's indefatigable president was not about to let what he termed a bunch of "dagos" and "homicidal corruptionists" stand in his way.

Conspiring with an ad hoc group made up of a wily French businessman and engineer named Philippe-Jean Bunau-Varilla and members of both the Panamanian independence movement and the Colombian junta, Roosevelt and company succeeded in buying up enough "revolutionaries" to create a phony uprising, seize control of the isthmus, and split Panama off from Colombia—all for the purpose of ensuring that the land for the canal could be sold off. Roosevelt even deployed the US Navy offshore to ensure that Colombia did not think too hard about putting down the "revolution."[12]

The president justified his role in these shenanigans by citing an 1846 treaty that had given the United States the right to use force in order to protect Colombia's sovereignty—yet at the same time, he was planning to seize a piece of that country for his canal and turn it into a colonial US possession. Later, in the midst of significant delays, along with disease and corruption on the canal site, Roosevelt tried to claim that he had taken Colombia's land and built the canal all for the sake of "civilization"—and that this somehow made it legal. Attorney General Philander C. Knox thought this laughable, and said as much to Roosevelt: "Oh, Mr. President, do not let so great an achievement suffer from any taint of legality." In 1903, Roosevelt signed a treaty with his fellow coconspirator, Bunau-Varilla, who had managed to secure legal ownership of the necessary strip of land, which covered an area of about ten by thirty miles. The Hay-Bunau-Varilla Treaty granted the United States control of the land in perpetuity "as if it were sovereign" in exchange for a onetime payment of $10 million plus $250,000 annually to the government of Panama along with a $40 million payment to Bunau-Varilla. It was, as a title of a 1970 documentary on the subject called it, "the treaty that no Panamanian signed."[13]

A spirited political debate about the canal followed Roosevelt's exploits—especially over the issue of so much money being paid to Bunau-Varilla—but the fact that the president may have twisted the truth to suit his purposes did not much enter into it. Roosevelt sought to cast the matter not only as one of US "national interests and safety" but also as involving "the interests of collective civilization," from which he claimed to have received "a mandate." When Roosevelt asked his secretary of state, Elihu Root, whether he had silenced his opponents by means of these explanations, Root replied, "You certainly have. You have shown that you were accused of seduction, and you have conclusively proved that you were guilty of rape."[14] (Roosevelt apparently surrounded himself with wiseacre advisers.) On the issue of whether Roosevelt could be trusted to tell the truth, a *Detroit Free Press* editorial opined that the word of a US president was "as good as anybody else's word." Whether this was true, then or ever, remains an open question at best.

Roosevelt's word would prove to be a decidedly expensive one to keep. Back in 1823, President Monroe, acting on the advice of Secretary of State John Quincy Adams, had proclaimed the "Monroe Doctrine," which attempted to put a stop to any further European colonization of the Western Hemisphere. The doctrine enjoyed no standing in US or international law and could not be meaningfully enforced, given the weakness of America's military at the time. (Adams imagined, correctly, that the Royal Navy had the same interest and would take care of matters until the United States became strong enough to do the job itself.) Even so, it had accrued considerable rhetorical power as the United States had grown in stature over time. In 1905, Roosevelt declared what has become known as the "Roosevelt Corollary" to the doctrine, asserting that the United States enjoyed the right to intervene in the internal affairs of other nations in its hemisphere in order to make sure they would "maintain order within their boundaries and behave with a just regard for their obligations toward outsiders." The corollary, like the Monroe Doctrine itself, had no legal authority; it was merely an excuse for the United States to do whatever it wanted in the hemisphere at any time. And that is just what happened. The United States ended up repeatedly sending troops around the hemisphere over the next dozen years, although it preferred to exercise control via political and economic levers.[15]

The ultimate significance of Roosevelt's lies about the Panama Canal ended up having little to do with the lies themselves. After all, these paled when compared to the lies Polk had told half a century earlier. What the Panama adventure demonstrated first and foremost was the degree to which America's unparalleled economic power and technological prowess could be put to use abroad in the creation of a new form of empire. Actually building the canal was perhaps the most demanding engineering feat ever completed at the time. Moreover, the near eradication of yellow fever and reductions in malaria in the area while the project was in progress were huge achievements, things no other nation could have contemplated at the turn of the twentieth century.[16]

Owing to their beliefs about white supremacy and the dangers they imagined from the mixing of different races and ethnicities, Americans did not wish to move to Panama, the Philippines, or Cuba (or Puerto Rico, or Guam, or American Samoa, or even Hawaii), or to integrate them into the United States as they had done with Louisiana, Florida, Texas, Oregon, and California. They had no desire to repopulate these places, either, and no particular interest in how the people living in them governed themselves. The last thing Americans wished to see was an invitation extended to the many nonwhite inhabitants of these places to join them as full citizens. The emerging American empire, then, was run not by armies, but by ambassadors, treasury officials, undersecretaries of state, and corporate executives. Military force was deployed only in extremis, by presidents generally claiming to be acting on the basis of Divine guidance or in the interests of "civilization," rather than for anything so vulgar as strategic interests or corporate profits. "Dollar diplomacy," a term Roosevelt coined only after his presidency had ended, allowed Americans to practice imperialism without colonialism, and to create an economic empire that, in historian A. G. Hopkins's description, would turn out to be "both formal and invisible."[17] If a few presidential lies were required to make it work, well, that was fine with most people so long as no wars or other disasters resulted—and so long as the United States got what it wanted.

Despite pauses here and there, the American economic juggernaut continued increasing its dominance during the early years of the twentieth century. And so, despite the nation's best efforts at denying them, its global responsibilities mounted. With these responsibilities came new forms of presidential deception.

Meanwhile, much of Europe stagnated, in part as a result of just the kinds of conflicts America's founders had warned against, and the US economy boomed beyond what any other nation had ever experienced. Statistics for the period remain imprecise, but it is clear that during the final years of the nineteenth century and in the early years of the twentieth, the United States became the world's largest producer of both agricultural and manufactured goods. Long a debtor nation, it became the world's wealthiest creditor.[18]

But Woodrow Wilson, America's twenty-eighth president, faced a very different set of challenges from his predecessors soon after taking office in 1913. Europe's "Great War," a massive global upheaval, began in August 1914. Though Wilson tried mightily to remain neutral "in both thought and action," the global power and influence that the United States had amassed in the nearly 140 years since its founding made that policy untenable. Regardless of whether Wilson and other American leaders wished to admit it, the United States had become a great power, and it needed to protect its interests not just in the hemisphere but on a global scale. The deeply moralistic Wilson cannot be said to have consciously lied to the American people as president—either when he sought to maintain America's neutrality between the European combatants, during the war's early years, or in the service of the war effort once the United States entered the conflict. But he did set up a series of government structures and agencies to lie for him, thereby keeping his personal record pristine.

When the United States finally entered the war in early April 1917, it did so with profound reluctance. Now in his second term, but having failed to maintain the neutrality he had so energetically preached during his first term in office, Wilson fully understood that once a people were led to war, as he himself had written, they could "forget there ever was such a thing as tolerance." Indeed, he added, "to fight you must be brutal and ruthless, and the spirit of ruthless brutality will enter into the very fiber of our national life."[19] Wilson helped to enable this brutality, however, by instituting a harsh regime of censorship and giving his cabinet members carte blanche to fire anyone they desired without explanation or due process. This instruction was understood, correctly, as a license to lie.

When Wilson signed the Espionage Act of 1917, its supporters pitched the measure as a means of protecting the military from radicals' efforts to interfere with its recruitment efforts and to inspire insubordination among the troops. The government deployed it, however, in the service of an extremely broad range of censorship and surveillance activities. At least seventy-five publications found themselves banned, including the *Catholic Register*, which had offended by quoting Thomas Jefferson. These publications were not by any definition genuine security threats to the United States or hindrances to its war effort. The government simply didn't like their politics, and so it lied about the phony "security threat" they allegedly represented.

Even more outrageous were the actions the Wilson administration undertook under the aegis of the Sedition Act of 1918. This law made it a crime to say anything "scornful or disrespectful" of the US government, its Constitution, its flag, or even its soldiers' uniforms. Essentially, it gave the administration the ability to punish and silence anyone it wished, for whatever reason. All that was necessary was for an official to call something someone said or wrote "disloyal." Not surprisingly, abuse was rampant. Socialist presidential candidate Eugene V. Debs received a ten-year prison sentence for opposing the war despite having received a million votes in the presidential election of 1912. Hollywood producer Robert Goldstein received a ten-year sentence (later reduced to three) and was fined $5,000 for including a scene in his movie about the American Revolution that reflected badly on Britain, which was now America's ally. A Wisconsin official received a thirty-month sentence for criticizing a Red Cross fundraising drive. Here again, calling these acts "seditious" was a lie, and the cases were undertaken in President Wilson's name and with his assent. That the president did not personally lie about them does not change this fact.[20]

Among the worst abuses were those carried out by Wilson's attorney general, A. Mitchell Palmer. In the spring of 1919, anarchists had carried out a series of bombings, including two against Palmer at his Washington, DC, home. That fall, beginning on the second anniversary of the victory of the Bolshevik Revolution, November 7, Palmer therefore instituted a sometimes-violent roundup of thousands of mostly (but not exclusively) Russian-born radicals and allegedly dangerous aliens—all of whom he planned to deport. The ensuing raids lasted for two years. Working with J. Edgar Hoover, who was only twenty-four years old at the time but had been tapped to head up the Justice Department's newly established General Intelligence Unit, he ordered the arrests of five thousand people in a single day. It was the largest police action in American history at the time, and it remained so for the next half century. Almost all those arrested were innocent of any crime, even as it was defined by the Sedition Act itself. Among those arrested, as author Adam Hochschild noted, were dancers at the Tolstoi Club in Manchester, New Hampshire; patrons at the Tolstoy Vegetarian Restaurant in Chicago; thirty-nine bakers in Lynn, Massachusetts; Polish Americans raising money for a funeral in New Jersey; and members of the Lithuanian Socialist Chorus in mid-rehearsal in Philadelphia.[21]

Much to Palmer's chagrin, the acting secretary of labor, Louis Freeland Post, whose position gave him responsibility for the Bureau of Immigration, demonstrated an impressive commitment to due process in these cases. Only forty-three of Palmer's arrestees were deemed sufficiently "guilty" to warrant deportation. Palmer attacked Post for his "habitually tender solicitude for social revolution and perverted sympathy for the criminal anarchists of the country," but to no avail. When the newly formed National [later American] Civil Liberties Union took the government to court, Massachusetts District Court judge George Anderson declared the arrests to have been illegal. "A mob is a mob," he explained, "whether made up of government officials acting under instructions from the Department of Justice, or of criminals, loafers, and the vicious classes."[22]

Wilson also created America's first propaganda agency, the Committee on Public Information (CPI), to support the war effort. Established in April 1917 and led by the energetic George Creel, the CPI was America's first dip into the business of information dissemination and marked an important moment in the history of mass communication.

The CPI published a great deal of material, and some of it, inevitably, included lies. For instance, it published one pamphlet, titled "The German-Bolshevik Conspiracy," that presented forged documents pretending to demonstrate that Vladimir I. Lenin and Leon Trotsky had actually been paid by the Germans to withdraw Russia from World War I. The committee also provided false information to newspapers regarding the progress of US war efforts, which led the *New York Times* to nickname it "the Committee on Public Misinformation." But owing to the enormous scale of the effort—which included twenty separate bureaus operating in nine countries around the world—the CPI maintained a surprisingly impressive record when it came to adhering to the truth, especially given that it was operating during a war and had been created for propaganda purposes. Although its news releases and films (prepared for theater showings) were rarely scrupulously accurate, they were probably no less reliable than most newscasts were at the time. But to lie infrequently is not the same thing as being entirely honest. Journalistic wunderkind Walter Lippmann, who worked for the committee while still in his twenties, characterized its "general tone" as "one of unmitigated brag accompanied by unmitigated gullibility, giving shell-shocked Europe to understand that a rich bumpkin had come to town with his pockets bulging and no desire except to please."[23]

Ironically, the most significant lies the Wilson administration told the nation were not those offered in support of the war effort. Rather, they concerned the condition of the president himself. Here again, the *presidency* was lying without the president himself being the one to utter the words.

The topic of presidential health is a tricky one: an individual's right to privacy can easily conflict with the public's right to know about a leader's fitness to carry out the demands of the office. In many instances prior to Wilson's tenure, US presidents had prioritized their own self-interest above that of the larger public when it came to revealing debilitating illnesses or injuries. For instance, Zachary Taylor, America's twelfth president, who assumed office on March 5, 1849, following his victories in the Mexican-American War, soon contracted what was judged to be cholera. He and his administration denied this fact right up until the moment the disease killed him in July 1850. Three decades later, in 1881, Chester Arthur succeeded the murdered James Garfield as president. He quickly contracted Bright's disease, which attacks the kidneys and today is called "nephritis." Worried that news of the president having a debilitating, fatal illness would undermine his ability to be an effective executive, he pretended to be in perfect health, despite the fact that he could barely function. Not long afterward, Grover Cleveland, who served noncontiguous terms as the nation's twenty-second and twenty-fourth president, was diagnosed with cancer of the jaw during his first term. Rather than risk the news of his surgery leaking to the press and public, he arranged for an operation on a yacht out at sea. The surgery was therefore undertaken under almost incalculably risky conditions made even more dangerous by the president's obesity. Cleveland ended up with a vulcanized-rubber prosthesis designed to disguise the fact that a considerable portion of his upper left jaw and part of his palate had been removed. As far as the world outside the boat knew at the time—including virtually everyone in the US government—Cleveland was happily vacationing at his Cape Cod summer home. Five days after the operation, Dr. Joseph Bryant, Cleveland's personal physician, who had made the original cancer diagnosis, held a press conference in which he announced that the president had concealed his operation—not for cancer, however, but for "rheumatism." The lie held for most of the summer, until Cleveland's dentist let it slip to a doctor friend without knowing it was still supposed to be secret. The doctor told a reporter, who broke the story later that summer. Although the article was perfectly accurate, Cleveland's advisers, panicky about the potential economic impact of the truth being revealed, denounced it as fantasy. The doctor's story failed to capture much attention anyway, and so the lie ultimately proved inconsequential—save for the precedent it helped to set when it came to Wilson's far more serious situation decades later.[24] But in those cases, the deceptions mattered far less than in Wilson's day, in significant measure because America and its presidency mattered far less.

Unfortunately, the lies about Wilson's health came at a crucial moment in the course of his presidency and, as fate would have it, in the history of the world. America's twenty-eighth president was not a well man even before he assumed the duties of office in 1913. Wilson's doctor, Admiral Cary T. Grayson, was known to be extremely concerned about the president's demanding work habits. Six years later, as Wilson barnstormed the country in a desperate attempt to whip up support for the League of Nations, he began having trouble eating and sleeping. He grew weaker every day and started to endure a series of debilitating headaches. Advised to return to Washington immediately for tests, he refused. Then, on the night of September 25, 1919, at a train stop in Pueblo, Colorado, Edith Wilson found her husband twitching uncontrollably and screaming in pain, in the throes of what was almost certainly a stroke.

Wilson's private secretary, Joseph Tumulty, announced that the president was suffering from "a nervous reaction in his digestive organs," and the president's train turned around and headed back to Washington. A few days later, however, on October 2, an even more serious medical event occurred, though it is difficult to describe exactly what happened in detail because both Edith Wilson and Dr. Grayson lied about it continuously. A Philadelphia neurologist named Francis X. Dercum, whom Grayson brought in for a consultation, pronounced the president to have experienced what would later be called an "ischemic stroke," which is caused by clotting in the brain and causes the sufferer to temporarily lose consciousness. It was likely the fourth stroke he had suffered and certainly the most serious.[25]

In the Cabinet Room that day, Secretary of State Robert Lansing met with Tumulty to figure out who would assume the duties of the president. Lansing read Article II, Section 1, of the Constitution aloud: "In Case of the Removal of the President from Office, or of his Death, Resignation, or Inability to discharge the Powers and Duties of the said Office, the Same shall devolve on the Vice President." He apparently expected Grayson to certify Wilson's inability to carry out his duties. Alas, Tumulty said that Grayson would "never certify his disability." The doctor arrived, confirmed this, and, together with Tumulty and Edith Wilson, promised to personally repudiate anyone who said otherwise.

The *Washington Post* characterized the president's illness merely as "nervous exhaustion," but rumors of syphilis and insanity ricocheted around the capital. Meanwhile, Edith Wilson herself took charge of the government, refusing to allow cabinet members or members of Congress in to see the president. Miraculously, the Volstead Act, outlawing the production, sale, and transport of alcoholic beverages, somehow received the signature of a president who was at the time incapacitated, hemiplegic, and, in the words of a physician quoted by Wilson biographer Kendrick A. Clements, "subject to 'disorders of emotion, impaired impulse control, and defective judgment.'" The First Lady and Dr. Grayson were the only people in regular personal communication with the president during this time—though the conspiracy succeeded in significant measure because Vice President Thomas Marshall was willing to play along: he did not demand that the cabinet follow the constitutionally mandated path for dealing with a disabled president.[26]

Wilson did eventually recover, but in a decidedly diminished capacity both mentally and physically.[27] He had to abandon his dream of a League of Nations led by the United States that would keep the world's peace and ensure self-determination for all people. The Senate Foreign Relations Committee chair, Henry Cabot Lodge, a Republican from Massachusetts, offered up a series of fourteen reservations to the treaty whereby the United States would have joined the League of Nations, mimicking the fourteen points that Wilson had put forth as his plan for the peace. Lacking the energy to deploy the persuasive talents that had served him so well in the past, Wilson was unable to reach an agreement with Congress. The United States never joined the League of Nations, and hence the League proved to be too weak to stand up to challenges it faced from Nazi Germany and fascist Italy, among others, in later decades. As Wilson's admiring biographer John Milton Cooper (who does not posit a single untruth spoken by the president in nearly six hundred pages of text) rightly observed, "If there have been times in the nation's history that have cried out for strong presidential leadership, this was one of them."[28] And if Wilson's wife, doctor, and advisers had not lied to hide his medical condition, the nation might have gotten it.

3

Franklin D. Roosevelt

THE "JUGGLER"

America's thirty-second president, Franklin Delano Roosevelt, lied repeatedly and without apology. He liked to call himself a "juggler," by which he meant, "I never let my right hand know what my left hand does."[1] Roosevelt readily admitted that he was willing to lie in order to win World War II, but in fact he was willing to engage in deliberate deception on just about any matter. Yet FDR ranks today—both in the opinion of presidential historians and among the general public—just below the sainted Abraham Lincoln and George Washington as America's most admired president. Yes, Roosevelt lied, but he lied effectively. And because he did so in the service of a victorious war, history has rewarded him.

No doubt the most historically significant lies that Franklin Roosevelt told as president were offered in the service of the political pretense that the United States could avoid going to war with

Germany and Japan. These appear awfully perspicacious with the hindsight of history and greatly complicate any arguments for absolute presidential truthfulness as a hard-and-fast rule. Campaigning for reelection in 1936 and 1940, Roosevelt repeatedly promised to keep the country out of war—even though he knew, well before the Japanese attack at Pearl Harbor on December 7, 1941, that this would likely be impossible. Surely he was aware that to articulate the truth aloud would have panicked the nation and undermined his party—it could even, conceivably, have cost him reelection.

As Nazi Germany and its allies grew stronger in the years leading up to World War II, nativist and isolationist sentiments in the United States put more and more pressure on the president. According to a 1934 survey, 95 percent of Americans felt the United States should avoid engagement in a future European war for any reason. Congress naturally reflected these sentiments and stood ready to oppose any effort by Roosevelt to involve the country in the brewing conflict. Once war broke out in Europe, journalists, pro-German business interests, peace groups, women's groups, and "America Firsters" joined to create what was then the largest peace movement in the nation's history, focusing all their efforts on preventing Roosevelt from aiding the Allies against the Axis powers. This commitment to self-enforced isolationism remained strong right up to the moment of the Pearl Harbor attacks, which, together with Germany's declaration of war shortly thereafter, finally made it irrelevant.

Despite being politically hampered by the intensity of these sentiments, Roosevelt was able to replace the expiring 1937 Neutrality Act in late 1939 with a "cash-and-carry" policy that allowed the United States to sell the British all the weapons they could afford—significantly increasing America's role in the war while allowing it ostensibly to remain neutral. During a special session of Congress following the September 1, 1939, Nazi invasion of Poland, the president assured the country that the new policy offered "far greater safeguards than we now possess or have ever possessed to protect

American lives and property," when in truth he was deliberately inching closer to war. Next, FDR promised, in 1940, to lease obsolete US destroyers to Great Britain in exchange for British naval bases in the Caribbean. Ironically, in defending his decision privately to reporters, he cited Thomas Jefferson's Louisiana Purchase as a legal precedent, explaining that it was similarly undertaken without congressional or explicit constitutional sanction.[2] To the larger public, the president compared the deal to loaning one's neighbor a garden hose when his house is on fire, with a promise that it would be returned when the fire was put out. But as FDR knew quite well, Britain's economy was struggling merely to survive beneath the burden of the war; there was no possibility whatsoever that America's "neighbor" would be able to repay this debt, even were it as simple to return a destroyer as to return a garden hose.

Roosevelt also frequently exaggerated America's vulnerability to attack. In April 1939, he warned newspaper editors that "the totalitarian nations...have 1,500 planes today. They cannot hop directly across our 3,000 miles but they can do it in three hops....It would take planes based at Yucatan, modern bombing planes, about an hour and fifty minutes to smash up New Orleans." A year later, before the same audience, he repeated the warning, claiming this time that America's foes "could put 5,000 bombing planes into Brazil." To support these assertions and many others, Roosevelt repeatedly referred to documents he claimed to have in his possession proving that Germany was planning to invade Central and South America in preparation to attack the United States. Of course, no one ever saw these documents, because they did not exist.[3]

Not long after the September 1, 1939, Nazi Blitzkrieg in Poland, a reporter asked the president at a midmorning press conference whether the United States could hope to "stay out" of the conflict. Roosevelt replied, "I not only sincerely hope so, but I believe we can and that every effort will be made by the Administration to do so." This, too, was almost certainly false. British prime minister Winston

Churchill later told his War Cabinet that he had secretly met with the president in August 1941 aboard a warship off the coast of Newfoundland, and that Roosevelt had vowed to "wage war, but not declare it," because of isolationist opposition in Congress. The president, according to Churchill, had also promised "that he would become more and more provocative. If the Germans did not like it, they could attack American forces."[4]

FDR believed, as an aide explained, that it would "appear to be preferable to have the people push the President into danger than to have them pulled into it by him." Hoping to engineer just such a push, he allowed US ships to engage German and Italian warships on the high seas. This resulted in a dramatic exchange in September 1941, when a US destroyer, the *Greer*, tracked a German U-boat on and off for nine hours, constantly signaling its location to British forces. Its captain had been issued secret orders to escort British convoys and to aid in their efforts to sink German submarines, but to avoid doing any of the firing himself. The Germans fired a torpedo at the *Greer* but missed. In an eerie foreshadowing of the imaginary Second Gulf of Tonkin incident thirty-four years later, the *Greer* escaped unharmed. FDR used the incident as an excuse to escalate tensions with the Germans. Pretending that the "attack" was part of a plot by "Hitler's advance guards," Roosevelt proclaimed "the blunt fact" that the "German submarine fired first...without warning and with deliberate desire to sink [the ship]." The Nazis were, he insisted, working with Hitler's "avowed agents," his "dupes among us" and other, unnamed "rattlesnakes of the Atlantic" seeking to undermine the United States from within. He then took advantage of the incident to order a new "shoot-on-sight" policy for the US Navy against German submarines.[5]

During the 1940 campaign, which took place more than a year before the United States finally entered the war, Roosevelt repeatedly assured Americans that he would not send their sons to fight in "foreign wars," even though he fully expected to do so. When his friend and speechwriter Samuel Rosenman wondered why the president had left the caveat "except in case of attack" out of his speech, when it had appeared in the printed text handed out to reporters, FDR resorted to obvious sophistry: "If we're attacked, it's no longer a foreign war." Even so, Roosevelt then dropped the word "foreign" from this promise as he continued to offer it up on the campaign trail. "Your President says this country is not going to war, period," he said. The gadfly Republican congresswoman Clare Boothe Luce of Connecticut would later insist that Roosevelt had been "the only president who ever lied us into a war because he did not have the courage to lead us into it."[6] A more generous interpretation of his actions is that he was trying to keep England alive long enough to ready the United States for war. Given the hindsight of history, FDR's choices appear not merely far-sighted but positively prophetic. They required lying, yes, but his lies can honestly be said to have saved civilization from the Nazi barbarians and their allies who sought to destroy it.

Roosevelt's record in responding to the Nazi genocide remains his most controversial presidential legacy, and appropriately so. There is no question, as historians Richard Breitman and Allan J. Lichtman concluded, that "the president and his administration did not forthrightly inform the American people of Hitler's grisly 'Final Solution' or respond decisively to his crimes." This was especially true of the State Department, which actively "sought to prevent some information about the Nazi extermination of the Jews from reaching the American people." The motivation for this, the authors surmised, was that the president "feared that his involvement in publicity about what we call the Holocaust would divide the American people and add to the widespread perceptions at home and abroad that Jews manipulated his policies."[7]

Roosevelt did reluctantly agree to a meeting on December 8, 1942, with the understandably panicked leaders of American Jewish institutions to discuss his response—or lack thereof—to the news of the mass slaughter (which, it must be admitted, was being met with a shameful lack of alarm in almost all official and other potentially powerful communities in the United States at the time). The meeting lasted twenty-nine minutes. In certain respects, the president was remarkably honest. He explained that the United States would not bomb gas chambers or the death camps' transportation networks, lest such an effort slow progress in winning the war. The reason he offered his guests—which many historians support today—was that the best way to save Jewish lives was to win the war as quickly and efficiently as possible. The president did not get much argument on this point that day. Like Roosevelt himself, Jewish leaders were extremely wary of giving the impression that the United States was making any special effort to save Jews—which could, they feared, lead anti-Semites to campaign against the war and undermine the nation's morale. In the end, FDR did make a vague promise: "We shall do all in our power to be of service to your people in this tragic moment."[8]

But the truth was that he did nothing at all. Roosevelt did not even order his own State Department to fulfill the tiny quotas allowed under the nation's recently revised immigration laws to help save the lives of Jews fleeing the Holocaust. Instead, he left the matter in the hands of an old navy crony, Assistant Secretary of State Breckinridge Long. Under Long's authority, visa applications from Jews were almost always rejected. The very fact of an applicant having family remaining in nations under fascist or communist rule was frequently offered as grounds for refusal. Long attacked what he called "liberal attitudes," which he insisted "discount[ed] the 'risk' involved in admitting refugees," who might be "Nazi, Italian or Communist agents." He even applied this logic to orphaned children. Despite the fervent lobbying of Eleanor Roosevelt and many others who insisted that at least the children be saved, the president backed the cruel strictures of his State Department all the way, forgoing the opportunity to save possibly hundreds of thousands of Jews who would perish in places like Auschwitz and Dachau.[9]

A second significant stain on Roosevelt's record during World War II involved his account to the American people of the agreements he negotiated with Joseph Stalin and Winston Churchill regarding the postwar order at the Crimean resort of Yalta in February 1945, while the Allied armies were closing in on Berlin. The problem with Roosevelt's performance was not in the deals he negotiated, as so many conservatives and other anti-Roosevelt voices have since claimed; rather, it was that he lacked the will, or the courage, to tell the truth about them afterward. Almost all his compromises at Yalta appear eminently reasonable, given the hand that fate had dealt him. The war had left Stalin's armies in control of much of Eastern Europe, and the Soviets had suffered two devastating German invasions in fewer than twenty years. Therefore, the Soviet dictator was not about to allow democratic—and therefore potentially hostile—governments into any nation bordering the Soviet Union, no matter what the United States said or did. But at Yalta, the United States did not say much about these issues. The president and his men sought stability in Europe, not democracy. Regarding the latter, they demanded only rhetoric.

Roosevelt went much further than was necessary merely to protect his achievements and purposely misled Americans about the level of Soviet cooperation he had been able to achieve at Yalta. He promised Americans a pipe dream of peaceful cooperation and national self-determination in Eastern Europe that had no hope of realization. In an emotional speech to Congress following his return from Yalta—the first time Roosevelt was ever seen in public being wheeled in his chair—the president told the country of the results of his secret negotiations. But instead of taking advantage of the enormous goodwill and political capital he had earned in the impending victory in Europe to level with Americans about the kinds of concessions any country must make in the world of great power politics and diplomacy, he sugarcoated the agreements beyond recognition. And in doing so, he inadvertently laid the groundwork for the atmosphere of Cold War paranoia that would paralyze American politics for years to come.

Roosevelt misled Congress and the American people about almost all the key points of the agreements he had reached. He portrayed for Americans a future filled with global cooperation and understanding, insisting that the nation's victory in the war "spells the end of the system of unilateral action and exclusive alliances and spheres of influence and balances of power." In fact, the Yalta accords ensured that these very sorts of arrangements would become the norm. The agreements reached there literally divided up the world into spheres of influence where the United States, the Soviet Union, Britain, and China could determine the future of their respective neighboring nations without having to concern themselves about any bothersome interference from the others. He promised that the governments that met in Yalta would "see to it that interim governments...will be as representative as possible of all democratic elements in the population, and that free elections are held as soon as possible thereafter," but this was also false.[10] The Soviets attached no such meaning whatsoever to the understandings they made with the United States and Britain and made no pretenses to the contrary. Roosevelt also proudly promised a free government in Poland in spite of the fact that the Soviets, again, signaled no intention of allowing one. The accord's language regarding Poland was written so loosely that Roosevelt's chief of staff, Admiral William Leahy, complained that it was "so elastic that the Russians can stretch it all the way from Yalta to Washington without ever technically breaking it." Roosevelt responded, "I know, Bill....But it is the best I can do for Poland at this time."[11]

Roosevelt no doubt expected to be able to convince Stalin to relax his stranglehold on Poland just enough to satisfy most of the American public (if not its extremely vocal Polish American population), and he may well have been right about this. The Soviets liked Roosevelt, and even the notoriously paranoid Stalin appeared to trust the working relationship the two men had established. They viewed his commitment to working out issues of mutual concern with "full confidence," in the words of the Soviet foreign minister, Vyacheslav Molotov.[12] But given how short the rest of the president's life turned out to be, history would take a decidedly different turn.

Another series of lies Roosevelt told in his speech to Congress involved Asia. "Quite naturally, this conference concerned itself with the political problems of Europe—and not the Pacific war," he informed the nation.[13] This lie was entirely justifiable at the time. In fact, Roosevelt had made significant territorial concessions to the Soviet Union in East Asia in exchange for a Soviet promise to turn to the war in Japan once the European war ended. This agreement made absolute sense from a military perspective. So, too, did the need to keep it secret. The Joint Chiefs of Staff were especially insistent on the need for Soviet participation in the war against Japan, so as to take some of the pressure off what was expected to be a brutal fight for its surrender. It was the atom bomb, of course, that ended up securing Japanese surrender, in August 1945, but at the time it remained mired in secrecy and uncertainty, and it was not at all yet clear that it would work, much less force Japan to capitulate. Even so, Roosevelt should be held accountable for his refusal to share this secret with those who needed to know it, most particularly the man who succeeded him upon his death just six weeks after he gave this speech. In fact, Harry Truman did not even know Roosevelt was in Yalta as the conference was taking place. By the time he ascended to the office on April 12, 1945, the new president had met with his predecessor exactly twice as vice president and never alone.

Given how soon Roosevelt died after returning home, we can now see that the problems arising from his lies about Yalta were exacerbated greatly by his lies about his health. These lies were of a different order, however, and deserve to be considered independently of what has become known as FDR's "splendid deception" in the matter of his polio, which he contracted in 1921 at age thirty-nine. That condition was less a lie than it was a topic to be discussed only privately. The newsreels never captured it. The White House press corps never mentioned it. Photographers assigned to the president would go so far as to block the vision of anyone who tried to violate the unspoken rule of not portraying his condition, never allowing anyone among their ranks to take a picture of the president as he was sometimes literally carried from place to place where wheelchair access was lacking. It's hard to see what's wrong with this behavior. Public figures are, after all, entitled to some degree of privacy, and Roosevelt's confinement to a wheelchair does not seem to have impeded his ability to carry out his presidential duties in any way. The far more significant problem with FDR's deception was that it emboldened him to lie about other health problems that really did affect his fitness to serve.

Like Woodrow Wilson during the latter stages of his presidency, Roosevelt was not at all a well man during his final election campaign. But FDR proved so adept at hiding his infirmities that his personal physician, Dr. Ross McIntire, confided in his diary, "It made me doubt my accuracy as a diagnostician." In December 1944, just a month after his final election victory, a new physician, Dr. Robert Duncan, conducted a thorough examination of the president and gave him only a few months to live. This prognosis was apparently due to a "hardening of the arteries of the brain at an advanced stage." We can see at least one important result of his infirmity in the fact that, according to biographer Robert Dallek, "Roosevelt's cardiologist 'begged Eleanor time and again not to upset her husband' with complaints about State Department appointments of anti-Communist conservatives."[14] It so happens that these appointees were the very same people who slammed the door shut on refugees from Hitler's

Holocaust. The question of whether his health affected his performance at Yalta cannot be put entirely to rest. FDR could work for only a few hours at a time during his final months, and he was hardly at his best when he did. In retrospect, however, the problems that arose with the Soviet Union in the aftermath of the war did not result from Roosevelt's having been hoodwinked at Yalta, much less from any nefarious attempts to undermine him by pro-Soviet members of the US delegation there, as so many have since charged. Rather, it was that in securing the best deal he could, Roosevelt apparently lacked the energy to tell anyone—for example, his vice president— about what he had agreed to and why he had done so.

In the paranoid politics of postwar America, Roosevelt's secrecy cast suspicion on the whole postwar order. As the Soviets eliminated independent governments one by one on their borders, often liquidating their opponents and imposing their tyranny on those remaining, "Yalta" came to be seen as the cause of America's alleged betrayal of Poland and the rest of the Eastern bloc. The victory of the Chinese communists in that nation's civil war in October 1949 gave further credence to this argument, however lacking in firm evidence it may have been. As the columnist Raymond Swing would observe in the *New York Times* in February 1949, the word "Yalta" had "become a byword for failure, folly and treason."[15] Some opponents blamed Roosevelt's health for the "sellout" they saw there. Others contended that there had been more nefarious forces at work. Conservatives appeared to settle on a story during the extremely well-publicized 1948 perjury trial of Alger Hiss, who was an American translator at Yalta and is now assumed by most historians to have been a spy for the Soviets. The story concocted by conspiracy-minded anti-FDR Republicans was that Hiss somehow manipulated the sickly and confused president into giving away the store to the communists.

By the time of his second trial—the first one ended in a hung jury—Hiss had become president of the Carnegie Endowment for

International Peace and an icon of what remained of Roosevelt's liberal, New Deal order. His 1950 conviction for perjury gave Cold War conservatives all the evidence they needed (or wanted) to blame FDR's secret Yalta agreements undermining freedom in both Europe and Asia as the cause of the Cold War. The Hiss case, in the eyes of many, discredited liberalism. It also jump-started the political career of Richard Nixon and fueled the fires of McCarthyism. After Hiss was found guilty, Nixon, then a two-term California congressman, offered up a four-hour lecture on the significance of the case on the floor of the House of Representatives, indirectly blaming Hiss for the fact that "today there are 800,000,000 in the World under the domination of Soviet totalitarianism," far more than the alleged 540,000 he claimed for "our side." As a result, he insisted, the United States was in danger of losing the Cold War. Two weeks after Nixon's address, the junior senator from Wisconsin, Joseph McCarthy, was scheduled to give a speech to the Ohio County Republican Women's Club of Wheeling, West Virginia. He had planned to focus on issues related to health care, housing, and aid to the elderly. But inspired by Nixon's eloquence, he changed his mind and lifted much of his material directly from the congressman's address. McCarthy deemed Hiss "important not as an individual any more, but rather because he is so representative of a group in the State Department" whom McCarthy insisted were hell-bent on selling out the United States to communism.[16] What we call "McCarthyism" is, in this respect, a direct outgrowth of the lies Franklin Roosevelt told about Yalta.

4

Harry Truman Fights a "New Fanatic Faith"

The Cold War offered US officials what they understood to be an invitation to deceive the public in the service of also deceiving their Soviet enemies. But if you give politicians license to lie, no matter what the reason, you can almost always bet they will do so in their own interest rather than in the interest of their country. This is what happened repeatedly during the early Cold War, as one US president after another lied to the nation under the aegis of "national security." Presidential lies were deemed to be a crucial and unavoidable weapon in the arsenal of America's Cold War commanders in chief. These presidents were charged, after all, with protecting the nation against a foe whose capacity for evil apparently knew no limits. If their own leaders were lying, Americans were led to believe, it was for the country's—and humanity's—own good.

Harry Truman had almost no experience with foreign policy before becoming president and yet found himself faced with some of the most fateful decisions ever made by any leader anywhere and at any time:

how and when to use the atom bomb. Before assuming the presidency, his philosophy, such as it was, could have been summed up in one of his 1941 quotes: "If we see that Germany is winning the war, we ought to help Russia; and if that Russia is winning, we ought to help Germany, and in that way let them kill as many as possible."[1] At the time of President Roosevelt's death on April 12, 1945, there were probably waiters and cooks in the White House who were better acquainted with his thoughts about the world's postwar future than his successor was.

It was therefore one of the great accidents of history that a man so unprepared for such responsibility was asked to make the decision about the atom bomb. Truman was not briefed on the Manhattan Project until April 25, 1945, thirteen days after he became president.[2] Despite the awesome weight on his shoulders, he never agonized over his decision. He may not even have seen it as a decision at all. Rather, the issue as it was presented to him by Roosevelt's military team was not "whether" to use the atomic bomb, but how best to use it in order to end the war, and thereby avoid what everyone expected to be a horrifically bloody invasion of Japan.

The *Enola Gay*, an American B-29 bomber, flew its fateful mission over Japan on August 6, 1945, carrying the "Little Boy," a bomb weighing nearly ten thousand pounds with the explosive power of about fifteen thousand tons of TNT.[3] The administration issued a carefully worded press release shortly afterward alerting the country to the fact of the attack, but it was not until three days later, in a speech largely devoted to news about the Potsdam peace conference, that Truman sought to explain to Americans what had happened in any detail. During a radio address on the evening of August 9, following the second bombing, of Nagasaki (although Truman did not mention the second city), he suddenly switched topics to explain the shock that the United States had just given Japan and the world: "The first atomic bomb was dropped on Hiroshima, a military base," he announced. "That was because we wished in this first attack to avoid, insofar as possible, the killing of civilians." But Hiroshima was not a "military base." Although the city did contain a military base, over 90 percent of the people killed there were civilians. This particular deception had been planned. At the preparatory meetings for the bomb's use, discussion had focused on those civilian targets that would produce "the greatest psychological effect against Japan." Secretary of War Henry Stimson advised Truman that "we should seek to make a profound psychological impression on as many of the inhabitants as possible." Truman said he understood and agreed.[4]

Today, the number of fatalities caused by the bomb dropped on Hiroshima remains unknown—and the same is true of the weapon dropped on Nagasaki three days later. The Nagasaki bomb on August 9 had a far more devastating impact than the one that had been used on Hiroshima three days earlier. Nagasaki was home to numerous factories but had no military bases, and the bomb caused an estimated seventy-five thousand deaths in the immediate aftermath plus another one hundred eighty thousand or so over the ensuing years as a result of long-term radiation effects. However, it is impossible to calculate an accurate figure. The lingering uncertainty in both cases is due, in large part, to the decision by the director of the Manhattan Project, Lieutenant General Leslie Groves, to censor truthful reports about the bomb's radiation effects—and even to order up false reports as substitutes—in an effort to keep the weapon viable for use in future conflicts. But according to what we do know, up to perhaps one hundred fifty thousand people died in the immediate aftermath of the Hiroshima bombing alone. It is also difficult to estimate the long-term death toll from the effects of radiation. A "Life Span Study" of approximately one hundred twenty thousand Japanese bomb survivors began in 1950 and remains ongoing, but it started too late to provide reliable mortality figures.[5]

It was not only the challenging question of the bomb that flummoxed Truman. His ignorance of Roosevelt's myriad diplomatic demarches, especially those related to the agreements reached at Yalta, left him largely at sea when it came to making the big decisions that the war's end demanded. Truman never fully understood what Roosevelt had committed the country to at Yalta. Add to this his lack of patience and his consuming desire to be perceived as a decisive leader, and the result is quite a few ill-considered decisions, coupled with a significant number of lies to defend them. One of these missteps that has received decidedly little attention, even from most historians, is Truman's decision to engage in a step-by-step repudiation of the Yalta accords.

While most histories of the Cold War blame the Soviet Union for the collapse of the Yalta accords, in fact the United States was guilty of the first unambiguous violation. Churchill, Roosevelt, and Stalin had agreed at Yalta that only countries that had declared war on Nazi Germany by March 1, 1945, would be admitted to the General Assembly of the soon-to-be-created United Nations. The United States chose to ignore this restriction when it voted to seat Argentina even though that nation had failed to meet the Allies' rather generous deadline. Argentina had not only maintained its diplomatic relations with the Nazis for two full years after the United States had entered the war, but it had served as a base for Axis espionage and subversion around the hemisphere. One *Washington Post* writer speculated that the United States cast its vote for Argentina because it was planning "more for the next war than the upcoming peace."[6]

Truman consistently found himself shocked by the brutality of the Soviet Union's behavior—such as its decision to replace the Polish government with one to its own liking, along with Stalin's willingness to summarily execute anyone who dissented. Yet he somehow failed to understand that nothing in the Yalta accords was intended to prevent such actions. Secretary of State James Byrnes told his boss that he should not blame himself for Roosevelt's "duplicity and hypocrisy," but also that, as a result, Truman had no choice but to embrace the same strategy.[7]

Roosevelt's lies about the secret concessions he had made to the Soviets in the Far East also left Truman in a bind. In exchange for a Soviet promise to invade Japan soon after the defeat of Germany, Roosevelt had agreed to allow the Soviets to resume Russia's pre-1905 position in the Far East (prior to its defeat by Japan in the Russo-Japanese War). This included an endorsement of Soviet claims to the return of South Sakhalin (which had been ceded by Japan to Russia in 1875 by treaty, but retaken by Japan in 1905); recognition of existing Soviet hegemony in Outer Mongolia; approval of the lease of Port Arthur, Manchuria, as a naval base; agreement with the preeminence of Soviet commercial interests in Dairen (now Dalian, in Liaoning Province, China), which was to be made a free port; and acceptance of joint Sino-Soviet operations of the Manchurian railways connecting the Soviet Union with Dairen.[8]

Byrnes desperately tried to alter these agreements in private while simultaneously denying any knowledge of their existence in public. When, after Byrnes's resignation, Acting Secretary of State Dean Acheson finally admitted the existence of the deal to Congress, he, too, lied about its actual terms. The administration followed up with the crazy-but-possibly-accurate excuse that literally nobody in the government could find a copy of the agreement. The Soviets, who must have been watching the Americans squirm with a mixture of both glee and alarm, ended these shenanigans by publishing the relevant portions of the secret protocol and occupying their new Far Eastern possessions.[9] Because Truman administration officials refused to ever come clean about these accords, they paved a path by which Yalta could be spun into an ever more nefarious tale of duplicity and even treason. As a result, the conspiracy-mongers who pushed these stories would soon find themselves in the driver's seat of US foreign policy as they agitated for constant confrontation abroad and anti-communist hysteria at home.

What we know as "the Cold War," and the presidential lies it engendered, grew out of this moment. Becoming ever more impatient with the Soviets' refusal to adhere to his blinkered interpretation of what Roosevelt had managed to achieve at Yalta, Truman instructed two young aides, Clark Clifford and George Elsey, to draw up an indictment that would list every Soviet violation to date. The so-called Clifford-Elsey Report of August 1946 was intended to demonstrate the degree to which the Soviets were "chiseling" on their word. Unfortunately, the Soviets were not chiseling at all. The Joint Chiefs of Staff noted that the USSR had adhered to its wartime accords. General Lucius Clay, the US commander in occupied Germany, admitted the same. Dean Acheson, speaking for the State Department, was also unable to locate any Soviet violations. Stuck, Clifford and Elsey found themselves forced to admit that they found it "difficult to adduce direct evidence of literal violations" by the USSR of any of its postwar agreements.[10]

Without any genuine evidence to build their case, the authors took refuge in rhetoric. They laid it on particularly thick, because Truman, as Clifford readily admitted, liked things in "black and white." The combination of Soviet power and communist ideology, the authors argued, represented so great a threat to the United States that just about anything could be justified in response. The memo drew heavily on the arguments laid out by the diplomat and Russian scholar George F. Kennan that had proven so influential in his famous "Long Telegram" of February 1946. In July 1947 it was published in *Foreign Affairs* under the title "The Sources of Soviet Conduct," with the author identified only as "X." It described the Soviets as "committed fanatically to the belief that with US there can be no permanent modus vivendi [and] that it is desirable and necessary that the internal harmony of our society be disrupted, our traditional way of life be destroyed, the international authority of our state be broken, if Soviet power is to be secure."[11]

However little basis in observable fact they may have enjoyed, the Clifford-Elsey arguments, when codified into "United States Objectives and Programs for National Security," or NSC 68, became the official

US government position. Although the document remained classified until 1975, it functioned as the government's operational blueprint for the Cold War. As such, it justified whatever lie a president chose to tell in the name of "national security." After all, if you are facing an adversary while in the grip, as NSC 68 put it, of a "new fanatic faith," seeking "absolute authority over the rest of the world," it becomes possible to justify "any measures, covert or overt, violent or non-violent, which serve the purposes of frustrating the Kremlin design." In such a context, who could object to a little presidential lying?[12]

Americans had largely dispensed with their isolationist illusions following Pearl Harbor; most of the public now accepted that to protect the homeland, they would need to operate militarily on a global scale. As the publishing magnate Henry Luce put it in 1941, in his famous *Life* magazine "The American Century" manifesto, the time had come to reject the "virus of isolationist sterility." The American people, he continued, were above all concerned with making "the society of men safe for the freedom, growth and increasing satisfaction of all individual men." The essay reflected, as Luce biographer Alan Brinkley noted, a pressing desire "to spread the American model to other nations, at times through relatively benign encouragement, at other times through pressure and coercion, but almost always with a fervent and active intent." This credo would guide American presidential politics throughout the Cold War in thick and thin. It was given perhaps its most inspirational expression in John F. Kennedy's January 1961 inaugural address when he proclaimed, "Let every nation know, whether it wishes us well or ill, that we shall pay any price, bear any burden, meet any hardship, support any friend, oppose any foe in order to assure the survival and the success of liberty."[13]

No doubt many millions of people, including future presidents, were moved by the sentiments expressed in these words—but they did not have much relevance for presidential decision-making during the Cold War. For a more realistic explication of America's goals in this period, we must turn to its unofficial ideologist George F. Kennan. In February 1948, while serving as head of the State Department's Policy Planning Staff, Kennan penned a top-secret memo to the secretary of state in which he supplied a different take on American interests:

> We have about 50% of the world's wealth but only 6.3% of its population....In this situation, we cannot fail to be the object of envy and resentment. Our real task in the coming period is to devise a pattern of relationships which will permit us to maintain this position of disparity without positive detriment to our national security. To do so, we will have to dispense with all sentimentality and day-dreaming; and our attention will have to be concentrated everywhere on our immediate national objectives. We need not deceive ourselves that we can afford today the luxury of altruism and world-benefaction.[14]

It was this clear-eyed understanding of America's role in the world that demanded that US presidents go so far as to deceive themselves, their countrymen, and the rest of the world about the true purpose of US foreign policy. And given the nearly limitless scope of US national interests, and the allegedly unprecedented dangers posed by the USSR, a great deal of lying was deemed necessary in order to carry out this decidedly complicated mission.

The Truman administration's phony war scare of 1948 provides a window into how this new ethos allowed the president to hide his true political aims behind the veneer of "national security." Following the end of World War II, US airline manufacturers found themselves in danger of bankruptcy from the subsequent downturn in demand. The massive demobilization of the military left the generals and admirals well short of both the manpower and the weapons they sought for the deployments they anticipated the Cold War would demand. The State Department, moreover, was not getting the funds out of Congress that it needed to carry out an ambitious plan, proposed by Secretary of State George Marshall, to help the countries of Western Europe rebuild themselves, with the corresponding objective being to stave off the challenges those countries faced in resisting the appeal of their own internal Marxist movements and communist parties. And, to top it all off, Truman's election campaign looked to be in serious trouble. All these problems, however, had the same solution. As Clark Clifford laid out in a now-infamous memo: "There is considerable political advantage to the Administration in its battle with the Kremlin."[15]

In early March 1948, General Lucius Clay, now US commander of military forces in Europe, sent a telegram to Senator Henry Cabot Lodge Jr., a leader of the Republicans' internationalist wing, and therefore an ally of the administration in its funding efforts. The telegram informed Lodge that "American personnel are as secure here [in Berlin] as they would be at home." General Stephen Chamberlin, the director of army intelligence, visited Clay in Berlin and told him that in order to get Congress to reinstate the military draft, the administration needed a war scare. (That advice had been offered originally in an early 1947 meeting, when a formerly isolationist Republican senator from Michigan, who was now chair of the Senate Foreign Relations Committee, Arthur H. Vandenberg, had told Truman that to get the military aid he wanted out of Congress for Greece and Turkey, he would have to "scare hell out of the country."[16]) So Clay wrote a second telegram, this one to Chamberlin, to offset the earlier one. It read: "For many months,...I have felt and held that war was unlikely for at least ten years. Within the last few weeks, I have felt a subtle change in Soviet attitude which I cannot define but which now gives me a feeling that it may come with dramatic suddenness." Clay could not supply any new intelligence to support this about-face, so he relied instead on what he called "a feeling of a new tenseness in every Soviet individual with whom we have official relations." In reality, nothing had changed. The Joint Strategic Plans Committee was still reporting to the Joint Chiefs of Staff that war with the Soviets was "not probable for within the next five to seven years."[17]

Secretary of State Marshall and Secretary of War James Forrestal appeared before Congress to hype the nonexistent threat. Insider columnists (and brothers) Joseph and Stewart Alsop reported that "the atmosphere in Washington today is no longer postwar, it is a prewar atmosphere." As the historian Athan Theoharis observed back in 1972, "Truman's willingness to reject the Yalta formulas, while publicly proclaiming his commitment to them, added the element of distrust to diplomatic relations" between the two nations. He then proceeded to blame the Soviets for their breakdown. But as we have seen, the USSR had been careful to respect the letter—though obviously not the spirit—of the Yalta agreements, while the United States had violated both.[18] Even so, it worked. The draft was reinstated, the Marshall Plan was funded, and the US military budget skyrocketed, especially for the purposes of aircraft procurement.[19] Most important, in 1948, Harry Truman was elected president of the United States.[20]

5

Dwight Eisenhower's "Legacy of Ashes"

Harry Truman ended his only full presidential term with an approval rating so low that any attempt at reelection would have been an act of masochism. He was, however, eager to find a replacement who might improve his party's 1952 prospects. So Truman approached America's beloved war hero, General Dwight David "Ike" Eisenhower, then ensconced as president of Columbia University. It turned out that Ike had decided he was a Republican, but Truman was not the first Democrat to make that mistake. The leaders of the militantly liberal Americans for Democratic Action had actually approached Eisenhower to replace Truman as the Democratic nominee four years earlier.

Despite his confusing political identity—or perhaps because of it—Eisenhower enjoyed an almost-unparalleled reputation for common sense, honesty, and decency. The influential syndicated columnist Stewart Alsop professed to detect not only "grandeur" and "power" in the former army chief of staff and supreme allied commander for Europe but also "a curious brand of earnestness as well, which makes him a man remarkably difficult to disbelieve."[1] But Eisenhower lied frequently to Americans and turned out to be the first American president whose dishonesty was revealed to the entire world.

The Eisenhower presidency coincided with a deeply ironic period of American history, one of great success accompanied by an equally debilitating fear. The 1950s were a boom time for what has become known as "Americanism." The late historian Eric Hobsbawm, a proud member of the British Communist Party, toward the end of his life could not but admit that, in the period following World War II, the United States had sustained a path that led it to become

> by any standards the success story among twentieth-century states. Its economy became the world's largest, both pace- and pattern setting; its capacity for technological achievement was unique, its research in both natural and social sciences, even its philosophers became increasingly dominant, and its hegemony of global consumer civilization seemed beyond challenge.[2]

And yet the same historical moment found the nation's politics gripped by senseless paranoia about the ability of its geopolitical and ideological adversary, the Soviet Union, to somehow take it all away. The fever began under Truman, and by the end of his term it had so captured the Republican Party that even the man who had led the Allied armies to victory over Hitler lacked the courage to take it on.

Eisenhower's dishonor in this regard can be traced to his first presidential campaign, during which, at a crucial moment, the war hero proved a profile in cowardice. Wisconsin's demagogic junior senator, Joseph McCarthy, had accused General George Marshall, then President

Truman's secretary of state and Eisenhower's good friend, of incompetence and disloyalty in allegedly allowing hundreds of subversives and spies to serve under him in the State Department. Marshall, like Eisenhower, was among the most admired men in America, and McCarthy's charges against him were transparently meritless. Eisenhower grew so furious that he decided to travel to Wisconsin to defend Marshall on McCarthy's home ground. In doing so, he would demonstrate to the country that he planned to reclaim the Republican Party from the moral disgrace and political hysteria that McCarthy and his allies had helped to foment across America. When the crucial moment arrived, however, Eisenhower choked. Instead of denouncing McCarthy, he stood beside him and endorsed his destructive crusade. "I want to make it very clear about one thing," the man who was soon to be president said. "The purposes he and I have of ridding this Government of the incompetent, the dishonest and above all the subversive and the disloyal are one and the same. Our differences have nothing to do with the end result that we are seeking. The differences apply to method." It stretches credulity to believe that this savvy leader could have been so naïve as to take the pathological liar, McCarthy, at his word about "the end" he sought. McCarthy was not attempting to rid the government of spies or even of communists, but of anyone who refused to go along with his deliberate smears.[3]

To further seal this dishonorable deal, Eisenhower allowed McCarthy the honor of introducing him to the crowd at a campaign stop in the senator's hometown of Appleton. The draft of Eisenhower's speech, including his defense of Marshall, was released to the press in New York and Washington. But when it came time to speak, Eisenhower made no mention of Marshall, leaving his friend to fend for himself. The false release may have been an accident, but it resulted in a far more flattering picture of Eisenhower than his actions merited. Eisenhower's conspiracy of silence here was a lie of omission. President Truman idolized Marshall and turned on Eisenhower in fury as a result, accusing him of associating himself with "a wave of filth" and of appeasing "moral pygmies." His "surrender" to Mc-Carthy, Truman insisted, made Eisenhower "unfit to be president."[4]

As with all Cold War presidents, the lion's share of Eisenhower's dishonesty was undertaken in the service of America's now nearly infinite definition of its "national security" needs. Literally nothing outweighed the need to proactively prevent the spread of Soviet influence anywhere and everywhere in the world, regardless of the consequences for those who fell into the crossfire. And the battlefield on which this ideological struggle would be fought was almost unimaginably vast, given how much America's informal and undeclared empire had now grown. By the end of Eisenhower's second term as president, according to historian Greg Grandin, the US security frontier "ran, starting in the northern Pacific, from Alaska around Japan, southern Korea, and Taiwan, across Southeast Asia (Indonesia to be added later, after its 1964 CIA-supported coup), and back under Australia, New Zealand, Latin America, southern Africa (with more countries from that continent to be included as decolonization from Europe proceeded), up to the Persian Gulf, especially Iran and Saudi Arabia, to Turkey and Pakistan, then across the Elbe to Scandinavia and back around to Canada."[5] A "win" anywhere for the Soviet Union was considered a loss for the United States and therefore not to be tolerated, and few nations anywhere on earth were deemed too insignificant as to be allowed to decide their own fates. The administration's top officials believed so thoroughly that the interests of US corporations meshed with the nation's own interests that it was often hard to tell who was in the driver's seat. This was particularly true when it came time to do the dirty deeds necessary to ensure the cooperation of independently minded foreign leaders. And woe unto those who failed to understand just how stark a choice they faced.

In the oil-rich nation of Iran, one company, Britain's quasi-official Anglo-Iranian Oil Company (AIOC), had enjoyed an unchallenged monopoly on the extraction and refining of its petroleum reserves since 1901. AIOC retained almost all the profits, save for what was necessary to pay in bribes. When, in October 1952, Iran's democratically elected prime minister, Mohammad Mosaddegh, announced plans to nationalize his country's oil industry, it was the British who first raised the idea of a coup. Iran's nationalization law was passed in March 1951 by a strong majority of Iran's parliament and promised to compensate AIOC for the cost of its wells and refining equipment. Mosaddegh noted at the time that Britain had recently nationalized its own coal and steel industries. No matter. What was sauce for the goose was poison for the gander. Britain's spy agency, MI6, attempted a coup but bungled it, and so Mosaddegh was able to proceed with his plans.

US officials were initially divided on the wisdom of an anti-Mosaddegh putsch. The CIA, urged on by then deputy director Allen Dulles, was game, but President Truman was not. The United States itself had no oil interests in Iran, and try as they might, neither the CIA nor MI6 could produce convincing evidence of ties between Mosaddegh and Moscow. Iran's Marxist Tudeh Party was not even cooperating with Mosaddegh, and its membership stood at a paltry 2.3 percent of voters, according to a US National Intelligence Estimate (NIE). As the NIE concluded, the communists did not represent "a serious threat."[6] But the CIA's top man in the Middle East, Kermit Roosevelt—grandson of Panama coup plotter Theodore Roosevelt—would not be deterred. He told the British to be patient so that the CIA could ensure that the deed was done properly.

In fact, the agency already had a number of operations underway in Iran. In the spring of 1951, for instance, it had instituted a multipronged program of domestic subversion against Mosaddegh. Working with the Shah of Iran, Mohammed Reza Pahlevi, who had always proved extremely sympathetic to the needs of both Anglo and American interests—especially as they poured what would eventually become billions of dollars into his family's private fortune—CIA officials oversaw the selection of candidates for parliament and recruited journalists, clerics, and politicians, up to and including vetting the résumés of potential prime ministers. The CIA offered covert support to various Islamic organizations looking to attack Mosaddegh supporters and hired thugs to beat them up. The campaign, which started under the Truman administration but continued into the Eisenhower years, also included "poison pens, personal denunciations, and rumor mongering [in the Iranian media]"—actions that fell under the category of "moral sabotage."[7] Eisenhower became president in January 1953, and orders for a second coup attempt went out that August with his assent. But this coup failed as well, as the bulk of the army remained loyal to its elected government.

Dulles and the rest of the CIA were ready to call it quits and try to make a deal with Mosaddegh. But Kermit Roosevelt, who had traveled to Tehran for the coup, was determined to somehow save it. Ignoring instructions from Washington, he redoubled US support for the coup plotters. This renewed effort involved more bribery, bombings of government buildings by both Iranian and CIA planes, and a massive propaganda blitz to spread the lie that the Mosaddegh government was in the pocket of the Soviets. The third time proved the charm. Soon enough, the Shah was back on his golden throne, the generals were in control, Mosaddegh was in jail for life, oil profits were flowing back to Britain, and Persian democracy was consigned to the dustbin of history. It took the US government fully six decades to admit that any of this actually happened. "The military coup that overthrew Mosaddegh and his National Front cabinet was carried out under CIA direction as an act of US foreign policy, conceived and approved at the highest levels of government," the agency's official history admitted in 2013. Britain's MI6, meanwhile, remains stoically silent about its role to this day.[8]

President Eisenhower was kept abreast on the coup while on vacation, and it pleased him mightily. He told the public that "Iran threw off a threat of Communist domination and came strongly to our side." In his diary, however, he admitted, "The things we did were covert. If knowledge of them became public, we would not only be embarrassed in that region, but our chances to do anything of like nature in the future would almost totally disappear."[9] The autocratic regime the United States imposed on Iran would last through 1979, when its corruption and cruelty inspired the Islamic Revolution that overthrew it. Relations between the United States and Iran have remained toxic ever since.

Within the Eisenhower administration and its ever more ambitious national security establishment, the US overthrow of Iran's democratically elected government was considered not merely a success but a model, and the president was eager to apply it elsewhere. When Jacobo Arbenz Guzmán ascended to the presidency of Guatemala in 1951, he was only the second leader to be elected during what has become known as that nation's "democratic spring." His election marked the first peaceful transfer of power in its history. But "democratic" was a decidedly relative term in mid-twentieth-century Guatemala. At the time, the United Fruit Company (UFC) administered the country's primary harbor, and its subsidiary, the International Railways of Central America, controlled virtually every mile of the country's railroad tracks as well as its telegraph and telephone infrastructure. In his inaugural address, Arbenz promised "to convert our country from a dependent nation with a semi-colonial economy into an economically independent country," and "to convert Guatemala from a country bound by a predominantly feudal economy into a modern capitalist state."[10]

In June 1952, Arbenz devised a plan to expropriate mostly fallow and underused land from large estates, much of it owned by the UFC, and divide it into small parcels that could then be sold to landless peasant farmers. He planned to compensate the corporation to the tune of $1.185 million, an amount matching the company's own valuation of the land for taxation purposes. A *New York Times* editorial called the plan "long overdue," but United Fruit's executives begged to differ. The corporation enlisted the services of Edward Bernays, known today as the "father of public relations." Bernays had learned his trade working for George Creel's Committee for Public Information during World War I, and he had headed up groundbreaking advertising campaigns for a number of major corporations. For United Fruit, Bernays painted a picture of a nation in chaos—and therefore an easy target for communist subversion. Referring to Mosaddegh's attempt to nationalize Iran's oil industry, Bernays warned that "Guatemala might follow suit." It was all part of what a Democratic congressman from Massachusetts, John McCormack, called, on the House floor, "the Kremlin's design for world conquest."[11]

When *New York Times* reporter Sydney Gruson provided the paper's readers with reasonably accurate coverage of events on the ground in Guatemala City, minimizing the (largely nonexistent) communist presence and noting the nationalist fervor developing in favor of Arbenz in the face of the US / United Fruit propaganda onslaught, Allen Dulles, now the agency's first-ever civilian director, made his displeasure clear to the paper's publisher, Arthur Hays Sulzberger. Gruson soon got a one-way ticket back to Times Square. In fact, Guatemala's Communist Party boasted a membership of just a few hundred, and its adherents in the country's sixty-one-seat legislature languished in the low single digits. The Soviets did not even have diplomatic relations with Guatemala at the time, and a classified State Department report judged the country's tiny Communist Party "indigenous." Publicly, however, the department issued a report saying just the opposite. Admitting that "the Communists are not seeking open and direct control of the Guatemalan Government," the report nevertheless maintained that their tactics demonstrated a desire "to convert [the country] into an indirectly controlled instrument of Communism."[12]

This nonsensical argument received a significant boost from Arbenz in April 1954, when he bought some decidedly obsolete and ill-functioning arms from Czechoslovakia—something that could only have happened with Moscow's approval. The CIA had captured

Arbenz in a trap that would become unmistakably familiar to leftist leaders during the Cold War: the United States would justify a coup or an invasion by citing a threat posed by that nation's reaction to the United States' threat of a coup or an invasion. Arbenz was the first but hardly the last to fall for it.

"Operation PBSuccess," which began two months later, in June 1954, turned out to be a bloody affair, with far greater loss of life and destruction of property than its Iranian prototype. When elements of the Guatemalan military attempted to defend their nation's sovereignty, CIA-funded forces bombed their barracks and strafed them with machine guns. They attacked numerous targets all over the country, including Guatemala City's airport and fuel storage facilities, causing fires that quickly spread into civilian areas. When the coup appeared to teeter, Dulles convinced Eisenhower to send in more bombers. The president told an aide, "If at any time you take the route of violence or support violence, then you commit yourself to carrying it through, and it's too late to have second thoughts." Meanwhile, the secretary of state, John Foster Dulles (the brother of the CIA director), lied—and it turned out to be only the first of many lies that he would tell Americans during the course of the coup. On this occasion, he announced to the country, on June 19, that the State Department had received reports of "a revolt of Guatemalans against the government." With impressive audacity, he would later explain in a radio address that "the Guatemalan government and Communist agents throughout the world have persistently attempted to obscure the real issue—that of Communist imperialism." Dulles deemed the concerns of the United Fruit Company to be "relatively unimportant." But as Arbenz well knew, his country's crime was "having enacted an agrarian reform which affected the interests of the United Fruit Company."[13] Arbenz went into exile, and soon afterward, the CIA's handpicked leader, a colonel named Carlos Castillo Armas, handed United Fruit back its land.

Eisenhower would later elaborate on the lies his administration told in his memoir, creating a fully fictional account of the coup. He

78

dated the beginning of the crisis to 1944, the year of Guatemala's first free election, and blamed communist infiltration of the nation's labor unions, peasant organizations, and media. He called Arbenz "merely a puppet manipulated by Communists." He then invented a scenario in which "the agents of international Communism in Guatemala continued their efforts to penetrate and subvert their neighboring Central American states[,]...fomenting political assassinations and strikes [abroad]" while "answer[ing] protests [at home] by suspending constitutional rights, conducting mass arrests, and killing leaders in the political opposition." When "Arbenz had declared a state of siege and launched a reign of terror," Eisenhower said, he finally felt forced to act. In his characterization, the United States merely supplied "a small amount of air support" to the coup. Even so, he insisted that the coup was driven not by the CIA's ambitions, but instead by "the disaffection of the Guatemalan armed forces and the population as a whole with the tyrannical regime of Arbenz."[14]

In fact, overthrowing Arbenz not only destroyed democracy in Guatemala but also dealt a significant setback to hopes for free elections across much of Latin America. Potential peaceful reformers, revolutionaries, and aspiring autocrats all learned the same lesson: Washington wanted malleable, cooperative governments in its backyard, not potentially troublesome democratic ones, no matter what level of corruption or human rights abuses took place as a result. One revolutionary who learned this lesson was a young, recently graduated Argentinean physician named Ernesto "Che" Guevara, who happened to be visiting Guatemala during the coup. Two years later, he traveled to Cuba to help Fidel Castro mount his anti-imperialist revolution there. Guevara considered this a model revolt and would attempt to export its methods to other nations, including Bolivia. But he would be assassinated in that country in 1967 with the help of the CIA. Guevara's death transformed him into a global symbol of resistance to American military and political power—Eisenhower's and Dulles's lies had created exactly the danger they had invented to justify them. The very day after the Bay of Pigs invasion of Cuba—aided and directed by the United States during the Kennedy administration—failed so miserably, the president's adviser for national security, McGeorge Bundy, lamented to his young aide Marcus Raskin, "Well, Che learned more from Guatemala than we did."[15]

Meanwhile, in Guatemala, the results of the coup turned out to be nearly forty years of unbroken military dictatorship coupled with human rights abuses and the brutal suppression of nearly all forms of civil liberties. Once Castillo Armas became president, he immediately declared a new law establishing the death penalty for a series of political "crimes." At the same time, he disenfranchised three-quarters of Guatemala's voting population; outlawed all political parties, labor confederations, and peasant organizations; and indefinitely postponed all future presidential elections. Guatemala became a country led by military-backed terrorists, and the military became a caste unto itself, with its leaders enjoying vast ranches in an area called the "Zone of the Generals." They regularly sold Mafia-style protection to the country's feudal landowners. Semiofficial death squads terrorized virtually every sector of civil society, murdering lawyers, schoolteachers, journalists, peasant leaders, priests and other religious workers, politicians, trade union organizers, students, and professors. They carried out these activities with de facto impunity. Indeed, during the 1980s, the government exterminated more than two hundred thousand people, mostly Mayans, committing what the 1999 UN-sponsored Historical Clarification Commission termed "genocide." That same commission credited "the United States government and US private companies" with "exercising pressure to maintain the country's archaic and unjust socioeconomic structure."[16]

In the Eisenhower administration, meanwhile, the coups in Iran and Guatemala were perceived as successes, which stoked a desire for more coups. Oil-rich Indonesia, an archipelago stretching across three thousand miles of the Indian and Pacific Oceans, fought off Dutch rule to gain its independence in 1949. Secretary of State John Foster Dulles considered its elected leader, Sukarno, to be "dangerous, untrustworthy and by character susceptible to the Communist way of thinking." In fact, Sukarno sought to court both sides of the Cold War simultaneously, pretending to offer each what it wanted and implicitly threatening to bolt if his needs were not satisfied. At the same time that he invited communists into his government, he explained to the US ambassador to his country, Howard P. Jones, that he personally was "a nationalist but no Communist," adding that "nationalism is the fire that is sweeping Asia." But, here again, virtually no one in the US government or political establishment took this distinction seriously.

First, the CIA pumped millions of dollars into Indonesia's elections. When this policy failed to achieve the agency's goals, it opted for more direct measures. The initial operation began in 1957. Eisenhower approved the plan, but insisted, for purposes of plausible deniability, that no Americans be involved in the actual fighting. CIA director Allen Dulles ignored these instructions, however, and ordered agency bombing raids against both civilian and military targets. The operation could hardly have failed more spectacularly. Not only was a US pilot shot down, but the uprising pushed Sukarno to embrace his country's Communist Party. John Foster Dulles, meanwhile, had lied yet again when, speaking to reporters, he denied knowledge of the failed coup and any involvement in it. Eventually, this debacle would inspire a far more extensive and successful CIA sabotage operation in 1965, this time in support of Sukarno, who proved a nimble pawn in the bloody Cold War chess match and was once again ready to switch sides.[17]

Variations on the same theme were taking place on other continents, such as Africa, where events in what is now the Democratic Republic of the Congo (formerly the Belgian Congo, the Republic of the Congo, and Zaire), for example, were similar. In an extremely complicated, ongoing political crisis resulting from the nation achieving its independence in June 1960, while in the throes of civil war, Prime

Minister Patrice Lumumba, an internationally recognized leader of the Pan-African movement, facing a coup, appealed to the United States for help. He was rebuffed, however, and so turned to the Soviet Union. The coup succeeded, and Lumumba was imprisoned and tortured by his opponents within the republic. Then, during the final forty-eight hours of Eisenhower's presidency, in January 1961, Lumumba was assassinated. Historians remain divided about whether Eisenhower ordered his death or it was CIA director Allen Dulles who took the decisive action on his own. Or Dulles may have merely assumed these were Eisenhower's orders based on the latter's musings in the style of "Will no one rid me of this meddlesome priest?" In 1975, a congressional investigation found that Dulles had told his subordinates that Lumumba's murder was an "urgent and prime objective," and budgeted $100,000 for the job. Although the precise degree of CIA responsibility for the plot remains unclear, the result was that Lumumba was dead, his government was over, and the army chief of staff, Joseph-Désiré Mobutu, was now in power. Mobutu ruled as a dictator and remained the country's leader for almost thirty-seven years, up to his death in 1997. Belgian and British intelligence were also deeply involved, and of course the plotters had their own ambitions. But Mobutu had already been on the CIA's payroll, receiving both funds and arms, and following the coup the agency dispersed at least another $500,000 to him and his allies.[18] Like Che Guevara, albeit on a smaller scale, Lumumba would become a martyr to the cause of anti-imperialism and inspire countless revolutionaries to follow his path. And like Guatemala and Iran, Zaire (the name of the country under Mobuto from 1971 through 1997) became a US-supported kleptocracy. Its corrupt leaders made a practice of enriching themselves via the sale of natural resources and jailed and tortured anyone who got in their way. The hope for democracy, meanwhile, remained a brief, dreamlike memory.

The great irony of these coups and assassinations is that they not only upended genuinely democratic governments, and made liars of Eisenhower and his subordinates, but also undermined the CIA's ability to carry out the job for which it was actually created: the collection and analysis of intelligence. On January 5, 1961, just two weeks before Eisenhower left office, the president's Board of Consultants on Foreign Intelligence Activities admitted, "We are unable to conclude that, on balance, all of the covert action programs undertaken by CIA up to this time have been worth the risk of the great expenditure of manpower, money and other resources involved." According to the board, these activities "tended to distract substantially from the execution of [the agency's] primary intelligence-gathering mission." To Eisenhower, this failure constituted what he termed an "an eight-year defeat." At the end of his term, he admitted to Allen Dulles that he regretted leaving what he called a "legacy of ashes" to his successor, President John F. Kennedy.[19]

By far the most personally painful lie Eisenhower told as president was the one in which he got caught. During a 1955 summit in Geneva, the president had proposed an "Open Skies" program to Soviet premier Nikita Khrushchev whereby each nation would be permitted to fly over the other's territory without warning in order to keep an eye on each other's nuclear facilities. The idea, he said, was that such a practice would enhance deterrence. The Soviets saw the deal as a transparent espionage proposal. Eisenhower, Khruschev observed, "could hardly expect [them] to take this seriously."[20] Eisenhower knew that this would be their response, and the entire point of the exercise was to publicly contrast American openness with Soviet secrecy. The gambit worked perfectly as a propaganda ploy and redounded to the president's benefit at home. Meanwhile, there was little progress at the summit on any issue of substance.

Without permission to conduct legal overflights, the CIA began them anyway, deploying the U-2, a plane capable of flying at a high enough altitude to evade Soviet ground-based radar, to carry out these missions. It was crucial that the overflights go undetected, as the unauthorized invasion of Soviet airspace would certainly be understood as an act of war. The administration started sending out these planes in 1956 and continued until May 1, 1960, when a Soviet surface-to-air missile downed a U-2 piloted by Francis Gary Powers near the city of Sverdlovsk in the Ural Mountains. Powers ejected and parachuted safely to the ground only to be captured by local authorities.

Four days afterward, Khrushchev disclosed to the world that an American plane had been shot down over Soviet territory. In response, the administration concocted a story about a "weather research plane" that might have accidentally drifted into Soviet territory from Turkey, saying that Powers, whom the White House assumed to be dead, had been a civilian employee of the Lockheed Corporation. A State Department spokesperson insisted that the poor fellow had apparently just "blacked out." He then reiterated that "there was absolutely no—N-O—no deliberate attempt to violate Soviet air space. There never has been." The clear implication was one of Soviet perfidy and paranoia. It was then that a smiling Premier Khrushchev appeared before a Communist Party gathering to tell the world, "I must let you in on a secret. When I made my report two days ago, I deliberately refrained from mentioning that we have the remains of the plane—and we also have the pilot, who is quite alive and kicking." Laughter followed when Khrushchev revealed that the Soviets had recovered the plane's aerial camera system as well as "a tape recording of the signals of a number of our ground radar stations—incontestable evidence of spying." Upon hearing this, Eisenhower turned to his private secretary and admitted, "I would like to resign."[21]

A US president caught in a bald-faced lie and exposed by the leader of his country's greatest adversary was something decidedly new in history. No one close to the president had any idea how to deal with it. So they improvised. At the State Department, a spokesperson insisted the flight was a rogue adventure, unauthorized in Washington. This was another lie, as the president himself had not only initiated the program but had signed off on its flight schedule and targets. Eisenhower pretended to "heartily approve" of a proposed congressional investigation of the incident, but at the same time he instructed both the CIA and the Joint Chiefs of Staff to quash it. The White House staff secretary, General Andrew Goodpaster, instructed Christian Herter, who had become secretary of state after John Foster Dulles's death in 1959, to lie under oath to Congress when questioned, explaining that the "president wants no specific tie to him of this particular event."[22] So when Herter testified that the U-2 flight program had "never come up to the president," he was committing perjury on orders from the president's top aide.[23] The fallout from the incident included the cancellation of the US-Soviet summit in Paris, which had been scheduled to discuss the ongoing situation in divided Germany, as well as the possibility of an arms control or test ban treaty along with a general relaxation of tensions. The Soviet Union convicted Powers of spying and sentenced him to three years in prison and seven more of hard labor, but he was later traded for a captured Soviet spy.

In retirement, Eisenhower admitted that he deeply regretted this dissimulation. The first time he said this was in a filmed interview with CBS News in 1961, but his son, Lieutenant Colonel John Eisenhower, demanded that it be cut before the segment aired. A year later, a reporter for the *Miami Herald*, David Kraslow, visited Eisenhower at his Gettysburg farm and asked him to name his "greatest regret." Eisenhower replied, "The lie we told. I didn't realize how high a price we were going to have to pay for that lie. If I had to do it all over again I would have kept our mouths shut."[24] It is telling that Eisenhower refers only to the lie he was caught telling. But he needn't have worried. His popularity remained untouched by the crisis, and his historical reputation remains no less stellar today than it was when he turned his office over to his young successor, John Fitzgerald Kennedy, on a snowy January 20, 1961.

6

John F. Kennedy and the "Right" to Lie

Dwight Eisenhower was the first president to be caught in an unambiguous lie to the American people, but John Kennedy was the first whose administration actively argued for the government's "right"—indeed, duty—to mislead the country. Kennedy demonstrated no less compunction about lying than any of his predecessors and perhaps had more reasons to do so. No president ever defined America's sense of global responsibility more expansively than Kennedy did in his famous inaugural address, when he promised that the nation would "pay any price, bear any burden, meet any hardship, support any friend, oppose any foe to assure the survival and the success of liberty." But "liberty" for foreigners was not really what Kennedy wished to see the United States bear its burdens for. And in most of the myriad places that the United States had come to define as within its sphere of vital interests, America's involvement, whether covert or overt, required a great deal of lying to be carried out.

John F. Kennedy and the "Right" to Lie

Kennedy came into office already set up to lie by his predecessor, Eisenhower, who had left him with the poorly planned Bay of Pigs invasion of Cuba ready to go. Add to this Kennedy's personal problems, deriving from his horrific health issues; his incautious connections to organized crime; and his almost-impossible-to-believe sexual shenanigans, and you have a president for whom lying was an ongoing necessity. As with Franklin D. Roosevelt, with whom he was often compared, some of Kennedy's most significant lies may have saved millions of lives by preventing nuclear war; on these matters, we can only be grateful today for his farsightedness. And yet, like FDR, Kennedy, in the end, lacked the courage to tell the American people the truth about what he had done in their service.

The Kennedy administration first asserted its "right to lie" during the Cuban Missile Crisis, when the Soviet Union began constructing missile sites in Cuba. On October 19, 1962, Assistant Secretary of Defense for Public Affairs Arthur Sylvester told the press (and therefore the country): "The Pentagon has no information indicating the presence of offensive weapons in Cuba." In fact, just three days earlier, top US military officials had been urging President Kennedy to undertake a full-scale invasion of the island to counter these very weapons. Sylvester would later explain his decision not to acknowledge the truth: "It's inherent in [the] government's right, if necessary, to lie to save itself," he insisted. "News generated by the actions of the government…[are] part of the arsenal of weaponry that a President has." Kennedy's press secretary, Pierre Salinger, would later endorse this view: Lies and disinformation were the means by which "democracy…defends itself in a cold-war situation against an enemy which can operate in secret."[1] Here we see the logic of NSC 68 reasserting itself—logic that Kennedy effectively exploited in his abbreviated presidency but that would undermine his successor, Lyndon Johnson. The difference was that Kennedy's lies were told in the service of victory, while Johnson's were told in defeat.

It is not as if the Kennedy administration had been in any doubt about its "right to lie" before the missile crisis. Immediately after the failed 1961 Bay of Pigs plot, in which CIA-backed Cuban exiles invaded the island only to be abandoned by the Kennedy administration and slaughtered by Castro's forces, Arthur Schlesinger Jr., the liberal intellectual and activist whom Kennedy employed as a special assistant, authored a memo advising that "when lies must be told, they should be told by subordinate officials," in order to protect the president's plausible deniability. "At no point should the President be asked to lend himself to the cover operation," Schlesinger wrote. It would be preferable, he wrote, to have "someone other than the President make the final decision and do so in his absence." Thus, a subordinate's "head can later be placed on the block if things go terribly wrong." When this memo was released to the public more than a decade after it was written, it caused mere snickers, rather than outrage, in the post-Watergate political press, whose members had grown relatively inured to the notion of a lying president. William F. Buckley, for instance, writing in the *New York Post*, asked, "Could Nixon have improved on that one?" His answer: "No sir, this is Grade A, Harvard BA, Harvard Ph.D. Quality Lying." (Ironically, Schlesinger, who like his father had been a Harvard University professor of history before working at the White House, never did earn a PhD.[2])

The fact is that few presidents have had more reason to lie to the public than John Fitzgerald Kennedy. He would never have become president had he not consistently misled the public about his health, or about his astonishingly voracious libido. At the time of his election, neither of these issues were considered appropriate for public discussion or respectable journalistic investigation. The press had purposely hidden FDR's affairs as well as his physical condition, and suppressed news of his wife Eleanor's likely lesbian relationship with her friend Lorena Hickok. Even so, Kennedy's philandering would likely have shocked not only FDR but almost every other president before him. But as with his predecessors, Kennedy's most profound and influential lies were told in the context of his desire to further the country's Cold War empire and its all-but-infinite definition of its "national security" needs.

Kennedy's road to the White House was hardly a straightforward one, much less an honest one. But surprisingly for such a closely contested election, both Kennedy and his Republican opponent, Richard Nixon, ran relatively truthful presidential campaigns in 1960. The most significant policy lie JFK told as a candidate arose from the so-called US-USSR missile gap. The Cold War had begun to feel so warm to Americans by this time that their top priority was electing a president tough enough to take on the Soviets by whatever means necessary, up to and including the credible threat of nuclear war. The alleged advantage enjoyed by the Soviets in the realm of intercontinental ballistic missiles (ICBMs) during the late 1950s was a major issue for the Kennedy campaign. According to the candidate's claims, the Eisenhower administration, in which Nixon served as vice president, had allowed the Soviets to accumulate nearly twenty times the number of missiles the United States had, and experts were predicting the Soviets' advantage to grow to nearly 100-to-1 within three years. In reality, the Soviets had fewer than four operational ICBMs capable of reaching the United States at the time—and may not have had any at all. The United States, meanwhile, possessed at least forty such missiles, and they were capable of striking back in the event of an attack. The United States would retain its enormous military advantage right up through the 1970s, especially given its supply of nuclear-armed bombers and submarines.[3]

In a similarly sly and dishonest vein, Kennedy attacked Nixon for allegedly standing idly by as Fidel Castro established a communist beachhead in Cuba, even though he had been fully briefed on the CIA's plans to try to overthrow Castro in the coming Bay of Pigs operation.[4] Nixon was effectively unable to respond to these charges—just as he was unable to rebut Kennedy's false claims about the supposed missile gap—because doing so would have meant revealing classified information he had received as vice president. He received no help from President Eisenhower, who appeared to be secretly enjoying his vice president's humiliation.

Kennedy also lied repeatedly to the public about his health, both as a candidate and as president. Throughout his life, he had suffered through a remarkable array of injuries and illnesses, and he had demonstrated remarkable strength and stoicism as he endured them. But, needless to say, neither Kennedy nor anyone else ever told the truth about his maladies until after his assassination. In this respect, the Kennedy presidency mirrored those of two Democratic administrations preceding him: those of Woodrow Wilson and Franklin Roosevelt. In each of those cases, the results of the lies had been disastrous. In Kennedy's case, such a judgment is much more difficult to make.

Robert Dallek, who remains the only historian ever to be given access to the slain president's medical records, wrote that Kennedy's various maladies constituted "one of the best-kept secrets of recent U.S. history." But they were less "secrets" than lies. According to Bill Walton, a Kennedy family friend, JFK was followed everywhere during the 1960 presidential campaign by an aide with a special bag containing the "medical support." When the bag was misplaced during a trip to Connecticut, Kennedy telephoned the governor of that state, Abraham Ribicoff, and said, "There's a medical bag floating around and it can't get in anybody's hands....You have to find that bag." If the wrong people got hold of it, he added, "it would be murder." (The bag was recovered.) When, during the primary campaign, aides to his opponent, Senate Majority Leader Lyndon Johnson, told the press—correctly—that Kennedy suffered from a potentially life-threatening case of Addison's disease, the Kennedys publicly denied the allegation and released a letter from two of JFK's doctors describing his health as "excellent." Not everyone bought this story, however, and in the fall of 1960, as Kennedy and Nixon battled one another in what would turn out to be, as of 2019, the closest popular vote in history, thieves ransacked the office of New York endocrinologist Eugene J. Cohen. When they failed to find Kennedy's records, which were filed under a code name, they tried unsuccessfully to break into the office of Janet G. Travell, an internist and pharmacologist who had also treated Kennedy.[5]

Had Kennedy's medical records been accurate and comprehensive—and made public—they would likely have been as thick as a Manhattan phone book. Even today, it remains difficult to keep track of the various ailments that simultaneously afflicted him, to say nothing of the effects of the myriad misguided treatments administered by the countless physicians and others who attended to him. In Dallek's recounting, we learn of a childhood marred not only by the childhood diseases that were typical at the time, including chicken pox, ear infections, German measles, measles, mumps, and whooping cough, but also scarlet fever, bronchitis, and possibly osteoporosis and degeneration of his lumbar spine. In 1954, while he was in the US Senate, Kennedy chose to undergo a life-threatening operation in which a metal plate was inserted to stabilize his spine. The procedure ended up putting him in a coma, during which, for the second time in his brief life, a priest was summoned to perform last rites. Treatments, according to the records that Dallek reviewed, included "ingested and implanted DOCA [deoxycorticosterone acetate] for the Addison's, and large doses of penicillin and other antibiotics to combat the prostatitis and the abscess. He also received injections of procaine at 'trigger points' to relieve back pain; anti-spasmodics—principally Lomotil and Trasentine—to control the colitis; testosterone to keep up his weight (which fell with each bout of colitis and diarrhea); and Nembutal to help him sleep." At one point, his cholesterol reached an amazing level of 410. (A reading of 240 is considered unhealthy.) All this, needless to say, was kept from the public. When asked about his health, Kennedy and his representatives lied outright, repeatedly and without exception.[6]

Winning the 1960 presidential election did not cure Kennedy of his multiple maladies, and so the deception continued. Responding to a reporter's question a day after the election, Kennedy pronounced himself to be in "excellent" shape and dismissed all talk of Addison's. Robert Kennedy, soon to be his brother's attorney general, supplied false information to the American Medical Association journal *Today's Health*, which, according to a summary published in the *New York Times*, found the president to be in "superb physical condition" and more than ready to assume the duties of the presidency. In fact, Dallek noted, Kennedy was receiving treatments from an allergist, an endocrinologist, a gastroenterologist, an orthopedist, and a urologist along with at least three other dispensers of medicine and medical wisdom, including, most notoriously, Max Jacobson, also known as "Dr. Feelgood," who would regularly administer shots of amphetamines and adrenaline to the likes of Andy Warhol, Marilyn Monroe, Elvis Presley, and the president of the United States.[7]

It is impossible to say just how all these afflictions and treatments affected Kennedy. During both the Bay of Pigs incident and the Cuban Missile Crisis, Kennedy was, according to Dallek, simultaneously under the influence of "steroids for his Addison's disease; painkillers for his back; anti-spasmodics for his colitis; antibiotics for urinary-tract infections; antihistamines for allergies; and, on at least one occasion, an anti-psychotic (though only for two days) for a severe mood change that Jackie Kennedy believed had been brought on by the antihistamines."[8] Nevertheless, Kennedy somehow handled both crises with remarkable aplomb, demonstrating what might fairly be called superhuman strength and endurance. How he did it will forever remain another mystery in Kennedy's already profoundly mysterious life.

John Kennedy was obviously not the first philanderer elected to the presidency. But he was undoubtedly the most energetic. His only competition may have been Warren Harding.

John F. Kennedy and the "Right" to Lie

America's twenty-ninth president, who died in office in 1923, ran a deeply corrupt administration and is almost always ranked by historians as among America's worst presidents. He would not disagree. He was, in his own estimation, a man of "limited talents from a small town" who could never "seem to grasp" that he was president. But one area in which he excelled was in having illicit sex in and around the White House. His escapades as president included a long-term affair with Nan Britton, with whom he allegedly had a son he never met; another long-term affair with Carrie Fulton Phillips, who received a $5,000 hush-money check monthly from the Republican National Committee; another affair with Marion Louise Hodder, who claimed yet another child of the president's; and yet another with his staff secretary.[9]

Sex, meanwhile, for John Kennedy served less as an expression of emotion than a form of medication. In 1961, he told Prime Minister Harold Macmillan of Britain that if he did not have sex at least every three days, he would get a terrible headache. According to one former partner, Kennedy approached fornication with workmanlike dedication. "He wasn't in it for the cuddling," she observed. Nor did he evince much concern for the potential impact of his sexual escapades on his marriage, on his political career, or on the national security of the United States. In August 1963, for instance, a West German embassy worker named Ellen Rometsch found herself expelled from the United States. She was suspected of being an East German spy. But she was also rumored to be one of Kennedy's many sex partners in the White House. As a result, either Attorney General Robert Kennedy or the FBI director, J. Edgar Hoover, had her deported.[10]

Judged in political terms, Kennedy's most significant paramour was undoubtedly Judith Campbell (later Judith Campbell Exner). She claimed to have regularly carried envelopes back and forth between her lover, Kennedy, and Sam Giancana, the top man in the Chicago Mafia, and Johnny Roselli, Giancana's Los Angeles lieutenant.

Exner, who was in her midtwenties at the time, also said she helped arrange numerous face-to-face meetings between Kennedy and Giancana, including one in the White House. There is no way to confirm these stories, and it is hard to believe the president could be *this* reckless. But despite insistent denials of the affair by Kennedy aides, White House logs were later found to contain roughly seventy phone calls between Exner and Evelyn Lincoln, Kennedy's personal secretary.[11] And these do not include the calls to Kennedy's personal phone numbers—ones that changed each week but were given to his Mafia-connected girlfriend.

According to Exner, as told to the tabloid-style (but not unreliable) biographer Kitty Kelley, she began her side career as a Kennedy courier in April 1960. Exner claimed that with Jackie away, pregnant, in Florida, she and then presidential candidate Kennedy had sex in his Georgetown home before he asked her to set up a meeting with Giancana, because, as Kennedy explained, "I think I may need his help in the campaign." According to FBI wiretaps, significant Mafia donations to JFK's West Virginia campaign were subsequently disbursed by Kennedy's friend Frank Sinatra, a mutual friend of the senator and the mobster. Those funds were then used for payoffs to local politicians to get the Kennedy vote out during that state's crucial primary, which Kennedy won in a squeaker. Giancana also took credit for manipulating the vote in Kennedy's favor in Cook County, Illinois, during the general election, where the Democratic candidate prevailed over Nixon by fewer than nine thousand votes.[12]

The story grew even more bizarre when Attorney General Robert Kennedy made Giancana a top-priority target for the Justice Department, resulting in agents putting a tail on Exner as well. Exner said that John Kennedy confided to her that he thought the surveillance was "part of [J. Edgar] Hoover's vendetta" against him—and that he called the FBI director "a queer son of a bitch." She claimed he also told her not to worry about Giancana's fate, because "you know he works for us." Why Kennedy allowed his brother to undertake this risky investigation is all but impossible to explain. In any case, the affair with Exner was over by early 1962, and Kennedy found a new love, Mary Pinchot Meyer, sister-in-law to his close friend Ben Bradlee and the ex-wife of a CIA agent, Cord Meyer. (Kennedy's rejection of Exner, followed by his assassination, sent her into a tailspin that ended with a lengthy stay in a sanitarium following a suicide attempt, and Pinchot Meyer was mysteriously murdered in 1964.) At one point, finding himself hassled in Chicago's O'Hare International Airport by FBI agents, Giancana lashed out, "I know all about the Kennedys....You lit a fire tonight that will never go out. You'll rue the day."[13] Kennedy was remarkably vulnerable to the Mafia as a result of whatever dealings he (and his father and brother) may actually have had with Giancana, Roselli, and whoever else may have been involved, but the president had no reason to fear that his sexual affairs, at least, would be exposed in the press. When asked about the rumors, he denied them, but this happened only rarely. Any discussion of the president's sex life would have violated what were then the rules of respectable reporting. What's more, most of the journalists who covered Kennedy revered him; his legendary charm worked almost as well on men as it did on women.

One of the few people in Washington immune to the president's charm was FBI chief J. Edgar Hoover, who neither liked Kennedy nor believed in turning a blind eye to anything he could use to enhance his own power and that of the bureau. At a luncheon meeting in March 1962, Hoover questioned Kennedy about Exner and her connections to Giancana and Roselli, and the meeting is understood by historians to have led Kennedy to sever his ties to Sinatra. When Kennedy stood up Sinatra—who had had a helipad built especially for Kennedy at his Palm Springs home—and chose to stay at the Republican crooner Bing Crosby's house instead, it infuriated the singer so much that some of his friends credit the snub with inspiring the singer's switch from left-wing Kennedy acolyte and civil rights champion to right-wing Nixon booster. But the story is also significant because that evening at Crosby's was apparently the only time that Kennedy and screen goddess Marilyn Monroe were alone together, presumably consummating their relationship. The tryst was arranged by the president's brother-in-law Peter Lawford. It is possible that this was another reason why Kennedy moved his stay to Crosby's home, as Sinatra, a former lover of Monroe's himself, might not have been so accommodating (or closed-mouthed).[14] Hoover's warning, meanwhile, can be seen as a warning for the president's political benefit, but it might just as well have been Hoover's way of warning the president against trying to replace him as head of the FBI. And given the decades of damage Hoover caused, not only to Kennedy's presidency but to the nation itself—up to and including his attempt to drive Martin Luther King Jr. to suicide by threatening to expose his extramarital affairs—it is not hard to see just how consequential the results of the lies were that Kennedy needed to tell to protect his "privacy."

In June 1975, long after Kennedy's November 1963 assassination, Sam Giancana was scheduled to testify before the House Select Committee on Assassinations when he was found with seven bullets in his skull in his Oak Park, Illinois, kitchen. His murder remains unsolved. Roselli appeared before the committee, however, and told its members about the role of the Mafia—and especially that of Giancana—in the CIA's countless failed attempts to kill Cuba's communist dictator, Fidel Castro, which were apparently directed by Robert Kennedy. Did RFK hide these efforts from his brother, the president? It is possible, but doubtful, especially since documents later surfaced that, according to investigative reporter Seymour Hersh, writing in his 2018 memoir, "made it clear that the continuous pressure to assassinate Fidel Castro emanated from Jack Kennedy." Roselli's body was fished from a fifty-five-gallon oil drum floating in a waterway outside of Miami just three months after his testimony.[15] Who, exactly, ordered these hits remains unknown. This, after all, was the business they had chosen.

The attempted outsourcing of Castro's assassination to members of the Mafia was only one of the many threads hidden from Americans and the world in the deeply dishonest accounting of events the administration offered about the Cuban Missile Crisis. The story that US officials told at the time—and repeated for decades thereafter—went like this: The United States was minding its own business when the Soviet Union decided to place missiles in Cuba in a bid to gain an upper hand in the strategic balance of power between the two nations. President Kennedy, faced with the possibility of having to invade Cuba to take out the missiles—which could easily have led to a nuclear war, killing untold millions—chose instead to blockade the island nation and give the Soviets an ultimatum wrapped inside a minor concession: if they removed the missiles, the United States would not invade Cuba. This was not really a concession, because the United States never had any intention of invading the island. Nevertheless, the gambit worked, because it allowed Soviet premier Nikita Khrushchev to unilaterally withdraw the missiles and save face at the same time. And so it was Kennedy's unique combination of toughness and psychological insight, along with the "credibility" of America's willingness to risk nuclear war to remove the missiles, that saved the day, and therefore the world.

But virtually every aspect of this story was false. As noted above, the missile crisis was the first occasion when a US official asserted the government's right to lie. And the claim inspired almost no controversy because it was made in defense of Kennedy's masterful diplomatic maneuvering designed to prevent a nuclear holocaust. And who, really, can object to a presidential lie or two if they help save humankind? Kennedy's far more problematic lies came immediately following the crisis, and these had the effect of distorting the future of US politics to a degree that, even more than a half century later, is difficult to measure.

What Winston Churchill once called the "bodyguard of lies" necessary to protect the truth was forced to work overtime to shield all the various lies constructed for the Kennedy administration's cover story. In fact, few countries in modern history have ever had greater reason to wish to defend themselves from invasion than Cuba did from the United States during Kennedy's presidency. Following the failure of the 1961 Bay of Pigs invasion, Robert Kennedy had instructed the CIA director, John McCone, to make overthrowing Castro "the top priority in the US Government," insisting that "no time, no money, effort or manpower is to be spared." The result was "Operation Mongoose," a series of increasingly bizarre plans to bring down or murder the Cuban leader. In March 1962, the Joint Chiefs of Staff put forth a series of shocking proposals, including the sabotage of the American space program and the mass murder of US citizens—up to and including the downing of a plane ferrying US college students for a trip to study abroad. The idea was to hire mercenaries to carry out these attacks and then blame them on Castro in order to provide the president with a pretext for an invasion. The CIA had its own menu of what Richard Helms, a successor to McCone, would later characterize as "nutty schemes." Just days before the missiles in Cuba were discovered, Robert Kennedy complained to National Security Council members that the president was demanding "more dynamic action" against Castro. Despite all this, during the crisis and its aftermath, US officials peddled the lie that the whole ordeal was a result of what Pentagon officials, quoted in the *Chicago Tribune* at the time, called "the aggressive designs of the Communists...while for 60 years the United States has shown that it has no desire to subvert the Cuban government."[16]

But the biggest lie that President Kennedy and his advisers and acolytes told about the missile crisis came afterward, when they insisted that the Soviets had offered a swap whereby the Soviet missiles in Cuba would be dismantled in exchange for the United States taking down its missiles in Turkey, which were aimed at the Soviets—and that Kennedy, in no uncertain terms, had refused. Kennedy did, in fact, agree to the swap, but he conditioned it on the Soviets' willingness to accept the public humiliation of embracing the administration's phony narrative in public.

News coverage of the deal was unanimous in purveying Kennedy's expertly created myth. According to *Time* magazine, Khrushchev initially "proposed his cynical swap [to] pull his missiles out of Cuba if Kennedy pulled his out of Turkey" in a "long, rambling memorandum...remarkable for its wheedling tone—that of a cornered bully." Fortunately, *Time* reported, "Kennedy bluntly rejected the missile swap and increased the speed of the U.S. military buildup." According to Arthur Schlesinger Jr., writing in 1965, Kennedy had been "perplexed" by Khrushchev's offer to trade; the president, he said, had "regarded the idea as unacceptable and the swap was promptly rejected." In reality, as Schlesinger would explain in his biography of Robert Kennedy, published thirteen years after the crisis, the president had actually instructed his brother to make a secret deal on the Soviets' terms and informed almost none of his closest advisers of what he had done.[17]

Although President Kennedy allegedly forbade bragging after the end of the crisis, he could not help telling intimates, "I cut [Khrushchev's] balls off." Media accounts communicated a similar sense of self-congratulation. According to *Newsweek*, "By the way it handled the situation, the United States has...gained a new sense of confidence in charting the perilous course through the cold war." The USSR, in contrast, stood as "a liar before the world, a reckless adventurer for trying to upset the balance of power." *Time* concluded that "generations to come may well count John Kennedy's resolve as one of the decisive moments of the 20th century. For Kennedy was determined to move forward at whatever risk. And when faced by that determination, the bellicose Premier of the Soviet Union first wavered, then weaseled, and finally backed down." "For the first time in twenty years," wrote Walter Trohan, Washington bureau chief for the deeply conservative *Chicago Tribune*, "Americans can carry their heads high because the President of the United States has stood up to the premier of Russia and made him back down.... Mr. Kennedy ended a course of appeasement."[18]

The United States soon began disassembling the missiles in Turkey, but continued to lie about it. The president told the *New York Times* foreign correspondent Cy Sulzberger—who was later accused of being a CIA asset—that the Soviets "could not have thought of really getting us to dismantle Turkey," and claimed that he "simply could not understand" what it was the influential columnist Walter Lippmann had in mind when he proposed such a trade during the crisis. Secretary of Defense Robert McNamara, Assistant for National Security McGeorge Bundy, and Secretary of State Dean Rusk, along with every other administration official questioned, told the same lies to Congress. Bundy even had the nerve to lecture the great French political philosopher Raymond Aron that those "who would spread rumors" about a secret trade "must be pretty far gone in their mistrust of the United States to start with." The lengths that the Kennedy brothers went to in order to protect and reinforce their lies were nothing short of extraordinary. The president even personally edited a fiction-filled *Saturday Evening Post* account of the crisis by Stewart Alsop and Charles Bartlett billed as an "exclusive, behind-the-scenes report" and an "authoritative account of top-secret sessions of the National Security Council's Executive Committee." John Kennedy undermined the career of a Soviet diplomat who helped pass along the messages, and he trashed the reputation of his UN representative, Adlai Stevenson, for supporting the idea of a missile swap during their internal deliberations. ("Adlai wanted a Munich" was the devastating phrase the president used to the press under the cover of anonymity.)[19]

The net result of all these lies was the wholesale misinterpretation of what had happened and what it all meant. Kennedy solved the crisis by conceding the legitimacy of Soviet concerns and making concessions to address them in a spirit of pragmatism and flexibility. It was sold, however, as exactly the opposite: the triumph of Kennedy's willingness to stand firm, to offer no concessions, and to back up his demands with force, including nuclear force.

Meanwhile, Khrushchev's willingness to keep the deal secret, even long after Kennedy's assassination, "cost him dearly," according to longtime Soviet ambassador to the United States Anatoly Dobrynin. "The whole world was under the impression that Khrushchev lost because he had given in to the pressure of a strong president, that he had taken everything out of Cuba and gotten nothing in return," Dobrynin wrote in 1996. "No one knew anything about the agreement regarding the missiles in Turkey."[20] Within two years, Khrushchev was removed from power. His fall would usher in a period of superpower instability, putting an end to US hopes for the relaxation of tensions. According to Averill Harriman, who had been the US ambassador to the Soviet Union in the early 1940s and served as assistant secretary of state for East Asian and Pacific affairs under Kennedy, the Soviet leader had been eager to reduce military spending in order to free funds to modernize Soviet agriculture. Khrushchev felt he had "quite enough missiles," but he required US cooperation if he was to "curb the appetite" of his military.[21] Because of the need to demonstrate continued "toughness" based on the false rendering of the crisis Kennedy sold to the world, the Soviets responded instead with a massive nuclear arms buildup, in order to at least reach parity, and possibly to surpass the United States in the quantity and quality of nuclear weapons. They felt it was necessary to be able to threaten their adversary by means of a dangerous and expensive nuclear arms race. Its inspiration? As the Soviet deputy foreign minister Vasily Kuznetsov warned John J. McCloy, his counterpart in the post-crisis negotiations: "You Americans will never be able to do this to us again."[22]

Thanks in part to an extremely influential 1971 book titled *The Essence of Decision* by Graham T. Allison, a political scientist who

taught at Harvard's John F. Kennedy School of Government, the
Cuban Missile Crisis became one of the most studied and discussed
historical events in American academic circles. Many hundreds of
scholarly articles about the crisis in dozens of disciplines were published and debated, all of them based on the administration's fictional
version of events. Harvard treated Allison's book as a foundational
text and instructed thousands of future government officials according to its mistaken precepts. Foreign policy experts in both political
parties adopted the book as the paradigmatic example of what the
influential international relations scholar Alexander George would
call "coercive diplomacy." This doctrine held that threatening an adversary with increasingly painful penalties—usually associated with
military force—was the most effective means of achieving a desired
diplomatic result. Soon, as the diplomat and scholar of the crisis
James Nathan observed, "the ability to oversee force became the
coin of an exclusive realm."[23] This logic was directly applied to the
conflict in Vietnam. Cyrus Vance, who became Kennedy's secretary
of the army and Johnson's deputy secretary of defense (and later,
Jimmy Carter's secretary of state), would later recall, "We had seen
the gradual application of force applied in the Cuban Missile Crisis,
and had seen a very successful result. We believed that if this same
gradual and restrained application of force were applied in…Viet-
nam, that one could expect the same kind of result; that rational
people on the other side would respond to increasing military pressure and would therefore try and seek a political solution."[24]

Unsurprisingly, the Kennedy brothers had kept Vice President
Johnson in the dark during the missile crisis, just as FDR had done
with Truman during Yalta. And yet again, a president's untimely
death and his successor's ignorance would have extremely costly results for that successor, the country, and the world. Having no idea
what had really happened during the crisis, Johnson was forced to
conduct his Vietnam policy in the shadow of Kennedy's mythical
victory and the hawkish Cold War lessons it imparted. The politics

birthed by Kennedy's deception reinforced this tendency. Aware that Johnson was particularly sensitive about his minimal role in the Cuban crisis, some in Washington sought to exploit his insecurity to demand a ratcheting up of the war in Vietnam. Senator Bourke Hickenlooper, quick to compare Vietnam to Cuba, wrote during the Johnson administration that "Cuba was a bold and dangerous operation as far as Washington is concerned. No one knows what would have happened had we not reacted. Is it possible this [Vietnam] follows the same route? If we don't react, what kind of position does that put us in with the North Vietnamese?"[25] The pundit Joe Alsop, a Kennedy intimate, taunted Johnson, saying, "Vietnam is what the second Cuban crisis was for John F. Kennedy. If Mr. Johnson ducks the challenge, we shall learn by experience about what it would have been like if Kennedy had ducked the challenge in October 1962."[26] Kennedy did not "duck" the challenge, but neither did he meet it in the manner that Alsop was implying. The gulf between what really happened during the missile crisis and what people were led to believe about it would therefore haunt Kennedy's successor in a nation thousands of miles from the United States and determine the direction of US foreign policy for decades to come.

Lyndon Johnson's "Credibility Gap"

Lyndon Johnson holds the distinction of being the first occupant of the Oval Office to be viewed by a majority of Americans as a habitual liar, and hence to lose the ability to lie to them effectively. The cause, appropriately, was Vietnam. Johnson and his advisers lied so frequently about so many aspects of the war effort that members of the media were forced to devise a special way of referring to the lies, lest they appear disrespectful by telling the truth about them. The chosen phrase was the "credibility gap": that is, the "gap" that arises when someone says something that listeners know to be a lie and is therefore not "credible." By 1967, three years into the conflict that would last at least eight more, with nearly five hundred thousand US soldiers serving in the jungles of Southeast Asia, Gallup was reporting that nearly 70 percent of Americans believed that the Johnson administration had lied about the war. A Harris poll the same year concluded that Americans' most "serious criticism" of the president was that "he was not honest about sending troops to Vietnam."[1]

Lyndon Johnson's "Credibility Gap"

Arguments for the importance of a speaker's credibility before an audience, and the complicated components that go into it, date as far back as Aristotle's *Rhetoric*, in the fourth century BCE. More recently, the political scientist Francis Fukuyama defined "trust" as "the expectation that arises within a community of regular, honest, and cooperative behavior, based on commonly shared norms, on the part of other members of that community."[2] Trust allows people to carry on all kind of societal functions—from economics to culture to the most personal of relationships—without the interference of lawyers, contracts, private investigators, and who knows what else? It also keeps the day-to-day debate of politics within parameters that are mutually understood and beneficial to all sides. All earlier presidents enjoyed this advantage, the trust of the public, however undeserved it may have been in many cases. But Lyndon Johnson was the first to lose it.

The Johnson administration told Congress and the nation any number of falsehoods about the Vietnam War. The fact of his willingness to lie in support of the ongoing war in that nation was hardly unprecedented among previous presidents. The country's Vietnam policy was already built on a mountain of lies by the time Johnson succeeded Kennedy in November 1963. The Eisenhower administration had refused to abide by the 1954 Geneva accords, which had called for nationwide free elections across Vietnam, and had lied about its reasons for doing so. As always, Cold War logic ruled. From its beginnings, the Eisenhower administration's primary purpose in Vietnam was to create an "effective bulwark against further Communist aggression in Southeast Asia," as CIA officer Edward Lansdale, whom Eisenhower had appointed to take charge of the US effort there, cabled his superiors in July 1954. To achieve this objective, Lansdale explained, "the United States must accept a dominant and direct role in aiding the country." The US Joint Chiefs of Staff admitted at the time that "free elections would be attended by almost certain loss of [Indochina] to

Communist control." President Eisenhower predicted a landslide of "possibly eighty percent" of the vote for the Communist leader, Ho Chi Minh, were the United States to allow elections to proceed—and so they did not. When the authors of the *Pentagon Papers*—the top-secret history of the war commissioned by Secretary of Defense Robert McNamara in 1967 and exposed by the *New York Times* in 1971—wrote that "South Vietnam (unlike any of the other countries in Southeast Asia) was essentially the creation of the United States," they were telling a truth that no US president would publicly admit. Johnson was therefore lying when, in 1965, he told the country, "The first reality is that North Vietnam has attacked the independent nation of South Vietnam. Its object is total conquest." There was no "independent" nation of South Vietnam and never would be.[3]

The second overarching lie that haunted Johnson's presidency was his insistence that America was not losing the war, when in fact, it clearly was. This lie had begun under Kennedy. In late 1961, as the effort was already turning sour, Secretary of State Dean Rusk had cabled the Saigon embassy with a warning: "Do not give other than routine cooperation to correspondents on coverage of current military activities in Vietnam," lest the truth become known to readers and viewers of the news back home.[4] Johnson then took a losing hand and bet the ranch.

One of the most painful (and poignant) ironies of Lyndon Johnson's disastrous decision to commit to war in Vietnam was the fact that no one knew better than he did how unhappily it was likely to end. And yet he believed himself to have no choice. Transcripts of taped conversations reveal the pain the president experienced as he failed to find a path out of the dilemma. In late May 1964, Johnson told his assistant for national security affairs, McGeorge Bundy, "I stayed awake last night thinking of this thing....It looks to me like we're getting into another Korea....I don't think that we can fight them 10,000 miles away from home....I don't think it's worth fighting for and I don't think we can get out. It's just the biggest damned mess that I ever saw."[5] Johnson also confided to his close friend and political ally Richard Russell, the powerful chairman of the Senate Armed Services Committee, that the war in Vietnam could prove "the damnedest mess on earth." He believed the war would sink the United States "in quicksand up to its neck." "I don't think [Americans] know much about Vietnam," Johnson told Russell, "and I think they care a hell of a lot less." Russell, a famously hawkish southerner, concurred, saying, "It'll be the most expensive venture this country ever went into." Russell predicted that the effort would require "a half a million men" and that they would likely "be bogged down in there for ten years." But Russell refused Johnson the political cover he needed in sanctioning an American withdrawal. Kennedy had committed the original American "military advisers" to the cause in Vietnam, and he may very well have been planning to remove them after the 1964 election, as many historians have argued. But without Russell's blessing, Johnson felt trapped. Both men believed it necessary to demonstrate their macho bona fides to the nation no matter what the costs. Russell told Johnson that if he chose withdrawal, he did not see "how you tell the American people you're coming out [of Vietnam]. They'll think that you've just been whipped, you've been ruined, you're scared. It'd be disastrous."[6]

And so, despite his fateful premonition, the president continued down what he knew to be a ruinous path. Sounding very much like Franklin Roosevelt in 1940, just days before the November 1964 election Johnson said, "We are not about to send American boys 9 or 10 thousand miles away from home to do what Asian boys ought to be doing for themselves." But however much he wished he could avoid it, Johnson likely knew that was exactly what he was going to do.[7] Imprisoned by a combination of his own psychological insecurities and the impossibly expansive definition of America's "national security" needs that he, like all Cold War presidents, had adopted, Johnson felt he had no choice but to pursue the war and to pursue it dishonestly. For the only thing Lyndon Johnson feared more than entering a pointless and costly war—one that the United States might very well lose for the first time in its history—was an honest democratic debate about whether to fight it in the first place.

Given the difficult position he had created for himself and the country, Johnson felt compelled to lie virtually every time he discussed the war. So did his advisers. And so did his generals. In doing so, they doomed not only his presidency and his ambitions but also much of the historical trust that Americans had once felt for their elected leaders. As the German émigré philosopher Hannah Arendt would later observe, while reading the *Pentagon Papers*, the administration's "policy of lying was hardly ever aimed at the enemy...but was destined chiefly, if not exclusively, for domestic consumption, for propaganda at home, and especially for the purpose of deceiving Congress."[8]

Detailing the countless lies that Johnson and his advisers told about Vietnam could easily fill a book the length of the one you are reading and then some. I will therefore focus on just one—and perhaps the most important of them all: the lie that began the war and led to the now-infamous Gulf of Tonkin Resolution passed by Congress on August 7, 1964. Ironically, Johnson did not know he was misleading the nation when, at 11:37 p.m. Eastern Standard Time on August 4, 1964, he had appeared on all three national television networks to announce that he had just ordered US forces to bomb North Vietnam. He may have believed, as he said, that the "aggression by terror against the peaceful villages of South Vietnam has now been joined by open aggression on the high seas against the United States of America." But even given what he thought he knew at the time, Johnson was offering an extremely misleading version of events. By insisting on breaking into the nighttime newscasts to announce the attacks on television before US planes had even reached their targets—much less before the navy could confirm the fact of the attacks themselves—Johnson not only significantly widened the war on the basis of false pretenses but also alerted the North Vietnamese in advance. This gaffe likely contributed to their success in downing two of the planes and killing one of the pilots, leaving the other to be tortured and imprisoned for the following eight years. For the fact was that Johnson's broadcast was monitored in Hanoi by a radio-listening unit in the Foreign Ministry, which informed the air defense forces to expect an impending American attack. Shortly afterward, a radar station detected the incoming planes. Hanoi managed to shoot down two of the attacking aircraft. Lieutenant Richard C. Sather was killed over North Vietnam. Lieutenant Everett Alvarez was captured (after fracturing his back in the crash) and sent to a prison camp, where he suffered physical and mental abuse for more than eight years.[9]

Johnson may have knowingly lied about the timing of the US attacks, but at the time he had every reason to believe that the other part of his message was accurate—that the North Vietnamese had indeed carried out an attack of some sort on US ships in the Gulf of Tonkin. But of course this, too, was false, as Johnson would have discovered himself had he been in less of a hurry to announce the bombing. Bundy later admitted that "the Gulf of Tonkin incident was seized by the president as a time for him to take his resolution on Vietnam to the Congress." The result was "a quick decision [made] on an incompletely unverified event."[10]

It is impossible to prove a negative. But philosophical caveats aside, we can say with extremely high confidence that the alleged Gulf of Tonkin attack on August 4, 1964, on the destroyers USS *Maddox* and USS *Turner Joy* did not take place. There was no attack—just a lot of confusion, panic, and inexperience on the part of a young sonarman on the *Maddox*, along with extreme eagerness on the part of Secretary of Defense McNamara and the president to believe in it.

South Vietnamese troops, under a program called "Operation Plan 34A" (or OPLAN 34-Alpha), had begun conducting a series of attacks on North Vietnam in January 1964 using US-supplied weaponry. These attacks were under the authority of US "military advisers" with US Navy ships holding back in support. When the North Vietnamese responded with some small-scale retaliation, John Herrick, commander of the USS *Maddox*, wired his superiors in Honolulu that his mission now represented an "unacceptable risk." He asked that his orders be immediately terminated. But they responded that doing so would fail to "adequately demonstrate United States resolve to assert our legitimate rights in these international waters," and the request was denied.[11]

Herrick's concerns were borne out on August 2, 1964, when a tiny fleet of North Vietnamese PT boats approached the *Maddox*. While confusion remains about who fired first, and what the North Vietnamese were trying to accomplish, it would have been a rather pitiful attack if that was what they had in mind. This was the "first Gulf of Tonkin incident," which Johnson chose to ignore, but whose details US officials would later cite in order to try to confuse the issue as to whether there had been a second incident two days later. All the North Vietnamese vessels approaching US ships on August 2 either fled or were quickly sunk by the vastly superior US destroyers. Most of the men on the American side found the attack to be, at the very least, irrational, save for the possibility that the North Vietnamese felt the need to make a purely symbolic gesture in response to the OPLAN 34-Alpha commando raids that had taken place just two days earlier.[12]

Undersecretary of State George W. Ball, who played the role of a dovish devil's advocate at the time, later explained that the administration was operating on the basis of "a feeling that if the destroyer got into some trouble, that would provide the provocation we needed."[13] Assistant Secretary of Defense for International Security Affairs John T. McNaughton had written a draft "Plan of Action for South Vietnam," in which he suggested that the United States "provoke a DRV [Democratic Republic of Vietnam, i.e., North Vietnam] response" and then "to be in a good position to seize on that response" to mount its own attack.[14] At a White House dinner on July 26, Johnson had spoken to his friend J. William Fulbright, chairman of the Senate Foreign

Relations Committee, whom he would soon ask to shepherd the Gulf of Tonkin Resolution through the Senate. The now-infamous resolution was designed to give the president the power to expand the war. To Fulbright, he had insisted that the South Vietnamese regime was in danger of collapse, and that a resolution in support of the war effort might be necessary to shore it up. The following day, July 27, the US ambassador to South Vietnam, General Maxwell Taylor, told General Nguyen Khanh, the top Vietnamese military officer at the time, that US air attacks on North Vietnam might begin any day.[15]

The initial reports about the alleged second Gulf of Tonkin incident on August 4 confused almost everyone. Shortly after having mistakenly reported that the *Maddox* was under attack, Commander Herrick followed up with a second cable that read, "Review of action makes many reported contacts and torpedoes fired appear doubtful. Freak weather effects on radar and overeager sonarmen may have accounted for many reports. No actual visual sightings by *Maddox*. Suggest complete evaluation before any further action taken." Johnson would have none of this, however, and Defense Secretary McNamara encouraged his natural impatience. The president wanted to break into the eleven o'clock news that night with his statement, and the possibility that nothing had happened in the Gulf of Tonkin was not about to stop him. He had, after all, spent the day preparing leaders in Congress for just such an announcement. "Some of our boys are floating around in the water," he had lied.[16]

Ignoring both the "knowns and unknowns" of this non-incident, McNamara and Bundy gave a series of deliberately deceptive briefings to members of Congress after the event. McNamara, for instance, testified before the Senate Foreign Relations Committee on August 6 that the ships were attacked while cruising at least thirty miles from the North Vietnamese coast. This was double the real distance from the coast where the imaginary attack took place. McNamara also said that the guns on the North Vietnamese boats were twice their actual size. As for the OPLAN 34-Alpha raids, he dismissed their scope and significance, reporting, "We think there were very few civilian casualties because these bases and the depot were in isolated portions of North Vietnam." In fact, the depot in question was in Vinh, the highly populated capital of the province of Nghe An.[17]

The day after he ordered the bombing mission, Johnson gave a long-planned address at Syracuse University in which he once again condemned the "deliberate, willful and systematic aggression" that had "unmasked its face to the world." Two days later, responding to an official protest from Soviet Premier Khrushchev, he repeated the claim, saying that the United States had "complete and incontrovertible evidence" of North Vietnamese aggression. The US ambassador to the United Nations, Adlai Stevenson, made a similarly misleading statement before the UN Security Council. And two days later, the State Department issued an equally false account, insisting that US ships had been attacked at locations "indisputably in international waters."[18]

Johnson's aides had a tougher time maintaining these lies in Congress, owing to the fact that at least one senator had been tipped off that the whole story was a house of cards. McNamara lied repeatedly in response to questions from the skeptical Democratic senator from Oregon, Wayne Morse. In particular, he promised that "our Navy played absolutely no part in, was not associated with, was not aware of, any South Vietnamese actions, if there were any. I want to make that very clear to you. The *Maddox* was operating in international waters, was carrying out a routine patrol of the type we carry out all over the world at all times….I say this flatly; this is the fact." Under subsequent questioning by Morse, McNamara repeated versions of this statement in the most categorical terms possible, even going so far as to claim that he possessed intercepted North Vietnamese communications that substantiated his account. But these, he explained, remained too sensitive for anyone to be allowed to see them. He ordered the Joint Chiefs to send a "flash" message to the commanders of all US units involved in the action asking for evidence that might "convince United Nations Organization that the attack did in fact occur." But the commanders could not produce what did not exist. Later, in 1966, nineteen members of the North Vietnamese Navy who had been on the PT boat in the gulf that day were captured. But before they could be questioned about the disputed events of August 4 two years earlier, US Pacific Headquarters sent an urgent message ordering that the men be sent back to Vietnam with no questions asked.[19]

The lies worked in the short run (as they so often do). The narrative, after all, had long ago been firmly established. Once again, the United States was boldly—and selflessly—standing up to the bad guys on behalf of our scrappy, democracy-desiring allies abroad. The story just about wrote itself, though many media accounts were good enough to invent melodramatic details to give it more color. *Time* magazine went so far as to endow the *Maddox*'s radar systems with the power to track torpedoes, though this was technically impossible at the time. "There were at least six of them," the magazine's correspondents wrote,

> Russian-designed "Swatow" gunboats armed with 37-mm and 28-mm guns, and P-4s. At 9:52 they opened fire on the destroyers with automatic weapons, this time from as close as 2,000 yards. The night glowed eerily with the nightmarish glare of airdropped flares and boats' searchlights. For 3½ hours, the small boats attacked in pass after pass. Ten enemy torpedoes sizzled through the water. Each time the skippers, tracking the fish by radar, maneuvered to evade them.

Newsweek described a PT boat that "burst into flames and sank" and added that "another PT boat exploded and then the others scurried off into the darkness nursing their wounds." Public opinion naturally followed the news: before the incident, 58 percent of those polled had a negative view of the Johnson administration's handling of Vietnam policy; afterward, 72 percent approved.[20]

The Gulf of Tonkin Resolution passed unanimously in the House, and only Morse and Ernest Gruening, a Democrat from Alaska, dissented in the Senate. It empowered Johnson to "take all necessary measures to repel any armed attack against the forces of the United States and to prevent further aggression [in Vietnam]." As Johnson famously quipped, the resolution was like "grandma's nightshirt. It covered everything."[21]

In Hanoi, the raids inspired a more belligerent posture in the war. The North Vietnamese well knew the American pretext had been a phony one, but if war was what the United States wanted, war was what it would get. In South Vietnam, General Nguyen Khanh took advantage of the confusion surrounding the crisis a day after the alleged attack to declare a state of emergency and have himself appointed president. Within ten days, opposition had spread across the nation, particularly among Buddhists and students, culminating in protests and riots. Both groups had already been protesting the war as well as the repression they had been experiencing under the US-supported military regime. Khanh, a Catholic, apparently suffering a breakdown, resigned. He agreed, however, following intense US lobbying, to return to power as fighting between Buddhists and Catholics threatened to tear the nation apart. The net result was that the post–Gulf of Tonkin bombing, which US officials had long planned with the idea that it would stiffen the backbone of the South Vietnamese leadership and frighten its adversaries, accomplished just the opposite.[22]

Meanwhile, at home Johnson's lie had the effect of awakening Fulbright's conscience, as the Tonkin fable was hardly the only one Johnson was telling the American public about foreign relations at the time. In April 1965, the president ordered the US Marines into the Dominican Republic to support a right-wing coup that had recently overthrown the democratically elected reformist leader there. Johnson insisted that the military intervention, which eventually involved 40,000 troops, was necessary to "protect American lives," as US citizens were being evacuated at the time. Soon enough, however, he was telling the same types of lies he had told about Tonkin, this time in the service of preventing "another Cuba." According to the president's entirely fictional account, "1,500 innocent people were murdered and shot, and their heads cut off, and six Latin American embassies were violated and fired upon over a period of four days before we went in....As we talked to our ambassador to confirm the horror and the tragedy and the unbelievable fact that they were firing on Americans and the American Embassy, he was talking to us from under a desk while bullets were going through his windows." Johnson insisted that a "thousand American men, women, and children" had begged for the United States to intervene. He told the Senate Majority Leader, Montana Democrat Mike Mansfield, "The Castro forces are really gaining control," even though McNamara had told him and others there was no evidence of Castro's involvement. Fulbright later explained that he found this case to be "marred by a lack of candor and by misinformation."[23]

Upon learning the details of the deception Johnson and company had undertaken in the Dominican Republic, and becoming ever more aware of the bill of goods Johnson had sold him vis-à-vis the Second Gulf of Tonkin incident, Fulbright decided that both he and the nation he served had been unconscionably betrayed. "We were just plain lied to," he explained, and as a result, the country had lost a "form of democracy."[24] In January 1966, Fulbright informed Secretary of State Dean Rusk that "there was no legal basis for what the Government was doing in Vietnam." He started planning to expose what he considered to be the crimes committed under the authority of "grandma's nightshirt."[25]

The "Fulbright Hearings," held under the auspices of the Senate Foreign Relations Committee, which Fulbright chaired, began in February 1966. They were inspired, the chairman said, by the president's decision to resume bombing raids against the North Vietnamese. Over Johnson's objections, the hearings were originally carried live on NBC and CBS—at considerable cost to each network in lost advertising revenue. Millions of Americans tuned in to watch. Fulbright's own history as a southern segregationist and skeptic of liberal internationalism gave him a peculiar political authority as a critic of the war, since he could not easily be pigeonholed among the doves who opposed the war on moral grounds. Moreover, the witness list for the hearings featured such widely admired figures as General James Gavin, who served as assistant chief of staff of the army, and the "Father of Containment," George Kennan. Their testimony proved to be a powerful factor in turning the foreign policy establishment against the Johnson administration. "The United States will never extricate itself with honor from its Vietnam involvement," the *New York Times* editorial page insisted, "unless it achieves a better comprehension of how it became entrapped."[26]

Johnson grew increasingly unhinged as the hearings proceeded. He prevailed upon J. Edgar Hoover to have the FBI investigate whether Fulbright—whom he called "Senator Half Bright"—and the committee were receiving information from communists. Fulbright was put under strict surveillance, and the bureau allegedly discovered many "parallels" between statements made by committee witnesses and "documented Communist Party publications or statements of communist leaders." This entire notion was not merely false, it was crazy. Johnson was clearly cracking under the strain of losing the war and with it his presidency. But no one stopped him or even tried to, for fear of becoming the next target of the president's vindictive paranoia.[27]

Though he had grown to despise Fulbright and had little but contempt for the other members of the Foreign Relations Committee, Robert McNamara agreed to testify. The examination lasted over seven hours. McNamara doggedly stuck to the same story he had told more than two years earlier. He repeated the falsehood that there had been visual sightings of an attack in the Gulf of Tonkin, including "gunfire against the patrol." The notion that the United States might have intentionally provoked the attack, he said, was both "inconceivable" and "monstrous." He read to the committee from what he called an "unimpeachable" North Vietnamese source regarding the alleged attack—but when Fulbright asked to examine the cables himself, correctly suspecting that they had been intercepted on August 2, during the first, inconsequential encounter, rather than on August 4, 1964, when the allegedly significant attack took place, the secretary refused and immediately reclassified them.[28]

The Fulbright hearings not only illuminated the lies told about August 4, 1964, but also shook the truth from people who had previously been silenced. Fulbright's staff started receiving mysterious reports from an anonymous author who said he knew that the second attack never took place. "In all that time," he wrote, "I have never been able to find a way to disclose this information to a responsible person or organization who could and would use it constructively." He charged that the "U.S. Navy patrols in the Gulf of Tonkin were undertaken apparently to bait the North Vietnamese." The author, who later revealed himself to be Commander Jack Cowles, had been stationed in Flag Plot, the navy's "war room," on August 4. His willingness to come clean was rewarded by his superiors with a forced psychiatric examination, followed by the suggestion that he retire on "physical disability" for his own good. He refused and ended up with a make-work job until he reached mandatory retirement age in 1969, following a full decade without promotion. Another clue appeared in December 1967, when the *New Haven Register* published a letter from a Connecticut high school teacher named John White, who noted that he had served in August 1964 as a commissioned naval officer aboard the USS *Pine Island* in the Pacific. White wrote that he recalled "confusing radio messages" sent back and forth at that time between the US destroyers—"confusing because the destroyers themselves were not certain they were being attacked." He added that he had spoken to the chief sonarman of the *Maddox*, who had told him that there had been a negative reading on the sonar scope picture, "meaning that no torpedoes were fired." White went on: "Yet the Pentagon reported to the President that North Vietnam had attacked us and the President reported it to Congress. Why?...[I]n a moment of panic, based on false information, the President was given unprecedented powers, which today enable him to conduct an undeclared war involving over a half million men and costing billions of dollars."[29]

Events came to a head in March 1968, when the *New York Times* reported that Johnson was considering a request from General William Westmoreland of the US Army for an additional 206,000 troops for Vietnam—together with the news that the president believed he did not require any congressional sanction beyond the original Gulf of Tonkin Resolution to meet Westmoreland's request. Fulbright publicly declared the resolution to be "null and void" like "any contract based on misrepresentation." He apologized to the nation for having guided it through the Senate, admitting, "I regret it more than anything I have ever done in my life."[30] On the Senate floor, a dozen of his colleagues rose to applaud his speech and to call for a full-scale debate on the war. Johnson announced his decision not to seek reelection at the end of that month, at which time 20,000 Americans had already died in Vietnam, 4,000 of them in the previous two months alone.[31]

Americans were tired of the constant chaos the war created at home. The president had made himself unpopular not only with the war's opponents but also with its supporters. Many Americans of all stripes were furious about a 10 percent income surtax Johnson had imposed to pay for the war. Meanwhile, Johnson was unleashing J. Edgar Hoover and the FBI on lawful American citizens, violating civil liberties, and ignoring the Constitution. To his aides, he sounded paranoid. Student anti-war organizations were being secretly funded and infiltrated by the FBI. Government agents posing as demonstrators were inciting others to violence for the purpose of entrapment and political gain. Civil war or violent repression seemed a genuine possibility at the time. The anti-war movement provided the fuel for the explosion of a youthful New Left whose leaders had little but contempt for the older liberal leaders who had helped guide America into the disastrous war. They spoke casually of revolution and devoted themselves to acts of increasingly confrontational protest. Many of those demonstrations turned violent. As the author Thomas Powers would observe, "The violence in Vietnam seemed to elicit a similar air of violence in the United States, an appetite for extremes: people felt that history was accelerating, time was running out, great issues were reaching a point of final decision."[32]

Johnson's Great Society programs—legislation on education, health care, urban renewal, and transportation—were meanwhile dying for lack of funding and attention owing to the war. Not only tens of thousands of US soldiers but countless Vietnamese, Cambodians, and others had lost their lives as a result of the catastrophic combination of hubris, corruption, incompetence—and perhaps, most significantly, dishonesty—characterizing America's folly in Southeast Asia.

The Tonkin effect, if it might be so described, had perhaps its most profound impact on the soldiers themselves. As an institution, the US military was deeply wounded by Vietnam, as its morale and professionalism all but disintegrated under the strain of the war. "From the beginning everything about it was a lie," John F. Terzano, president of the Vietnam Veterans of America Foundation, would later write. "From the fabricated attack on the destroyers *Turner Joy* and *Maddox* . . . through the call to arms to my generation to preserve 'freedom and democracy' for a government that jailed citizens who spoke against it."[33] Johnson's lies had poisoned not only his presidency and his war but American political life itself. Ironically and tragically for the country, instead of seeing his catastrophe as a cautionary tale, his successor, Richard Nixon, would double down on both the war and the dishonesty necessary to defend it.

8

Richard Nixon

"IT'S A WIN. SEE?"

Lyndon Johnson's presidency was undone by America's unrealizable imperial ambitions and the necessity of consistently lying about them. And in refusing to face up to the factors that precipitated his downfall, he helped lay the groundwork for the ascendancy of Richard Nixon's catastrophic presidency.

Even more than his disgraced predecessor, Nixon, with his obsessive and aggressive dishonesty, placed the issue of presidential lying front and center before the American public. Such erratic behavior from two presidents in a row led many to wonder if the office was just so demanding that it drove its occupants crazy. Then again, the country itself appeared to be undergoing a collective nervous breakdown. Perhaps the institution was simply mirroring the nation it was supposed to serve.

Like Lyndon Johnson, Richard Nixon was a lifelong politician whose personal and political character arose from multiple warring components of his personality. "There was no true Nixon," explained his assistant for national security, Henry Kissinger (who would eventually become secretary of state). Nixon and Kissinger enjoyed, if that be the word, a remarkably tortured codependent relationship—both to one another and to the truth. Practicing what he himself called "obsequious excess," Kissinger frequently wrote notes to Nixon thanking him "for the privilege" of serving him, for "the inspiration" Kissinger experienced in observing Nixon's "fortitude in adversity and [his] willingness to walk alone." Behind Nixon's back, however, Kissinger would refer to his boss as "that madman," and "our drunken friend" with the "meatball mind." The president more than returned the compliment. He complained to other subordinates that Kissinger was "goddam difficult for us to deal with" owing to a "personality problem" that might be termed "pathological" or "psychotic." Moreover, Nixon complained, Kissinger was "Jewish, Jewish…Jewish as hell," and "a rag merchant," and referred to him as "my Jewboy" in the presence of fellow anti-Semites.[1]

We have seen any number of presidents fool themselves into believing their own self-constructed myths. But even in such company, Nixon stands out. During one Thanksgiving weekend, the president sat alone at the Camp David presidential retreat and jotted down a series of resolutions under the heading "Goals for 71–72." It began: "1. President as moral leader—conscience of the nation… bring nation together…End war." It's fair to say that this description is literally the opposite of what the rest of the world saw when it looked at Richard Nixon. This was not the only way in which Nixon's understanding of himself clashed with reality. "With regard to delegation," he informed his chief of staff early in his first term as president, "I am exactly the opposite of [Grover] Cleveland. Cleveland read every bill…he got so enmeshed in the details that he could not take the long view." In reality, no president, Cleveland included, was ever so "enmeshed in detail" as Richard Milhous Nixon. Two years before his 1972 reelection campaign, Nixon dictated literally hundreds of pages of notes and conducted meetings with his advisers that lasted as long as six hours at a time. White House Chief of Staff H. R. Haldeman recorded in his diary that both the notes and the meetings contained an "amazing array of trivia" deriving from the president's "obsessive boring-in." Few leaders in history have done more to demonstrate the truth of Friedrich Nietzsche's observation that "the most common sort of lie is the one uttered to one's self."[2]

Nothing obsessed Nixon quite so much as his public image. When members of the media failed to give him the credit he felt was his due, he would go so far as to personally dictate phony letters to reporters and editors. In one particularly sad but illustrative instance, he decided that a nonexistent Georgetown University graduate student should send a letter to John Osborne of the *New Republic* and copy it to Max Frankel at the *New York Times*. Writing on New Year's Eve 1970 under this alias, Nixon complained to Osborne: "I thought this was really the time the press would get to this S.O.B [meaning himself]....It was a shocking disappointment. Can't you do something to get smarter people in the press corps?....He chopped his questioner to bits." A letter dictated later that same not-so-festive night to the *Washington Star*'s James Doyle explained, "I write this letter, not in any sense of anger, but simply one of sorrow...that you and your colleagues had utterly struck out when you tried to take the President on in his press conference."[3] This is the president of the United States taking time out from war, economic emergencies, and other matters of grave importance to send phony, poison-pen letters to a bunch of scribes.

On another, equally sad occasion, the president dictated a memo to his wife, Pat, regarding an article for which she was about to be interviewed, titled "Nixon the Man." Writing "RN to PN," he instructed her to tell its author, "He is so thoughtful of all of us. He is always planning little surprises and little gifts for us. He is not a cold man. I have never seen anyone more thoughtful than he is....

He does little things that mean so much. He is also very thoughtful about the criticisms he receives....Dick has a marvelous sense of humor....And also some people just don't want to write about it because they think it makes him seem more human and likable." In fact, Nixon was famously cold and cruel to "PN." According to the investigative journalist Seymour Hersh, citing White House counsel and assistant to the president for domestic affairs John Ehrlichman and others, Nixon beat her on at least two occasions, one of them badly enough to send her to the emergency room.[4]

At least on one level, Nixon was sufficiently self-aware to understand that he was a hard man to like. This worry haunted him even as he reached the zenith of political ambition, and he consistently engaged in humiliating rituals in an effort to imitate how he imagined a genuinely likable human being might act. For instance, after receiving a twenty-seven-page memo on the topic from a PR consultant, Nixon agreed to pretend to like pizza and dogs.[5]

Lying was standard operating procedure inside the Nixon White House. In July 1970, Nixon met with a group of aides and Republican operatives to discuss plans for that year's midterm elections. One of these was Harry Dent, a former segregationist Democrat from South Carolina who had joined the Republicans. He had helped them implement Nixon's "Southern Strategy" to draw angry whites into the party following the passage of LBJ's civil and voting rights legislation, and he was now employed as Nixon's special counsel. Dent was assigned to write the official memo about the meeting for the files—but he also wrote a second memo detailing what was really discussed at the meeting, and this was judged sensitive enough to be locked away in a safe. The second memo referred to a discussion about the illegal distribution of secret campaign funds collected from wealthy donors, as well as a list of bribes the campaign had received specifying which donors campaign staff anticipated could be stiffed without consequence. The lying extended to literally everything. When Nixon's daughter Julie was married, the White House published the cake's alleged recipe for the public. It turned out to be entirely inedible.[6]

In addition to being a shameless liar, Nixon was also an inveterate hater, though it should hardly surprise anyone that he lied obsessively about this as well. After being forced to resign, Nixon called his staff together for one final farewell. He talked about his mother and father and then advised, "Always remember, others may hate you. But those who hate you don't win unless you hate them, and then you destroy yourself."[7] The by-this-time-ex-president should have known this better than anyone, for nothing, and no one, undermined Richard Nixon's presidency as much as his bottomless capacity for hatred.

Thanks to the fact that Nixon was operating a secret taping system in the Oval Office, and these tapes were preserved after his presidency, his virulent anti-Semitism is no longer secret. There are dozens of examples in the tapes, often spoken in raw, vulgar terms. His loyal friend, lawyer, and former business partner Leonard Garment recalled that whenever something angered Nixon, he could be heard yelling, "God damn his Jewish soul!" Asked what kinds of people he wanted appointed to his administration during his second term, he replied, "No Jews. We are adamant when I say no Jews." Nixon admitted to the Protestant evangelist Billy Graham that he thought the "stranglehold" of Jewish influence "has got to be broken" (in Graham's words). He told Graham he believed that prominent Jewish leaders "don't know how I really feel about [them]." And while many Nixon defenders have excused these outbursts as the president merely blowing off steam, this was clearly not the case. For instance, one day in July 1972, Nixon was musing with his aides Haldeman and Ehrlichman about the potential value of reviving the House Un-American Activities Committee [HUAC]. "You know what's going to charge up an audience," Nixon said. "Jesus Christ, they'll be hanging from the rafters. Going after all these Jews. Just find one that is a Jew, will you."[8]

In addition to his anti-Semitism, the president was also motivated by a deep racial animosity. According to Haldeman's diary, while discussing how to implement his "law and order" agenda, Nixon told him, "You have to face the fact that the whole problem is really the blacks....The key is to devise a system that recognizes this while not appearing to." Speaking of Jamaica's government, he mused, "Blacks can't run it. Nowhere, and they won't be able to for a hundred years, and maybe not for a thousand....Do you know, maybe one black country that's well run?" Nothing revealed Nixon's vicious racism more than the sight of an African leader defying the United States in the United Nations. After watching one vote in October 1971 in which a few nations opposed the United States' preferred outcome, Ronald Reagan, then governor of California, called Nixon to express his exasperation about having "to see those, those monkeys from those African countries." Reagan continued, "Damn them, they're still uncomfortable wearing shoes." Nixon was so impressed with the future president's cleverness that he told his secretary of state, William Rogers, to share it, adding that Reagan told him he saw "these, uh, these cannibals on television last night, and he says, 'Christ, they weren't even wearing shoes.'" For some reason, Nixon felt compelled to repeat the story to Rogers two hours later. Crediting Reagan again, he informed Rogers that the governor had complained of "these cannibals jumping up and down and all that....This bunch of people who don't even wear shoes yet, to be kicking the United States in the teeth." These conversations—which did not become public until forty-four years after Nixon left office, and more than twenty years after the end of Reagan's presidency—provide "a stark reminder," according to Timothy Naftali, former director of the Richard Nixon Presidential Library and Museum, "of the racism that often lay behind the public rhetoric of American presents."[9] (Nixon passionately hated Indians, too, as we shall see below.)

Perhaps what most doomed Nixon's presidency, even more than his crimes, was the degree to which his true character was revealed through the publication of the Watergate tape transcripts. These were finally made public in August 1974, following a seesaw court battle. Nixon's racist rhetoric as recorded on the tapes shocked and horrified even many of his staunchest supporters. Although white supremacy had been a fundamental characteristic of presidential politics since America's founding, the success of the civil rights movement in the 1960s and 1970s was rapidly changing many minds about both racial equality and acceptable social mores. What had been common parlance decades earlier was by the early 1970s judged to be beyond the pale of civilized discourse, at least in public. Senate Minority Leader Hugh Scott, a Republican from Pennsylvania, called what he heard in the tapes "a deplorable, disgusting, shabby, disgusting immoral performance," adding that he was "enormously distressed that there is not enough showing of moral indignation that would have been expected under the circumstances." The columnist Joseph Alsop, who had been one of Nixon's strongest, last-ditch defenders, wrote of the "sheer flesh-crawling repulsion" he felt after reading the transcripts and compared the atmosphere in the Nixon White House to "the back room of a second-rate advertising agency in a suburb of Hell."[10]

True to his character, Nixon arrived in the Oval Office in January 1969 on the back of a massive lie: one that, even today, contains the power to shock. The proximate cause of Nixon's treachery was the possible success of the 1968 Paris Peace Accords between the United States and North Vietnam, with the goal of bringing US troops home and the war to a negotiated end. Henry Kissinger was attached to the US negotiating team, and he was leaking the contents of its secret discussions to Nixon's aide, Richard V. Allen (who later became Ronald Reagan's assistant for national security affairs).[11] Nixon had been polling comfortably ahead of the Democratic nominee—LBJ's vice president, Hubert Humphrey—but the gap was closing, from fifteen points in September down to just two points right before the election. The announcement of a Vietnam peace deal would likely have sealed Humphrey's election.

Nixon had good reason to worry. Kissinger had secretly informed Nixon's campaign chairman, John Mitchell, that there was "a better than even" chance that Johnson would order a bombing halt in Vietnam. Upon hearing that South Vietnam was feeling considerable pressure from the Johnson administration to agree to whatever was hammered out in the negotiations, Nixon asked whether there was "any other way to monkey wrench it." There was. It was for this purpose that the campaign enlisted Anna Chennault, a well-connected Republican socialite and fundraiser, to pass a message to Bui Diem, South Vietnam's ambassador to the United States. Chennault told the South Vietnamese, "Hold on. We are gonna win." When Johnson learned of Chennault's efforts via surveillance by the FBI and the National Security Agency (NSA), the super-secretive agency that operated the government's spy satellites, he called Senate Minority Leader Everett Dirksen in a fury: "It's despicable," he said. "We could stop the killing out there....But they've got this...new formula put in there—namely, wait on Nixon. And they're killing four or five hundred every day waiting on Nixon." He then added, "I'm reading their hand, Everett....This is treason." Dirksen said he agreed.[12]

The day before the election, Johnson called in the members of his national security team to help him decide whether to go public with Nixon's subterfuge. Just as Barack Obama would decide to keep quiet about Russian interference in the presidential election of 2016, however, the men chose not to risk appearing to throw the election—especially since, at the time, they had no clear evidence of Nixon's personal involvement. What's more, Johnson was hardly eager to reveal his illegal domestic spying. Finally, it is far from clear that Johnson preferred a Humphrey victory to a Nixon one, ironically, because he thought Nixon, the alleged "peace candidate," to be less likely to give up on Vietnam than his own vice president. So the plot worked: South Vietnam announced a boycott of the talks, which killed Humphrey's momentum and ensured Nixon's paper-thin electoral victory.[13]

Nixon lied about these events for his entire life. When Johnson first confronted him about them, Nixon replied, "My God. I would never do anything to encourage [South Vietnam] not to come to the table." Asked about these events by the British journalist David Frost in 1977, he lied again. "I did nothing to undercut them.... As far as Madame Chennault or any number of other people," he averred, "I did not authorize them and I had no knowledge of any contact with the South Vietnamese at that point, urging them not to." Nixon insisted that this had been an important point of honor for him: "I couldn't have done that in conscience," he claimed. (Note the caveat. Here, for once, Nixon may have been telling the truth.) Nixon's conscience aside, whether or not he was guilty of treason, he was certainly in violation of the 1799 Logan Act, which forbids citizens from contacting foreign governments if such contact interferes with US diplomacy. Moreover, Nixon's actions left him—and therefore the US government—open to blackmail. In his memoir, *A Tangled Web: The Making of Foreign Policy in the Nixon Presidency*, William Bundy, brother to McGeorge Bundy and one of the early war planners in the US State Department under Kennedy and Johnson, decried the fact that South Vietnamese President Nguyen Van Thieu became "convinced that Nixon owed him a great political debt." Thieu "attached great weight to it throughout" Nixon's presidency, he added. Bundy called this "the most important legacy of the whole episode."[14]

The cost of this secret proved itself during 1972, when the South Vietnamese refused to cooperate with Nixon and Kissinger's attempts to reach a deal with Hanoi. To try to shore up South Vietnamese support, Nixon ordered up "Operation Linebacker II," popularly known as the "Christmas Bombing" of North Vietnam. In this operation, US pilots dropped over 20,000 tons of explosives on North Vietnam for eleven days, December 18–29, 1972—and this was only a fraction of the 207,000 tons it had dropped on the country that year. The number of soldiers and civilians who died in the campaign is still unknown. The formerly pro-war *Washington Post* editorial page, growing more dovish by the day, called it "the most savage and senseless act of war ever visited, over a scant ten days, by one sovereign people over another." When Nixon finally told the country about the bombing, he said it had been "very, very effective." But atop the secret memo he received describing its allegedly positive results, he wrote in large letters a single word: "Zilch."[15]

The Nixon administration's dishonesty on matters relating to Vietnam was vast and wide-ranging. In one of its more inventive episodes, Nixon's men sought to rewrite the history of the war by creating a Soviet-style phony historical record. The idea was to blacken President Kennedy's reputation in order to weaken the appeal of Senator Ted Kennedy, the late president's brother, whom Nixon expected to challenge him for the presidency in 1972. In September 1971, CIA officer E. Howard Hunt, soon to become infamous for his role in the Watergate break-in, manufactured a series of backdated cables pretending to prove that the Kennedy administration had participated in the assassination of South Vietnamese president Ngo Dinh Diem. Using decommissioned White House and State Department typewriters as well as a 1963 date stamp, Hunt sliced up photocopied versions of cables to make his fake documents appear authentic. His plan had been to arrange for *Life* magazine to publish an exclusive article based on the "revelations," but *Life* ceased publication before it could run the story. Instead, NBC News jumped at the chance. After the story ran, the *New York Times* reported that the program left "the viewer with little doubt about the extent of United States implication" in Diem's death. In fact, Kennedy did not plan or even actively approve of the coup—but neither did the US embassy in Vietnam do much to try and prevent it, despite having known about it in advance.[16]

Nixon had to lie about the past in part because the future looked so bleak. The consistent failure of the Nixon/Kissinger strategy in Vietnam made him reluctant even to entertain the idea of telling the truth about the war. Nixon believed that "the press and the editors are against the war," a consequence, no doubt—in his mind—of the fact that so many members of the media were Jewish, and Jews were by definition "disloyal." "Generally speaking," Nixon said, "you can't trust the bastards." And so "the main thing" when discussing the war, he told Kissinger, was to ignore the truth and claim victory: "I don't care what happens there, it's a win. See?" If reporters were angered by the fact that they were clearly being lied to, that was just an added benefit. Nixon wanted to see reporters leave thinking, "That was a very poor briefing." He went on, "That's what we want the cocksuckers to have."[17]

Throughout the Cold War and beyond, presidents would use the threat of war, and sometimes the prospect of peace, as a means of bolstering their chances for reelection. For conservatives, war was quickly becoming a largely symbolic exercise, a performance meant to appease an entirely hypothetical audience made up of people who were eager to shout "cowardice" and "lack of resolve" at the first sign of retreat, or even in response to any reconsideration of what was clearly a failed strategy. A nation facing so many responsibilities around the world needed a strong, experienced hand at the tiller, went the argument, especially when the enemy was so eager to exploit internal division. Ever since James K. Polk complained that Abe Lincoln and his allies were giving "aid and comfort" to the enemy, presidents have sought to exploit citizens' natural patriotism, trusting in the office of the presidency for their own nefarious purposes. But none played this game more cynically than Richard Nixon. In an almost-perfect mirror image of John Adams undermining his own reelection efforts during the campaign of 1800, by negotiating a last-minute peace deal with France, Nixon, fearful of a South Vietnamese collapse should a deal be signed, further extended the Vietnam War to ensure his second term.

Nixon's original hope had been to withdraw all US troops by the end of 1971. Kissinger, however, warned that doing so could result in a period of instability (or worse) in Saigon right around the time of the 1972 presidential election. He therefore recommended that they delay the withdrawal until at least the autumn of 1972—"so that if any bad results follow they will be too late to affect the election." Nixon and Kissinger required "a fairly reasonable interval," as Kissinger explained it to Soviet Ambassador Anatoly Dobrynin, between the time the United States withdrew its troops and North Vietnam overran South Vietnam. This cynical strategy, presidential biographer Robert Dallek sardonically noted, "had nothing to say about the American lives that would be lost in the service of Nixon's reelection," or about the American prisoners of war who would continue their needless suffering if they prolonged the war. Its goal was merely to allow Nixon and Kissinger to evade responsibility for losing the war once the North finally conquered the South. Naturally, Kissinger lied about this when asked by a journalist, insisting that "there is no hidden agreement with North Vietnam for any specific interval after which we would no longer care if they marched in and took over South Vietnam." Nixon termed Kissinger's handling of the Paris Accords to be "a brilliant game we are playing," as "Henry really bamboozled the bastards."[18] In this case, the "bastards" were those Americans who believed their president when he said he was honestly seeking to end the war.

Vietnam brought out the worst in Nixon, and his lies about the war there were, by far, the most damaging lies he told during his presidency, at least for America's standing in the world. But the dishonesty that he and Kissinger displayed in that instance was far from unusual. Among the many other lies they told were lies about genocide. One particularly disturbing example occurred in March 1971. At the time, Pakistan's military dictatorship had just been roundly defeated in an election, after having suspended its National Assembly a year earlier. Facing deep and mounting public anger, the dictatorship launched a military attack on the independence-seeking population of East Pakistan (now Bangladesh). US personnel stationed there were horrified by what they saw and sent a telegram back to Washington accusing the US-supported Pakistani government of "Selective Genocide." This missive was followed by a second one two weeks later, authored by the US consul general, Archer Blood. It was signed by twenty officials stationed in Pakistan and later endorsed by numerous South Asia experts in the State Department. Titled "Dissent from U.S. Policy Toward East Pakistan," and dated April 6, 1971, it accused Nixon and Kissinger of "moral bankruptcy" for their failure "to denounce [the Pakistani government's] atrocities." But it was not merely a failure to denounce. It was positive support. For instance, Kissinger demanded that Robert McNamara, who by this time had become the president of the World Bank, continue an aid program for Pakistan as if nothing unusual were happening while the massacres were taking place.[19]

In his February 9, 1972, State of the World report to Congress, Nixon said the "United States did not support or condone this military action." Another lie. Nixon and Kissinger at the time were secretly planning their diplomatic overture to China, and General

Yahya Khan, the president of Pakistan, was their chosen middleman. Nixon told Kissinger that the United States should "not do anything to complicate the situation for President Yahya or to embarrass him." Meanwhile, as the historian Gary Bass has demonstrated, Kissinger sought—unsuccessfully—to find examples of massacres the Bengalis had committed, in order "to generate a moral equivalence that would exonerate Yahya," and offered not a word of discouragement to the Pakistani president regarding the massacres. Archer Blood was recalled from his post, and like those officials who tried to tell the truth about the Gulf of Tonkin non-incident, was demoted and placed in the bureaucratic equivalent of Siberia: the department's personnel office. Within a year, meanwhile, India and Pakistan went to war. The United States professed neutrality, but in reality it tilted heavily toward Pakistan. Kissinger noted the administration's indebtedness to Yahya Khan and joked to Nixon about the genocide, quipping, "Yahya hasn't had such fun since the last Hindu massacre." In favoring Pakistan over its rival, India, Nixon had many motivations, but a powerful one was his intense personal prejudice against both Indians in general and the country's leader, Indira Gandhi. In his conversations with Kissinger, he called her "that bitch," that "goddamned woman," and that "old witch." Nixon added that "what the Indians need—what they really need— is a mass famine." This was no one-off remark spoken in the heat of the moment. Nixon and Kissinger agreed at various times that the Indians were "a slippery, treacherous people," "cowards," and "savages." Nixon found himself wondering aloud, "I don't know why the hell anybody would reproduce in that damn country, but they do."[20]

Having been Dwight Eisenhower's vice president during the height of the Cold War, Nixon was certainly not opposed to the use of coups against democratically elected governments when they displeased him. And more coups meant more lying. The case of Chile is, sadly, representative of Nixon and Kissinger's tendency to employ covert military means to pretend to pursue one policy while secretly pursuing its opposite. Under Kennedy and Johnson, the CIA had sought to undermine the 1964 democratic elections in Chile, to prevent the Frente de Acción Popular (Popular Action Front), and especially its presidential candidate, Salvador Allende, from winning. The CIA funded anti-Marxist candidates pretty much wherever there were Marxist candidates, so this was hardly unusual. In the Chilean case, the CIA provided roughly half of pro-American centrist Eduardo Frei's campaign funds, to say nothing of the vast amount it spent on anti-Allende propaganda and other dirty tricks. Frei ended up winning with 57 percent of the vote without any of this being publicly revealed.

When Nixon was first elected in 1968, he announced "a new spirit and a new approach" to South America, promising that the United States would be "changing our attitude to accommodate the forces of change." His policies, he said, would promote "independent, self-reliant states linked together in a vital and useful association" in which "the United States should contribute, not dominate." He promised that the United States would show "respect for national identity and national dignity."[21] These were all lies. Under Kissinger's guidance, Nixon fought persistently to undermine Chilean identity, dignity, and everything else related to the successful practice of democracy.

It's not that Nixon or Kissinger had reason to care about Chile per se. Prior to Allende's 1970 election, the US government's Interagency Group, made up of representatives of every significant branch of the national security bureaucracy, had concluded that "the United States has no vital national interests within Chile." Furthermore, it said, "the world military balance of power would not be significantly altered by an Allende regime, and an Allende victory in Chile would not pose any likely threat to the peace of the region."

Rather, the effects of such a victory, according to the report, would have been largely "psychological" for members of the Organization of American States and "other countries." The US ambassador to Chile, Edward M. Korry, a Johnson appointee, also advised against any action designed to reverse the results of the election, despite his distaste for the Marxist Allende and his followers. Chile was "one of the calmer and more decent places on earth," he pointed out. "Its democracy, like our own, has an extraordinary resilience."[22]

The US government was hardly alone in wanting to influence the election. Ironically, Fidel Castro's communist Cuban government and the US-based corporation International Telephone & Telegraph each reportedly spent $350,000 on the election. By supporting opposite sides, they canceled each other out. PepsiCo, run by Nixon's friend and funder Donald Kendall, had also invested heavily in defeating Allende, and removing him, if necessary. Nixon and Kissinger were not exactly difficult to convince on this point. Speaking both of Chile specifically and as a matter of a deeply held personal conviction, Kissinger complained that he did not "see why we need to stand by and watch a country go Communist due to the irresponsibility of its own people."[23] When the Chileans chose Allende, Nixon eagerly embraced plans to prevent that country from carrying out the results of the election—and if that failed, to help see it overthrown.

At first, the CIA embarked on a plot to try to bribe members of the Chilean Congress before they voted to ratify the popular vote, as was the custom. When this tactic failed, the White House instructed the agency to "prevent Allende from coming to power or to unseat him" through a combination of "propaganda," "economic pressure tactics," and the "resolve of the Chilean military to act against Allende." Nixon had also approved a $10 million plan to "make the [Chilean] economy scream" in anticipation of the Chilean Congress's vote. All this was done without informing or consulting the US State Department or Defense Department. Kissinger also ordered the US embassy to facilitate a "military takeover [of] the government," and to promise the opposition that it would be showered with money in return for the "maintenance of our close relationship." Ambassador Korry was apoplectic when he found out what was afoot and cabled back that he was "appalled to discover that there is a liaison for terrorists and coup plotting." When the Chilean military's commander in chief, René Schneider, refused to go along with the plan, the CIA arranged to have him kidnapped, blaming it on "leftists." This ploy failed, too, and so Schneider was murdered by Venezuelan agents armed with CIA-supplied submachine guns. (Decades later, the CIA admitted its own role, including having made a $35,000 payoff to the kidnappers—though it insisted, with impressive chutzpah, that the payment was made for "humanitarian reasons.") When news of Schneider's killing broke, Nixon professed to be "shock[ed]" by this "stain on the pages of contemporary history" and spoke of his "sorrow that this repugnant event has occurred." When, resisting Nixon and Kissinger's bribes and threats, the members of the Chilean Congress voted to seat Allende's government, Kissinger issued one of the most shameless press releases in the history of shameless press releases. It noted that it was "of course, up to the new government and the people of Chile to choose and shape the nation's future and policy.... [F]ew nations have more justification for pride in political and intellectual freedom than Chile....We would, therefore, hope that Chile will not violate its own democratic and western tradition."[24]

The coup finally came on September 11, 1973. As bombs fell on the presidential palace, Allende shot himself in the head rather than allow himself to be taken by the plotters. The CIA was aware of the coup-plotting but was instructed by the White House not to interfere. Once it was over, Nixon complained to Kissinger that the press was "bleeding because a pro-Communist government has been overthrown." Kissinger, egging him on, replied, "Isn't that something?" Continuing his rant, Nixon mused, "I mean…in the Eisenhower period we would be heroes." He then asked Kissinger, "Our hand doesn't show on this one?" Kissinger answered, "We didn't do it," but still he could not resist taking some credit. "I mean we helped them [and] created the conditions," Kissinger offered. The State Department immediately sent a cable to Santiago instructing US diplomats there to "welcome" the coup's plotters and to make clear the United States' "desire to cooperate with the military Junta and to assist in any appropriate way." Richard Helms, director of the CIA, would later be convicted of lying to Congress about these activities. After pleading no contest to the charges, he received a two-year suspended prison sentence and a $2,000 fine, and he was met with a crowd of cheering conservatives as he emerged from the courtroom. The *New York Times* editorialized in favor of his lies, claiming that Helms had been "caught between his duty to obey the law and his duty to protect the secrets." The *Times* uttered not a word about the illegal killings or the purposeful destruction of Chilean democracy.[25]

Chilean democracy would disappear for the next seventeen years. Augusto Pinochet's vicious military dictatorship, a regime lasting from 1974 until 1990, rounded up, tortured, and killed thousands of its perceived opponents, many of whom were neither Marxists nor Allende supporters but apolitical constitutionalists and centrists of the kind the United States had previously supported. As many as 1,500 people were summarily executed. Two of these murders took place in Washington, DC, in September 1976, when Orlando Letelier, a Chilean diplomat, together with Ronni Moffitt, a twenty-five-year-old American scholar at the Institute for Policy Studies who was working as Letelier's assistant, were gunned down in broad daylight by a Chilean hit squad. No charges were ever leveled in the United States for this crime. Meanwhile, another 28,000 Chileans were tortured but not killed. In 1990, the Chilean National Commission on

Truth and Reconciliation charged the Junta with "the murder, disappearance and death by torture of some 3,197 citizens" through its program of "state-sponsored terror."[26]

Nearly half a century after it took place, what we call Nixon's "Watergate scandal" remains firmly rooted in the American collective historical memory. What is not nearly so well remembered is the degree to which the scandal was the product of a nexus of Nixon's personal and political qualities that empowered his eagerness to abuse the power of the presidency and then lie to Congress and the country to try to hide his crimes.

The simplest place to begin the Watergate story is on May 9, 1969, when *New York Times* reporter William Beecher wrote about the US bombing of Cambodia—a country with which it was allegedly at peace—for nine weeks. (The confusing headline read, "Raids in Cambodia by US Unprotested.") US pilots would eventually drop between 2.5 million and 3 million tons of bombs on that country, killing countless civilians. They are countless, in part, because the Nixon administration instructed the air force to destroy its records and replace them with phony reports of bombings within South Vietnam. Upon seeing the *New York Times* story revealing the truth about the raids, Nixon demanded of Kissinger, "What is this cocksucking story? Find out who leaked it and fire him!" Kissinger replied, "We must crush these people! We must destroy them." At Nixon and Kissinger's behest, the FBI director, J. Edgar Hoover, soon agreed to wiretap the phones of thirteen people, including five of Kissinger's top aides and four reporters, with Beecher among them.[27]

Nixon approved a full-scale US invasion of Cambodia a year later, at which point he made the almost comically dishonest claim that the United States had always "scrupulously respect[ed] the neutrality of the Cambodian people." Though both men denied it in their memoirs, Nixon and Kissinger privately admitted to one another that the bombing of Cambodia had been a disaster—not because it killed innocents or led to genocide, but because, as Kissinger would later write, "it pushed the North Vietnamese deeper into Cambodia." Kissinger would later lie to the media when questioned about his role in helping to pick out the wiretap targets following the leak of the bombing story, insisting that he was only following Nixon's orders. When Nixon read this, he again grew furious. "Henry ordered the whole goddam thing....He read every one of those taps....[H]e reveled in it, he groveled in it, he wallowed in it."[28]

In the aftermath of the *Washington Post*'s initial reporting of the now-famous break-in at Democratic National Committee headquarters at the Watergate Hotel on June 17, 1972, Nixon did not appear terribly concerned. Five men had been arrested for the break-in: three of them were Cuban exiles; one was a Cuban American; and the fifth was James McCord Jr., a former CIA officer who had become a salaried security coordinator for Nixon's Committee for the Re-election of the President (CREEP). But Nixon's reaction was to tell his aides, "The country doesn't give much of a shit about it....It's politics." Special Counsel Charles Colson suggested that the White House try to blame the break-in on the CIA, and Attorney General John Mitchell, Nixon's former and future campaign chief, supported the plan, noting that it would provide a useful pretext for shutting down what could be an extremely worrisome FBI investigation. The central figures involved in planning the break-in, former FBI agent and ex–White House aide E. Howard Hunt and ex-CIA officer G. Gordon Liddy, who had become CREEP's finance counsel, were to be paid off, promised pardons, and told to disappear. That sounded fine to Nixon, who approved the plan and convinced himself that he had the situation well under control. He received reassurances as well from Haldeman, who informed the president that the wealthy right-wing Greek American Tom Pappas was good for "the continuing financial activity in order to keep [the defendants] in place." He added, "And he's able to deal in cash," so long as Nixon kept the US ambassador to Greece, Henry Tasca, on the job in Athens. Nixon replied, "Good. I understand. No problem."[29]

Once again, this *Godfather*-style tough talk was just the way this White House did business. Pappas was known in the White House as "the Greek bearing gifts"; he had funneled $549,000 from Greece's ruling military junta into Nixon's 1968 presidential campaign as a "gift" to Nixon for naming the corrupt governor of Maryland, the Greek American Spiro T. Agnew, as his running mate. Agnew was accepting illegal payoffs, not only before Nixon chose him but even during his vice presidency.[30]

A full accounting of crimes committed by Nixon and his henchmen would prove shocking even to his die-hard defenders. For instance, on June 30, 1971, Nixon instructed Charles Colson to commit a burglary of the Brookings Institution: "I want the break in....[Y]ou're to break into the place, rifle the files and bring them in....[J]ust go in and take it." He added to Haldeman and Kissinger, "Goddammit, get in and get those files. Blow the safe and get them." And he would not let it go. Tape recordings captured Nixon a day later demanding of Haldeman, his chief of staff, "Did they get the Brookings Institute raided last night? Get it done. I want it done." In response to this presidential demand, Liddy and Hunt came up with a plan to buy a fire engine, dress their (Cuban) agents in firemen's outfits, and then blow the place up. Thoughtfully, they would do this "at night so as not to endanger lives needlessly." That plan was eventually shelved over the fact that it was "too expensive."[31]

It is not likely that Nixon ordered or even had specific knowledge of the Watergate break-in in advance. His entirely reasonable reaction to the news of the failed break-in was to call Special Counsel Colson and ask: "No one in our operation could be this stupid, could they?" At the time, Haldeman said to Nixon, "The great thing about this is that the whole thing is so totally fucked up and so badly done that nobody believes—" Nixon interrupted him, adding, "that we could have done it." Yet, according to White House Counsel John Dean's

2009 judgment, "It was the quest to get the very information [on potential Democratic opponents] that Nixon had wanted and repeatedly requested that resulted in the bungled bugging and burglaries at the DNC." John Ehrlichman's July 8, 1972, diary entry records that he and the president's other advisers had warned Nixon that unraveling the true story of the Watergate break-in likely "would involve the activities which were perfectly legitimate but which would be hard to explain." Ehrlichman, who was apparently operating on the basis of a decidedly expansive definition of the term "perfectly legitimate," added in his diary entry, "From that day forward Nixon knew everything I knew about Howard Hunt's activities—the attempts to pile more blame on President Kennedy for the failure of the Bay of Pigs and the assassination of President Diem."[32]

Fortunately for American democracy, Nixon's confidence turned out to be misplaced. On March 19, 1973, just before he was about to be sentenced for his conviction on eight counts of conspiracy, burglary, and wiretapping, James McCord wrote a letter to the presiding US District Court justice John J. Sirica admitting to having perjured himself during his trial. That got the ball rolling. The big break in the case came the following month, with Dean's decision to turn state's evidence. Worried about this very possibility, Nixon had tried to blackmail Dean, telling Ehrlichman that Dean needed to remember "that there is only one man who can restore him to the ability to practice law in case things go wrong....He has got to have that in the back of his mind." Nixon had requested that Dean conduct an investigation of Watergate and write a full report of what took place, knowing full well that Dean had been an enthusiastic participant in countless Watergate-related crimes. A week later, in a prime-time Oval Office speech, Nixon told the American people that Dean had already finished his "full-scale investigation." Dean later recalled that he "damn near fell off the bed" upon hearing this. The president claimed that Dean had informed him that all activities undertaken on his watch as White House counsel were fully legitimate. But what was really happening was that he was being set up to take the fall. Nixon was preparing to say that he had been misled by Dean, and that Dean had kept the illegal activities secret so as to conceal his own role in them. Dean decided then and there to flip, thereby setting off the series of events that would eventually lead Nixon onto his path of disgrace, denial, and eventually resignation.[33]

The process took over a year, but the end for Nixon finally came on August 8, 1974, just as a grand jury was about to indict him on charges of bribery, conspiracy, obstruction of justice, and obstruction of a criminal investigation. Republican senators had informed the president that they were prepared to turn on him: he would not only be impeached but also be convicted and removed from office. Nixon seized on the loss of support as a face-saving rationale for his resignation—as if he were a European party leader who had lost a "no-confidence" vote. "To continue to fight through the months ahead for my personal vindication would almost totally absorb the time and attention of both the President and the Congress in a period when our entire focus should be on the great issues of peace abroad and prosperity without inflation at home," he announced, thereby becoming the first American president to voluntarily leave office.[34] Naturally, he did so with a lie.

After Nixon told his new chief of staff, Alexander Haig, of his decision to resign, Haig went to see Vice President Gerald Ford to sound him out about a potential deal for a pardon. Ford did not reply immediately, saying that he wanted to think about it. Soon after Ford took the oath of office as president, the pardon came, without any admission of guilt on Nixon's part or even an explanation for his actions. Ford began his presidency under the shadow of Watergate, and he was never able to escape from it entirely. The new president's poll numbers plunged precipitously in the aftermath of the pardon, making him the first president to receive a negative poll rating in his first month in office.[35] Fittingly, perhaps, Nixon's lies undermined the presidency of his successor as well as his own.

9

Gerald Ford

A TIME FOR MORE LYING

As president, Gerald Ford was almost universally celebrated as the "Not-Nixon." He was a simple man who made his own breakfast and still had a listed phone number on the day of Nixon's resignation; he was nothing like the tortured psychopath whose uncontrollable hatred and paranoia had torn the country apart. The new era was, as Ford would call it in the title of his memoir, "a time to heal." Ford bet correctly that the nation's desire to move on from the Nixon scandals would spare him from any tough questioning about what actually had been discussed in advance regarding his Nixon pardon. But this turned out to be a devil's bargain. In failing to confront the rumors surrounding the pardon, Ford failed to free himself from Nixon's web of criminality and deception. Ford repeatedly insisted that "there was no deal, period, under no circumstances," but he failed to convince the millions who doubted his word that this was the truth.[1]

Though he appeared to share none of his predecessor's patholog-ical tendencies, Ford was nevertheless subject to some of the same political pressures. He inherited the remains of a soon-to-be-lost war in Vietnam that had long ago lost its raison d'être. US policymakers were unable to figure out how to evade responsibility for the loss and all its horrific consequences, whether for the US military, the country at large, or the Vietnamese. Ford and Kissinger thus felt compelled to restore what they imagined to be "credibility" as a military super-power, whether to allies or adversaries, and grew obsessed with the need to demonstrate America's toughness wherever the opportunity might present itself. This obsession determined how they faced virtu-ally every issue that arose during Ford's brief presidency.

Ford's first opportunity to show his mettle came just days after the April 30, 1975, fall of Saigon. On May 12, less than a month after the murderous Khmer Rouge, Cambodia's communist movement, took over Cambodia and renamed it "Kampuchea," a commercial ship named the *Mayaguez*, owned by a subsidiary of the American tobacco company R. J. Reynolds, was running cargo for the US military and diplomatic corps when it was seized by the Cambodian navy off that nation's coast. Within the White House, the captured ship and crew were viewed exclusively as a political opportunity, albeit a risky one.

The men sitting around the table at the National Security Council meetings were terrified of nothing so much as a situation like the one the Johnson administration had confronted when, in January 1968, North Korea had captured a US spy ship called the *Pueblo*. The North Koreans had proceeded to kill some of the *Pueblo*'s crew, starving and torturing the rest, and only released them after the United States agreed to issue a humiliating apology.[2] Since the United States had no diplo-matic relations with the Khmer Rouge, it had no reliable information about what was going on in Cambodia. When the US soldiers dis-patched to rescue the *Mayaguez* crew invaded the island of Koh Tang on the second day after the seizure, they were met by a hundred or so hostile Khmer Rouge soldiers who had been stationed there to resist the Vietnamese, but none of the *Mayaguez*'s crew members. By the time Ford had actually ordered the attack, the Cambodians had already freed the crew members. The Cambodians had previously announced that they had "no intention of detaining [the ship] permanently," explaining that they had "no desire to stage provocations." They "only wanted," they said, "to know the reason for its coming and to warn it against violating our waters again." In what was almost a catastrophe for all concerned, Ford ordered US pilots to fire on a patrol boat that was initially believed to be hostile, but turned out to be transporting the *Mayaguez* crew to return them to their ship. Fortunately, the pilot happened to notice who was on the boat before carrying out the order.

For the duration of the three-day-long incident, Ford spoke not a word to the nation. The White House did issue a press release that called the seizure of the ship an "act of piracy," but this was a made-up claim insofar as maritime law was concerned. When *Mayaguez* crew members later sued the captain of the ship as well as the company that owned it, the terms of the settlement suggested that the skipper had likely been negligent in "recklessly venturing into known dangerous and hostile waters of foreign sovereignty (Cambodia)." Moreover, the *Mayaguez* was not flying a flag at the time it was seized and was sailing just two miles off the Cambodian coast. The press release asserted "that the vessel has been recovered intact and the entire crew has been rescued. The forces that have successfully accomplished this mission are still under hostile fire, but are preparing to disengage." This, too, was false.[3]

Ford and his advisers sought to use the incident to project steadiness, strength, and resolve on the part of the president, regardless of how profoundly his actual behavior contradicted this image. In his memoir, Ford wrote, "Rhetoric alone, I knew, would not persuade anyone that America would stand firm. They would have to see proof of our resolve." The reality, however, was chaos. When Ford gave the

orders to shoot at the Cambodian boat that turned out to be carrying the *Mayaguez* crew, it was countermanded by the secretary of
defense, James Schlesinger, only to be snuck out through his National
Security Council staff and given to the pilots, who then fortunately
ignored it when the time came to do the actual firing. The fighting
that did take place, however, resulted in the unnecessary deaths of
three US soldiers, with forty-nine wounded and three missing in action. The Cambodians said their death count was fifty-five, though of
course that number was impossible to independently verify.

What is clearly evident about this crisis is the fact that the Ford
administration placed an extremely low priority on actually rescuing
the captured crew members. Kissinger's initial reaction was "God-
damn it. We are not going to sit here and let an American merchant
ship be captured at sea and let it go into the harbor without doing a
bloody thing about it." Vice President Nelson Rockefeller demanded
"a violent response," adding, "The world should know that we will
act and that we will act quickly." Ford was operating in a political
environment in which Ronald Reagan, his right-wing challenger for
the 1976 Republican presidential nomination, was all but calling him
a wimp and a weasel on a nearly daily basis. In the aftermath of the
incident, the super-hawk senator Barry Goldwater, the party's 1964
presidential nominee, insisted that if Ford had "not done what he
did, every...half-assed nation in the world would be taking shots at
us, and now I think they're going to think twice before they try it."[4]

From a purely public relations standpoint, the lying worked. The
president's approval rating rose eleven points in the immediate aftermath of the "rescue" because most of the major news outlets reported the incident just as the president and his advisers wished, Gulf
of Tonkin–style. C. S. Sulzberger of the *New York Times* admired
"Ford's resolute and skillful leadership," which he said had "destroyed
a polluting American image of lassitude, uncertainty and pessimism."
According to *US News and World Report*, the president's response
"was meant as a signal to US allies and adversaries. In essence: Don't

take us lightly. The humiliating setbacks in Indo-China…have not paralyzed America's will to play its role as a global power." To *Newsweek*, it was "a daring show of nerve and steel…swift and tough… and it worked." *Time*'s Hugh Sidey weirdly called it "a lovely bit of rascality." The *New York Times* further reported that eleven Republican governors had banded together to congratulate the president for "rescuing the American ship and crew which was seized by the Cambodian pirates," and added, "This example of valor and a strong U.S. foreign policy will promote the safety of American citizens throughout the world. We commend and thank you for your strong action." To a questioner who praised his performance at a public forum, Ford replied, "That, I think, should be a good warning to any country that thinks they can challenge us. If any country does any act of that kind, I think the *Mayaguez* incident and the action we took ought to be a fair warning to them on the decisiveness of the Ford Administration."[5]

As with both the Tonkin Gulf and the Cuban missile crises, this time as farce, braggadocio over the *Mayaguez* was based on a mountain of baloney. When the US General Accounting Office (GAO) issued a report a year and a half later that accurately described what had happened—crediting Chinese diplomacy, rather than the bungled US military action, with ensuring the safety of the crew—Ford responded, "I don't believe the American people will believe somebody who, with the luxury of 18 months afterwards, can sit back and write a report. I think they will believe a president who was there and had to make the tough decisions on an incident that was important to the American foreign policy." Ford was probably correct here, despite the fact that his statement was nonsensical even on its own terms. No less paradoxically, he dismissed the nonpartisan GAO report as "another example of partisan politics." And when the Democratic presidential nominee, Georgia governor Jimmy Carter, raised the report during a presidential debate, Ford again insisted that "every possible diplomatic means was utilized," which was also false. Ford repeated this lie over and over. At a 1976 news conference, he said, "I can assure you that this administration has taken a firm action wherever we have been confronted with any illegal international action. The best illustration is, of course, what we did in 1975 in the *Mayaguez* incident."[6]

Of course it was all for show. Later that year, Henry Kissinger, meeting the foreign minister of Thailand, asked him to relay the message to the Cambodians that "we will be friends with them. They are murderous thugs, but we won't let that stand in our way." He would later muse, in his memoirs, "We had entered Indochina to save a country and ended by rescuing a ship."[7] It was a decidedly modest claim, but that did not make it true. The only successful rescue operation performed was the decidedly brief rescue of Gerald Ford's reputation.

The civil war that erupted in the African nation of Angola following Portugal's decision to grant it independence in 1974 presented the Ford administration with yet another opportunity to demonstrate its alleged toughness and resolve. It was in another deadly Cold War skirmish without any discernible threat to US national security. And once again, a combination of incompetence and the administration's inability to sensibly explain its actions led to yet another series of lies that begat more lies and chaos.

In order to do battle with the Soviet- and Cuban-backed Marxist guerrillas in Angola, who were called the MPLA, for the Portuguese name meaning People's Movement for the Liberation of Angola, the Ford administration, in a secret plan masterminded by Kissinger, spent $32 million arming anti-Soviet guerrilla forces. These were led by Holden Roberto of the FNLA (National Front for the Liberation of Angola) and Jonas Savimbi of UNITA (National Union for the Total Independence of Angola). Zaire's murderous US-supported dictator, Mobutu Sese Seko, acted as the middleman between the United States and the warlords. The *New York Times* broke the story of the administration's participation in a secret war but hid its own scoop, placing it within a larger contextual article that focused more on the conflict than on the secret US role in it—or the administration's lies.[8] While the news failed to excite many US citizens, it did command attention within Congress, which the administration had consistently kept in the dark.

Called before the Senate Foreign Relations Committee, CIA director William Colby found himself forced to admit to the full scope of American involvement, and he apologized for deliberately misleading Congress about it. But as with the *Mayaguez* crisis, the administration's primary (really its only) concern was its ability to assert American power in order to boost the country's "credibility."[9]

The administration's efforts failed in nearly every respect. Democratic senator Dick Clark, who chaired the Subcommittee on Africa of the Senate Foreign Relations Committee, traveled to the region to assess the situation and quickly realized that the administration had been lying to Congress about virtually every aspect of its efforts there. US-backed forces enjoyed little to no chance of success despite far greater involvement from the United States in their military activity than anyone in the Ford administration had so far admitted. More than anything else, it was the administration's lies that infuriated Clark and ultimately pushed him to try to end the program entirely.[10]

Ford and Kissinger fought furiously to defeat the "Clark Amendment" (which was actually sponsored by California Democrat John Tunney). But during congressional hearings, administration officials were forced to admit that the lying had been more extensive even than CIA director Colby had admitted. So Congress passed the Clark Amendment as an attachment to the Arms Export Control Act of 1976, which made it politically impossible for the president to exercise his veto, shutting down the program in question, though this, too, was something of a ruse. In fact, then CIA director George H.W. Bush refused to concede that his agency's efforts in Angola would cease as a result, and soon, according to those involved, turned to Israel to replace the United States as an arms pipeline to the FNLA through Zaire.[11]

Even so, Kissinger accused Congress of inviting the Soviets "to take advantage of our own continuing domestic division and self-torment" to upset "some form of equilibrium between the great powers." An-gola, he argued, represented "the first time that the United States has failed to respond to Soviet military moves outside their immediate orbit." Ford simply said that the amendment's passage proved that Congress had no "guts." Neither man considered that their own con-sistent dishonesty played any role in their defeat. Why, after all, did it matter to US national security which group of guerrillas ended up on top in Angola? It didn't. The appearance of toughness was the entire policy. Meanwhile, Kissinger eventually admitted that the effort had been just for show. "We are not opposed to the MPLA as such," he explained in a news conference near the end of 1975. "We can live with any of the factions in Angola." His justification for the US inter-vention, the lies, and the lives lost rested entirely on the importance of projecting strength: "Failure to resist can only lead other countries to conclude that their situation is becoming precarious."[12] Angola itself did not matter, and neither, of course, did the truth.

As the *Mayaguez* and Angolan episodes clearly demonstrate, Presi-dent Ford was hardly averse to lying to the country when he thought it suited his political purposes. The logic of Cold War national secu-rity ideology had made these kinds of lies so commonplace that they were deemed barely worthy of mention in the nation's political press. It was therefore deeply ironic that the "lie" that ruined him politi-cally was not a lie at all, just a dumb mistake he could not bring him-self to admit having made. During the final 1976 presidential debate with Jimmy Carter, Ford insisted that "there is no Soviet domination of Eastern Europe and there never will be under a Ford adminis-tration." Ford began his election campaign polling fully thirty-three points behind Carter. He had cut this gap down to just two points by the October 6 debate, and clearly enjoyed momentum going into it.

It's not as if Ford was given a trick question. A reporter asked him whether the Soviets were "using Eastern Europe as their own sphere of influence in occupying most of the countries there," while US allies like France and Italy appeared to be "flirting with Communism." That's when Ford blew it. "I don't believe…the Yugoslavians consider themselves dominated by the Soviet Union," he said, and he went on to repeat the very same sentence regarding both the Romanians and the Poles. "Each of those countries," Ford insisted, "is independent, autonomous: it has its own territorial integrity and the United States does not concede that those countries are under the domination of the Soviet Union."[13]

In the aftermath of the debate, Dick Cheney, who was then Ford's chief of staff (and later would serve six terms as a Republican congressman from Wyoming before being named secretary of defense under George H.W. Bush and being elected vice president under George W. Bush), attempted to assure the press that "the American people will understand" what the president meant. This was perhaps true, albeit not at all in the manner Cheney meant it. The ensuing press coverage attempted to clarify the matter for confused Americans: yes, the Soviets really did dominate these countries. Ford, journalists speculated, was probably just trying to pay tribute to the spirit of Eastern European independence that lived in the hearts of those citizens, whose nations were most definitely politically and militarily dominated by the USSR. But that was not what Ford said. It may be that one reason Ford refused, repeatedly, to admit how wrong he had been was the fact that, immediately following the debate, Henry Kissinger, to whom Ford always looked for advice, congratulated the president on his "magnificent performance."[14] To the rest of America, however, Ford just looked darned confused. Did he realize that what he was saying made no sense at the time? It's impossible to know. But whatever the reason, his stubbornness, together with the Nixon pardon, almost certainly cost him the election, as it painted him as the same kind of liar as his predecessor had been. The times had changed, and the sorts of lies that had won elections for presidents in the pre-Vietnam era were now losing them.

10

Jimmy Carter "Will Never Lie to You"

The presidencies of both Lyndon Johnson and Richard Nixon ended in disgrace, at least in part owing to their lies and policy failures. In their aftermath, Jimmy Carter, a little-known former one-term governor of Georgia, fashioned a come-from-nowhere presidential campaign based largely on one virtue-signaling promise: "I will never lie to you." Carter would learn, however, that while the idea of a president who did not deceive the public was an attractive campaign gambit, in practice such a commitment was all but impossible for him to honor as the president of a nation that had become accustomed to lies. What's more, it was a nation that had long ago redefined its national security needs as nearly infinite, and had therefore found itself aiding and abetting regimes so abhorrent that to admit the truth of it all would have created an endless cascade of public scandal. These matters put the president in an all-but-impossible position, demanding of him a willingness to elide the truth—by omission if possible, and by lies if not.

Jimmy Carter "Will Never Lie to You"

Without a 180-degree reversal of US foreign policy, lies were necessary simply to maintain US commitments in any number of countries in Latin America, Asia, Africa, and elsewhere—as Carter was soon to learn once he took office in January 1977. Many of those countries were led by brutal dictators who had been put in power with the understanding that so long as they sided with the United States against the Soviets, and protected US corporations from expropriation of their properties, nobody would bother them about "human rights." Ensuring the continued rule of these cruel, kleptocratic regimes—such as the Somozas of Nicaragua, the Marcoses of the Philippines, and the Shah of Iran—could not be explained in a manner consistent with Americans' self-understanding. The nation's citizens had, for decades, if not centuries, been repeatedly told that they lived in a nation that defended democracy, promoted freedom, and fought against tyranny abroad as well as at home.[1] The country's popular culture and educational system constantly reinforced these beliefs. Nixon was understood to be an aberration, and Carter the correction. And so a president, even one who promised never to lie, was left with no choice but to pay tribute to those illusions. Fairy tales, after all, have a purpose for adults as well as for children.

Candidate Jimmy Carter surely knew that almost all of us lie sometimes and that successful politicians do so rather more often than that. His own mother admitted to reporters that her son was not averse to telling "white lies," if only to spare the feelings of those around him. Carter offered his campaign pledge to never lie at a moment when, as one White House correspondent, James Deakin, noted, "lying had become official policy of the American government."[2] Thanks to Richard Nixon, reporters were, according to *New York Times* columnist Tom Wicker, "more skeptical of politicians than ever before, anxious to demonstrate their skepticism and

prove their independence, and in a mood to challenge every statement, question every act of those who sought the public's trust."[3]

Moreover, because most journalists, like most well-educated urban voters, tended to pull the lever for Democrats when they voted
at all—and conservatives had already latched onto this notion as
a powerful line of attack on the news media—many were eager to
demonstrate their bona fides as equal opportunity tormentors. This
meant, ideally, finding a way to prove that the sanctimonious, Bible-
toting Jimmy Carter was just another lying pol like Nixon or Johnson. These same reporters and editors could hardly fail to notice
that the Watergate scandal had made *Washington Post* reporters Bob
Woodward and Carl Bernstein into wealthy celebrities. Woodward
got to see himself played by Robert Redford in *All the President's
Men*, the movie based on his and Bernstein's book; Bernstein had to
settle for Dustin Hoffman, but soon got to date Elizabeth Taylor.[4]

Another problem Carter faced from the get-go as president de-
rived from the culture clash he represented, coming as he did from
rural Georgia and now placed directly into the thick of worldly Washington intrigue. It didn't help that he demonstrated an undeniable
self-righteousness in this regard, believing himself to be uncorrupted
by Washington's wicked ways. Part of the problem was stylistic.
Time's Hugh Sidey called it the "yahoo" or "cornpone" syndrome.
Newsweek's Meg Greenfield disparaged this notion but nevertheless
helped to popularize the image of "bare-chested, peanut-feeding ya-
hoos" fouling the White House grounds.[5] The larger issue, however,
was the fact that it was simply impossible for the president of a
superpower with interests and commitments all over the world, or
even for a leader of the Democratic Party, to adhere to Carter's moralistic posture. In his inaugural address, Carter proclaimed, "Our
commitment to human rights must be absolute," a statement more
appropriate to a pope than a president. And it made Carter appear a
perfect hypocrite when, to take just one instance, on New Year's Eve

1977, almost a year after taking office, he toasted the brutal Shah of Iran for his "great leadership."[6]

Carter had gotten his first taste of the treatment he would receive as president during the Democratic primary campaign, when the journalist Steven Brill published a cover story in *Harper's* provocatively titled "Jimmy Carter's Pathetic Lies." Brill did not come up entirely empty-handed, but neither did he justify his headline. Most of his examples were either trivial political exaggerations or examples of the kinds of things that a person running for office in Georgia might say, but that one running to represent the entire Democratic Party would wish he had not. In the former category, Carter referred to himself as a "nuclear physicist" and a "peanut farmer" when he was not exactly either one. In reality, Carter had taken classes in nuclear engineering and nuclear physics while in the navy's nuclear submarine training program at Union College, but received no degree. His family owned a peanut farm upon which he grew up, together with a warehouse, which he turned over to a blind trust upon becoming president. The candidate also consistently exaggerated his success as Georgia's governor and walked back a bunch of statements he had made there. Many of these claims were decidedly ambiguous, however. Back in Georgia, Carter had called the war criminal William Calley—a lieutenant in the US Army who had led his troops in butchering, raping, and murdering hundreds of Vietnamese civilians, including infants and young children, in a village called "Son May" (but referred to as "My Lai" by Americans)—a "scapegoat." Later, as a presidential candidate, he denied that he had ever thought Calley "anything but guilty." Although no investigatory sleuths could locate transcripts of the speeches the governor had made on "George Wallace Appreciation Day," they allegedly contained some decidedly problematic utterances from the perspective of his presidential ambitions. The Carter campaign apparently had his official records scrubbed for exactly this reason. There is no question that Carter was shading the truth as he reinvented himself from a moderate in Georgia to a politician who was at least liberal enough to win the Democratic presidential nomination. But neither is it clear that these examples justify Brill's term "pathetic lies." Was calling Calley a "scapegoat" the same thing as denying his guilt? Was it fair to say that the war he now called "racist" made his earlier view that American servicemen had "our complete backing" a lie? Is "I was never a liberal" the opposite of "I've always been a liberal on civil rights and social needs"? These questions are valid only in light of Carter's "I will never lie to you" promise (later revised to "I will never mislead you"). Otherwise they would be called "politics."[7]

Carter was also the victim of a post-Watergate infatuation among journalists with unsubstantiated gossip, led by the Nixon-slaying *Washington Post*. This tendency led to a number of clearly silly stories designed to take Carter and his people down by exposing typical personal foibles and to an increased reliance on anonymous and often self-interested sources. Len Downie Jr., who would succeed Ben Bradlee as the top editor at the *Washington Post*, later admitted that "after Woodward and Bernstein became household names...a number of journalists lost their perspective. Too many got caught in the thrill of the chase. And it was a very, very dangerous period when a lot of people got burned."[8] The fact that Carter and his advisers knew almost no one from the Democratic establishment—and did not appear eager to court them, much less offer the tribute of flattery to which they had grown accustomed during election years—further exacerbated his administration's vulnerability to political assassination by anonymous-source quoting.

Any fair assessment of Carter's presidency would have to conclude that he and the members of his administration were far more frequently lied about than they were liars themselves, and these lies were frequently relayed to the American people by the very news outlets that had, under Nixon, done their best to ferret out the truth. They now went to great lengths to try to paint Carter and company as no more honest than their predecessors. News reporters and editors failed repeatedly and embarrassed themselves in the process, but along the way they inflicted considerable damage to Carter's presidency. The *Washington Post*'s Sally Quinn, for example, reported that Carter's chief of staff, Hamilton Jordan, gazed ostentatiously down the dress of the Egyptian ambassador's wife in order to "see the twin pyramids of Egypt," as Quinn quoted him.[9] Both Jordan and the Egyptian ambassador denied Quinn's report, and Quinn was in fact not there at the time of the supposed incident. The *New York Times* later reported that most of the guests who were in a position to witness it found the allegation "ridiculous," according to one couple who shared their table.[10] Nor did Jordan spill his drink on the head of one woman and down the shirt of another, as was reported almost everywhere.[11] Neither did Jordan, or Press Secretary Jody Powell, do cocaine at Studio 54. (The source who made up this story turned out to be Joe McCarthy's consigliere, Roy Cohn, who later became Donald Trump's mentor.) Nevertheless, that lie required an independent counsel investigation and a grand jury vote of 24–0 to disprove, with oceans of ink spilled on the lie in the process.[12]

Carter tried, and largely failed, to escape the truth trap set by America's global interests and the devious means necessary to maintain them. The problem, however, was baked into the office of the presidency, leaving him vulnerable to the Washington powers that were gunning for him. In his 1999 book *Shadow: Five Presidents and the Legacy of Watergate*, Bob Woodward went to great lengths to show that Carter had lied about an incident involving CIA payments to Jordan's King Hussein. Carter had ended the payments shortly after taking office while continuing to keep all these efforts secret. On February 14, 1977, barely more than three weeks into Carter's presidency, Bob Woodward, still at the *Washington Post*, told Carter he planned to publish an exposé of the CIA's plans, creating an early crisis for his presidency, still in its infancy. Part of the problem was that Carter had set impossible standards for himself as a candidate. He had gone much further than the central "I will never lie" promise—writing, for example, in a campaign position paper, "We must never again keep secret the evolution of our foreign policy from the Congress and the American people. They should never again be misled about our options, commitments, our progress or our failures." He had personally pledged that "if the CIA ever makes a mistake, I'll be the one, as President, to call a press conference, and I'll tell you and the American people, this is what happened." These promises were remarkably naïve on Carter's part, if indeed he meant to keep his word. Given the enormous range of covert actions undertaken by the CIA, "mistakes" were inevitable, as were cover-ups to hide them. In this case, Carter did not want to announce his mistake just as his secretary of state, Cyrus Vance, was about to land in Jordan to meet with the king. Woodward had the story, however, and, meeting with both the reporter and his editor, Bradlee, Carter asked the newspaper to hold off on publishing it until after Vance's visit. He noted that the payments had "been in existence for twenty years." In fact Carter had been unaware of them before Woodward contacted him, and it was only then that he learned that, although CIA officials had reported what they termed these "bribes," and the Intelligence Oversight Board, established by President Ford, had deemed them "improper," Ford had done nothing. The president told Woodward and Bradlee that he could not "undo the past or be responsible for all the past." He also added that he had just learned of the payments himself. Unusually for a president in a position like this one, Carter refused to utter the magic words "national security" that previous presidents had so frequently used to kill inconvenient news stories. Even more modestly, he added that although he had made his preferences clear, "I can't tell you how to run your business"—as if no one who had occupied his office would ever imagine such a thing.[13]

Woodward and Bradlee refused Carter's entreaty and ran the story just as Vance's plane landed in Amman. Asked about it by congressional leaders, Carter sidestepped the larger question by replying that he had "not found anything illegal or improper" in any ongoing CIA operation, which was technically true, if misleading, since Carter had by then ended all payments to the king. In his 1999 book, Woodward demonstrated his hostility to Carter by accusing him of offering one impression during their meeting and giving a "rather different impression" during the press conference. He added, "Carter lied about his meeting with us....His account of our meeting to the Congressional leaders was not accurate and reflected a mood and manner that did not exist." Conveying a different "mood" or "impression" is hardly synonymous with telling a lie. Nevertheless, Woodward went on to conclude that "Carter's policy of openness fell far short of his campaign pledges."[14]

The reason why was obvious: Woodward, like many other Washington actors at the time, knew that Carter's campaign pledges were just that. They were never meant to be taken entirely literally, as even Carter's mother once admitted. But when it came to Jimmy Carter, Bob Woodward, like so much of the Washington political establishment, pretended not to know this. The entire episode can be said to mark, as well as any, the beginning of a new trend of elite political journalists seeking to prove their journalistic bona fides by being extra-tough on Democrats and liberals in the face of far greater transgressions by Republicans and conservatives. This double standard was soon weaponized by Republicans and conservatives. In addition to enjoying salacious stories themselves, mainstream journalists were eager to demonstrate their credentials as "savvy" political insiders like Woodward and Bradlee. This quality, as defined by media scholar Jay Rosen, would come to define inside-the-Beltway political journalism and punditry in the coming decades. It implies, in Rosen's diagnosis, a cultish desire by journalists to be perceived as "shrewd, practical, hyper-informed, perceptive, ironic, 'with it,' and unsentimental in all things political." The savvy, Rosen wrote, are "winners," or at least know "who the winners are," while "the unsavvy are hapless, clueless, deluded, clownish, or in some cases extreme."[15] As the kid-glove treatment of Carter's immediate successors, Ronald Reagan and George H.W. Bush, would clearly demonstrate, in the post-Watergate era Republicans were, with the help of this emerging journalistic ethos, able to indulge in dishonesty much more easily than Democrats were, lacking as they did the qualities of earnestness that interfered with its success. And in doing so, they took what we may now recognize as the first steps on the path to the presidency of Donald Trump.

11

Ronald Reagan

AMERICA'S "MAGIC TOTEM"

When then Texas governor George W. Bush instructed Senator John McCain, during a 2000 presidential primary debate, that "it is not Reaganesque to say one thing and do another," he may not have been purposefully lying, but he just as surely was not telling the truth. In fact, almost nothing could be more "Reaganesque" than to say one thing and do another. And until Donald Trump became president, thirty-six years after Ronald Reagan's first electoral landslide, no one had ever done it more effectively. After all, Reagan, an avatar of "family values," rarely saw his own children or grandchildren. The champion of the conservative Christian Coalition almost never set foot in church. The die-hard supporter of the military could not be bothered to don a uniform during World War II (though he did care enough to lie about it).[1]

Reagan displayed a seamless and surprisingly successful penchant toward shameless hypocrisy in politics. As governor of California, the right-wing, anti-tax, small-government crusader repeatedly raised taxes and more than doubled the state's spending, increasing the size of the state government by thirty-four thousand employees. The "pro-life" politician signed a law legalizing abortion.[2] And yet, because he never admitted that he did these things—indeed, he repeatedly denied their reality or blamed others for his own actions—he has somehow managed to remain a conservative hero.

It is impossible to address the question of Reagan's serial dishonesty as president without simultaneously raising the issue of his mental health. This question was studiously avoided during Reagan's presidency, but when journalists finally allowed themselves to address the president's mysterious state of mind, they relied heavily on the word "disengaged." At the time, the humorist Calvin Trillin mocked the frequent use of this term, comparing the notion of a "disengaged president" to a "disengaged blonde" or ten-pound "disengaged-bells." But there was rarely much to find funny in the subjects of Reagan's lies. True, some of them were simply self-serving, such as when Reagan repeatedly pretended to have participated in the liberation of German death camps at the end of World War II, despite having remained comfortably ensconced in sunny Culver City, California, for the duration of that operation. But some had the potential to instigate wars, even nuclear ones. Almost all of them reinforced some right-wing fantasy at odds with reality. Reagan once claimed to have received what he called "a verbal message" from the pope in support of his Central American proxy wars, which was news to everyone at the Vatican. He announced one day in 1985 that South Africa—though still ruled by the vicious apartheid regime of P. W. Botha—had somehow "eliminated the segregation that we once had in our own country." And perhaps most frightening of all, he claimed that intercontinental ballistic missiles could be recalled once they had been launched. "For a while," as

Neal Conan of National Public Radio (NPR) observed at the time, the media kept a "running record of his malapropisms, his mistakes and things that he'd gotten wrong, facts he'd remembered from the movies that he presented as real. After a while, they stopped because people didn't care." Reagan's adviser, the sometime journalist David Gergen, defended his boss on the grounds that "Reagan was telling larger truths," advising reporters not to "try to use every one of these stories as an absolute truth," but "to see them in parables."[3]

One of Reagan's advisers once described his former boss as follows: Reagan liked to "build these little worlds and live in them." One of his children concurred: "He makes things up and believes them." Reagan suffered from Alzheimer's for years before he died in 2004, and to this day it remains unclear when the disease first began to affect his mind. Certain episodes from the beginning of his presidency point to the possibility that it may have begun much earlier than has so far been acknowledged. For instance, Reagan failed to recognize his own secretary of housing and urban development early in his presidency, and he introduced himself to his son Michael at the young man's high school graduation. His other son, Ron, recalled that during the 1987 Iran-contra scandal, he found his father to be "lost in a fog of depression and denial." By the time Reagan was put under oath about the scandal during the criminal trial of his former aide John Poindexter, just a year after he left office, his memory was apparently long gone. He spoke as if he had no knowledge whatsoever of his own policies as president.[4]

By the time these events took place, most members of the media had long ago given up on holding Reagan to the standard of any typically sentient adult. They preferred instead to treat his refusal to recognize reality as some strange sort of superpower. *Newsweek*'s Washington bureau chief, Morton Kondracke, described the president as "a magic totem against the cold future."[5] In 1986, a *Time* cover story lauded Reagan as both "a sort of masterpiece of American magic," a "Prospero of American memories," and "a kind of magician who carries a bright, ideal America like a holograph in his mind and projects its image in the air." Around the same time that *Time*'s hagiographic hymn appeared, in July 1986, Reagan gave a press conference in which almost everything he said was false. His aides did what they always did, which was to "clarify" his comments. The issues they had to straighten out for the press covered a variety of topics, ranging from the future of the post-*Challenger* space-shuttle program to the status of the Strategic Arms Limitation Talks (that is, SALT II, dealing with a nuclear arms control treaty with the Soviets). Afterward, a White House aide said he could not believe "how easy the press was on him," treating him "almost reverentially." He added, "He's gone from [being] the Teflon President to the boomerang President. Nobody wants to throw anything at him, because it comes back and hurts them."[6]

Mainstream American journalists were decidedly unprepared for Reagan's presidency. Former *Washington Post* assistant managing editor William Greider later recalled what a shock Reagan's election had been, saying, "It was a sense of, 'My God, they've elected this guy who nine months ago we thought was a hopeless clown.'" His boss, Ben Bradlee, attributed the phenomenon to "a subconscious feeling...that we were dealing with someone this time who really, really, really disapproved of us, disliked us, distrusted us, and that we ought not give him any opportunities to see he was right." After Watergate, Bradlee recalled, millions of Americans were skeptical of the elite media—in his words, it was as if they were saying, "Okay, guys, now that's enough, that's enough." He continued: "The criticism was that we were going on too much, and trying to make a Watergate out of everything. And I think we were sensitive to that criticism much more than we should have been, and that we did ease off." The net result was that the *Post*—along with virtually every other mainstream media institution—according to Bradlee, was "kinder to President Reagan than any President."[7] Following John Hinckley Jr.'s March 30, 1981, failed assassination attempt on the president, coverage became not merely "reverential" but nearly beatific.

This development was particularly ironic given how petty and unrelenting members of the elite media had been in their efforts to expose the "lies" of Jimmy Carter and his administration—none more so than the *Washington Post*. This stark contrast should be understood, at least in part, as the result of a persistent complaint from conservatives about alleged "liberal bias" in the media—along with a strong desire on the part of media institutions to appease them. This remarkably successful strategy of "working the refs" would quickly become standard operating procedure in Republican politics and has now been in use for nearly half a century.[8] But its result, during the 1980s, was that America's great newspapers, newsmagazines, and broadcast networks purposely made themselves complicit in Reagan's efforts to mislead Americans about the right-wing fantasies that defined his ill-informed beliefs.

Even more than Nixon and Kissinger, whom he considered to be weak and overly solicitous of Soviet interests and sensitivities, President Reagan felt that the Cold War should be fought on every possible front. Reagan and the members of his team saw the world exclusively in terms of a contest between the uniquely virtuous United States and the Soviet "Evil Empire," and they defined virtually every other nation in the world as a pawn in that struggle. And as a result, before long, both the lies and the number of dead rose to new heights—indeed, to levels that would have been difficult to imagine at the end of the Vietnam War.

Immediately upon taking office, the Reagan administration began looking for opportunities to turn the Cold War hot again. It did not matter whether US national security was meaningfully menaced. The administration's sole objective was to restore what it understood to be the credibility of US military power in the world's eyes. Reagan and company were therefore willing to pick fights in places that most Americans had never even heard of. The biggest obstacle his administration faced was the fact that Congress and the American people remained in the grip of what members of the media had named the "Vietnam Syndrome"—that is, a decided reluctance to allow a president to get the country stuck in yet another foreign "quagmire" where the United States had no significant interest and faced no genuine threat. As a candidate, Reagan had specifically renounced this notion when speaking to the Veterans of Foreign Wars, stating that, owing to the constraints it placed on the use of the US military abroad, "we find ourselves increasingly in a position of dangerous isolation. Our allies are losing confidence in us, and our adversaries no longer respect us."[9] Yet Americans' reluctance to embark on another adventurous war in which a genuine threat was not immediately evident remained strong. Bumper stickers and protest signs arose around America with the slogan "El Salvador is Spanish for 'Vietnam.'" And given the fact that these views were powerfully represented in Congress, the Reagan team decided that it would have to try to fight its wars in secret.

Reagan's first target was the Central American nation of El Salvador, a country entirely unknown to most Americans at the time. But that did not matter, since the battlefield was really in the minds of men. "If we cannot defend ourselves there," Reagan told a special 1983 joint session of Congress, called to drum up support for his unpopular Central American policies, "we cannot expect to prevail elsewhere. Our credibility would collapse, our alliances would crumble, and the safety of our homeland would be put in jeopardy."[10] This was nonsense. El Salvador mattered not in the slightest to the safety of the American homeland. But the meaning of "national security" was now so expansive that US intervention was deemed crucial, even without the slightest evidence that anyone was paying attention, save perhaps its victims.

Despite El Salvador's tiny size, its citizens became the victims of American hubris and presidential dishonesty during the Reagan/

Bush years. A military junta there had been conducting a brutal campaign of extermination against a peasant population in an effort to tamp down the flames of a Marxist-inspired rebellion led by Cuban- and Nicaraguan-supported guerrillas. The Carter administration had helped the junta avoid what many would view as a communist takeover, but it did so extremely reluctantly, given the Salvadorans' awful human rights record. Reagan turned this reluctance into enthusiasm. From the first moments of his presidency, Reagan and his advisers acted as de facto public relations flacks for the junta and its murderous generals. "We are helping the forces that are supporting human rights in El Salvador," Reagan claimed. In fact, to remain in power, the junta relied on the efforts of allegedly independent "death squads" to kill not only its opponents but anyone who might even think of supporting its opponents, including numerous nuns, priests, and even children. And far from being authentically independent, the death squads were in truth out-of-uniform soldiers directed by the very same generals the United States was so eagerly funding.[11]

In December 1980, shortly before Reagan's inauguration, these forces raped and murdered a group of Maryknoll sisters and one lay missionary who had been based in the Massachusetts district represented by Democratic Speaker of the House Tip O'Neill. The nuns had been serving as missionaries in El Salvador at the time of the killings. When Reagan took office, his team responded by trying to find a way to blame the victims for their own deaths. Jeane Kirkpatrick, Reagan's United Nations representative, called them "political activists." Secretary of State Alexander Haig speculated that perhaps the murder victims had fired at their assassins while running a roadblock. The US ambassador to El Salvador, Robert White—a Carter holdover—sent a confidential cable to Secretary Haig that read, "It is amazing to me that the department can state publicly that the investigation of the nuns' deaths is proceeding satisfactorily. This is not backed up by any reporting from this embassy. I reiterate for the record that in my judgment there is no sign of any sincere attempt to locate and punish those responsible for this atrocity." He was immediately fired. Undersecretary of State Walter Stoessel Jr. later admitted that the department had "no evidence that the four American missionaries were engaged in political activity." It would eventually turn out that all the administration's claims about this incident were false. Nevertheless, it continued to aid and abet the Salvadoran military's campaign of mass murder against its own people, a campaign that eventually killed an estimated seventy-five thousand people. (Decades later, in July 2002, two Salvadoran generals who had earned the support of the United States during this period were ordered by a West Palm Beach jury to pay $54.6 million to three torture and kidnapping victims, setting a precedent in the prosecution of human rights law.)[12]

A similarly shocking set of events occurred in early 1982, when reporters from the *Washington Post* and *New York Times* received a tip that Salvadoran soldiers, using US-supplied weaponry, had murdered nearly one thousand civilians—mostly women, children, and senior citizens—and buried their bodies in mass graves in and around an isolated village called El Mazote. State Department officials vehemently denied that any massacre had taken place. Deploying what had by this time become traditional McCarthyite tactics, they attempted to cast aspersions on the alleged political sympathies of the reporters who broke the story. Once again decades later, investigators for El Salvador's postwar Truth Commission uncovered the victims' graves and identified roughly five hundred bodies, mostly women (many of whom had apparently been raped), the aged, and young children. In a pattern that would repeat itself over and over in the coming decade, Reagan's assistant secretary for inter-American affairs, Thomas Enders, eventually admitted that "the materials that we and the embassy passed on to the Congress [during the cover-up] were wrong."[13]

These horror stories, and many more like them, took place in a context of violence and lawlessness that can be difficult to imagine.

At one point, the death squads were killing more than two hundred people per week, which, given El Salvador's tiny population, would have been the equivalent of more than twelve thousand political murders a week in the United States. It was during this time that President Reagan, still hoping to find a way to send US troops into battle there, invented the baseless conspiracy theory that the killings were not the work of "so called murder squads" aligned with the right-wing junta, but of left-wing "guerrilla forces" who thought they could "get away with these violent acts." Their motivation? "To try and bring down the government," because "the right wing will be blamed for it." Days later, Vice President George H.W. Bush flew to El Salvador's capital city, San Salvador, to convey a very different message. He explained to junta members and military officials that "every murderous act" committed by "right-wing fanatics… poisons the well of friendship between our two countries," adding that allowing the "death squad murders" to continue could cost the killers "the support of the American people."[14] Reagan, permanently ensconced in his right-wing fantasyland, continued to speak as if the rebels were staging the murders of their own supporters to garner global sympathy.

As horrific as these events were, the citizens of nearby Guatemala were facing even greater brutality, which the Reagan administration supported with an even more egregious set of lies. In 1999, after a five-year investigation that included some nine thousand witnesses, Guatemala's United Nations–backed Commission for Historical Clarification issued a report. The country's dictator at the time, General Efraín Ríos Montt, it said, had carried out "acts of genocide" against the indigenous people in the Ixil region of the department of Quiché—located in the country's heartland, northwest of Guatemala City—with the knowledge of the US government.[15]

Among the genocidal general's most enthusiastic boosters during this campaign was the neoconservative provocateur Elliott Abrams, who, as if plucked from a George Orwell novel, had recently been appointed Ronald Reagan's assistant secretary of state for human rights. On the *MacNeil/Lehrer Report*, Abrams credited Ríos Montt with having "brought considerable progress" on human rights issues, and even went so far as to insist that "the amount of killing of innocent civilians is being reduced step by step," before telling Jim Lehrer that Congress should provide the regime with advanced arms, because its alleged "progress need[ed] to be rewarded and encouraged." He said the dictator had brought about "tremendous change, especially in the attitude of the government toward the Indian population."[16] Promoted to assistant secretary of state for inter-American affairs in 1985, Abrams repeatedly denounced the continued protests from Democrats and human rights activists in the United States against Reagan's silence over the atrocities that the genocidal general and his no-less-bloodthirsty successor, President Vinicio Cerezo Arévalo, had committed. In one village during the latter's reign, for instance, "the army herded the entire population into the courthouse, raped the women, beheaded the men, and took the children outside to smash them to death against rocks," according to the historian Walter LaFeber.[17] When the *New York Times* published an op-ed challenging the official State Department account of the mass murders underway—by a woman who had witnessed a death-squad assassination in broad daylight in Guatemala City that had never been mentioned in the press—Abrams responded by lying outright. In a letter to the editor, he cited an imaginary story in a nonexistent newspaper to insist that the man's murder had, in fact, been reported. While Abrams may have been the point man on the general's team, its captain, unsurprisingly, was President Reagan, who judged Ríos Montt to be "totally dedicated to democracy" and "a man of great personal integrity."[18]

El Salvador and Guatemala notwithstanding, the truest object of Ronald Reagan's affection were the "contras" in nearby Nicaragua. In the wake of that country's Marxist revolution in 1979 against the US-supported dictator Anastasio Somoza García, American conservatives were furious that the Carter administration had not sent in troops to stand by their man. Somoza's father was the subject of a famous, though possibly apocryphal, quote from Franklin Roosevelt—"He may be a sonofabitch, but he's our sonofabitch"—following his 1936 overthrow of Nicaragua's former government and installation of his family's dictatorship there. Somoza had come to power as part of a US-created and -supported Nicaraguan National Guard, which had defeated the Nicaraguan general Augusto Sandino. Sandino had led the resistance to the US Marine occupation in the 1920s and 1930s and had given the Marxist "Sandinista" movement its name. The Reagan administration hoped to overthrow the Sandinista regime by arming and equipping the contras, a group made up largely of formerly Somoza-supporting soldiers and mercenaries, whose leaders were to be recruited and paid by the CIA. Reagan apparently convinced himself that this motley army of so-called freedom fighters represented "the moral equal of our Founding Fathers and the brave men and women of the French Resistance." Before an enthusiastic audience of conservatives, he insisted, "We cannot turn away from them for the struggle here is not right versus left, but right versus wrong." He went on to demand that Congress fund the rebels by providing $14 million in military aid.[19]

Frustrated by both the legal limitations Congress placed on its involvement and a decided lack of enthusiasm for actual warfare on the part of the contras, the CIA often took matters into its own hands by secretly carrying out attacks itself. One such operation came to light in early 1984, when the Nicaraguan government announced that the CIA had been placing mines in its harbors, an obvious act of war. The news did not inspire much interest, however, until months later, when a Soviet oil tanker hit one of the mines while entering Managua's Puerto Sandino. The Soviets condemned the explosion as a "grave crime" and "an act of banditry and piracy." In the ensuing weeks, ships from Japan, Panama, Liberia, the Netherlands, and the USSR suffered mining damage at Nicaragua's three main ports. Fifteen sailors were injured, and two fishermen were killed.[20]

The entire episode unfolded as if it were yet another rerun of the Gulf of Tonkin incident, but transported in time and space, and almost comically farcical. Just as the United States had pretended that the South Vietnamese were solely responsible for the 1964 OPLAN 34-Alpha raids against North Vietnam, which in reality the US military had planned, equipped, and guided, the government was now seeking to credit its client with military operations that US military and intelligence forces had clearly both planned and executed. The entire mining operation was overseen by CIA "mother ships" operating out of a secret base on Tiger Island in neighboring Honduras. Agents were ferried by helicopter from CIA ships—positioned twelve miles offshore, just beyond the reach of Nicaragua's jurisdiction—to the ports where they were placing the mines. When these logistical arrangements proved too difficult to maintain, the CIA turned the work over to US Navy SEALs. Yet Secretary of Defense Caspar Weinberger, echoing the dishonesty of his predecessor in the job, Robert McNamara, declared outright, "The United States is not mining the harbors of Nicaragua." Publicly, US officials defended the mining operation (without admitting to the degree of the US role) by claiming that the United States was merely exercising its right of "collective self-defense" against Nicaragua. But as one administration official admitted of that defense at the time, "Unfortunately, it's bullshit."[21]

The next sequence of lies came in October 1984, when news reports revealed that the CIA had published and distributed what later became known as a "murder manual." This manual recommended the "selective use of violence" for the purpose of "neutralizing" Nicaraguan government officials. The story of the murder manual broke just days before a scheduled presidential debate between Reagan and the Democratic nominee, Walter Mondale, and the president was therefore forced to speak to the issue. In doing so, Reagan offered up an extremely convoluted explanation that attempted to lay the blame for the manual on the accidental printing of "twelve copies" of the booklet in question that mistakenly included the pages encouraging murder that were supposed to be excised. It was not, he insisted, submitted to the CIA for proper vetting before its accidental publication. His account was false from start to finish. The manual had been written by a CIA contract employee. Nothing was ever excised save a single line advising the contras to hire criminals. The agency distributed three thousand copies, not twelve, and the contras printed up to two thousand more.[22] Reagan, of course, was reelected anyway, in a landslide even bigger than before. The victory—the final tally gave him 58.8 percent of the popular vote and 525 out of 538 electoral college votes—empowered Reagan not only to continue his secret wars but to substantially ratchet up the US commitment to their successful conclusion.

In March 1986, the administration decided to create yet another contra crisis with yet another obvious lie, this one mimicking Teddy Roosevelt's shenanigans in Panama a century earlier. This time, the Reagan administration announced that between 1,500 and 2,000 Nicaraguan troops had invaded Honduras. The Hondurans themselves, however, professed to be unaware of any invasion of their country and refused to ask for help. Their recalcitrance infuriated State Department official William Walker, who screamed at his embassy personnel in Honduras, "You have got to tell them to declare there was an incursion!" "You don't have a choice in this one," the US ambassador to Honduras, John Ferch, informed the president of Honduras. "You've got to get a letter up there right now....They're going bonkers up there. This is absurd, but you've got to do it." Ferch was forced out soon afterward.[23]

Reagan's most egregious lies came in the service, appropriately, of his most egregious actions. While he promised the nation that "America will never make concessions to terrorists," as doing so "would only invite more terrorism," his underlings were simultaneously supplying sophisticated weapons to Iran—which the State Department deemed to be a "terrorist" nation—as ransom for the American hostages. And so great a breach of so important a declared presidential policy could only be carried out dishonestly.[24]

The policy grew out of the Reagan administration's desperation to free the hostages, who were being held by the Hezbollah organization in Lebanon. The organization, more powerful than the Lebanese government, was allied, politically and ideologically, with Iran. With Israel acting as middleman, Reagan secretly agreed to sell missiles to Iran in exchange for the hostages. At the same time, in a plot masterminded by the NSC and the CIA, Iran was vastly overcharged for its weapons so that the excess proceeds could be skimmed off and used to secretly—and illegally—fund weapons for the Nicaraguan contras—as Congress had, by law, specifically and repeatedly enjoined the administration from doing.

Reagan's administration had by this time already experienced an extraordinary number of legal and financial scandals affecting top cabinet members, advisers, and even Attorney General Edwin Meese.[25] What became known as the Iran-contra affair was in many respects a culmination of the corrupt culture Reagan had fostered. The scandal also represented a near-perfect confluence of the president's fanatical devotion to the cause of anti-communism in Central America and the outsized role that casual lying had come to play in the way the administration conducted its business.

When, on November 3, 1986, a Lebanese weekly newspaper called *Ash-Shiraa* broke the story of the secret missile sales, the president's staff set about concocting a cover story, in order to throw the media and the Democrats in Congress off the scent. This story kept changing as parts of it collapsed over time, but it never fully disappeared. Congress appointed a special prosecutor and a joint committee of investigation, with dramatic, high-profile hearings before television cameras and, at least initially, much talk of Reagan's potential impeachment. The result, however, would turn out to be a long, slow descent into a world of mercenaries, factions, and right-wing adventurism that proved almost impossible for most citizens to follow, much less remain outraged over. CIA director William Casey did his fellow conspirators the favor of dying following a lengthy hospitalization for a brain tumor not long after the initial revelations, and so proved a convenient fall guy.

With no James McCords or John Deans in the administration to upend the cover-up, virtually everyone involved continued to lie to the press, to Congress, to Special Counsel Lawrence Walsh, and even, in many cases, to the judges and juries they faced once Walsh secured their indictments. Some, including Reagan's two assistants for national security, Robert McFarlane from the first administration and John Poindexter from the second, and their staffer Colonel Oliver North, were convicted and sentenced to prison. Defense Secretary Caspar Weinberger, State Department official Elliott Abrams, and three CIA officers were also found guilty of various crimes. But as the proceedings dragged on into George H.W. Bush's presidency, and the White House refused to cooperate with Walsh's subpoenas, and then, after the 1988 election, as President George H.W. Bush—who was himself vulnerable to some of the same charges—pardoned some of the targets, many of the cases were dropped. When Caspar Weinberger's diaries appeared to implicate Bush in both the crimes and the lies that had characterized the scandal, Weinberger received a preemptive pardon before a jury could decide on his guilt or innocence. This marked, as a furious Lawrence Walsh would later note, "the first time a president ever pardoned someone in whose trial he might have been called as a witness." Meanwhile, from the time that the Iran-contra scandal was first exposed until long after he left office, Reagan lied virtually every time he ever spoke about the affair.[26]

Today, Ronald Reagan remains revered as the man who restored America's confidence in itself with his genial smile and simple, homespun wisdom. True, Reagan lied a great deal, but he never said anything truer than when he was accused by an opponent of being "only an actor." In response, he wondered aloud about "how you could be President and not be an actor."[27] This aspect of Reagan's presidency—the "acting" on the basis of his own fantasies rather than reality—would become the modus operandi of subsequent Republican presidents and presidential candidates.

Moreover, during the Reagan presidency, the members of the mainstream media often found themselves becoming passive purveyors of presidential lies, but they refused to call them out as such and merely cited the opposing views of "the other side." In this way, they left it to their readers, listeners, and viewers to decide who and what to believe. Increasingly, Republicans would discern in this model an opportunity to make up whatever stories and justifications they wished to convey on behalf of their policies, just as Reagan did. This strategy would balloon over time with the ascension of right-wing talk radio, with wealthy funders backing think tanks, and with other new media institutions rising to reinforce them. Eventually, America witnessed the creation of an enormous and multifaceted conservative media establishment that could challenge the very notion of reality as reported by its mainstream competition. In the meantime, with so many journalists afraid of giving ammunition to accusations of "liberal bias"—and most of them committed to an almost-robotic form of "objective journalism"—the political lies that conservative Republicans told began to earn the same respectful treatment as the truth. This, as much as any particular policy, was the primary legacy of Ronald Reagan's presidency.

George H.W. Bush
DON'T READ HIS LIPS

George H.W. Bush's pre-presidential career was marked by a series of metamorphoses designed to suit a shifting cast of political patrons. It began in the mid-1960s when he won two terms in Congress. He was a Republican, but moderate by Texas standards—for example, he supported Planned Parenthood and civil rights. And it ended with him becoming Reagan's loyal VP and successor, and thus the party's choice to carry the torch for the American revanchist right wing. Many of Bush's political flip-flops would turn out to be trivial, but almost all of them involved taking a more conservative position than before. This makes perfect sense when one considers that Bush—who, educated at Andover and Yale, was born the scion of the Connecticut patrician Republican senator Prescott Bush—had transplanted himself to Texas to make his fortune in the oil business. By the time he entered the world of politics, conservatism in that state was growing like sagebrush. Pressed about one of his more significant flip-flops, his (accurate) characterization in 1980 of Ronald Reagan's supply-side economics plan—an updated version of typical Republican "trickle-down economics"—as "voodoo economics," he replied, "I'm not going to get nickel-and-dimed to death with detail."[1] And, true to his word, he rarely was.

Until Iraq invaded Kuwait on August 2, 1990, Bush's presidency appeared relatively inconsequential. It was characterized by the same sorts of lies he had told as Reagan's vice president, particularly about allegedly having been "out of the loop" on all the major Iran-contra decisions.[2] The reality was that he had been at the meetings and had approved of the decisions made in them, although the evidence for this remained under wraps until it appeared in former defense secretary Caspar Weinberger's journal. The journal was not made public until Weinberger's criminal trial, and then Bush—as president—preemptively pardoned him.[3] Bush would not turn over his own diary and notes until 1992—nearly five years and two presidential elections after Special Counsel Lawrence Walsh had subpoenaed them. Walsh concluded that "the criminal investigation of Bush was regrettably incomplete." Nevertheless, the diary demonstrated that Bush had repeatedly lied about his own involvement, as he was "fully aware of the Iran arms sale."[4]

Bush famously insisted that policies be made on the basis of "facts... facts...facts."[5] But needless to say, he was no more honest about his role in Iran-contra during the 1988 presidential campaign than he had been before it. The Bush team was lying about the Iran-contra scandal at the same time that it was hyping the story of an African American rapist and murderer named Willie Horton. Horton had been furloughed from a Massachusetts prison in 1986 under a program established under a Republican governor in 1972. But the state's governor at the time of the release was Bush's Democratic opponent, Michael Dukakis. Horton violated the terms of the release, which was supposed to be for the weekend, and went on to commit more crimes, including rape, assault, and car theft, in Maryland. Shortly after his crime spree, he had been apprehended by police in Maryland, and he ended up being convicted and sentenced to more jail time in late 1987. The Bush campaign succeeded in distorting the truth about the furlough program with nakedly racist advertisements designed to play on white fears about African American men. Bush successfully maintained his patrician, country-club-style Republican image in the tradition of his father and was able to evade responsibility for the advertisements: his famously Machiavellian campaign manager, Lee Atwater, had the political sense to arrange for a cutout—an organization ostensibly unconnected to the campaign—to buy the advertisements, giving his candidate plausible deniability in the face of outraged accusations by civil rights leaders and others. But the ads nevertheless had the intended effect, raising white fears of black men and crime—especially violent, sexualized crime—and successfully connected it all to the Democrats.[6]

Bush continued his implicit racial scapegoating in the White House when, during a nationally televised speech in September 1989, he held up a packet of crack cocaine and announced that it had been "seized a few days ago by Drug Enforcement Administration agents in a park just across the street from the White House." He raised it before the cameras and proclaimed, "We need more prisons, more jails, more courts, more prosecutors."[7] In order to be able to make that claim, Bush's staff had arranged to have the park police lure an eighteen-year-old African American drug dealer to the park for the purpose of arresting him. The poor fellow did not even know where the White House was, or who lived in it.[8] Does this gimmick constitute a lie? In this case, Bush demonstrated how a president can lie while technically telling the truth. By this time, though, such shenanigans, however deceitful, had come to be considered unremarkable for a US president, and so few people even raised a metaphorical eyebrow about the media's willingness to treat Bush's shameless stunt seriously.

Naturally, Bush, a former director of central intelligence and ambassador to China, felt himself most at home when acting on the world stage. And it was here that he did his most consequential lying. Although the Cold War was winding down during Bush's presidency, the American empire was not. Soviet leader Mikhail Gorbachev had become a friend and almost an ally in the midst of his unintentional-but-effective dismantling of the Soviet Union and the individual Soviet Socialist Republics under its hegemony. The United States' new enemy was the Iraqi dictator Saddam Hussein, who, just months earlier, right up through the Reagan administration and the first part of Bush's presidency, had been considered a valuable American asset.

Saddam had previously been quite popular with conservative Republicans, who viewed his brutal dictatorship as an effective bulwark against the spread of neighboring Iran's Islamic Revolution. The result was the purposeful indulgence of the very behavior that would in the future be cited as a justification for his overthrow. President Reagan, for instance, had been personally and repeatedly presented with evidence of Iraq's widespread use of universally banned poison gas shells, including ones filled with sarin, tabun, and mustard gas, in its war with Iran, which lasted from September 1980 through August 1988. The war had cost Iran and Iraq in excess of five hundred thousand (combined) battlefield deaths; the number of civilian casualties is still unknown. When written briefings went ignored, the CIA tried to convey the information cinematically—Reagan's favorite medium—but to no greater effect. And so the United States continued to provide Saddam's horrific regime with the tactical intelligence it needed to deploy its poison gas against the Iranians. Making matters worse, many of the Iranian "soldiers" were teenagers who were forcibly sent into battle with no training and virtually no weapons.[9]

If Reagan's vice president—a former CIA director—did not know of these efforts, which is decidedly unlikely, it could only be because he did not want to know. To be fair to Bush, the policy, however dishonestly defended, was not at all unpopular among Republicans at the time. In the spring of 1990, shortly before Iraq—under Saddam—invaded Kuwait, a group of farm-belt senators visited the

Iraqi dictator. Bob Dole, explaining that he was speaking for the president, assured Saddam that Bush "want[ed] better relations with Iraq." The senators reassured the Iraqi leader that the US government was with him. One of them, the Republican senator Alan Simpson of Wyoming, told him that any criticism coming from the United States was the fault of a "haughty and pampered [American] press," adding, "They all consider themselves political geniuses." Not long afterward, April Glaspie, US ambassador to Iraq, instructed Saddam that the US government had "no opinion on the Arab-Arab conflicts, like your border disagreement with Kuwait."[10]

When Iraq invaded the tiny, oil-rich kingdom of Kuwait on August 2, 1990, claiming it as part of the Iraqi nation, Bush initially gave no indication that he thought Saddam's aggression merited a US military response. This was before he met British prime minister Margaret Thatcher at an Aspen Institute gathering three days later, however. There, she gave him what his aides would later call a "spine transplant."[11] His initial plan was merely to prevent Saddam from pushing past Kuwait into Saudi Arabia and attempting to take over the far more plentiful oil resources of that desert kingdom. But Bush eventually changed his mind yet again, deciding that Saddam Hussein's troops had to be expelled from Kuwait, and that the only way to achieve that goal was with a US-led war.

Bush biographer Jean Edward Smith called Bush's argument for a war in the desert a deliberate "ruse." True, Smith noted, Bush's position "won overwhelming support." "But at bottom," he added, "it was not true." Upon announcing his decision to begin bombing on the evening of January 16, 1991, Bush exclaimed his decision as follows: "Why act now? Why not wait? The answer is clear. The world could wait no longer."[12] Of course, it is no simple epistemological task to determine what "the world" thinks of anything. But in Bush's case, his insistence had been repeatedly undermined by those much closer to the situation and with far greater expertise. James Schlesinger, for example, who had at various times been secretary of defense, director of the CIA, and secretary of energy under both Democratic and Republican presidents—and had stayed a hawk in all three positions—testified to Congress that the harsh economic sanctions imposed on Iraq by the UN Security Council immediately after the invasion were "working much more rapidly than originally anticipated." (The sanctions had banned all trade with Iraq save for medicine and foodstuffs.) With massive numbers of US troops being deployed to Saudi Arabia—the number would eventually top 540,000—Joint Chiefs of Staff chairman Admiral William Crowe and air force chief of staff General David C. Jones both testified in late November 1990 that Bush was exaggerating the need for war. Jones told the committee he "would have stayed with the lower number [of troops] until we gave sanctions a little more time to work." Crowe complained that "our dislike for [Saddam] Hussein seems to have crowded out many considerations."[13] Even General H. Norman Schwarzkopf, commander of US forces in the region at the time, had told a *Los Angeles Times* interviewer, shortly before the war began, that "if the alternative to dying is sitting out in the sun for another summer, that's not a bad alternative."[14]

It's hard to say just how much lying Bush and company did once the fighting began, because the government employed an unprecedented degree of censorship over the conflict. Rather than let reporters roam the battlefield at their own risk, as was the case in Vietnam and Central America, during the Gulf War the Pentagon demanded that they be "embedded" with individual troop units and not allowed anywhere near the battlefield without permission. Members of the media protested loudly against this curtailment of their ability to report honestly from the battlefield. The veteran broadcaster Walter Cronkite, famously known as "the most trusted man in America," wrote that "with an arrogance foreign to the democratic system, the US military in Saudi Arabia is trampling on the American people's right to know. The military is acting on a generally discredited Pentagon myth that the Vietnam War was lost because of the uncensored press." He concluded: "An American citizen is entitled to ask 'What are they trying to hide?'"[15] We still cannot answer that question with confidence.

Domestically, the most significant controversy of Bush's tenure occurred in September 1991, when he nominated Clarence Thomas to a spot on the US Supreme Court. In defending the nomination, he lied again when claiming, "The fact that he is black and a minority has nothing to do with this sense that he is the best qualified at this time." In fact, Thomas had been a judge for fewer than sixteen months at the time, and the American Bar Association gave him extremely low grades for fitness to serve on the court.[16] Bush's lie was the kind that everyone knew was a lie, and so it was considered just "politics." Obviously, Bush had nominated Thomas because he was one of the few dependable African American conservatives in the American legal world. Thomas would be replacing the court's only black justice (Thurgood Marshall, who had retired), but was judged by many observers not to be qualified intellectually. After his nomination, Anita Hill, a lawyer who had worked for Thomas, accused her former boss of extensive and demeaning sexual harassment, and she was called in to testify to the Senate in televised public hearings. The hearings led to a kind of Kulturkampf between men and women, liberals and conservatives, blacks and whites. The wounds inflicted on both sides have never fully healed. In the end, the Senate approved the nomination. As Bush knew as well as anyone, in politics a win is a win. Bush's lie about his reason for choosing Thomas was therefore seen as a savvy political play rather than the dishonest political ploy it really was. Thomas, meanwhile, went on to become one of the Supreme Court's most influential justices—as well as its most ideological—and thereby shaped the destiny of the nation on matters of race, gender, and corporate power over the coming decades to a far greater degree than the man who appointed him.[17]

Meanwhile, history took an ironic turn when Bush's most politically damaging "lie" turned out to be a statement that was not a lie at all, but merely a changed response to changed circumstances. During his 1988 campaign for the Republican nomination, Bush had sought to quell conservative objections to his relatively moderate record and Brahmin demeanor with a faux-Clint-Eastwood-style pledge: "Read My Lips: No New Taxes." But in May 1990, when the federal budget grew radically unbalanced, and the Democrats in Congress proposed raising $134 billion in "tax revenue increases," Bush reluctantly went along. House minority whip Newt Gingrich, a Republican from Georgia, called it a "betrayal," which perhaps it was—though, of course, one based on new information. Rupert Murdoch's *New York Post* went further, with the incendiary headline: "Read My Lips: I Lied." By the time the Democrats' tax increases reached the president's desk, Bush had been so thoroughly shamed that he vetoed the continuing resolution, leading to a federal government shutdown. This decision proved profoundly counterproductive. The US economy was entering a downturn, and Bush's inability to control his party, along with his ill-conceived attempt to force Congress to bend to his will, had the effect of painting him as weak and incompetent. Bush's approval rating fell from 91 percent following the victory against Iraq to just 29 percent during the summer before the 1992 election.[18] Without the Cold War to frame America's actions in support of its empire, Americans felt no need to stand behind the commander in chief who had been so successful in faraway lands, but appeared to be so clueless at home. Yes, Bush had "won" the war, but he had "lost" the economy. And in the future, the party would belong to the likes of Gingrich, whose willingness to lie to Americans in pursuit of political power would make Bush look like Saint Francis of Assisi.

13

Bill Clinton

DEFILING THE TEMPLE OF JUSTICE

In 1998, Bill Clinton became the first elected US president ever to be impeached by the House of Representatives. (Donald Trump is the second.) The ostensible reason for this extraordinary action was that he lied about his sexual relationship with a twenty-two-year-old White House intern, Monica Lewinsky. And of this, he was undoubtedly guilty. According to US District Court justice Susan Webber Wright of Arkansas, Clinton also gave "false, misleading and evasive answers that were designed to obstruct the judicial process" while defending himself against a sexual harassment lawsuit filed in 1994 by Paula Jones. Jones, a former employee of the state of Arkansas, had claimed that Clinton, as governor, had exposed himself to her three years earlier and demanded oral sex in a hotel room in Little Rock. It was during his sworn testimony in this lawsuit that the president insisted that he had never been alone with Monica

Lewinsky or engaged in sexual activity with her. Later, as part of his negotiated plea, Clinton agreed that he had made these false statements "knowingly." Prosecutor Robert Ray—who had by this time replaced Special Counsel Kenneth Starr in investigating Clinton—agreed to close the case on this basis. Clinton paid Jones a fee of $850,000 but admitted no liability, or even any memory of the incident that Jones alleged to have taken place. So ended the infamous Clinton-Lewinsky scandal.[1]

According to Starr's report, a key moment in Clinton's alleged crime of perjury—which led to his impeachment—occurred at approximately 2:00 a.m. on December 17, 1997, when the president telephoned Lewinsky to inform her that she was on the witness list for the investigation into the Paula Jones sexual harassment lawsuit. In Starr's words, the president

> suggested that she could sign an affidavit and use—under oath—deceptive cover stories that they had devised long ago to explain why Ms. Lewinsky had visited the Oval Office area. The President did not explicitly instruct Ms. Lewinsky to lie. He did not have to. Ms. Lewinsky testified that the President's suggestion that they use the pre-existing cover stories amounted to a continuation of their pattern of concealing their intimate relationship. Starting with this conversation, the President and Ms. Lewinsky understood, according to Ms. Lewinsky, that they were both going to make false statements under oath.[2]

This was both stupid and arrogant on the president's part. Clinton was well aware at the time that Starr and his staff were closing in on his past escapades in their effort to prove a pattern of reckless sexual behavior in order to lend credence to Jones's accusations. Women were coming out of the woodwork. Clinton's longtime aide Betsy Wright called these "bimbo eruptions." Their accusations may or may not have been true—we will probably never know for certain—but none at the time appeared to represent a credible threat to the future of Clinton's presidency. Jones's case was in the process of falling apart from a combination of scant evidence and the internal inconsistencies of her story. In retrospect, it appears entirely possible that Clinton had been telling the truth about Jones when he hatched his plan to encourage Lewinsky to lie. Meanwhile, according to investigative reporters Joe Conason and Gene Lyons, authors of the book *The Hunting of the President: The Ten-Year Campaign to Destroy Bill and Hillary Clinton*, Gennifer Flowers, a second, much-publicized accuser, "was unable in hours of cross-examination to specify a single time and place where she and Clinton had ever been alone together."[3] Clinton and Lewinsky had apparently convinced themselves that having avoided actual intercourse allowed them to truthfully deny the existence of a "sexual relationship." This notion has long been popular among adulterers of both sexes and among women eager to preserve physical evidence of their virginity. But it was not exactly a notion that Kenneth Starr and the US courts in general were going to agree with.

The independent counsel leveled a number of other charges against the president as well, though some of them spoke more to Starr's personal pique toward Clinton than to any violation of the US Constitution or legal code. For example, Starr's report complained that "surrogates of the President attempted to convince the Congress and the American people that the [Lewinsky] matter was unimportant"— as if voicing this widely held opinion were somehow against the law.

Starr's investigation was compromised from the start by its Javert-like tactics. His staff psychologically terrorized Lewinsky at her most vulnerable point, convincing her close friend Linda Tripp to wear a wire and secretly record their conversations in the bar at the Four Seasons hotel. As she was "crying, sobbing [and] screaming" in a hotel room, Justice Department agents with Starr's team confronted her and threatened to send her and her mother to prison if she refused to help them entrap the president. When the terrified and traumatized young woman asked to be allowed to speak to her mother, Starr's staffer Jackie Bennett mocked her fears: "You're 24, you're smart, you're old enough, you don't need to call your mommy." Lewinsky repeatedly said she wanted to call an attorney, but was told that if she called one, she would be in far bigger trouble and all negotiations would end (though Starr's investigators helpfully offered to give her a lawyer of their own choosing). By the time she mustered up the courage to exercise her constitutional right to counsel, it was after five o'clock in the evening and her family lawyer's office was closed for the three-day weekend of the Martin Luther King Jr. holiday. She had been held for twelve hours.

There's no question that Clinton lied to the prosecutors, to the country, to his wife, and to his staff about his relationship with Monica Lewinsky. Clinton lied when he famously insisted to America that he "did not have sexual relations with that woman, Miss Lewinsky," and he lied again, jabbing his finger in the air for emphasis, when he said he "never told anyone to lie, not a single time, never." He lied a third time when he added, "These allegations are false." He and Lewinsky did have sexual relations by any reasonable understanding of the term, as well as by the terms defined to him in gruesome detail by Starr's almost comically prurient investigators.[4] He also asked Lewinsky and his secretary Betty Curry to lie. He was, in short, a coward when it came to love—or at least sexual temptation.

Starr played the role of a present-day Torquemada. "You cannot defile the temple of justice," he declaimed to reporters while posing for the camera before his front-lawn trash cans. "There's no room for white lies. There's no room for shading. There's only room for truth."[5] This was posturing of the most transparent kind, but it appealed to Washington insiders who were eager to blame Clinton for morally debasing their community and the country at large— whether they believed he truly had done so or not. "I'd like to be able to tell my children, 'You should tell the truth,'" Stuart Taylor of the *National Journal* said on NBC's *Meet the Press*. "I'd like to be able to tell them, 'You should respect the President.' And I'd like to be able to tell them both things at the same time." William J. Bennett, who had worked in the Reagan and Bush administrations, also went on *Meet the Press*. He professed to detect a "moral and intellectual disarmament" of America in Clinton's failure to provide "a decent example" and teach "kids the difference between right and wrong." The story, ABC and NPR pundit Cokie Roberts insisted in the *New York Daily News*, was about reinforcing the lesson for children "that people who act immorally and lie get punished."[6]

Savvy Washington insiders distrusted the backwater-born Bill Clinton from the start, just as they had distrusted the previous Democrat in the Oval Office, peanut farmer Jimmy Carter. They were particularly offended by what many believed were the airs and ambitions of First Lady Hillary Clinton. The level of hostility that the couple faced from the most influential members of the punditocracy was truly a wonder to behold. Writing in the *New York Times Magazine* just eighteen months into Clinton's presidency, the influential insider journalist Michael Kelly said he discerned "a level of mistrust and even dislike of [Bill Clinton] that is almost visceral in its intensity." Kelly himself evinced these feelings in the extreme. Clinton was, he wrote, "a liar, a fraud, a chronically indecisive man who cannot be trusted to stand for anything—or with anyone," owing to his "profound immaturity, his pathological selfishness, his cynicism, above all his relentless corruption."[7]

The insider case against the Clintons was given its most revealing treatment in a 3,500-word missive in the *Washington Post* Style section by Washington socialite and sometime-journalist Sally Quinn on behalf of what had come to be known to many as "The Village." This was the name given to the group of permanent Washington insiders who considered themselves to be the rightful defenders of proper Beltway etiquette and the proprietors and protectors of its institutions. The Village was not shocked by lies or by adultery, but it had unspoken rules about what kinds of lies it embraced and the types of adulterous affairs to which it was willing to turn a blind eye. Had Clinton lied for reasons of "national security" or to preserve control over far-flung locations in the American empire, all would have been understood. If he'd had an old-fashioned affair with a woman of style and stature, the whispers would have been muted and likely approving. There was little hand-wringing in the Village, for instance, but much excited gossip, when in the late 1970s the *Washington Post*'s executive editor, Ben Bradlee, left his wife and family for the glamorous young reporter Sally Quinn. But Clinton's affair with Lewinsky offended these sensibilities, and Village denizens were determined to make him pay for it.

"THIS IS THEIR HOME," Quinn wrote, referring both to herself and the journalists, lobbyists, lawyers, and permanent government officials who made up her social circle. "This is where they spend their lives, raise their families, participate in community activities, take pride in their surroundings. They feel Washington has been brought into disrepute by the actions of the president." Quinn, quite properly, included the people who made up the government as well as the ones who sought to influence it on behalf of their corporate clients, along with journalists, who, at least theoretically, were there to hold the first two groups accountable. Again, this was appropriate for the time and place she was writing about, as it would have been hard to tell which players were on which teams, even with a scorecard. How, for instance, to devise a shorthand identification for someone like David Gergen, who was a former aide to Republican presidents (Nixon, Ford, and Reagan) as well as to a Democratic one (Clinton), in addition to having been a journalist (*US News and World Report*, CNN, *Parade*, *The MacNeil/Lehrer Report*) and an academic (Harvard's Kennedy School)? "We have our own set of village rules," Quinn quoted Gergen expounding. "Sex did not violate those rules. The deep and searing violation took place when he not only lied to the country but co-opted his friends and lied to them. That is one on which people choke." Much the same could be said of Chris Matthews, who had jumped from being chief of staff for the Democratic Speaker of the House, Tip O'Neill, to becoming a columnist for two San Francisco newspapers and hosting a show on MSNBC. In the wake of the Lewinsky scandal, Matthews said the president had violated the trust that reporters had placed in him: "Clinton lies knowing that you know he's lying. It's brutal and it subjugates the person who's being lied to."[8] These people, who shuttled between government, journalism, academia, and what Washington insiders called "buckraking"—that is, earning enormous speaking and "advisory" fees from corporations seeking good publicity and legislative advantages—had come to feel that Washington belonged more to them than to whoever showed up every four years following a presidential election. They demanded a degree of respect, sometimes bordering on fealty, from whoever might be temporarily occupying the offices of government. And as the complaints of Quinn and her fellow Villagers demonstrated, they could react with fury when they felt they did not receive their proper due. Clinton had "fouled" the Village nest by telling the wrong kind of lie. And the Village intended to make him pay.

Clinton had already earned a reputation for being willing to play fast and loose with the truth before becoming president, and the Lewinsky scandal only made it worse. His detractors in Arkansas were calling him "Slick Willie" as early as 1980.[9] But except for the lies that led to his impeachment, a close examination of his record as president reveals precious few falsehoods. Clinton was no stranger to the sort of exaggeration and rose-colored predictions that characterize virtually every successful politician, but in terms of knowingly misleading the country, examples are surprisingly sparse. And here, once again, the clearest of them stems from the demands of America's empire and its ever-expansive definition of "national security."

In his January 27, 1998, State of the Union address, Clinton laid the groundwork for the missile attack on Iraq that he would launch nearly a year later during his impeachment proceedings. He did so by claiming that Iraqi dictator Saddam Hussein had "spent the better part of this decade…developing nuclear, chemical, and biological weapons and the missiles to deliver them." Days later, speaking at Ohio University, Secretary of State Madeleine Albright said much the same thing: "[Saddam Hussein] is producing weapons of mass destruction, and he is qualitatively and quantitatively different from other dictators."[10]

What both the president and the secretary of state were saying was false. Inspections of Iraq's weapons were incomplete and at an impasse at the time of the US attacks in December 1998, and it would later become clear that Iraq had been in the process of destroying its weapons of mass destruction, not developing them. Scott Ritter was a United Nations weapons inspector in Iraq from 1991 to 1998 when he was ordered out of the country so that the US attacks could proceed. In 2005, Ritter told *Democracy Now!*'s Amy Goodman that as early as October 1992, he "personally confronted the C.I.A. on the reality that we had accounted for all of Iraq's ballistic missile programs." He added, "That same year they had an Iraqi defector who had laid out the totality of the Iraqi biological weapons program and had acknowledged that all of the weapons had been destroyed. The C.I.A. knew this." By 1995, he continued, "there were no more weapons in Iraq, there were no more documents in Iraq, there was no more production capability in Iraq, because we were monitoring the totality of Iraq's industrial infrastructure with the most technologically advanced, the most intrusive arms control regime in the history of arms control."[11] And if the CIA knew, we can safely assume that the president (and his secretary of state) did, too. Their insistence that Saddam Hussein was producing weapons of mass destruction would unfortunately help lay the groundwork for George W. Bush's administration to launch his campaign of relentless and purposeful deceit in order to build support for what would turn out to be a catastrophic preemptive war on Iraq. Yet this was the kind of lie that post–World War II presidents had always told. As far as most insiders were concerned, telling lies about war and peace was part of the president's job description.

Part of the reason for the explosion of interest in the Clinton-Lewinsky affair was that it would turn out to be excellent business for the media industry. On January 18, 1998, for instance, even though the story was still just a rumor based on anonymous leaks, the affair accounted for fully 47,500 words in fifty-seven separate stories on the *Drudge Report* and in the pages of the *Washington Post*, the *New York Times*, and the *Los Angeles Times* alone.[12]

Virtually none of the initial reports about the Clinton-Lewinsky affair were based on information provided by named sources. Seventy-two percent of the statements about the scandal made on *Good Morning America* and *World News Tonight* during the early days were based on anonymous sources or fell into the category of mere speculation. For NBC News, it was 81 percent; for CBS, 70 percent. ABC's *Nightline* did fifteen shows in a row on the scandal, but with slightly more reliably sourced reporting—only 48 percent of it was based on anonymous sources or speculation. Robert Kaiser, the *Washington Post*'s assistant managing editor, admitted that when it came to the Clinton scandals, the paper frequently ran stories with "only the vaguest sourcing." "We're in a new world in terms of the way information flows to the nation," said James O'Shea, deputy managing news editor for the *Chicago Tribune*. "The days when you can decide not to print a story because it's not well enough sourced are long gone."[13]

The Clinton administration was the first to be subjected to the intense scrutiny of a new amalgam of conservative media institutions that would soon develop into the most powerful and influential force in American politics. In 1987, under the Reagan administration, the Federal Communications Commission abolished a policy known as the "Fairness Doctrine," which had required broadcasters to cover the news in a way that balanced different political perspectives. Getting rid of the rule allowed AM talk radio to become dominated by extremist conservatives and conspiracy nuts who were able to juice their ratings by demanding that the Republican Party take ever more outrageous positions—in many cases based on the lies spread by the radio hosts themselves—or face the wrath of their listeners. They would be joined by a conservative media establishment that soon consisted of opinion magazines like William F. Buckley's *National Review* (funded by Buckley's admirers and supporters), Emmett Tyrrell's *American Spectator* (funded by Richard Mellon Scaife), and William Kristol's *Weekly Standard* (funded by Rupert Murdoch); heavily trafficked websites like the *Drudge Report*; and Robert Bartley's *Wall Street Journal* editorial page (owned at the time by the Bancroft family, and later purchased by Rupert Murdoch). But by far the most significant influence in the creation of the fact-free environment of political debate was Murdoch's 1996 launch of Fox News. All these forces grew together like Japanese movie monsters shot with radiation as they fed on the Lewinsky scandal. Fox News soon became the largest, most influential, and (by far) most profitable cable news station in America, its audience increasing by as much as 400 percent once the scandal began.[14] All these outlets regularly trafficked in misinformation, disinformation, bald-faced lies, and what Princeton philosophy professor Harry Frankfurt termed "bullshit."

The most influential of these voices, at least initially, were those belonging to the *Wall Street Journal* editorial writers. Long before Monica Lewinsky became a household name, its authors and editors had convinced themselves that Bill and Hillary Clinton were engaged in a massive conspiracy involving all manner of lawbreaking, potentially up to and including drug-running and murder.

Nearly twenty years later, David Brooks, its op-ed editor at the time, confessed that even he "couldn't follow all the actual allegations made in those essays." "Speculation," he said, "became the national sport." Brooks also noted, with considerable understatement, that "in retrospect the entire matter seems overblown."[15] When they were finally published in book form, the *Journal*'s editorials on the Arkansas-related crimes the Clintons and their cronies had allegedly committed came to just under three thousand printed pages in six volumes—approximately a thousand more pages than Leo Tolstoy's *War and Peace* and *Anna Karenina* combined.

Many more stories were driven by "reporting" paid for by the far-right heir to the Mellon fortune, the billionaire media magnate Richard Mellon Scaife. Obsessed with the Clintons, Scaife funded an outfit called the "Arkansas Project" at the *American Spectator* to the tune of $4 million, and it was designed specifically for the task of bringing down Bill Clinton. The project was best known for the deeply dishonest scandal-mongering of the right-wing hatchet-man and commentator David Brock. As Brock would later relate in a book-length confession, he "had stumbled onto something big, a symbiotic relationship that would help create a highly-profitable, right-wing Big Lie machine that flourished in book publishing, on talk-radio, and on the Internet in the 90s." Operating under the conviction that "right-wing journalism had to be injected into the bloodstream of the liberal media for maximum effect," Brock leaked a copy of his dishonestly sourced "Troopergate" story to CNN and was "astonished to see how easy it was to suck [them] in." The story alleged that, as governor, Clinton had instructed state troopers to pick up women and bring them back to him for sex. Brock's baloney-filled story led evening newscasts and was picked up by other outlets from there. Scaife liked what he saw and continued to pony up millions more in funding to fill the national discourse with baseless allegations and conspiracy theories. The Paula Jones story, which Brock also published, even though he didn't believe it at the time, proved to be an extremely effective strategic intervention. George Conway, then a $1-million-a-year law partner, and already husband to far-right pollster Kellyanne Conway, worked pro bono with Jones and her lawyers. The Conway team was, it turned out, planning to grill Clinton under oath about his consensual sex life in order to embarrass the president, undermine his agenda, and set him up with a perjury trap for the purposes of an impeachment trial.[16] To almost everyone's shock and amazement, the scheme worked.

Scaife lavished millions of dollars on countless right-wing groups working to discredit liberalism in general and the Clintons in particular.[17] The "cast of characters" listed in journalist Jeffrey Toobin's 1999 book on the impeachment conflict, provided to help the reader keep track of everyone materially involved, lists fifty-one people— lawyers, pundits, billionaires, freelancers, and lost souls with nothing more constructive to occupy their time—who made it their primary business to try to either entrap or convict Clinton of perjury, not including the many members of Congress who took it upon themselves to try to finish the job. That number also does not include the hundreds of people who worked for those fifty-one, or the hundreds, perhaps even thousands, of journalists who made it their professional duty to cover the proceedings, and in many cases to try to dig up even more dirt themselves.[18] Kenneth Starr's investigation, meanwhile, eventually encompassed twenty-eight lawyers, seventy-eight FBI agents, and countless private investigators. It cost $80 million and generated well over one hundred thousand news stories and many thousands of hours of television coverage, all of it over an adulterous affair between the president and his intern.

The entire panic and the Clinton impeachment proceedings appear even odder in retrospect than they did at the time. It's not merely that Clinton's sins pale in comparison to those of Donald Trump, with regard to both his sex life and the scale of his lying. It was widely known at the time of the Lewinsky scandal that many of the people who had undertaken the responsibility of investigating and ultimately impeaching Clinton were themselves liars about all manner of criminal activity, including sex crimes far more serious than mere adultery. The House Judiciary Committee that led the impeachment inquiry was chaired by Representative Henry Hyde, a Republican from Illinois, who—owing to the efforts of the man whose marriage he broke up—was later forced to admit to having had an affair with a married mother of three children while married himself. Hyde chalked up the affair to a "youthful indiscretion" committed when he was just an innocent lad of forty-one. The final proceedings leading to the impeachment vote began on a decidedly dramatic note when the Republican House Speaker–elect, Bob Livingston of Louisiana, announced that he was resigning from Congress over his own four adulterous affairs, which were about to be exposed by *Hustler* magazine. Livingston had been chosen by Republicans to replace Newt Gingrich, who had been forced to resign over financial improprieties. Gingrich, however, was no less vulnerable to exposure than Livingston over the issue of adultery: the most recent of Gingrich's numerous affairs had been conducted with a twenty-three-year-old congressional aide who would become his third wife.[19]

To replace Livingston in the Speaker's chair, Republicans chose Congressman Dennis Hastert of Illinois. Unknown to Republicans or to the press at the time, their new leader was secretly paying off at least six young men whom he had repeatedly raped while serving as their high school wrestling coach, in exchange for their silence about his crimes. The youngest was fourteen at the time. US District Court judge Thomas M. Durkin termed Hastert "a serial child molester," sentencing him to fifteen months in prison, after which he would be barred from possessing "any sex-related telephone numbers," have to install (and pay for) computer software recording all his online activities, and not be permitted to be alone with anyone under eighteen. In Congress, meanwhile, Livingston was succeeded by his fellow Republican and Louisianan David Vitter, who was later forced to resign from Congress over his role in a local prostitution ring. And Tom DeLay, who was the Republican majority whip during the impeachment fight (later replacing Hastert as House majority leader), may not have been involved in a sex scandal, but he was soon to spend three years inside a Texas prison for illegally plotting to funnel corporate contributions to Texas legislative candidates, along with another five years on top of that for money laundering (later negotiated down to ten years of community service). Kenneth Starr himself was later forced out of his job as president of Baylor University for turning a blind eye to a remarkably vast sexual assault scandal involving alleged rapes, including gang rapes, by thirty-one Baylor football players.[20] Later, he joined the legal team of child-rapist Jeffrey Epstein, helping him secure a shockingly lenient sentence that allowed him to go on committing his sexual crimes against vulnerable young women. Starr's legal team also included Brett Kavanaugh, who in 2018 was credibly accused of repeated sexual attacks in both high school and college—and, despite that, is now a member of the US Supreme Court.

Journalists are not (and should not be) subject to the same sort of scrutiny as public officials, but it seems worth noting that an impressive number of those who guided the coverage of the Clinton sex scandals, often expressing moral outrage over the president's lies, were themselves later embroiled in significant sex scandals—and lied to cover them up. Aggressive coverage of the Lewinsky and Paula Jones stories in the *New York Times*, for example, was directed, from its Washington bureau, by Michael Oreskes, but NPR put Oreskes on indefinite leave in the fall of 2017, when allegations emerged that he had earlier engaged in inappropriate sexual behavior with members of his staff as well as with job candidates at the *Times*. The influential inside dopester Mark Halperin, who was political director of ABC News at the time of the Clinton impeachment and later became a political analyst for MSNBC, was extremely harsh on Clinton during the scandal. In the fall of 2017, he, too, was reported to have sexually harassed and assaulted several women, including in company bathrooms. The bathroom was also said to be the favored location for Leon Wieseltier's bestowal of unwanted physical affection on young women in the offices of his allegedly liberal magazine, *The New Republic*. These incidents, which he was reported to have carried out in between writing his scathing editorials about Bill Clinton and Monica Lewinsky, led to his dismissal as well.[21]

And the exposés of 2017 were not yet over. In late November, over at NBC, the network's $20-million-a-year *Today* host, Matt Lauer, was said to be serially harassing young women. Although he admitted to some of the inappropriate behavior, he emphatically denied the allegations, in one case, of rape. Moreover, according to the investigative reporting of Ronan Farrow, who was later employed at NBC, the news division's president, Andrew Lack, had "pursued sexual relationships with underlings and talent." Lack, too, denied the allegations—and as of late 2019, he was still at the helm of NBC News and MSNBC. Reports of such behavior were decidedly unremarkable at the station's top echelons. A number of other important figures at NBC would be caught up in the scandal as well, accused by women at the network of "harassment or worse," according to Farrow. These included the network's star anchor, Tom Brokaw (who denies these charges); his close confidant and producer, Matt Zimmerman; *Hardball* producer Phil Griffin (who later became president of MSNBC); and *Hardball*'s extremely outspoken host, Chris Matthews.

At CBS, talk-show host Charlie Rose was apparently greeting young female assistants naked in his home when he was not forcing them to scrub his toilet. In this respect, Rose was evidently following the lead of accused sexual predators Les Moonves, the head of CBS, as well the abusive chief of that network's news magazine show *60 Minutes*, Jeff Fager, who was later fired for having "engaged in certain acts of sexual misconduct" with colleagues and failing to stop similar misbehavior by others. Fager replaced Don Hewitt, whose longtime alleged sexual abuse of a female colleague cost CBS at least $5 million in payouts as part of an agreement that had to be repeatedly amended to account for new information and accusations.[22]

Over at Fox News, top executive Roger Ailes and television host Bill O'Reilly, among many others, were accused of casually and repeatedly demanding sexual favors of their younger female colleagues. (Ailes had made his way to Fox after being forced out of NBC for calling a fellow executive there a "little fucking Jew prick.") Thirteen women accused Ailes shortly before his death in 2017. He was said to have pressured some of these women to service his friends and business associates as well, in a manner not dissimilar to that of the criminal sexual predator Jeffrey Epstein. Ailes was reportedly aided in these efforts by his wingman, Fox News copresident Bill Shine, who resigned from the network in mid-2017 and was named President Trump's director of communications in mid-2018. The political commentator Sean Hannity, also at Fox, was accused by a female guest in 2017 of making advances that she found "weird and creepy"; she said she rebuffed him (he denied her allegations).[23] All these people had repeatedly passed moral judgment on Bill Clinton during the Clinton impeachment era, shaping the public narrative about the nature and importance of his lies while, at a minimum, concealing their own actions from their employers, employees, friends, and families— and, more likely, frequently lying about them. This trend—of allegations, denials, firings, and resignations—widely commented on in social media, acquired the label #MeToo.

Owing at least in part to this hypocrisy, a decided disconnect developed over the significance of the Clinton-Lewinsky affair, with

Washington insiders—especially those in media circles—on one side, and most of the rest of the country on the other. When Clinton finally came clean following his four hours of videotaped testimony before a federal grand jury in mid-August 1998, he spoke contritely before condemning what he rightly insisted were the considerable excesses on the part of Starr's staff in their pursuit of him. Within the Beltway and in television commentary that night, the reaction was almost uniformly severe disapproval. The American people, however, according to the polls, were largely supportive of the president.[24] Perhaps they shared the view of Dale Bumpers, a former divorce lawyer and senator from Arkansas (he also served a term as Arkansas governor), who said that while "the president suffered a terrible moral lapse of marital infidelity," his actions were "not a breach of public trust, not a crime against society." In 1999, during the impeachment hearings, Bumpers, defending the president, said that lying about infidelity is common in divorce cases:

> In all those divorce cases [that Bumpers handled as an Arkansas attorney], I would guess that in 80 percent of the contested cases perjury was committed. Do you know what it was about? Sex. Extramarital affairs. But there is a very big difference in perjury about a marital infidelity in a divorce case and perjury about whether I bought the murder weapon, or whether I concealed the murder weapon or not. And to charge somebody with the first and punish them as though it were the second stands our sense of justice on its head.[25]

Bumpers's view of Clinton's lies may be contrasted with that of, say, Henry Hyde, the adulterer and home-wrecker who was considered by most in Washington to be something of a wise man within the context of the Republican impeachment effort: "Have you been to Auschwitz?" he asked his colleagues during a December 1998 session of the impeachment hearings focusing on Clinton's adulterous lying. "Do you see what happens when the rule of law doesn't prevail?"[26] Nevertheless, the 1998 midterm elections made clear that the public was siding with the likes of Bumpers. Although Newt Gingrich had predicted a Republican gain of anywhere from ten to forty seats in the House, the Democrats picked up five seats. Indeed, the 1998 midterms became only the second time since the Civil War when the president's party actually improved its standing in Congress in a midterm election during a second term in office. The Senate put an end to the shenanigans with a 50–50 vote on February 12, 1999, to reject the charge of obstruction of justice against the president, and a 45–55 vote rejecting the perjury charge. Both would have required a two-thirds majority to pass. In the wake of his impeachment, Clinton's approval rating rose to an astronomical 73 percent.[27]

Although the Republicans did not succeed in removing Clinton from office, the impeachment effort crippled Clinton's ability to pass legislation in the final years of his presidency, just as he might have finally been able to turn to the progressive agenda he had promised his supporters back in 1992. The impeachment also contributed to upending Al Gore's presidential campaign, which took a decidedly passive-aggressive, semi-adversarial stance toward an extremely popular president with a booming economy behind him. The impeachment therefore paved the way for the 2000 election, which was so close and so riddled with voting glitches that the Supreme Court ended up shutting down a vote recount in Florida, ensuring a Republican win. George W. Bush would replace Clinton, and his lies to the American public would turn out to be of far greater consequence than any of Bill Clinton's.

The Republicans ultimately failed to remove President Clinton from office. Their efforts left him far more popular among the voters than when it all began, severely damaging their own popularity in the process. But it is evident in retrospect that the impeachment inquiry represented an important turning point in the decline of truth in America and another giant step on the road toward the Trump presidency. With Newt Gingrich deposed from his House Speaker's perch and out of Congress, one could have been forgiven for believing that his style of slash-and-burn politics, with no concern for the truth, had been dealt a serious setback. But one would have been wrong. Gingrich, together with conservative talk-radio and Fox News hosts such as Rush Limbaugh, Sean Hannity, and Bill O'Reilly, revolutionized the Republican Party along with the right-wing movement that increasingly controlled it. Impatient with the relatively soft-spoken leadership of the Republican old guard in Congress during its lengthy sojourn in minority governance, Gingrich used his leadership post and media ubiquity to turn the party into a twenty-four-hour-a-day attack machine on Democrats and liberals. From the time he first entered Congress as a junior member, he instructed his colleagues to consistently compare the Democrats to Soviet Politburo members and liken their values to those of child murderers. He encouraged them to pepper their speeches with the words "corrupt," "traitor," "abuse of power," "shame," "pathetic," "steal," and "lie" when describing their opponents. His success in mapping out a Republican strategy for taking the House in 1994 made Gingrich the leading voice for Clinton's impeachment. But at the same time, he was violating the House ethics rules himself and committing adultery with far greater frequency than his target. It was the kind of performance that can "give chutzpah a bad name." In Gingrich's case, it brought attention and publicity. He was *Time* magazine's "Person of the Year" in 1995 and the leading voice in the Republican Party three decades running.

Until his forced resignation from the Speaker of the House position in 1999 on corruption charges, Gingrich was able to lead Republicans with an iron grip. Suffice it to say that telling the truth was not a highly valued tactic in this struggle, especially on those myriad occasions when it conflicted with Gingrich's battle plans. In his campaign against Clinton, Gingrich saw himself as "what stands between us and Auschwitz." He instructed Americans to guard against "a gay and secular fascism in this country that wants to impose its will on the rest of us." When the filmmaker Woody Allen had an affair with his girlfriend's young daughter, Gingrich claimed these actions "fit the Democratic platform perfectly." When a woman in South Carolina drowned her two children, Gingrich intoned that "the only way you get change" to prevent that sort of thing was to "vote Republican."[28] Instead of becoming an embarrassing liability, or a sign of emotional instability, or mental illness, these statements became a template for conservative Republican politics. Gingrich found himself being treated as a statesman, an experienced political "wise man" in the mold of people like former officials Clark Clifford, Bill Moyers, and Henry Kissinger. As the historian Julian Zelizer has observed, "Gingrich made his biggest impact on the GOP by defining what partisanship should look like and by expanding the boundaries of what was permissible in the arena of congressional warfare." He "legitimated ruthless and destructive practices that had once been relegated to the margins," and as a result, the future of American politics "would be dominated by ongoing accusations, vilification, investigations, resignations."[29] Clinton was the first president to fall victim to this new playbook, but he would not be the last. American politics had entered a new era. Guided by Gingrich and his heirs, Republicans would tear down the walls between truth and lies, between evidence and accusation, between reality and fantasy. And into that void would first come George W. Bush and a disastrous, dishonestly defended preemptive war against Iraq, and after that, the presidency of a dangerously unstable pathological liar.

14

George W. Bush
"WE'RE HISTORY'S ACTORS"

George W. Bush's presidency is perhaps best remembered for his having misled the nation into the catastrophic Iraq War in 2003 on the basis of false information. Well before this, however, the pundit Michael Kinsley put his finger on the Bush administration's remarkably casual attitude toward truth and falsehood. "Their lies," he wrote, "are often so laughably obvious that you wonder why they bother. Until you realize: They haven't bothered. If telling the truth was less bother, they'd try that too. The characteristic Bush II form of dishonesty is to construct an alternative reality on some topic and to regard anyone who objects to it as a sniveling dweeb obsessed with 'nuance.'"[1]

Kinsley was not identifying a mere quirk of Bush's character. Rather, it was a fundamental feature of his administration's approach to governance. The Bush Justice Department argued before the US Supreme Court that his administration should have the right "to give out false information...incomplete information and even misinformation" whenever it deemed it necessary. This formulation went well beyond the Kennedy administration's famous insistence on the "government's right, if necessary, to lie to save itself."[2] George W. Bush effectively extended that claim, replacing the words "if necessary" with "whenever we feel like it."

Bush became president on the basis of some extremely questionable pronouncements by Florida Republican officials—including the governor, who just happened to be his brother—as well as by the US Supreme Court, which included two justices appointed by his father. This was possible because Bush's supporters—including, especially, the now-infamous political adventurer and Trump confidant Roger Stone—helped to organize what *Wall Street Journal* editorial page editor Paul Gigot admiringly called the "Brooks Brothers riot" on November 22, 2000, in which hundreds of people demonstrated in Florida's Miami-Dade County, many of them allegedly paid by the Bush recount committee or sponsored by corporate interests. Voting discrepancies involving the infamous "chads" on paper ballots had necessitated a recount, and the protesters—who were banging on the windows where the recount was taking place, and in some cases, punching and kicking Democratic officials—were proud to have "scared the crap out of [those charged with undertaking the recount]." Bush had lost the national popular vote for president and, despite media reports to the contrary, could easily have lost Florida, and therefore the entire election, if the count had been allowed to continue. The Republican-dominated Supreme Court, with two of its members appointed by Bush's father, George H.W. Bush, saw fit to help Bush's Florida coconspirators curtail the vote counting, coming to a decision that—tellingly—it disavowed for the purposes of precedent.[3]

Bush's ostentatious lack of concern for veracity was evident from the start of his presidency. When, for instance, he began his first term by presenting a budget that would dramatically inflate the federal deficit—after having just campaigned as a fiscal conservative—he excused himself by explaining, "As I said in Chicago during the campaign, when asked about [when] should the government ever deficit spend: if there is a national emergency, if there is a recession, or if there's a war." In fact, it was his opponent, Al Gore, not Bush, who had offered these exceptions during the 2000 campaign. When *New York Times* columnist Paul Krugman pointed out that the administration's figures greatly underestimated the degree to which its budget plan would contribute to the deficit, the administration simply replaced the figures with new ones in a revised press release, with no admission of error. Later on, when quizzed about a series of Bush's statements that turned out to be false, his press secretary replied, "The President of the United States is not a fact-checker." Truth, as far as Bush was concerned, was whatever he or his trusted advisers wanted it to be. This was the meaning of a warning given to reporter Ron Suskind by a still-unidentified anonymous source who was (and is) widely believed to be Bush's senior adviser Karl Rove. The source schooled Suskind on the new ways of the world, particularly the meaning of "reality" as the Bush administration applied it. Mocking the presumption of what he contemptuously termed "the reality-based community," defined as individuals who "believe that solutions emerge from your judicious study of discernible reality," he instructed Suskind, "That's not the way the world really works anymore....We're an empire now, and when we act, we create our own reality. And while you're studying that reality—judiciously, as you will—we'll act again, creating other new realities, which you can study too, and that's how things will sort out. We're history's actors...and you, all of you, will be left to just study what we do."[4]

What was most alarming about this pronouncement was how little alarm it inspired. The Bush administration's blasé attitude about truth and lies was not much discussed in pre-9/11 America. To sophisticated observers, Bush was seen in those days as an overgrown frat-boy wearing his daddy's suits rather than a genuine threat to world peace or American democratic norms and civil liberties. Bush had never shown much interest in foreign policy as a candidate, and he appeared to be more interested in "clearing brush" in Texas than in the details of governance. The stories dominating the attention of mainstream media outlets for the most part featured either pretty young women who mysteriously disappeared somewhere, or the largely imaginary appearance of killer sharks on America's shores. The 9/11 attacks fundamentally transformed the political atmosphere. After September 11, few Americans were in the mood to question the judgment of their president, even if they had been mocking him the day before—and that included virtually all those who worked for the major media organizations. Anyone who suggested that the administration was no more trustworthy the day after the attacks than it had been the day before found themselves accused of being unpatriotic—even treasonous—in the face of a mortal threat. In one of many notorious examples, for instance, the political commentator Andrew Sullivan, then a fervent Bush supporter, wrote, in the aftermath of the attack, "The middle part of the country—the great red zone that voted for Bush—is clearly ready for war. The decadent Left in its enclaves on the coasts is not dead—and may well mount what amounts to a fifth column."[5] Thus was dissent from Bush's policies silenced and the lies he and the members of his administration told allowed to pass as akin to gospel.

In ideological terms, Bush made a 180-degree turn in the aftermath of the 9/11 attacks. He had taken office in January 2001 speaking of the necessity for humility on the world stage. "If we're an arrogant nation, they'll resent us," he said, but "if we're a humble nation, but strong, they'll welcome us." Guided by his vice president, Dick Cheney, by Secretary of Defense Donald Rumsfeld, and by their respective aides—including, especially, the prominent neoconservative thinker and Deputy Secretary of Defense Paul Wolfowitz, the post-9/11 version of George W. Bush embraced a more expansive definition of US national security and empire than any previous president. Bush put the rest of the world on notice: no longer would he "stand by while peril draws closer and closer." Never again would he "permit the world's most dangerous regimes to threaten us with the world's most destructive weapons." The United States was undertaking a crusade against "evil," and other nations needed to decide whether they were "with us or against us." America would now "take the battle to the enemy, disrupt his plans and confront the worst threats before they emerge." Defense Secretary Donald Rumsfeld, who had been a counselor to Richard Nixon and his ambassador to the North Atlantic Treaty Organization (NATO), as well as Gerald Ford's defense secretary after that, put the matter more bluntly in private. Speaking on the evening after 9/11, he insisted, "We need to bomb something else [other than Afghanistan] to prove that we are, you know, big and strong and not going to be pushed around by these kinds of attacks"[6]

The lies began immediately. For instance, in its eagerness to get the stock market trading again and avoid an economic free fall, the administration immediately informed New Yorkers that it was safe to breathe the air in and around what became known as "ground zero," where the attacks on the World Trade Center towers occurred. This turned out to be a lie, and it was one that would inflict lifelong health problems upon a vast number of the brave Americans who committed themselves to helping victims in the aftermath of the attack. The truth, according to a comprehensive study later undertaken by the Sierra Club, was that no one had made "any reasonable effort to evaluate the actual safety of breathing that air." Even when it was "confronted with information revealing harm," such as the fact that 9/11 dust was "highly caustic" to those breathing it in, the Bush administration failed to disclose this to the public—including those heroic volunteers and first responders answering their nation's call in its time of profound peril. These lies had deadly consequences. In June 2019, for instance, New York Police detective Luis Alvarez succumbed to cancer at age fifty-three following sixty-nine rounds of chemotherapy. His doctors blamed his condition on the time he spent as a first responder at ground zero. He was but one of thousands. Office workers continued to suffer the health effects for months and years afterward. According to Dr. Michael Crane, medical director of the WTC Health Program at Mount Sinai Hospital, nearly ten thousand people exposed to the site had developed cancer by 2018, and fifteen to twenty new patients were still entering the program each week. Over forty thousand people had filed health claims related to breathing the ground-zero air, and by the end of 2018 more people had likely died from long-term illnesses attributable to the attack than were killed during the attack itself and its immediate aftermath.[7] But given George W. Bush's newfound global ambitions, and the war that Dick Cheney and others would soon begin planning, the lying was just getting started.

In October 2004, a group of 650 international relations professors and other specialists calling themselves "Security Scholars for a Sensible Foreign Policy" signed an "Open Letter to the American People" that was published as a full-page advertisement in the *New York Times*. The group addressed the administration's deliberate dishonesty:

> Many of the justifications offered by the Bush Administration for the war in Iraq have been proven untrue by credible studies, including by U.S. government agencies. There is no evidence that Iraq assisted al-Qaida [in the 9/11 attacks], and its prewar involvement in international terrorism was negligible. Iraq's arsenal of chemical and biological weapons was negligible, and its nuclear weapons program virtually nonexistent. In comparative terms, Iran is and was much the greater sponsor of terrorism, and North Korea and Pakistan pose much the greater risk of nuclear proliferation to

terrorists....The Administration knew most of these facts and risks before the war, and could have discovered the others, but instead it played down, concealed or misrepresented them.

The arguments and evidence presented by people who actually knew something about Iraq and the scholarly study of foreign policy carried very little weight in the prewar debate. If they had, the United States and the world would have been spared one of the most egregiously counterproductive military operations in modern history, saving countless lives and trillions of dollars in the bargain.

Even including Vietnam, the invasion of Iraq stands alone as the worst self-inflicted strategic wound in the nation's history. It was also the conflict that necessitated the greatest degree of purposeful deception. Consider, for instance, Bush's September 2002 claim: "I would remind you that when the inspectors first went into Iraq and were denied—finally denied access, a report came out of the Atomic—the IAEA [International Atomic Energy Agency], that they were six months away from developing a [nuclear] weapon. I don't know what more evidence we need." In fact, the estimate Bush was referring to was more than a decade old at the time—it had been made before Iraq's military capabilities were decimated by his father's war to liberate Kuwait. Next, in a speech to the nation that October, Bush claimed that "Iraq could decide on any given day to provide a biological or chemical weapon to a terrorist group or individual terrorists," an alliance, he said, that "could allow the Iraqi regime to attack America without leaving any fingerprints." Here, Bush was specifically contradicting his own CIA's analysis, which was only revealed years later when the agency's investigation was finally declassified. As it happened, the entire US intelligence community had come to the exact opposite conclusion: Iraq and its allies in the terrorist world were not planning any attacks on the United States, but could easily be spurred on to do so in the event of a US invasion. In the same speech, Bush warned the nation that

Iraq possessed a growing fleet of unmanned aircraft that could be used "for missions targeting the United States." This was yet another lie. According to the CIA, Iraq had some "experimental" craft that might pose a "threat to Iraq's neighbors and to international military forces in the region"—but not to the United States itself.[8]

Just as Bush spoke of Iraq's allegedly "massive stockpile" of biological weapons, Vice President Cheney insisted there was "no doubt that Saddam Hussein now has weapons of mass destruction." In fact, a secret September 2002 report from the Pentagon's Defense Intelligence Agency had concluded that "there is no reliable information on whether Iraq is producing and stockpiling chemical weapons, or whether Iraq has—or will—establish its chemical warfare agent production facilities." Two years later, CIA director George Tenet admitted that the United States possessed "no specific information on the types or quantities of weapons agent or stockpiles at Baghdad's disposal." Over and over, Cheney and others in the administration hyped an alleged relationship between Iraq's leader, Saddam Hussein, and al-Qaeda. The only evidence they could muster was a report of a pre-9/11 meeting in Prague between an Iraqi intelligence official and a 9/11 plotter, Muhammed Atta. This report was widely taken up in the press as an "undisputed fact" by the likes of William Safire of the *New York Times* and others making the case for war. In reality, the report was already being disputed, and it was later determined, in 2004, that the meeting never happened, as Safire's newspaper later reported. In March 2004, after studying the administration's prewar claims, the minority staff of the House Committee on Government Reform issued a report concluding that just five top administration officials (including the president) had "made misleading statements about the threat posed by Iraq in 125 public appearances" in the time leading up to the US attack on Baghdad. The source material the committee provided to prove it cited "237 specific misleading statements."[9]

The truth was available to those willing to make the effort to search for it, but Bush, Cheney, and company purposely suppressed it when they could and ignored it when they could not. National Economic Council director Lawrence B. Lindsey was forced out of office in late 2002 after he estimated, honestly and rather conservatively, that the likely cost of the war would be between $100 billion and $200 billion (which would actually turn out to be but a fraction of its eventual cost). When the army chief of staff, General Eric K. Shinseki, accurately testified to Congress that the occupation of Iraq would likely require "something on the order of several hundred thousand soldiers," he found himself invited to take early retirement. When Bruce Hardcastle, a senior Defense Intelligence Agency official for Middle Eastern affairs, explained to Bush officials that they were misreading the evidence, he was removed from his post—which was itself subsequently eliminated.[10]

Well after its mendacity had been exposed by its own experts, the administration attempted to use false claims of imaginary weapons discoveries to maintain the fiction that Bush's prewar arguments and warnings had been well founded. When he was asked directly in the summer of 2003 where the weapons of mass destruction were, Bush replied, "We found them." Vice President Cheney also lied when, months later, he insisted that "conclusive evidence now demonstrates that Saddam Hussein did in fact have weapons of mass destruction."[11]

The Bush administration suffered no penalty in the mainstream media once its dishonesty was revealed. Incredibly, the very people it had tricked into publishing its lies thanked and congratulated them for it, thereby encouraging future presidents to lie in the same way, so long as their lies were consistent with the ideological sympathies of the journalists to whom they lied. Thomas Friedman at the *New York Times*, arguably America's most influential foreign affairs pundit, wrote, "As far as I'm concerned, we do not need to find any weapons of mass destruction to justify this war....Mr. Bush doesn't owe the world any explanation for missing chemical weapons (even if it turns out that the White House hyped this issue). It is clear that in ending Saddam's tyranny, a huge human engine for mass destruction has been broken." The *Washington Post* editorial board concurred: "While the Bush administration may have publicly exaggerated or distorted parts of its case," it wrote, "much of what it said reflected a broad international consensus." Leaving aside the editors' purposefully misleading euphemisms, the claim itself was also false. Despite the intense pressure that the Bush administration exerted upon them, most of America's closest allies, including France, Germany, and Canada, along with almost every nation in Latin America, Africa, and Asia, were strongly opposed to the war. Great Britain was the only nation that contributed significant numbers of combat troops, albeit against the wishes of the majority of its people. Unlike Bush, however, Prime Minister Tony Blair later expressed deep regret about having unwittingly passed along misleading information to his fellow citizens.[12]

Bush's well-established reputation for blurring the distinction between fantasy and reality actually worked in his favor, just as Reagan's similar reputation had worked for him. After the war, he proclaimed in a TV interview, "Did Saddam Hussein have a weapons program? And the answer is: absolutely. And we gave him a chance to allow the inspectors in, and he wouldn't let them in." The lie was so blatant that even a sympathetic reporter like CNN's Howard Kurtz, then already on his way to his natural habitat at Fox News, felt forced to admit that this assertion bore "no relation to reality." UN weapons inspectors had been making considerable progress in mapping Hussein's arsenal when the United States forced them to abandon their mission in order to begin bombing. But when Kurtz asked Dana Milbank at the *Washington Post* about Bush's lie, on his misnamed CNN program *Reliable Sources*, Milbank, who had established a deserved reputation as among the toughest and most critical of all the correspondents covering the Bush White House, responded, "I think what people basically decided was this is just the President being the President. Occasionally he plays the wrong track and something comes out quite wrong. He is under a great deal of pressure." Here again, as above, journalists were specifically stating that the president continuing to lie about a disastrous war— a war he had lied about in the first place to justify starting it—was of no particular interest or consequence to them, and that it should not be of interest to the rest of the nation either. A clearer example of what media scholar Jay Rosen termed the journalistic "cult of savviness"—or one with more catastrophic consequences for presidential truth-telling and journalistic accountability—would be hard to imagine.[13]

During the 2004 presidential election, Bush's reelection campaign faced a decorated combat veteran and deeply knowledgeable senator, John Kerry of Massachusetts, who offered voters what should have been a clear choice at the ballot box. Bush as a young man had avoided military service during the Vietnam War under decidedly murky circumstances, quite possibly with the direct intervention of political allies of his father. The election took a sharp turn when a group of wealthy Republicans spent millions of dollars publicizing lies about John Kerry's war record. These lies had been put forth by a group of far-right veterans who had served in Vietnam at the same time as the candidate—or at least around the same time, or, in some cases, as it would turn out, quite a bit after him. They called themselves the Swift Boat Veterans for Truth, and of the 250 people who signed their original complaint, exactly one had served with Kerry.

Honest investigative reporters debunked their phony charges, but Fox News and talk radio nevertheless trumpeted them nonstop. At some point, among the savvy, the issue became a "dispute" rather than a lie. The Bush campaign, meanwhile, refused to take any position on the matter, despite knowing, as all professionals did, that the charges were made up. As journalist Jason Linkins's 2018 retrospective story on the debate demonstrated, the persistence of their intervention "made for many a pleasing, process-driven thumbsucker in the political press," which effectively ignored the fact that the story was itself a lie. *"How effective are the ads? We have polling! How to assess the Kerry campaign's response? Kerry's been unable to make the story go away! What is it about these Swift Boat Veterans For Truth that makes them such a force in our politics?"*[14]

And so, the carnage in Iraq and the lies about it continued for another four years. Bush's repudiation came in 2008 with the election of Barack Obama, whose campaign all but ignored his actual opponent, John McCain, and focused instead on the legacy and lies of his now-discredited predecessor.

Accurate statistics for the cost, in terms of both lives and money, of the Iraq misadventure remain elusive. But current estimates hover between 500,000 to 600,000 dead, with another 2.5 million Iraqi refugees forced to seek refuge in foreign nations. These lives were lost and uprooted at an estimated cost to US taxpayers of more than $3 trillion. And the result, instead of the promised "liberation" of Iraq, was a vast increase in the region of Iran's destabilizing influence there. This phenomenon was underlined when the supporters of an Iranian-backed militia—a crowd that included members of Iraqi security forces—stormed the US embassy in Baghdad during the final moments of 2019. Chanting "Death to America," they burned the embassy's reception area, raised militia flags on its roof, and graffitied its walls following a US bombing attack targeting the militia. (Barely a day afterward, in the early hours of January 3, 2020, the United States carried out an attack that killed Major General Qassim Suleimani, leader of the Quds Force of the Islamic Revolutionary Guards Corps, in a drone strike at Baghdad International Airport. Four top officials from other Iraqi militias were killed in the attack as well.) Ultimately, the US response in the aftermath of 9/11 led to the rise of a horrific organization that would go on to menace the region in the ensuing years and murder countless more innocent people: ISIS. Bush's insistence on removing troops from the unfinished war in Afghanistan against the actual culprits of 9/11, al-Qaeda, in order to deploy them in Iraq allowed the terrorist organization to regroup and rebuild itself. US troops were still fighting what eventually became the longest war in the nation's history.[15]

The stories told by the Bush administration regarding the progress of this war would also turn out to be based on a massive campaign of deliberate deception, as a comprehensive internal Pentagon study would eventually reveal. That information was made public following what the *Washington Post* called a "three-year public records battle" between the *Post*, the National Security Archive, a nonprofit research institute based at George Washington University working with the newspaper on the project, and the Special Inspector General for Afghanistan Reconstruction (SIGAR), an agency charged with oversight of US spending in Afghanistan. In late 2019, more than eighteen years after the war began, the *Post* was able to publish a lengthy overview of the study's contents along with extensive excerpts from the study itself. *Post* reporter Craig Whitlock, summarizing the more than two thousand pages of documents and interviews the *Post* finally obtained, said that the US military's true understanding of the effect of the massive US military, diplomatic, and economic investment in that nation was at odds with what Americans had been told. He said, "The documents...contradict a long chorus of public statements from U.S. presidents, military commanders and diplomats who assured Americans year after year that they were making progress in Afghanistan and the war was worth fighting."[16] It is safe to say that this cascading series of catastrophes would not have grown so dire if Americans had been given the truth about the situation in Iraq and Afghanistan from the beginning—or if the president had not been so indulged by the members of the media as he and his aides repeatedly told their lies.

15

Barack Obama vs. the "Propaganda Feedback Loop"

The election of President Barack Obama in 2008 was nothing if not something new in American presidential politics. He was a liberal, an intellectual, a former constitutional law professor, and a community organizer with a fiery black Kenyan father and a free-spirited white anthropologist mother. The former disappeared when his son was just nine, and the latter took him with her to Indonesia while doing her dissertation fieldwork before deciding to park him with her parents to be raised in Hawaii. In short, he was a shock to the system: a previously unimaginable dream of multicultural America. He was also a reaction to the failures of George W. Bush's Republican conservatism.

Barack Obama was not perfectly honest with the American people. But for a two-term post–World War II president, he came awfully close. After Trump partisans complained to the editors of the *New York Times* about the paper's tracking of Trump's prodigious falsehoods, the *Times* sought to test the proposition that previous presidents—including Barack Obama—had been guilty of the same, but simply were not so scrutinized. Following an investigation of all eight years of Obama's presidency, its investigators found "six straight-up falsehoods in his first year in office." Then, the *Times* reported, "Across his entire second four-year term, we counted the same number, six, only one of which came in his final year in office." Sometimes these falsehoods were overstatements. Sometimes they were "careless exaggerations." In almost every case, however, when alerted that he had been mistaken, Obama did not repeat what he had said. "Over all," they concluded, "Obama rarely told demonstrable untruths as president. And he appears to have become more careful over time."[1]

In addition to the examples provided by the *Times*, there were other occasions where Obama's administration opted for deception, almost all of which involved the all-but-infinite definition of US "national security" he inherited from his immediate predecessors. Like Jimmy Carter, Obama tried to resist the frequent and predictable demands for a US military response to every perceived threat. But he was often unsuccessful—and truth was the loser. For instance, as president, Obama made extensive use of America's ability to kill individuals anywhere on earth with drones. His administration repeatedly claimed that these drone strikes only targeted members of al-Qaeda or those who posed an "imminent threat" to the United States. But leaked intelligence reports demonstrated that they were used far more widely. Similarly, Obama gave the order for US bombers to fire missiles in Libya in 2011, while at the same time maintaining that the United States was not engaged in active "hostilities" with that nation, in order to avoid triggering the conditions outlined in the War Powers Act. His own legal counsel insisted that this contention was false, but Obama overruled him. Moreover, when the *Washington Post* published the US government's own formerly classified study of what went wrong in the war in Afghanistan, one National Security Council official described what the *Post* termed to be "constant pressure from the Obama White House and Pentagon to produce figures to show the troop surge of 2009 to 2011 was working, despite hard evidence to the contrary."[2]

At home, following the revelations of the intelligence community whistleblower Edward Snowden, Obama's director of national intelligence, James Clapper, speaking in June 2013, was forced to concede that he had spoken untruthfully in March of that year while under oath before the Senate Intelligence Committee. Oregon senator Ron Wyden, a Democrat, had asked him, "Does the [National Security Agency] collect any type of data at all on millions or hundreds of millions of Americans?" Clapper said, "No, not wittingly," even though he was well aware that the NSA was specifically demanding that phone companies provide the information in question, called "metadata." Clapper later tried to argue that he did not understand the question, but Wyden had been clear and Clapper is an intelligent fellow, so it seems more likely that he decided to lie. Fortunately for Clapper, Obama did not appear to mind. The president also made extensive use of the 1917 Espionage Act to shut down leaks from his administration to journalists, even though the act had clearly been written to apply to spies and, with only one exception in the past century, had been used in a way that followed that limitation. The purpose of these aggressive prosecutions was clearly to hide the truth about programs like the NSA's spying operations from Americans and the rest of the world.[3]

Even allowing for these national-security-related exceptions, Obama's overall record for honesty frustrated Republicans and forced them to invent reasons why voters should distrust him. In doing so, they received invaluable help from the conservative media personalities who had risen to prominence during the previous two decades. Obama's election coincided with an explosion of right-wing media initially led by Rush Limbaugh and his fellow talk-radio hosts, but soon dominated by the increasingly angry revanchist conservatism of Fox News. And just as bad money drives out good, so, too, does bad information usually succeed in displacing truth in public discourse. Over time, lies succeeded in poisoning the political atmosphere in the United States to a degree that has few precedents in modern times. Repeated with sufficient frequency, these lies became "true enough" that the members of the mainstream media felt comfortable passing them along—often without bothering to mention their dubious origins. Once that cycle of repetitive reinforcement began, it didn't take long before the lies became conservative conventional wisdom.

In 2009, for example, right-wing operatives James O'Keefe and Hannah Giles conducted a "sting" operation against the community organizing group ACORN (Association of Community Organizations for Reform Now). Posing as a couple seeking to smuggle underage prostitutes into the United States from Mexico, they met with an ACORN staffer and secretly recorded their conversation. The ACORN employee actually called the police, but O'Keefe and Giles doctored their video to make it appear as if she had been eager to cooperate with their scheme. They subsequently sent the doctored recording to Fox News, where it ran on a seemingly endless loop. The ACORN employee eventually sued and was awarded $150,000 in two separate cases, but in the meantime, the organization she worked for was destroyed. Most of the government agencies and other institutions that had funded it pulled their support over the ensuing, entirely manufactured controversy. Fox succeeded in polluting not just its own broadcasts, but the entire political discourse. While interviewing President Obama, ABC's George Stephanopoulos felt obliged to ask about the imaginary threat from this now-defunct organization. "George, this is not the biggest issue facing the country. It's not something I'm paying a lot of attention to" was Obama's polite response. In the meantime, the poor and underrepresented in the United States lost a valuable voice for their political participation. And yet, even after ACORN was dead and buried, the lies about it lived on. By 2011, fully a quarter of Republicans questioned in one poll professed to believe with certainty that ACORN was planning to steal the 2012 election for Barack Obama, while another 32 percent said it was a possibility. These numbers were admittedly lower than the 52 percent who, in 2009, went on record accusing ACORN of having stolen the previous year's election for Obama, but given the fact that ACORN had by then ceased to exist, they remained rather substantial.[4]

At Fox, the willingness to lie about Obama was not a bug but a feature. On a 2009 fundraising cruise in the Mediterranean, Fox's managing editor, Bill Sammon, told his audience that of course he did not believe the silly things he said about the president on television. It was, he admitted, all "rather farfetched...mischievous speculation." Among the lies Sammon specifically mentioned: the notion that Obama's campaign platform was "tantamount to socialism," and that Obama, "in his own words, talks about being drawn to Marxists." To spread the stupidity, Sammon emailed his staff insisting that they highlight "Obama's references to socialism, liberalism, Marxism and Marxists" in his memoir *Dreams from My Father*. Sammon would later brag that his lies had become "a main point of discussion on all the channels, in all the media," and that he found himself "astonished by how the needle had moved."[5]

As a result of these and countless other equally fantastic stories masquerading as "news," millions of Fox viewers came to inhabit a parallel political universe, one in which reality played only a supporting role to ideology, fear, hatred, and prejudice. A libertarian scholar, Julian Sanchez, popularized the term "epistemic closure" to describe the process whereby Fox, together with an entire ecosystem of right-wing blogs, radio shows, websites, and now, of course, social media, defined what the political pundit and philosopher Walter Lippmann long ago characterized as "the pictures in our heads." Back in 1919, Lippmann warned that "the quack, the charlatan, the jingo, and the terrorist, can flourish only where the audience is deprived of independent access to information." By the beginning of Barack Obama's presidency, Lippmann's fears had come to fruition.

Millions of Americans relied on Fox and its allies for their news. The result, Sanchez noted, was that "whatever conflicts with that reality [created by Fox, or any other right-wing source] can be dismissed out of hand because it comes from the liberal media and is therefore ipso facto not to be trusted." This trend was borne out by the research of scholars Matt Grossman and David Hopkins, who found that, "compared to Democrats, Republicans are significantly less likely to trust what scientists say, more critical of political bias in academe and less confident in colleges and universities." During the 2008 election season, Republicans replaced these institutions, according to a team of scholars at the Massachusetts Institute of Technology Media Lab, with "an internally coherent, relatively insulated knowledge community, reinforcing the shared worldview of readers and shielding them from journalism that challenged it." The MIT researchers named this phenomenon a "Propaganda Feedback Loop," defined as a "network dynamic in which media outlets, political elites, activists, and publics form and break connections based on the contents of statements, and that progressively lowers the costs of telling lies that are consistent with a shared political narrative and increases the costs of resisting that shared narrative in the name of truth."[6]

Fox's achievement was particularly ironic—and absolutely mind-blowing in the chutzpah department—given the fact that its chief executive and guiding spirit, Roger Ailes, was later revealed to have run the place as if it were his own private shareholder-funded brothel, demanding sexual favors from female employees for himself and his friends as a condition of promotion. Reportedly, its star broadcaster, Bill O'Reilly, was hardly less aggressive in his pursuit of young female employees with no interest in seeing him naked. The alleged reluctance of Ailes and O'Reilly to take no for an answer ended up costing the network at least $65 million in payoffs to their victims, plus another $40 million to Ailes to get him to leave quietly.[7] And these two were not by any means alone in their predatory behavior, according to the many accusations widely publicized from

2016 through 2018: the entire culture at Fox appeared to encourage it. As we have seen, Ailes and O'Reilly had shown no compunction when pretending to be shocked at Bill Clinton's far tamer escapades.

Fox broadcasts regularly combined lies with hatred, racism, and incitement to encourage and enforce the extreme ideology overtaking the Republican Party during Obama's presidency. For example, the network regularly welcomed Ted Nugent, the rock guitarist and conservative icon who, in 2007, called Hillary Clinton a "worthless bitch" and President Obama "a piece of shit" before instructing him to "suck on my machine gun." During an earlier appearance leading up to Fox host Glenn Beck's August 2010 anti-Obama rally on the Washington Mall, he insisted that the president was hiding his "Islamic, Muslim, Marxist, communist and socialist agenda" in order that he might "continue with his jihad of America-destroying policies." And boy did Nugent have a sympathetic audience in Beck, who had noted on occasion that Obama exhibited a "deep-seated hatred for white people" (presumably including his mother and the grandparents who raised him). Beck referred to Obama on various occasions as a Marxist, a fascist, a Nazi, a Maoist, a Bolshevik, and a Trotskyite. He was all these (contradictory) things, Beck explained, because his ultimate goal was "destroying our economic system as we currently know it." In service of this mission, according to Beck, Obama created a "fascist" economic rescue plan for the nation in 2009 that amounted to a form of slavery—it was, as Beck put it, "Josef Stalin without the bloodshed."[8] Such talk did not discourage ostensibly respectable Republican politicians from signing contracts to join the network. In 2012, literally every Republican presidential contender who was not in elected office, save Mitt Romney, was getting a paycheck and free airtime care of Rupert Murdoch and Fox.

This attempt to portray America's first African American president as some kind of alien was hardly limited to Fox and its right-wing cohorts. Even ostensibly mainstream commentators joined in on the effort to tar Obama with the same brush that Joseph

McCarthy had used on alleged communists during the 1950s Red Scare. Pulitzer Prize–winning *Wall Street Journal* columnist Dorothy Rabinowitz titled one of her missives "The Alien in the White House." Best-selling author Charles Murray, a contributor to the *New Republic*, said of Obama: "Time and time again, he does things and says things that are un-American. Not evil. Not anti-American. Just un-American." George H.W. Bush's former chief of staff, an ex-governor of New Hampshire, John Sununu, said he "wish[ed] the president would learn how to be an American." But by far the most bizarre brief on Obama's allegedly alien qualities came from the man who happened to be the single most-booked guest on NBC's *Meet the Press* during the first year of Barack Obama's presidency: Newt Gingrich. The disgraced former House Speaker achieved a kind of peak lunacy when he turned volunteer publicist for the nutty theories of a racist provocateur and convicted felon, the pundit Dinesh D'Souza. In September 2010, D'Souza had published a cover story in *Forbes* in which he argued that, owing to the president's relationship with his father—whom Obama had neither seen nor spoken to since age nine—the United States was now "being ruled according to the dreams of a Luo tribesman of the 1950s." He added, "This philandering, inebriated African socialist, who raged against the world for denying him the realization of his anticolonial ambitions, is now setting the nation's agenda through the reincarnation of his dreams in his son." As even conservative writer Heather Mac Donald observed, the story was a "fever dream of paranoia and irrationality," and the fact that it would appear inside—much less on the cover of—a putatively respectable business magazine was, as she put it, "all too representative of the hysteria that now runs through a significant portion of the right-wing media establishment." And yet, according to Gingrich, D'Souza's article offered "the most accurate, predictive model for [President Obama's] behavior."[9]

It may be tempting to think that such bizarre conspiracies and purposeful dishonesty could have had little impact on "real politics."

But according to survey after survey, Fox News viewers were among America's most misinformed citizens. One team of political scientists addressed this question in December 2016 with a detailed multivariate analysis of the level of accurate information individuals possessed about current events. After surveying more than three thousand people, the researchers concluded that "relying on Fox News as a major news source significantly decreased a person's score more than relying on any other news source." And what did those people believe? A 2009 study by Democracy Corps found that a majority of Fox's audience believed "Obama is deliberately and ruthlessly advancing a 'secret agenda' to bankrupt our country and dramatically expand government control over all aspects of our daily lives," with the ultimate goal of "the destruction of the United States as it was conceived by our founders and developed over the past 200 years."[10]

During the Obama era, Republicans came to understand that they would rarely pay a price for lying to the country about his background, his policies—indeed, virtually anything related to his presidency. Incredibly, this strategy was frequently acknowledged, and even praised, by journalists eager to cast themselves as savvy, non-liberal, nonpartisan observers. They took the stance that they had no responsibility to judge the difference between truth and falsehood, but were merely interested in keeping score between two competing teams.

This destructive dynamic was most clearly on display during the 2012 Republican National Convention, which dedicated a full evening to purposely misrepresenting a single sentence spoken by the president. In a speech delivered on July 13 of that year at a campaign stop in Virginia, Obama had made the mundane point that, though it was important to root out wasteful government spending, it was also easy to take the principle too far. It was the government, after all, whose investments helped to lay the foundation that enabled the success of the private economy.

If you were successful, somebody along the line gave you some help. There was a great teacher somewhere in your life. Somebody helped to create this unbelievable American system that we have that allowed you to thrive. Somebody invested in roads and bridges. If you've got a business—you didn't build that. Somebody else made that happen. The Internet didn't get invented on its own. Government research created the Internet so that all the companies could make money off the Internet. The point is, is that when we succeed, we succeed because of our individual initiative, but also because we do things together.

Obama went on to cite the GI Bill, the Golden Gate Bridge, the Hoover Dam, and the moon landing as examples of the foundations of economic growth that for generations had supported America's great fortunes. These ideas were hardly controversial or even new.[11]

Republicans immediately seized on Obama's statement to make it appear that the president was claiming something he never said and obviously did not believe. Presumptive Republican nominee Mitt Romney complained that "to say that Steve Jobs didn't build Apple, that Henry Ford didn't build Ford Motors, that Papa John didn't build Papa John Pizza....To say something like that, it's not just foolishness. It's insulting to every entrepreneur, every innovator in America." But Romney's statement was just as foolish as Obama's was truthful. Nothing could be more obvious than the fact that the individuals Romney named did not "build" those companies alone. Not only did literally thousands of other people contribute in each case to making those companies into what they would become, but their success also rested on a system of laws, regulations, roads, bridges, post offices, schools, and taxes—just as Obama was saying. Here Romney, not Obama, was the one lying. Obama had challenged neither the visionary nature of these entrepreneurs nor the importance of their contributions. He merely made the mundane, factual, and almost tautological point that they did not do it "alone."[12]

On July 17, just days after the speech in question and well before the Republican convention began, the Obama campaign issued a statement clarifying that the word "that" referred to "roads and bridges" one sentence earlier. The president recorded an advertisement in which, looking into the camera, he explained, "Those ads taking my words about small business out of context? They're flat out wrong....Of course Americans build their own businesses." But Romney was far from the only one who didn't care about whether he was purposely misleading voters as to what Obama had said—many in the mainstream media were perfectly happy to play along. Despite a *Washington Post* fact-checker giving Romney's statement three (out of a possible four) "Pinocchios," and CNN calling it "a theme out of context," many others ate it up. The *Wall Street Journal* editorial page, which had also energetically defended the lies of the Swift Boat campaign against John Kerry in 2004, led the attack. One of its columnists went so far as to pretend that Obama's remark "was a direct attack on the principle of individual responsibility, the foundation of American freedom." A *Washington Post* blogger professed to see "a level of resentment toward the private sector that was startling, even to [Obama's] critics."[13]

In tribute to the effectiveness of their campaign, Republicans chose "We Built It" as the theme of the second night of the 2012 convention. Press coverage, for the most part, focused not on whether the theme was honest but on whether it worked. And most journalists decided not only that the attack was valid but that Obama had only himself to blame and should stop bothering them with corrections and complaints. As Aaron Blake wrote in a straight news story in the *Washington Post*, "The problem with Obama's latest exhortation that 'you didn't build that' is not that it's not true. The context of the remark makes it pretty clear that he's referring to government-funded things like teachers and roads that make entrepreneurship possible." Rather, the problem, Blake concluded, was his "emphasis." This was what invited Republicans to "label Obama as a big-government tax-raiser." *Slate*'s Rachael Larimore not only dismissed questions of truth and falsehood as beside the point but appeared to find them to be somehow morally objectionable. In an article with the subheading "It Doesn't Matter What Obama *Meant*. Here's Why," she admitted that Romney's statement was false, noting that she endorsed the fact-checkers' condemnation of it. Nevertheless, she went on to say, she was unsympathetic to the Obama campaign: "Obama supporters can complain all they want. They can argue that when he said 'that,' he was talking about the roads and bridges, not the business itself. It doesn't matter. And it's pointless to blame Mitt Romney or the RNC or anyone else for taking it out of context." She found comical the idea that Obama's supporters would "try telling [voters] what their president 'meant.'" The idea that it might be her professional responsibility to speak up for the truth and debunk falsehood was entirely alien to her—a quaint relic of a sadly bygone era. Chris Cillizza, a star reporter at the *Washington Post* (later recruited by CNN), explained it thusly: "My job is to assess not the rightness of each argument but to deal in the real world of campaign politics in which perception often (if not always) trumps reality. I deal in the world as voters believe it is, not as I (or anyone else) thinks it should be."[14] One could hardly ask Professor Jay Rosen's 2011 diagnosis of the "cult of the savvy" that had come to dominate insider political journalism. Ben Smith, a former reporter for *Politico* who became BuzzFeed's editor in chief, made much the same point when, in August 2018, he lamented his own role in pioneering what he now termed the "amoral, tactical coverage of American politics" that dominated the journalism of the Obama era.[15]

Even fact-checkers were not immune to these tendencies. For instance, Glenn Kessler, chief of the *Washington Post* fact-checking team, admitted to finding the Republicans' rhetoric "a bit odd, since it was devoted to the political exploitation of a single Obama gaffe—'You didn't build that'—[that they] blatantly misrepresent." And yet he went on to energetically defend a speech by vice presidential nominee Paul Ryan that even Matthew Dowd, who had been the 2004 Bush campaign's chief strategist, admitted repeatedly "stretched the truth." Why? The headline above Kessler's column was "The Truth? C'mon, This Is a Political Convention." In Ryan's defense, Kessler wrote that "the whole point is for the party to put its best foot forward to the American people. By its very nature, that means downplaying unpleasant facts, highlighting the positive and knocking down the opposing team." He did not explain why Ryan could not have done so without lying. Kessler did, however, go on to speculate that "Ryan was so quickly labeled a fibber by the Obama campaign that one suspects it was a deliberate effort to tear down his reputation as a policy expert." Amazingly, the "fact-checker" did not even pause to consider the possibility that Ryan was "so quickly labeled a fibber" because he was fibbing.

Like almost all mainstream political reporters of the moment, Kessler sought to create a sense of false equivalence between the Republicans—whose lies, by this time, had become endemic and central to their appeal—and the Democrats, whose arguments remained largely reality-based. He did so, however, without pointing out a single lie told at a Democratic National Convention. His best shot was to complain that during Barack Obama's fully accurate 2008 convention speech, the candidate "knocked McCain for voting 90 percent of the time with his own party." Kessler did not dispute the truth of Obama's contention. Rather, he faulted Obama for failing to mention that, in his brief career as a senator, he himself had "voted 97 percent of the time with Democrats." His argument appeared to be that the Democratic nominee for president should have berated himself at a Democratic convention for voting Democratic. And it was on this false foundation that Kessler somehow concluded that the 2012 GOP convention "was strictly in the mainstream for such party celebrations."[16]

This tendency would haunt the fact-checking process for the remainder of the election cycle. Repeatedly, fact-checkers would scour

Democrats' speeches for examples of anything that might be construed as even slightly inaccurate in order to balance out the avalanche of Republican lies, completely ignoring the actual imbalance in these numbers. The political scientists Theda Skocpol and Vanessa Williamson have described this phenomenon as follows: "America has right now a thousand-pound-gorilla media juggernaut on the right, operating nineteenth-century style, coexisting with other news outlets trying to keep up while making fitful efforts, twentieth-century style, to check facts and cover 'both sides of the story.'"[17] In almost every instance, the media downplayed misinformation, disinformation, bald-faced lies, and "bullshit" from Republicans while insisting on a strict adherence to the highest standards of truth-telling for Democrats.

Politically speaking, the most significant "lie" of President Obama's two terms most undoubtedly was his promise that "if you like your health care plan, you can keep it." He said this repeatedly during his campaign to pass the Affordable Care Act (ACA), which began in 2009, and it was not strictly true. In 2013, PolitiFact picked the promise as its "Lie of the Year."[18]

Obama understood that there were exceptions to this rule when he made the claim. His Health and Human Services secretary, Kathleen Sebelius, had already acknowledged as much three years earlier. Some people were in fact forced to change plans once the law went into effect because changing the rules for health insurance meant changing the health care plans. Some people would need entirely new ones. In almost all these cases, however, when plans were changed, they did so to meet the law's higher standards and therefore provided better coverage than those they replaced.

Therefore, Obama's statement does qualify as a lie. He made an unqualified claim that he knew, or should have known, was not completely accurate. Granted, it was not much of a lie, given the fact that his assertion was true for 98 percent of the population. Before giving it the honor of being the "Lie of the Year" in 2013, PolitiFact had twice rated the same claim to be half-true when Obama had made it on previous occasions, in 2009 and 2011. At one point PolitiFact had even rated it as entirely true. Obama's advisers later explained that he considered the statement to be a simplification of a complex situation rather than an attempt to mislead. Obama was at least partially to blame for the confusion, and certainly he should never have employed the unambiguous terms he frequently used when asserting it. If Obama had simply added the caveat that Americans could keep their plans, so long as it was sufficient to meet the higher standards of the new law, or else it would be replaced by a better one available at a similar cost, this would have done the trick, albeit far less pithily.

Obama apparently caught himself and apologized in November 2013 for his original overstatement: "We weren't as clear as we needed to be in terms of the changes that were taking place, and I want to do everything we can to make sure that people are finding themselves in a good position, a better position than they were before this law happened. And I am sorry that they are finding themselves in this situation based on assurances they got from me." He subsequently changed the plan to give state insurance commissioners some flexibility in the ACA's enforcement to address this concern.

But he had already given his enemies a sword. The imprecision of his less cautious statements had already been transformed into a Republican mantra. Conservative politicians and activists deployed it relentlessly to hammer away at the president's credibility, which, according to the polls of the moment, quickly fell by fifteen points. This was possible in large part because members of the mainstream media could not be bothered to read up on even the broadest details of most policy issues, preferring to focus instead on what had by then become the political equivalent of a food fight. A second problem was that Fox News (and its conservative allies both online and on talk radio) had by this time become so influential that it could drive the political conversation in any direction it wished.

(Fox's Sean Hannity put Obama's statements up there with Nixon's "I am not a crook" and Bill Clinton's "I did not have sexual relations with that woman.") And finally, a significant portion of the blame must go to PolitiFact for its intellectually indefensible "Lie of the Year" assignation. Its spokespeople eventually said they agreed that it wasn't much of a lie, and that it had been chosen because of its alleged political significance.[19] This explanation, one must admit, is an extremely lame excuse for so incendiary an accusation. But one suspects that PolitiFact, like the *Post*'s Kessler and the mainstream organizations that quoted their work, felt compelled to bend over backward to prove their impartiality to conservatives.

Although Republicans and media conservatives had ideological disagreements with Obama, that was not the only reason they lied about him. They were also in it for the money. The frequently dispositive power of money in US politics provides Republicans with an artificial election advantage entirely unrelated to—and frequently in conflict with—democratic norms and desires. The fact that Republicans are far more generous than Democrats to the super-wealthy—whether it is in their tax policies, the subsidies they offer corporations, their attacks on organized labor, or their obstinate willingness to trust "the market" above all else—naturally leads corporations and wealthy individuals to want to pay to keep them in power. During the 2016 election, fully 40 percent of television advertisements were funded by "secret money groups"—that is, organizations whose donors were able to legally remain anonymous.[20]

Money has almost always and everywhere exercised powerful political influence. But in the United States, its dominion has grown so large that it threatens to strangle democracy itself. The problem stems from a misunderstanding of the Constitution that has inspired the US Supreme Court to issue a number of decisions that have done extensive damage to the fabric of the nation's democratic character. Ironically, the problem dates back to a lie told in 1882 by attorney Rosco Conkling while representing the Southern Pacific Railroad Company. He argued against the State of California's right to tax the corporation on the basis of the Fourteenth Amendment, which he argued had been intended to designate corporations as "people." Conkling, a former senator and presidential candidate, was the last surviving member of the Joint Committee on Reconstruction, and so his word was accepted despite the fact that, as historian Jill Lepore has demonstrated, he was almost certainly not telling the truth. Later Supreme Court decisions that defined money as speech, such as *Buckley v. Valeo* in 1976, and *Citizens United v. the Federal Election Commission* in 2010, opened the floodgates to virtually unlimited spending by allegedly "independent" entities—both individual and corporate—and ensured that the wealthy and powerful would face few, if any, barriers when seeking to buy themselves the political outcome they desired.[21]

During Obama's presidency, corporations and conservative billionaires demanded that the recipients of their largesse declare war on Democrats and their ideas—and even on reality itself—and the result was an avalanche of lies about the president and his programs. In an effort to undermine the legitimacy of empirical scientific data, for example, they invested massive amounts of money into the creation of a panoply of pseudoscientific institutions whose "research" was specifically designed to confuse the public about issues relating to its health and safety. These organizations then shamelessly exploited the eagerness of the mainstream media to give equal say to "both sides" of any given controversy, regardless of their respective professional credentials, reputations, or expertise.

With their nearly $100 billion fossil-fuel-based fortune, the brothers Charles and David Koch led the way (the latter passed away in August 2019). Consistent with the interests of their massive business empire, these two men, and the fellow multimillionaires and billionaires they recruited to their network, funded more institutions designed to undermine honest science than anyone could count. To shield these activities from scrutiny, the Kochs used what the *Washington Post* in 2014 called a "labyrinth of tax-exempt groups and limited-liability companies" set up to "mask the sources of the money." The Koch network directed hundreds of millions of dollars to organizations with anodyne names such as the Center to Protect Patient Rights, Americans for Prosperity, and the American Future Fund, which ended up being little more than fronts for the Kochs' ideological and commercial interests. Meanwhile, their fortune increased by more than a thousandfold between 2005 and 2018. Just how much they ultimately spent on buying pundits and politicians is unknown. According to the political scientist Stan Oklobdzija, "There is no way to verify how or where the money [was] spent because most of its organizations are registered as non-profit groups which aren't required to detail their donors." Examining a data set of 2.35 million IRS tax documents, Oklobdzija concluded that the new "post Citizens-United rules" for anonymous giving had enabled "more extremist candidates" to win their party's nominations as well as to win general elections. Overall, he said, the new rules "empowered these ideologically motivated groups while hobbling efforts of more moderate party factions."[22]

The unending stream of falsehoods and phony data, often dressed up in the garb of pseudoscientific jargon, sought to undermine (or at least to cast doubt upon) genuine, peer-reviewed scientific studies and honestly produced news reports. A scientific consensus on climate change has existed for two decades.[23] At least 97 percent of climate scientists agree that "climate-warming trends over the past century are extremely likely due to human activities." The outliers, it would often turn out, had their research funded by industry sources, including, either directly or indirectly, the Kochs. The brothers' billions successfully turned this intermittent willingness on the part of some extreme voices into GOP orthodoxy—what Republican strategist Whit Ayres called "yet another of the long list of litmus test issues that determine whether or not you're a good Republican."

Fox News and talk radio repeatedly brought on personalities and phony experts who insisted that climate change was a hoax and who, more often than not, barred the voices of anyone who did not buy into that lie. One 2012 study found that 93 percent of Fox segments and 81 percent of *Wall Street Journal* editorials on the subject "attempted to broadly undermine the major conclusions of climate science."[24]

Rather than pushing back against these deceptions, the mainstream media cooperated by booking fewer actual scientists to discuss the problem and sticking almost exclusively to "he said, she said" debates between politicians. The result was the elevation of right-wing disinformation to the same status as scientific research. This tactic paralyzed honest debate. It also helped to justify the Republican Party's unyielding obstruction when it came to the Obama administration's attempts to pass environmental legislation. According to Kert Davies, director of the Climate Investigations Center, which monitors climate science denial in the media, "You'd have a carbon tax, or something better, today, if not for the Kochs. They stopped anything from happening back when there was still time." The Koch brothers spent a veritable fortune to kill Obama's cap-and-trade plan—one that Senator John McCain had endorsed—working through what *New Yorker* writer Jane Mayer termed "their network of allied donors, anonymously funded shell groups, think tanks, academic centers, and nonprofit advocacy groups, which Koch insiders referred to as their 'echo chamber.'"[25]

The network worked tirelessly to undermine public confidence in academic and government climate-change scientists through character assassination and the selective and misleading use of purloined documents. They received considerable aid in this effort from allies in the mainstream media. For instance, Bret Stephens, a *Wall Street Journal* columnist later hired by the *New York Times*, denounced concerns about global warming as a "mass hysteria phenomenon." Christopher Leonard, author of the nearly seven-hundred-page study *Kochland: The Secret History of Koch Industries and Corporate Power in America*, demonstrated, in Mayer's words, how "the Koch machine bought its way into Congress and turned climate-change denial into an unchallengeable Republican talking point." With the cap-and-trade bill out of the way, Mayer continued, "the planet continued heating, and the Kochs' net worth doubled." To address the climate-change crisis, Obama was forced to use executive orders, and even then, the progress he managed to make in that way was immediately undone by his successor. So successful were the lies told by big money about the environment that there was literally nothing in the way of legislation or regulation that Republicans would approve to protect the planet. And after the 2016 election, in which the party nominated a man who insisted that the "concept of global warming was created by and for the Chinese in order to make U.S. manufacturing non-competitive" (although, true to form, he lied about having done so in a presidential debate), Leonard wryly noted, "the politics that the Kochs stoked in 2010 became the policies that Trump enacted in 2017."[26]

Aided by its allies in the conservative media, the Republican Party's turn toward a strategy of deliberate deception would turn out to be the most significant political development of the Obama presidency. While Democrats did move slightly leftward during the Obama years, Republicans moved much further to the right. Scholars Keith Poole and Howard Rosenthal analyzed decades of data and attempted to quantify this shift. They concluded that the "polarization" in today's politics "is largely due to how far and relatively quickly Republicans have shifted to the right end of the ideological spectrum."[27]

This radical turn in the Republican Party developed into an ideology that could no longer be accurately called "conservatism." Rather, it became something else entirely—something for which we still do not have a name (save for the extremely imprecise and ultimately undefinable term "Trumpism"). Many Republicans attempted to sound an alarm. Writing in *Politico* in 2013, Scot Faulkner, personnel director for the Reagan/Bush campaign in 1980, and Jonathan Riehl, former speechwriter for the right-wing Luntz Global consulting firm, complained about the corrosive effects of a "Republican world view that was devoid of facts and critical thinking." David Frum, a former Republican speechwriter who proudly coined the term "Axis of Evil" for George W. Bush's 2002 State of the Union address, could not help but admit a year later that "in the past five years, the American right has veered toward a reactionary radicalism unlike anything seen in American party politics in modern times." Even former House Speaker John Boehner said in the spring of 2016 that his party had fallen into the hands of "knuckleheads" and "goofballs." Toward the end of Obama's presidency, John McCain's 2008 campaign chair, Steve Schmidt, concluded by 2018 that his lifelong political home had been transformed into "a white ethno-nationalist party, a blood-and-soil party that is protectionist, isolationist, that is rooted in resentment and grievance…fueled by constant lying to incite fervor and devotion in [its] political base."[28] That the party soon experienced a takeover by a candidate whose virulent racism was at the heart of his appeal, in retrospect, should not have surprised anyone.

Donald Trump's 2016 presidential campaign surfed to victory on a tidal wave of dishonesty and democratic dysfunction. It is telling, and rarely noted, however, that this pathologically dishonest huckster was welcomed into the Republican fold long before he captured its nomination. During the 2012 election, for instance, Mitt Romney enthusiastically accepted Trump's endorsement as the psychopathic liar accused President Obama of covering up a "felony or worse." Already a devoted "birther"—that is, someone who refused to believe, against all evidence, that Barack Obama was born in the United States, and was therefore eligible to be president—Trump continually insisted that he would eventually demonstrate "things you will not believe" about

Obama—and that America would "learn more about Obama when we look at those college records than any other thing that could happen."[29]

Trump was telling what philosophers called "bald-faced lies," but it was far from clear that his intended audience recognized their falsity. By the time Trump made these statements, in the summer of 2012, lying about Obama had become a prerequisite for aspiring Republican politicians. Trump was merely hammering on the lie that had proven most compelling to core Republican voters—the kind who show up to vote in primaries. So it is no wonder that the influential Republican senator Jim Inhofe of Oklahoma, an inveterate climate-change denier, would muse aloud that the birthers "have a point" and suggest that Republican candidates should pursue the issue. Nor was it a shock when Senator Richard Shelby, a Republican from Alabama, told a town-hall meeting, "Well, his father was Kenyan and they said he was born in Hawaii, but I haven't seen any birth certificate." The party's 2008 vice presidential nominee, Sarah Palin, said she thought the birther issue was a "fair question." And Georgia Republican Nathan Deal won the governorship of that state after he cosigned a letter demanding that Obama "release a copy of his birth certificate so we can have an answer to this question."[30]

The Republican Party leadership at the time proved a profile in cowardice.[31] Asked on NBC's *Meet the Press* whether Obama was a Christian or a Muslim, then Speaker of the House John Boehner could not bring himself to give a straight answer. "Listen," he told the host, David Gregory, "the American people have the right to think what they want to think. I can't—it's not my job to tell them." Majority Leader Eric Cantor did much the same, refusing to criticize those who were spreading malicious lies about the president and questioning his legitimacy.[32] And given the endless attention this nonsense received on national radio and television shows, hosted by the likes of Lou Dobbs, Sean Hannity, and Rush Limbaugh, it should hardly surprise anyone that as late as 2016, long after Obama reluctantly produced official Hawaiian records documenting his birth, fully

72 percent of Republican voters told pollsters they either doubted or actually did not believe that he had been born in the United States.[33]

But to give credit where it is due, no one did more to spread this poisonous lie than Donald J. Trump. He started touting the birther lie while still a private citizen, and, amazingly, it was through doing so that he found his way to political credibility—at least as it had come to be defined in an age of casual Republican dishonesty, hysteria, and hucksterism. In March 2011, Trump was invited to appear on ABC's *Good Morning America*, where he made wild speculations about the president's origins. "Growing up no one knew him," Trump claimed. "The whole thing is very strange." He then went on *The View*, where he announced, "I want him to show his birth certificate. There's something on that birth certificate he doesn't like." A few days later, on NBC's *Today Show*, Trump continued his campaign of slander and lies against the president: "Three weeks ago when I started, I thought he was probably born in this country," Trump said. "Right now, I have some real doubts."[34]

Even after Obama produced the evidence, Trump took credit for it. And then he continued to promote the racist birther lie, bragging on Twitter of "an extremely credible source" who told him the certificate was a "fraud." He refused to give up on the matter.[35] President Obama was surely right when, speaking soon after the election in 2016, he told *New Yorker* editor David Remnick, "We've seen this coming. Donald Trump is not an outlier; he is a culmination, a logical conclusion of the rhetoric and tactics of the Republican Party for the past ten, fifteen, twenty years.…There were no governing principles, there was no one to say, 'No, this is going too far, this isn't what we stand for.'" The economic historian Adam Tooze got to the heart of the matter when he explained that Trump's election "reveals a deep degeneration of American political culture."[36] The first and foremost cause of the crisis was that lies went unchallenged and begat more lies. Finally, they succeeded not only in burying the truth but in debasing the value of truth as a principle in American presidential politics.

16

Donald Trump's License to Lie

In the spring of 2019, the *Washington Post* fact-checking team reported that President Trump made the 10,000th "false or misleading claim" of his presidency, according to the paper's own ongoing database. It happened 828 days into his term, and the *Post* editorial page called it "a whopper." The editors explained, "The president, whose own administration imposed and then rescinded a systematic policy of wrenching migrant children from their parents, with no protocol in place to reunite them, now poses as a paragon of compassion that ended cruel laws in place before he took office. This is false."

Trump told that bald-faced lie during a live televised interview by phone with his private adviser and public cheerleader, Sean Hannity of Fox News. It was his predecessors, George W. Bush and Barack Obama, he insisted, who had begun the child separation policy. His administration was blameless: "We've been on a humane basis.... [W]e go out and stop the separations." But as the *Post* editors pointed out, Trump had indeed instituted the policy, and in "an act of singular cruelty," he had done so without making any meaningful effort to ensure the eventual return of those children to their parents or to see to their mental, physical, and emotional health. Many of the children were held in cages. As for his predecessors' alleged responsibility, Trump's own Justice Department had proudly called his policy "new" when announcing it. With his policy and the lies he told about it, Trump, not atypically, "fused inhumanity with incompetence," in the *Post* editors' words, while hiding behind a facade of apparent cluelessness about his own administration's actions.[1]

For the first few months of his presidency, Trump had managed to keep his falsehoods down to roughly 5 a day, but by the time of number 10,000, he was averaging an astonishing 63 per day. During just his friendly forty-five-minute phone chat with Hannity, the president set a personal record of one lie for every minute they spoke, including 6 in a period of just ninety seconds. They came so fast that it was nearly impossible for anyone to keep up—even those whose job it was to try.

There was no particular pattern to Trump's dishonesty. One could try to categorize his falsehoods by their settings. For instance, among the first 10,000, the *Post* team found that Trump had made 2,217 of the false statements at rallies, 1,803 on Twitter, and 999 in other contexts. One might also track what they were about. He lied about every topic his predecessors had and added countless categories of his own. He told lies about his health,[2] about sex,[3] about race,[4] about corruption,[5] and about his own election.[6] Owing to his ignorance of both history and public policy, it was often unclear whether he was passing on misinformation, disinformation, bald-faced lies, or some hitherto unseen combination of all three. Whatever their origins, however, Trump's extended musings most often ended up devolving into "bullshit" as he tried to pretend that he knew what he was talking about when he obviously did not. One such incident occurred following a spirited debate among the Democratic presidential candidates in June 2019 over the value of America's controversial (and discontinued) policy of desegregating school districts by busing students, when Trump was asked for his own views. His nonsensical reply clearly demonstrated that he had no understanding or even familiarity with the issue at all. When a reporter asked him about busing, Trump said, "I will tell you in about four weeks, because we're coming out with certain policy that's going to be very interesting and very surprising, I think, to a lot of people." When a second reporter asked a follow-up question, he added that busing was "certainly a primary method of getting people to schools." The first part of this answer was purposeful disinformation: there was no policy in the works, and Trump had to know it. The second part was "bullshit." Later during the same press conference, Trump was asked about Russian president Vladimir Putin's recent assertion that "Western-style liberalism" had been proved a failure and should be considered obsolete. Trump was clueless regarding Putin's use of this extremely common term. He assumed that the Russian president was referring to the western United States and went on to attack the local governments in Los Angeles and San Francisco.[7]

Trump's tendency toward "bullshitting" grew more pronounced throughout the first three years of his presidency, especially as the pressures of impeachment appeared to weigh on his psyche. Leaving aside all the paranoid, conspiratorial attacks and accusations he made against his adversaries in this period, his tweets and rallies and interviews were filled with bizarre ruminations so thoroughly soaked in "bullshit" that it would lead any objective leader to wonder about the president's sanity. For instance, on December 6, 2019, Trump told a group of representatives of "small businesses" that "people are flushing toilets 10 times, 15 times, as opposed to once. They end up using more water. So, EPA is looking at that very strongly, at my suggestion." Twelve days later, basking in the adoration of the members and funders of Turning Point USA—an organization that, appropriately, devotes itself to fighting the largely imaginary phenomenon of "professors who 'discriminate against conservative students, promote anti-American values and advance leftist propaganda in the classroom,'" and whose chief creative officer, Benny Johnson, was fired from BuzzFeed after "41 instances of plagiarism" were discovered in his work—Trump mused: "I never understood wind. You know, I know windmills very much. Gases are spewing into the atmosphere. You know we have a world, right? So the world is tiny compared to the universe. So tremendous, tremendous amount of fumes & everything?"[8]

It may be embarrassing to have so transparent a "bullshit" artist as president, but this is among the most trivial of concerns raised by Trump's pathological dishonesty. It could even be funny, if one could ignore how dangerous it is.[9] For Trump's worst lies have been cruel, threatening to undermine the American democratic republic. For better and for worse, American democracy has managed to survive the forty-four presidents who preceded him. But Trump is something new, and far worse.

As is clear from the previous chapters of this book, the problem of presidential dishonesty certainly did not begin with Trump. Even so, the scope of Donald Trump's dishonesty created a political crisis for the country without any discernible precedent.

One difference between Trump and previous presidential liars lay in the fact that, with the exception of Nixon, his predecessors lied in pursuit of goals consistent with their announced policy objectives and philosophies. Previous presidential liars were fanatics on certain issues, and few of them proved particularly scrupulous about the means undertaken to achieve their goals. But for the most part, they tended to allow the government bureaucracy to function on a relatively honest basis with usually competent, often dedicated experts and public servants, ensuring that policy expertise was respected and public welfare advanced. The administrations of Republican presidents Nixon, Ford, Reagan, and George H.W. Bush were filled with conscientious professionals who took their duties seriously. Their party's addiction to what ex-GOP senator Jeff Flake called "the sugar high of populism, nativism, and demagoguery" had not fully captured its members.[10]

But by 2016, nurtured by countless conspiracy theories, ideological obsessions, the demands of corporate and conservative donors, and the unchecked ambitions of its increasingly cynical leadership—all reinforced by a panoply of carnival-barking cable and talk-radio hosts and inflammatory Internet sites—the Republican Party had come to embrace a radical worldview largely driven by its hostility toward minorities and vulnerable people of all types. So-called Tea Party activists, who helped reshape the party in the wake of Obama's first election, had cast themselves as a movement narrowly focused on limiting government spending. The fact that the movement was largely underwritten by the libertarian billionaire Koch brothers and its network of funders helped to perpetuate this mistaken impression. In reality, Tea Partiers were far more motivated by fear and anger over the belief that "real Americans"—meaning white conservative Christians like themselves—were losing the country to the kind of people who made up Obama's victorious coalition. Their concern, as enunciated by the conservative pundit and early advocate of what would become Trumpism, Pat Buchanan, was the transformation of the United States into a "multicultural, multiethnic, multiracial, multilingual 'universal nation' whose avatar is Barack Obama," and how to stop it.[11]

Trump cannot be credited with creating this phenomenon. He simply stoked the anger and resentment that had been rising among Republicans for decades. Already well to the right of the general public on matters related to fairness and economic inequality, Republicans had, by the time of Trump's presidential campaign, become more extreme than even the ethno-nationalist conservative parties in Western Europe on issues related to its members' white and Christian identities. Max Boot, a neoconservative writer and former adviser to both John McCain and Senator Marco Rubio of Florida, was speaking to this transformation when he announced his departure from the party. Writing in the *Washington Post* in July 2018, he complained that Trump and his supporters had wanted "to transform the GOP into a European-style nationalist party that opposes cuts in entitlement programs, believes in deportation of undocumented immigrants, white identity politics, protectionism and isolationism backed by hyper-macho threats to bomb the living daylights out of anyone who messes with us." He noted that he had first made that complaint just after the 2016 election. But he believed that transformation was now complete.[12]

In early February 2017, just two weeks into Trump's term, the right-wing talk-show host Charles J. Sykes authored a column headlined "Why Nobody Cares the President Is Lying." In it, he acknowledged his own complicity in helping to fashion an ideological echo chamber for conservatives, who were now "conditioned to reject reporting from news sites outside of the conservative media ecosystem." But, after admitting the role he had played by "hammering the mainstream media for its bias and double standards," Sykes said, "The price turned out to be far higher than I imagined. The cumulative effect of the attacks was to delegitimize those outlets and essentially destroy much of the right's immunity to false information."[13] Ambitious Republican politicians opted to flatter their voters' ignorance and cater to their prejudices. But because most Americans do not share the radical ideological commitments that animate the party's political base, much less those of loudmouthed right-wing radio hosts and cable television personalities, Republican candidates had no choice but to dissemble before them as well. They lied to their supporters about reality and to everyone else about themselves. The most successful among them were, naturally, also the most brazen—and none more so than Donald J. Trump.

A key factor in the Republicans' political success during the decades of their radicalization, beginning first with Reagan's presidency and next with Gingrich's speakership, was the stubborn reluctance of almost all mainstream media institutions to adjust to the party's political transformation. This refusal was correctly understood by Republican candidates as a license to lie. For instance, in a September 2015 debate among Republican presidential candidates, pundits roundly declared former Hewlett-Packard CEO Carly Fiorina to be the winner—not because she had advanced the best policies, but because her lies were deemed to have been the most effective. According to Karen Tumulty at the *Washington Post*, "Pretty much everyone agreed that [Carly] Fiorina...had won the evening." Chris Cillizza, also at the *Post*, described her "emotional call to a higher moral authority when talking about Planned Parenthood" as "the most affecting moment of the debate."[14]

But Fiorina's "emotional call" was simply a lie. The moment the pundits found so powerful was when she described a video secretly taped inside a Planned Parenthood clinic and released by antiabortion activists. It showed, Fiorina claimed, "a fully formed fetus on the table, its heart beating, its legs kicking while someone says we have to keep it alive to harvest its brain."[15] In reality, the video contained none of these horrors. But for the journalists handicapping the evening's performance, the category of truthfulness appeared nowhere on their scorecards.[16]

These same media institutions also remained hamstrung by two other related issues: their stubborn reluctance to use the word "lie"—even when lies were the topic of discussion—and their commitment to the now all-but-obsolete journalistic goal of "objectivity," which almost always led them to blame "both sides" when, in fact, only one side was guilty. One can see both tendencies at work in a November 2015 *New York Times* article about the role of truth in the presidential campaign. Reporter Michael Barbaro rattled off a list of the GOP candidates' most brazen, bald-faced lies while using only euphemisms. Carly Fiorina "refused" to back down from a "roundly disputed" story. Ben Carson "appear[ed] to have shaded the facts." And Donald Trump "utter[ed] plenty of refutable claims." And so on. At the same time, Barbaro felt compelled to devote considerable space to arguing that "the tendency to bend facts is bipartisan." His evidence consisted of hidden affairs by presidential candidates Gary Hart (twenty-eight years earlier) and Bill Clinton (twenty-four years earlier), as well as the fact that Hillary Clinton, who was then running for the Democratic Party's nomination, once mistakenly said that four of her grandparents were immigrants, when in fact her paternal grandmother was born shortly after her family arrived in the United States—an error that Clinton quickly corrected on her website.[17]

Yet Barbaro's coverage of the debate was consistent with the prevailing professional ethos of the mainstream media at the time. To fail to criticize Democrats when pointing to dishonesty among Republicans would immediately inspire charges of "liberal bias" from conservatives and others. As the journalist Matthew Yglesias has noted, "The self-consciousness [of] journalists at legacy outlets" leads them to live in fear of "accusations of liberal bias [which] leads them to bend over backward to allow the leading conservative gripes of the day to dominate the news agenda."[18] This is why Republican efforts to "work the refs" remain effective despite having been repeatedly exposed over a period of decades.[19]

With Donald Trump and dishonesty, the question has never been "whether," but "how much." In his ghostwritten memoir, Trump admitted, "I play to people's fantasies....I call it truthful hyperbole." This admission, at least, was true, albeit understated. Trump came to adulthood in the world of the New York City real estate business—a place where self-aggrandizing liars need not feel shame: both lying and self-aggrandizement were not merely accepted but actually admired.[20]

Some of those who knew Trump best tried to send up red flags in advance of his election. Tony Schwartz, the ghostwriter of Trump's first and best-known book, *The Art of the Deal*, was so worried about the prospect of this unstable person being given such a powerful position that he violated a nondisclosure agreement to speak out. Schwartz noted that Trump "had a complete lack of conscience" about lying. And given that the rest of us are, at least to some degree, "constrained by the truth," Trump's lack of concern "gave him a strange advantage."[21]

But few people, even among those who knew him best, were prepared for the scale of Trump's dishonesty once it began to reveal itself. Yes, they knew he regularly stiffed both his workers and his suppliers in his real estate ventures, and that he had created a scam "university" and persuaded poor people to invest in a "get-rich-quick" Ponzi scheme.[22] But more importantly, the entire Trump narrative was a lie. During the campaign, Trump cast himself as a self-made billionaire who could bring his business sense to government. He admitted to having received a loan of about a million dollars from his real estate mogul father as a young man, but insisted that he had repaid it with interest. The rest of his wealth, he claimed, he had earned himself. Thanks to a voluminously documented 2018 *New York Times* investigation, we now know that the alleged $1 million loan was really the equivalent of more than $413 million today, and that much of it "came to Mr. Trump through dubious tax schemes he participated in during the 1990s, including instances of outright fraud." But that investigation barely skimmed the surface of Trump's deception. A second lengthy *Times* investigation discovered that he was likely the single biggest financial loser in America, possibly even the world, in the years between 1985 and 1994, with losses totaling $1.17 billion. The money he earned back derived primarily from a scheme Trump operated by buying certain stocks and then lying to reporters about alleged plans to launch a takeover. Once the rumor was floated and the stock rose in price, he would dump it before it returned to its initial value.[23]

Trump owed his fame as an alleged real estate mastermind almost exclusively to his genius for media manipulation. Failing at one business endeavor after another, he nevertheless succeeded in promulgating the myth of himself as a dealmaking wiz. The truth was that in order to stay afloat, Trump required his daddy's bagmen to secretly bail him out on deal after deal. Once, for instance, Trump Sr. sent someone to buy up $3.5 million in chips to hide his son's losses on a casino investment from the media.[24]

Donald Trump was, as is now widely known, a terrible businessman, a con man, a racist provocateur, a serial adulterer, an admitted sexual predator and credibly accused rapist, an absent parent, and an egomaniacal liar about all of it. He is the kind of person, if any other such examples can be said to exist, who shared a laugh with the vulgar radio host Howard Stern as he agreed that, yes, Trump's then twenty-three-year-old daughter Ivanka was, indeed, "a piece of ass." And the Trump Foundation, facing accusations in New York State of engaging in "a shocking pattern of illegality," had to "dissolve...and give away all its remaining assets under court supervision." The Trumps had allegedly used the charitable foundation to enrich and celebrate themselves with financial donations intended for children's cancer organizations, among other causes. (Some of the funds went to the purchase of a portrait of Trump himself, hung at one of his resorts.)[25]

Judged by virtually any traditional measure of character and decency, Trump has been a failure and a disgrace—a clown at best, and a criminal menace to society at worst. But all this was overshadowed by the fact that in the world of New York City's tabloid media, he was great copy. Trump created a codependent relationship with the gossip writers, tabloid TV hosts, and radio personalities, who loved to broadcast his self-inflating lies and baseless boasts. No junkie has ever needed a fix so openly or frequently as Donald Trump needed to read his name in boldfaced print or hear it on the lips of some radio shock jock. Trump would frequently pretend to be his own publicity assistant, the nonexistent "John Barron," or sometimes "John Miller." The two Johns would call reporters to obsessively share details about the alleged conquests, both sexual and economic, of their super-amazing boss. Everyone knew it was Trump at the other end of the phone line, but no one cared. The bottom line, as one editor put it, was just this: "He sold papers for us—no questions. That's a fact."[26]

Trump's fame was mostly confined to Manhattan-based gossip writers and broadcasters until 2004, when he teamed up with the television producer Mark Burnett to create *The Apprentice*. Jeff

Zucker, an NBC executive who later moved on to CNN in time for the 2016 campaign, gave the program the green light. Unlike Trump's real estate deals, his TV show was genuinely profitable. Absent *The Apprentice*, he would likely have disappeared into the dustbin of best-forgotten 1980s history with the likes of Milli Vanilli and Mr. T. Instead, he became a national sensation.

Once again, Trump's unique brand of braggadocio and "bullshit" proved irresistible to the tabloids—he was now the king of the relatively new and perfectly misnamed phenomenon of "reality TV." "The show was built as a virtually nonstop advertisement for the Trump empire and lifestyle," according to a 2016 Trump biography. Naturally, it was a lie from start to finish. *The Apprentice* was filmed in his offices in Trump Tower, but, as one of the show's producers told a reporter from the *New Yorker*, "We walked through the offices and saw chipped furniture. We saw a crumbling empire at every turn. Our job was to make it seem otherwise." According to a supervising editor on the show, the producers' "first priority on every episode…was to reverse-engineer the show to make it look like his judgment had some basis in reality." Writing for *CineMontage*, a journal published by the Motion Pictures Editors Guild, he added, "Sometimes it would be very hard to do."[27]

The Apprentice earned boffo ratings, at least initially, but the network rejected Trump's pitch for another reality show that would have pitted Caucasians against African Americans. Zucker was happy to go along with a second Trump show called *Celebrity Apprentice*, however, which featured its host jostling with Z-list celebrity has-beens of the kind usually relegated to car dealership openings and bar mitzvah appearances. It succeeded only in further expanding the boundaries of vulgarity and stupidity on American network television, along with its host's increasingly fantastic reputation.[28]

Trump entered the presidential race in 2015 at a moment when the always-tenuous line between "entertainment" and politics was rapidly and purposely being erased. And it was around this time that Jeff Zucker, a fan of televised sports and the profits they earned, landed the top job at CNN. "The idea that politics is sport is undeniable, and we understood that and approached it that way," he told a reporter. And just as sports broadcasters hire hosts who can make boring games sound interesting, and keep the audience entertained regardless of their level of expertise, so, too, Zucker chose pundits with no discernible qualifications whatsoever, save their willingness to sing the praises of Donald Trump. Zucker hired Jeffrey Lord, a journeyman conservative author who repeatedly compared Trump to Martin Luther King Jr., and Kayleigh McEnany, an attractive young law student who consistently argued that Trump "doesn't lie," but that instead, "the press lies." (McEnany was rewarded for these arguments with an appointment in 2017 as the Republican National Committee spokesperson, and, two years later, for the same position in Trump's 2020 reelection campaign.) According to Zucker's preferred metric, these hires were more than justified. "Everybody says, 'Oh, I can't believe you have Jeffrey Lord or Kayleigh McEnany,'" he said. "But you know what? They know who Jeffrey Lord and Kayleigh McEnany are"—as if this somehow justified their lies and the lunatic conspiracy theories they passed along to viewers. Zucker even proved willing to hire Trump's former campaign manager, Corey Lewandowski, in June 2016, not long after an incident in which Lewandowski was charged with misdemeanor battery following his physical attack against a female reporter whose question he did not like. (The charges were later dropped, though not before Lewandowski was accused by another Trump supporter of sexual assault.) Lewandowski had lost an internal power struggle within the Trump campaign, and with it his job. Such a hire would not normally be considered unusual in the incestuous world of cable TV commentary, but in this case, Lewandowski had signed a nondisclosure agreement that contained a nondisparagement clause before leaving the campaign. That meant he was legally enjoined from saying anything that might reflect badly on Trump—even if it was truthful.

Zucker did not care. Truth was not the metric: ratings were. (In September 2019, Lewandowski testified before the House Judiciary Committee investigating impeachment and admitted, "I have no obligation to be honest to the media because they're just as dishonest as anybody else." He was booked on CNN that same night.)[29]

Owing to the strong ratings that Trump-themed programming earned the network during the election season, Zucker constantly pressured his staff to keep the focus on his campaign. CNN was happy to broadcast the candidate's lies unmediated and uninterrupted, whether they were offered on the phone, in live interviews, or during rallies. According to the nonpartisan fact-checking site PolitiFact, which investigated 158 statements Trump had made on the campaign trail before June 2016, 78 percent of those statements were false, mostly false, or "pants on fire." Only about 3 percent of the statements it investigated were judged to be entirely true. The other 19 percent were half-true or mostly true.[30]

Trump did not even need to get out of bed to have his lies broadcast across the nation. The cable shows and the TV network Sunday shows were more than happy to air even his phone calls, giving him the equivalent of billions of dollars' worth of free airtime. And during the lead-up to a campaign rally, CNN would promote the event with live footage of an empty lectern and captions on the screen that read: "DONALD TRUMP EXPECTED TO SPEAK ANY MINUTE." No other candidate—Republican or Democrat—was treated with anything remotely like this degree of attention and pretend-news value. According to the calculations of data scientist Kalev Leetaru, Donald Trump was mentioned on CNN almost eight times more than any other Republican candidate. Sam Nunberg, a Trump strategist at the time, later credited CNN as a campaign "asset." The network's willingness to allow Trump to fulfill his goal to "saturate the airwaves," he noted, increased his credibility, especially early in the campaign, at a time when Rupert Murdoch and Roger Ailes were still trying to find a way to put the kibosh on his candidacy over at Fox.[31]

CNN enjoyed sky-high ratings and profits during this period. The other cable stations lusted after these Trump-driven ratings, and soon the broadcast networks did, too. Asked about his network's wall-to-wall Trump coverage, CBS chief executive Les Moonves—who, like Trump, has been credibly accused of being a serial sexual predator—replied, "The money's rolling in and this is fun." Trump's campaign "may not be good for America," Moonves allowed, "but it's damn good for CBS."[32]

The mainstream media's simultaneous indulgence and exploitation of Trump's lies were just one part of what made his presidency possible. Trump also enjoyed the support of a network of what Vox's Yglesias termed "organized, systematic" media shills who "abjure[d] anything resembling journalism in favor of propaganda." Among the most devious and devoted of these enablers was David Pecker, publisher of the supermarket tabloid *National Enquirer*. Hounded by prosecutors during Trump's presidency, Pecker eventually admitted to having conducted an illegal "catch-and-kill" operation at the *Enquirer* to benefit Trump, buying up the exclusive rights to stories from people with damaging information about Trump and then refusing to publish them. The most famous of these was its suppression of the story of Trump's affair with *Playboy* model Karen McDougal, "so as to prevent it from influencing the election." The *Enquirer* also paid a doorman who worked for Trump Tower for a story about a woman claiming to have given birth to Donald Trump's child, a daughter. Pecker then allegedly "ordered the...reporters to stop investigating" the matter. Meanwhile, together with its sister publication, *The Globe*, Pecker's *National Enquirer* ran no fewer than thirty-five anti–Hillary Clinton cover stories during the run-up to the election. The absurd headlines ranged from "Hillary: Six Months to Live!" to "Hillary Hitman Tells All."[33]

At the even more distant edges of respectability was the racist, misogynist, and occasionally anti-Semitic Breitbart News Network, which at the time was still run by the man who would become

Trump's third and final campaign chair, Steve Bannon. According to Andrew Anglin, founder of the neo-Nazi website the Daily Stormer, Breitbart was not so different from his own site: "The articles that they publish about blacks in America and about Muslims in Europe, it's basically stuff that you would read on the Daily Stormer."[34] And yet, with ninety-four million unique visitors, Breitbart was the third most shared site on Facebook during the election, just after the *New York Times* and CNN.[35]

These investments in Trump's candidacy, by Zucker, Pecker, Bannon, and others, were reinforced by an avalanche of fantastic lies that paid Trump trolls—including those operating from Russia and other east and central European nations—launched on social media platforms. Among the false stories promoted to millions of Facebook and Twitter users in the final weeks of the election were made-up tales of the allegedly mysterious murders of Clinton's foes, along with the almost comically crazy allegation that the Democratic nominee for president and former First Lady, senator, and secretary of state was actually running a child pornography site from inside a Washington, DC, pizza parlor. That tale inspired one deranged fellow to drive from North Carolina to Washington with a loaded weapon and start shooting at the restaurant, and another individual, this one from California, to set the place on fire. Only slightly less alarmingly, a December 2016 YouGov poll found that nearly half of Trump's voters believed this lunatic lie.[36]

On Facebook, such wholly incredible pro-Trump stories outperformed actual news from genuine media outlets during the final three months of the 2016 election, earning more clicks and shares. Among the most frequently shared lies was a story alleging that Hillary Clinton sold guns to ISIS, and another announcing Pope Francis's (fictional) endorsement of Trump. On a single day, one group of Russian operatives masquerading as concerned American citizens posted a staggering eighteen thousand pro-Trump tweets. According to Twitter's own data, between September 1 and November 15,

2016, there were at least fifty thousand automated accounts tied to Russia working on Trump's behalf. And Twitter said this figure was almost certainly understated, given its own inability to trace the origins of fully 12 percent of its accounts.[37]

In November 2017, five scholars working for a research lab at Microsoft examined the company's Internet search data and released a study titled "Geographic and Temporal Trends in Fake News Consumption During the 2016 US Presidential Election." They had found that "social media was the primary outlet for the circulation of fake news stories," and that the consumption of the information on these sites "strongly correlated" with the users' voting patterns. Another study, by scholars at the Berkman-Klein Center for Internet and Society at Harvard University, was based on over 1.25 million news articles published online during the year and a half before election day. It found that the "right-wing media network anchored around Breitbart…not only successfully set the agenda for the conservative media sphere, but also strongly influenced the broader media agenda, in particular coverage of Hillary Clinton." Its authors posited that the political media was not subject to a "left-right division, but rather a division between the right and the rest of the media ecosystem." Moreover, "the right wing of the media ecosystem behaves precisely as the echo chamber models predict—exhibiting high insularity, susceptibility to information cascades, rumor and conspiracy theory and drift to more extreme versions of itself." The net result was "a network of mutually-reinforcing hyper-partisan sites" in which "decontextualized truths, repeated falsehoods, and leaps of logic create a fundamentally misleading view of the world."[38]

The pro-Trump conspiracy theory website Infowars demonstrated just how eager Trump was to flatter the most extremist—and irresponsible—voices to be found almost anywhere in the US media. Alex Jones, who runs Infowars, famously insisted that the December 2012 Sandy Hook Elementary School shooting, in which twenty young children and six adult staff members were murdered, had been faked—and he encouraged his followers to harass the bereaved parents who lost their children. At various times he also warned his ten million or so viewers and listeners that chemicals were being put into water to turn frogs gay; that the Federal Emergency Management Agency (FEMA) was planning to force Americans into concentration camps; and that Hillary Clinton—who, like Barack Obama, he said was a literal "demon"—was doing her pizza-pedophilia thing. Jones was quick to sidestep responsibility for his lunatic ravings: when faced with a defamation lawsuit by Sandy Hook parents in 2019, he blamed his statements on what he termed "a form of psychosis." Perhaps. But none of this apparently bothered Donald Trump at the time. Appearing on Infowars in December 2015, just a few months after entering the presidential race, Trump congratulated Jones on his "amazing" reputation and promised, "I will not let you down." Trump even called to thank Jones on election night (according to Jones). Jones described his influence over the candidate thusly: "I put out a video…a message to Trump, and then two days later he lays out the case. It's like sending up the Bat Signal." The popular right-wing Internet aggregator Matt Drudge would often send his millions of readers to Infowars as well, thereby injecting Jones's demented malevolence into the mainstream of US politics. Drudge was particularly enthusiastic about a story claiming that Hillary Clinton's campaign chief, John Podesta, had participated in a secret Satanist dinner, during which he drank "bodily fluids." The article went viral on Twitter, generating over four hundred thousand tweets. The whole thing had started with an email to Podesta that turned up on WikiLeaks inviting him to dinner. The original email was from the performance artist Marina Abramovic, and was forwarded to Podesta from his art-collector (and lobbyist) brother, Tony Podesta. John Podesta probably did not even attend, and no bodily fluids were consumed or Satanic rituals enacted. Nevertheless, many of the tweets claimed that the email "prove[d] a secret link between the Clinton campaign and Satan worship," according to a *Washington Post* reporter, who apparently felt it necessary to add, "which, just to be clear right here, it does not."[39]

Although Fox News had inspired any number of imitators and challengers by the time of the 2016 campaign, the kings of the conservative media jungle remained Rupert Murdoch and Roger Ailes. Long before Trump's candidacy took off, Fox ruled the Republican Party the way England and France once ruled their colonies. The network promoted out-of-office Republican politicians and paid them off in accordance with lucrative (and exclusive) contracts. The network even built some of their favorites—including Sarah Palin—their own television studios in their homes, so as not to saddle them with the inconvenience of having to leave the house in order to pontificate on camera. Fox soon grew so influential with its ever-more-misinformed audience that, according to a detailed study published by the National Bureau of Economic Research, its support of a candidate could mean the difference between winning and losing the presidency. The share of the total vote count the authors could credit exclusively to a voter getting his or her information from Fox rose from an extremely modest 0.46 percent in 2000 to a 3.59-point boost in 2004, and then 6.34 points in 2008—more than enough to change the outcome in a close election.[40] One can safely conclude that the share continued to rise after that, given Fox's explosive growth in viewership. Murdoch and Ailes were truly powers of the party, and no one thought to cross them until Trump came along.

Murdoch and Ailes initially shared the belief of most Republican Party politicians and funders that Trump's candidacy could turn off voters and sink the party's hopes in 2016. Trump also represented the first genuine threat to Fox's right-wing hegemony since its founding twenty years earlier. Fox therefore had reason to seek to stop the Trump candidacy in its tracks, and these efforts appeared to come to a head in the party's first presidential debate in the summer of 2015.

In her questioning, Fox host Megyn Kelly confronted Trump about his references to women in the past as "fat pigs, dogs, slobs, and disgusting animals." But Trump would not cave, calling the question "ridiculous" and "off-base." The next night, on CNN, Trump said, "You could see there was blood coming out of her eyes. Blood coming out of her wherever." And the day after that, he tweeted the same comment. These comments amazed and revolted many people, especially those who interpreted Trump to be talking about menstruation. But his supporters did not care.[41]

At the same time, Murdoch and Ailes could not help but notice the ratings boost that Trump-centric programming was causing over at CNN. Worse still, Fox was losing a significant part of its online audience as Trump supporters flocked to Steve Bannon's Breitbart. Breitbart's racist, anti-immigrant, anti-Semitic coverage was proving far more popular with Trump supporters than the Murdoch empire's less inflammatory, albeit hardly less obvious, political biases. Eventually, Murdoch threw in the towel and tweeted an edict to the troops, saying that the GOP "would be mad not to unify" behind Trump. This midcourse correction did wonders for Fox's profits, producing the network's best ratings ever. As one "on-air personality" told *Politico*, "the Trump shit rates through the roof."

And Trump was the gift that kept on giving. Over time, Fox News and its website would double their ratings from the pre-Trump period, with the website easily besting the online presences of the *New York Times* and the *Washington Post*. It's no wonder, then, that Fox did Trump the courtesy of killing a story that one of its reporters uncovered: Trump's secret payoff to the porn actress Stormy Daniels shortly before the 2016 election. "Good reporting, kiddo," the reporter, Diana Falzone, was told. "But Rupert wants Donald Trump to win. So just let it go." The story was dropped, the reporter was demoted, and Trump won the election. And so began the most bizarre era of presidential dishonesty in the nation's 240-year history.[42]

"What You're Seeing and What You're Reading Is Not What's Happening"

True to form, Trump's first instinct after winning the 2016 election was to lie about it. "In addition to winning the Electoral College in a landslide," he tweeted, "I won the popular vote if you deduct the millions of people who voted illegally." This was nonsense. When the returns from the popular vote were tallied, Clinton had beaten Trump by over three million votes. His 46 percent share of the overall vote was lower even than that of recent losers, including Gerald Ford (1976), Al Gore (2000), John Kerry (2004), and Mitt Romney (2012). And yet this lie quickly became conventional wisdom in the pro-Trump media. A July 2017 Morning Consult / Politico poll found that 47 percent of Republicans believed that Trump had won the popular vote, just 5 percent fewer than those who knew the truth.[1]

Trump's lie proved to be a brilliant political stroke, as it addressed three problems simultaneously. First, for those who believed whatever he said, it eliminated any uncertainty about the legitimacy of his victory. Second, it advanced his false argument that undocumented immigrants were undermining America and doing so at the behest of media elites and Democrats. And third, it provided the foundation for future lies. When reporters finally asked Trump to support his claim with evidence, the president-elect reassured them that "the very famous golfer Bernhard Langer" was waiting to vote in Florida on election day, and was refused, but some people "who did not look as if they should be allowed to vote" were allowed to do so. In fact, Langer said he had never even spoken to Trump. The president-elect had heard some story literally sixth-hand and then passed it on to the rest of the country in the hope of undermining the nation's faith in its democratic procedures. When a *New York Times* reporter noted that no evidence could be found to support Trump's ludicrous claim, the new leader of the free world responded by retweeting a sixteen-year-old fan, who had asked, "What PROOF do u have DonaldTrump did not suffer from millions of FRAUD votes? Journalist? Do your job!"[2]

When Trump repeated his nonsensical claim about the allegedly illegal votes in a private, off-the-record meeting with congressional leaders shortly after his inauguration, their reports to the press of what he said inspired something of an existential crisis within the mainstream media. The president was obviously lying, but almost no publication was ready to say so in black and white. Among daily newspapers, as tallied by the *Atlantic*'s Adrienne LaFrance, only the *New York Times* crossed the line and employed the word "lie" in its headline. The rest ranged from: "Trump Wrongly Blames..." (AP) to "Trump Falsely Tells..." (*Chicago Tribune*), "Trump Still Pushing Unconfirmed Claims..." (*New York Daily News*), "Trump Repeats Unsupported Claim" (*Wall Street Journal*), and "Without Evidence, Trump Tells..." (*Washington Post*). At least two allegedly neutral sources, CNN and *The Hill*, also repeated Trump's lie without any qualification: "Trump Believes Fraud

Cost Him Popular Vote" (CNN), and "Trump Continues to Insist Voter Fraud Robbed Him of Popular Vote" (*The Hill*).[3] The problem with so many of these headlines was that they took no position on whether Trump's boast was true or not. The CNN and *Hill* headlines positively encouraged the lie. These news organizations apparently felt themselves helpless in the face of a phenomenon they had never faced before: a president who was an unapologetic, pathological liar and did not care who knew it.[4]

And yet the word "lie" remained off the table for most media institutions. As *New York Times* executive editor Dean Baquet would argue, "If you get loose with the word lie, you're going to look pretty scurrilous. Right? It's going to be in every story." Similarly, *Washington Post* executive editor Martin Baron, following in the footsteps of Ben Bradlee, refused during the election campaign to allow his news staff to call the would-be president a liar. "I think you have to actually have documentation, proof, that whoever you're saying lied actually knew that what he or she was saying was in fact false," Baron said. The then *Wall Street Journal* editor, Gerard Baker, concurred. Though he admitted in an interview at the Aspen Ideas Festival in 2017 that he thought "the president probably lies a lot," he was only interested, as editor, in "what my reporters can report as facts." Faced with complaints about this policy from his staff, Baker later added a clarification: "If we are to use the term 'lie' in our reporting, then we have to be confident about the subject's state of knowledge and his moral intent." Other journalists also worried about alienating Trump voters by telling the truth about his lies. "Every time he lies you have to point out it's a lie, and there's a part of this country that hears that as an attack," wrote *New York Times* media columnist Jim Rutenberg. "That is a serious problem." And so Trump's lies, the scale of which had no precedent in American political history, were treated like politics-as-usual. Although some opinion writers felt free to call the president a "liar," in news coverage readers were told that Trump appeared to "backpedal," or that he had made statements that were "belied by the facts" or "proved to be inaccurate." When Trump spoke in a "misleading" fashion, making statements whose "veracity" had already been "undermined," this was often attributed to his "rhetorical bluster," particularly when he found himself walking a "rhetorical tightrope" owing to his "overboard boasts"—and the like.[5]

Trump's lies about his inauguration clarified that the responsibilities of the office would do nothing to moderate his dishonesty. And the response to them appeared only to encourage his brazenness. Following the shockingly sparsely attended event on the morning of January 20, 2017, Trump demanded that his hapless press secretary, Sean Spicer, call in members of the White House press corps and berate them for their "deliberately false reporting" about the size of the crowd. They had just seen, Spicer told them, "the largest audience to ever witness an inauguration, period, both in person and around the globe." The following day, Trump made an impromptu appearance at CIA headquarters in Langley, Virginia, where he spoke in front of what for many in the agency was its most sacred setting, a wall with carved stars marking the lives of those agents killed in its service. Accompanied by an audience of staffers he brought along to stand in front of the CIA officers and cheer for him, Trump continued his obsessive lying about the previous day's crowd. "It looked like a million, a million and a half people," he said, more than quadrupling actual estimates. According to the National Park Service, the number of people in the crowd was not even a quarter of the number who had attended Obama's first inauguration eight years previously—there were far fewer in attendance, even, than those marching against Trump on the Washington Mall at the very moment he was speaking. Deploying his favorite technique—one familiar to anyone who has read George Orwell—Trump then accused those who had accurately identified his lies of lying themselves. "It's a lie," Trump said of the press reports that had given accurate estimates. "We caught [the media]. We caught them in a beauty." He then added that journalists were "among the most dishonest human beings on earth."[6]

Together with a never-ending barrage of lies and baseless conspiracy theories in the weeks and months that followed, Trump's ceaseless attacks on the news media would prove to be a central theme of his presidency. "Stick with us. Don't believe the crap you see from these people, the fake news," he shouted at one political rally. "What you're seeing and what you're reading is not what's happening." To help justify her boss's incessant lies, Counselor to the President Kellyanne Conway invented the nonsensical notion of "alternative facts." Asked during a television interview to justify this obviously fanciful term, her response was pure Michael Corleone: "Look," she said. "You got 14 percent approval rating in the media that you've earned. You want to push back against us?" Here was the essence of Trump's media strategy. He even admitted as much to CBS News' Lesley Stahl, saying, "You know why I do it? I do it to discredit you all and demean you all so when you write negative stories about me no one will believe you."[7]

In his ceaseless complaints about "fake news," Trump was often careful to carve out an exception for his friends at Fox, and this was no wonder. The network regularly broadcast lies that, more often than not, were identical to the ones Trump happened to be telling—though who got there first was often unclear. Staffers shuttled between jobs at the network and at the White House the way some people change summer and winter residences. Until he lost his job as White House deputy chief of staff for communications in March 2019, Bill Shine was still getting regular payments on his $15.4 million severance deal from Fox, where he was fired in May 2017 for his apparent role in enabling Roger Ailes's regime of sexual terrorism toward his female underlings to take place. While working in the White House, however, Shine coordinated Trump's media coverage with the staff members he had hired in both places.[8]

No matter who was running things in either place, Fox employees had become accustomed to taking direct orders from Trump administration staff regarding the content and timing of their stories, and even their tweets. Fox staffers sometimes gave the administration scripts of their shows and talking points for their interviews in advance, waiting for approval before proceeding.[9] It was all one big, unhappy family. In addition to Shine, other former Fox personalities given top-level posts in Trump's government included:

- John Bolton, who served as Trump's third national security adviser until he was unceremoniously fired
- Heather Nauert, who served as State Department spokesperson, and was then appointed to be Trump's UN permanent representative, but withdrew in a "personal decision," according to Secretary of State Pompeo, before actually assuming the post
- Morgan Ortagus, who replaced Nauert as State Department spokesperson
- Lea Gabrielle, appointed the State Department's "special envoy and coordinator of the Global Engagement Center"
- Mercedes Schlapp, White House director of strategic communications (who later joined Trump's reelection staff)
- K. T. McFarland, deputy national security adviser (briefly)
- Anthony Scaramucci, White House director of communications (incredibly briefly)
- Tony Sayegh, assistant secretary for public affairs, Treasury Department

Among the least defensible of these hires was that of Monica Crowley as the spokesperson for the Department of the Treasury. During the Obama presidency, she had been an enthusiastic "birther" who went so far as to claim that President Obama's "loyalties [were] to Islam" and that he took his orders from terrorists. Crowley had been expected to be appointed spokesperson for the State Department when it was discovered that her doctoral dissertation at Columbia University contained instances of plagiarism. Crowley insisted the charges against her were part of a "despicable, straight-up political hit job" and had been "debunked." This was a lie. After she was appointed to the Treasury position, Columbia University announced that it had found "32 revised passages that contained plagiarism or other citation deficiencies that required correction" in her doctoral thesis. It was a habit, according to the research of others, that Crowley allegedly had consistently engaged in throughout her career.[10] The train, meanwhile, traveled in both directions. Ex–White House aides Hope Hicks, Sarah Sanders, and Sebastian Gorka all landed contracts at Fox after having earned reputations for the kind of shameless dishonesty and slavish devotion to Trump required in both workplaces.

The porousness between Fox and the White House was only one aspect of the cozy relationship between the two institutions. Early in Trump's presidency, it became clear that the network was functioning as a Soviet-style propaganda channel for the Trump administration, though again, it was sometimes unclear who was in charge, as its pundits often gave the president advice and instruction, both on the air and in private. Trump's first tweet on his first morning as president, sent out the morning after he woke up in the White House on January 21, 2017, was a "thank you" to the network for his "GREAT reviews." It was one of 750 times in the next thirty-two months that he would beat the drum for the network, one of its shows, or one of its personalities on Twitter.[11] Trump sometimes even referred to the network in the first-person plural, speaking of "we" when critiquing its programming. He also personally intervened in Fox's personnel decisions. In March 2019, when Jeanine Pirro, a Trump supporter and frequent speaker at Republican fundraising events, was temporarily taken off the air following an advertiser boycott—inspired by her anti-Muslim criticism of Democratic congresswoman Ilhan Omar of Minnesota—"Trump called Rupert, and Rupert put pressure on the executives," a source told *Vanity Fair*. As a result, Pirro's job was saved.[12]

Fox News has never been an actual "news" channel. Since it first appeared in 1996, it has acted simultaneously as the Republican Party's propaganda outlet and its ideological enforcer. Fox has not really turned into "state television," as is often claimed, but has become a much stranger and more complicated phenomenon. Pre-Trump, the party was answerable to Fox, as often as not, rather than the other way around. With Trump in the White House and Roger Ailes no longer at the helm of Fox, the network morphed into a phenomenon for which political scientists and communications scholars have yet to find a name. Once it got behind Donald Trump, it was relentless, influential, and almost aggressively uninterested in truth. As Ailes biographer Gabriel Sherman observed on NPR's *Fresh Air*, the Trump presidency represented "the logical conclusion of entertainment and right-wing media taking over the Republican Party." Whatever one called it, it was effective. In an October 2019 Public Religion Research Institute survey, fully 55 percent of Republicans who relied on Fox News as their primary news source told pollsters that there was literally nothing the president could do that could cause them to abandon him politically. Just 29 percent of Republicans who chose other primary sources of news felt the same way.[13]

Trump's public schedule usually featured long blocks of time that the White House called "Executive Time," which journalists soon came to understand meant that Trump was tweeting while watching Fox News. This practice was particularly easy to identify in the morning hours during broadcasts of the network's ridiculous chitchat program *Fox & Friends*. Trump had been making regular appearances on the show since 2011. But after taking office, he began to call so often, and stay on the phone so long, that its hosts sometimes felt compelled to suggest that they hang up already, what with his being president and all. Researcher Matthew Gertz, who spent months studying the Trump-Fox feedback loop, found that many of Trump's tweets aligned almost perfectly with the nutty observations expressed by the "friends": they appeared in his feed just moments after they were broadcast on Fox, often without context, cohesion, or any remote connection to reality. Asked to defend them, the White House press office was forced, on occasion, to point reporters to the transcript of the show.[14] Approximately 15 percent of the eleven thousand tweets Trump sent out between January 21, 2017, and October 15, 2019, according to a *New York Times* analysis, "seemed to come directly from Fox News and other conservative media outlets."[15]

But as bizarre as Trump's reliance on the *Fox & Friends* knuckleheads may have been, it did not come close to the weirdness evident in his mind-meld with Sean Hannity, Fox's most popular host. Hannity shared Trump's attraction to conspiracy theories long before the latter entered politics. In November 2017, Vox reporter Alvin Chang compared the conspiracies aired on Hannity's show to over a thousand conspiracy postings on the news aggregation and discussion site Reddit. During the two-year period in question, November 2015 to October 2017, Chang found a remarkable level of coincidence between Hannity's discussion topics and lunatic Hillary Clinton–related conspiracy theories that appeared to have been lifted directly from right-wing Reddit forums (though undoubtedly a feedback loop existed between Hannity and many forum participants). It should surprise no one that Chang also unearthed countless examples of Trump tweeting out these same crazy stories within minutes of Hannity's broadcasts.[16]

Just before the 2018 midterm elections, the Trump campaign website announced that Hannity would be appearing onstage with Trump at a preelection rally. Hannity immediately sent out a tweet refuting the announcement: "I will not be on the stage campaigning with the president," he said. It was Fox's stated policy not to allow its commentators to show such open partisanship, and of course Hannity pretended to be an independent voice on his program. But hours later, Hannity was up there onstage with the president, conclusively demonstrating that any protestations he might have made to defend his—and Fox's—journalistic independence were nonsense. (In fact, Fox hosts regularly appeared at political and fundraising events for Republican candidates. A December 2019 *Washington Post* article noted, among the many other examples, that "[Jeanine] Pirro, the host of the weekly Fox News program 'Justice With Judge Jeanine,' appeared at an event hosted by the Volusia County Republican Party in Daytona Beach, Fla., last month [November 2019]. The keynote speaker at the gathering was Dan Bongino, a regular Fox contributor and sometime fill-in host for Hannity. Another Fox contributor, Tomi Lahren, keynoted the event in 2018. The next week, Pirro appeared at a fundraiser staged by the Seminole County Republican Party outside Orlando." The article also noted that the network said it did not "condone" such appearances, something its spokespeople said whenever asked about its hosts' "apparently routine" practice— the *Post*'s words—of flouting its own alleged regulations.)[17]

When Trump visited the Mexican border during the government shutdown over funding for his proposed border fence in January 2019, he gave the forty-second Fox interview of his presidency (he'd given just nine interviews to all the other networks combined). Per usual, Hannity posed questions to the president that merely repeated his own deceitful arguments. When, for instance, Trump claimed that the border wall would shut down the "pipeline for vast quantities of illegal drugs, including meth, heroin, cocaine, and fentanyl," Hannity responded, "There is no barrier. All those drugs get in if these guys can't cover every inch of, you know, the 2,000 miles." In fact, the vast majority of illegal drugs smuggled into the United States came through ports of entry. A border wall therefore would have been irrelevant to the problem. The very day of this publicity stunt, customs officials seized $1.7 million worth of fentanyl at the Port of Philadelphia, en route from China.[18]

In his seminal 1985 work, *Amusing Ourselves to Death: Public Discourse in the Age of Show Business*, media scholar Neil Postman warned that the politicians who entertain us can be just as dangerous as the ones who lie. Trump, as we have seen, redefined the limits of presidential behavior on both fronts, and in doing so he successfully enlisted the media in his web of mendacity. Trump had a genius for news generation—and more often than not, he was able to define its terms. Parsing out truth and falsehood in any given Trump story felt both tiresome and quarrelsome to many journalists who were themselves eager to entertain their readers and audiences. Moreover, many journalists did not want to offend the Trump supporters in their audience, who often did not care if the president was lying, just so long as they liked the lies. And most journalists retained what had traditionally been a strong sense of respect for the office Trump occupied. Yet they could not resist covering his antics, no matter how brazenly he lied about them. Rarely did mainstream media journalists challenge the president's lies on those rare occasions when he agreed to be interviewed by them. Instead, the accepted practice was to approach his lies and slanders as the kind of spectacle one would expect to see on a trashy TV program that happened to feature dishonest politicians. On December 11, 2018, during his feud with Democrats over the proposed border fencing, Trump purposely set up a phony clash on live television by inviting Democratic Speaker of the House Nancy Pelosi and Senate Minority Leader Charles Schumer to discuss the matter in the White House, and then staging a melodramatic walkout just three minutes in. CNN's Chris Cillizza analyzed it thusly: "The reality TV president just broadcast one hell of an episode."[19]

It is a truism that while technology, especially communications technology, may change rapidly over time, people rarely do. During the 1970s—that is, in the days when New York City tabloids set the tone for political and entertainment coverage—Trump rose to fame by enticing gossip columnists to publish his lies. Forty years later, he was able to drive coverage with social media all by himself, most frequently on Twitter, which provided him with a medium through which to spread his lies without mediation. With somewhere in the vicinity of sixty million Twitter followers—there is no reliable way to measure these numbers—Trump enjoyed direct access to many more people than any single news organization. Even so, these same organizations frequently passed along his Twitter rants without commentary or correction on their own Twitter feeds, thereby both amplifying the falsehoods they contained and adding to their apparent credibility. A 2019 study by Media Matters for America looked at the Twitter feeds of thirty-two major media outlets and found that they repeated Trump's false claims an average of nineteen times per day.[20] For most social media users, the media outlets' tweets, or the accompanying headlines, are all they will ever see. In another survey, this one conducted by four scholars associated with Columbia University and the French National Institute, as many as 60 percent of those questioned admitted that they paid attention only to news headlines, rather than to the content of the articles. The "click-through" rate on Twitter is less than 10 percent, meaning not even a tenth of people read the article connected to any given tweet that they see. Trump's tweets, and the headlines they produced, were therefore much more politically potent than the substance journalists reported on them, even if, in the fine print, journalists did ultimately explain that what he had said happened to be contradicted by all the known facts.[21]

On the topic of his incessant lying, Trump successfully wore down most of the media assigned to cover him. Daniel Dale, hired by CNN from the *Toronto Star* to continue his relentless focus on Trump's falsehoods, likened his task to "fact-checking one of those talking dolls programmed to say the same phrases for eternity, except if none of those phrases were true." He estimated that "Trump regularly makes 20 to 30 false claims in his rally speeches. But if you watched a network news segment, read an Associated Press article or glanced at the front page of the newspaper in the city that hosted him, you'd typically have no idea that he was so wholly inaccurate." This is Trump's greatest victory. "If a car salesman told you 36 untrue things in 75 minutes, that would probably be the first thing you told your friends about your trip to the dealership," Dale noted. But Trump's lies have become normalized by the mainstream media, in part because its members have themselves become accustomed to the onslaught, and hence do not even bother to mention it. Faced with the daunting task of slogging through lie after lie, most reporters and their editors have simply given up and given in. What's more, Dale added in an October 2019 Twitter exchange, these lies did double duty for Trump politically. "Trump starts the cycle by lying about trivial stuff, but some of his supporters end up seeing the cycle primarily as evidence of media pettiness/bias, fueled by such accusations from his professional allies. So the lie ends up a 'win' with his base even if widely debunked."[22]

Trump launched an assault on honest, accountability-minded journalism at a moment when the profession was already facing a number of existential challenges. Newspapers provide the lion's share of reliable reporting in America, especially when it comes to conducting investigative journalism matters that government and other powerful institutions prefer to keep hidden. But with just a few exceptions, the only newspapers likely to survive the digital destruction of their centuries-old business model are those owned by families or individuals willing to lose money on them. This exclusive club would include the *New York Times*, owned by the Sulzberger family for over a century; the *Washington Post*, purchased by one of the world's wealthiest men, Jeff Bezos, in 2013; the *Los Angeles Times*, purchased by billionaire physician Patrick Soon-Shiong in 2018; and Rupert Murdoch's *Wall Street Journal*, which he purchased from the Bancroft family in 2007—but not many others.

Between 2004 and 2018, some 1,800 American newspapers were forced to shut down. And most that have survived so far have done so as shadows of their former selves. Back in 2007, 85 percent of US newspapers reported making cuts in their editorial staffs, eliminating a total of 3,000 jobs and continuing a steady trend that had begun years earlier. In retrospect, these were halcyon days. Over the next decade, from 2008 to 2018, America's newspapers lost almost half of their collective editorial staffs, and the devastating trend would only accelerate from there. Digital behemoths Facebook and Google gobbled up almost all the advertisements that newspapers had historically relied upon to support the costs of reporting. Craigslist, meanwhile, pirated away what had been the financially crucial business of classified advertising in local newspapers.[23] News-oriented magazines experienced a similar, though slightly slower, contraction, also as a result of plummeting print advertising. And with the demands of video, podcasting, and other audience-attracting gimmicks, overworked journalists were increasingly under pressure to do more with less. The first cuts that understaffed newsrooms made, understandably, were the kinds of stories the First Amendment was written to protect: expensive, time-consuming investigative reporting that actually serves democracy by holding powerful people and institutions accountable.

Taken together, Trump's genius for distraction, self-pity, and entertaining idiocy, expressed on Twitter, at rallies, and in televised conversations with his "friends" and cronies at Fox, created a constant sense of chaos that exhausted the journalists charged with covering White House news. Steve Bannon has contended, convincingly, that Trump's "superpower" is that he "understands the overwhelming power of modern mass communications." Journalist Alexandria Neason, a *Columbia Journalism Review* staff writer, wrote in 2018 that "with every ban, every policy threat, every protest I covered, every executive order, every press conference (the entire newsroom plugged in, our eye rolls almost in sync), every alarmist headline, every controversial tweet and the inevitable backlash—I became increasingly exhausted and void of any energy to actually do my job. I'd spent it all just trying to keep up."[24] At the same time, the countless assaults that Trump and his cronies leveled against government institutions, and the protections these had historically offered vulnerable citizens, went largely unreported.

The mainstream media's inability to hold Trump accountable to readily observable reality was also a product of executive cowardice. In January 2019, for instance, when Trump demanded that the major television networks give him prime-time coverage for a speech full of lies and misrepresentations about an alleged immigration crisis, the executives acceded—although Barack Obama's request for airtime five years earlier, to give a (truthful) speech on immigration, had been denied. In defending the decision, one fearful TV executive said, "If we give him the time, he'll deliver a fact-free screed without rebuttal. And if we don't give him the time, he'll call every network partisan. So we are damned if we do and damned if we don't."[25] So they did. And Trump was invited to lie to the public over and over again, always without correction, and only occasionally with a "rebuttal" from Democrats. Truth was simply a matter to be squabbled over by "both sides."

It was certainly no coincidence that Trump's path to power and exploitation of the powers of the presidency proved coterminous with the rise of social media, which presented stiff competition to older, more reliable forms of news gathering and dissemination. Today, according to pollsters, Americans are more likely to rely on social media sources for their news than they are to read newspapers.

"What You're Seeing and What You're Reading Is Not…"

During the 2016 election season, more than four times as many Americans were exposed to disinformation on Facebook originating from Russia-based sources than own a print or digital subscription to an American newspaper. The stalwart refusal of social media sites to take full responsibility for the content posted by users invites manipulation by all manner of liars, scam artists, and, certainly, Russian intelligence agents seeking to illegally influence the course of US elections. Facebook CEO Mark Zuckerberg initially insisted that it was "crazy" to suggest that the lies transmitted on his site played any role in Trump's election. After Barack Obama spoke to him personally to set him straight, he began to take the issue a little more seriously. The company eventually admitted to finding as many as 583 million automated accounts, many of which turned out to be pro-Trump trolls and scammers.[26]

Facebook sought to scrub itself of phony profiles, but even then, it continued to insist that it bore no responsibility for policing its content for lies, save for those that purposely incite violence. Initially, the social media giant even fought to keep vicious hate-monger Alex Jones on the site, even after he called special counsel Robert Mueller a child rapist, claimed he aided and abetted other child rapists, and mimed, for his viewers, the act of murdering him with a pistol. The company subsequently reversed itself and kicked Jones off, but, according to the head of Facebook News Feed at the time, merely lying "doesn't violate the community standards." He went on to call Jones's incitements just one among many "points of view." He made these comments, ironically, at a presentation dedicated to Facebook's "work to prevent the spread of false news."[27]

Days later, Zuckerberg went even further and volunteered that, however distasteful he might find it personally, Holocaust denial was also permitted on Facebook because, as he put it, "I don't think that they're *intentionally* getting it wrong." In October 2019—just in time for the 2020 election—Facebook loosened its rules further to let advertisers lie with even greater impunity than before. "We can't be a policeman on the internet saying what is acceptable or what is absolutely true" was the excuse offered by its vice president of global affairs and communication, Nick Clegg. According to a study by three scholars associated with Princeton University and New York University, conservatives are at least four times more likely than liberals to share falsehoods on Facebook. Another study—this one undertaken by six researchers at Oxford University and the network analytics firm Graphica—demonstrated that conservatives frequently contribute to the spread of "deliberately… misleading, deceptive or incorrect information." At the same time, Twitter claims to host roughly 6,000 new tweets every second. Almost 4 million Google searches are conducted and 7 new articles are added to Wikipedia every minute. Roughly 1.5 billion people log onto Facebook each day, and they upload 243,000 photos per minute. Meanwhile, if Facebook ever decided to fact-check ads, there would be a lot of ads to check. The company reported that as of 2019 it had more than 7 million active advertisers.[28]

In the White House, the most powerful and influential liar in the world constantly demanded that these companies refrain from censoring almost anyone who supported him. Trump's pressure tactics were seconded by a constant barrage of complaints from dozens of Republican senators and representatives and countless cable and radio talk-show hosts. According to Joshua Bolten, who served as White House chief of staff to George W. Bush, efforts like those undertaken at Facebook to justify its decisions were necessary because "a lot of people on the right are suspicious of most media outlets and social media platforms." With Trump's encouragement, rightwing provocateurs insisted that any attempt to block hate speech on social media was tantamount to political censorship of conservative ideas. This relentless "working of the refs" had its intended effect. Like the mainstream media institutions, the executives at these platforms were desperate to demonstrate their "neutrality" to Trump. Facebook, for example, appointed former George W. Bush adviser

Joel Kaplan to be its vice president of US public policy in 2011. He later rose to become the company's VP of global public policy. In 2018, Facebook chose a former Republican senator, Jon Kyl of Arizona, to conduct a review of conservative complaints about liberal bias. Although he could not find any significant evidence to support the accusations, his report nevertheless repeated their "concerns that hate speech policies would work against conservatives."[29]

No one at Facebook was willing to explain to the White House and its allies that the problem was not Facebook's regulations (which were, in reality, incredibly loose). The problem was the preponderance of pro-Trump voices whose posts tended toward hate speech and incitements to violence. Nevertheless, for Zuckerberg, the problem was that "conservatives don't trust that our platform surfaces content without a political bias." So, in addition to hiring Kaplan and Kyl, in 2019 Zuckerberg convened a series of secret dinner meetings with the likes of radio talk-show host Hugh Hewitt, Tucker Carlson of Fox, and Senator Lindsey Graham, a Republican from South Carolina—along with a whole panoply of other far-right, Trump-friendly media personalities—in order to find out how Facebook might further address their complaints. Not long afterward, he announced that political advertisements on Facebook would not be monitored for lies. This decision had the double advantage of appealing to Trump supporters (who consistently used the site to lie) while boosting the company's bottom line, along with Zuckerberg's own multibillion-dollar stake in its profits. In December 2019, the *Wall Street Journal* revealed the hitherto secret close relationship Zuckerberg enjoyed with the pro-Trump, right-wing extremist billionaire Peter Thiel, the site's first outside investor and longtime board member. A denier of the settled science of climate change and outspoken champion of Trump's 2016 campaign (and attendant conspiracy theories), Thiel arranged an October 2019 dinner meeting for just himself, Zuckerberg, and Trump, and, not coincidentally, was reported to have been influential in the company's refusal to monitor lies in the political advertisements from which it profited. The Trump campaign, unsurprisingly, took the opportunity to immediately flood the site with millions of dollars' worth of dishonest advertisements, all of them expertly targeted, with the help of Facebook's algorithms, to reach the kinds of voters likely to believe them. When questioned in October 2019 by New York congresswoman Alexandria Ocasio-Cortez, Zuckerberg allowed that, personally, he did "think lying is bad." He just didn't think Facebook should be required to prevent politicians from using his site to do so. Following this appearance, the *Washington Post* editorial board chided Zuckerberg, writing that, if Facebook did have to monitor ads, "Mr. Trump and other conspiracy-mongers might chafe at their inability to poison the public conversation with such precision at such scale." But Trump supporters were pleased, and so were Facebook shareholders. And, judging by Zuckerberg's actions, rather than his words, these were apparently his only genuine concerns.[30]

The other social media behemoths were hardly any less accommodating to right-wing misinformation than Facebook, and no less responsive in the face of Trump supporters' relentless campaign to "work the refs." Google's US director of public policy, Adam Kovacevich, expressed his concerns in a company meeting, saying, "I think one of the directives we've gotten very clearly from Sundar [Pichai, Google CEO at the time, now CEO of Google's parent company, Alphabet]…is to build deeper relationships with conservatives. I think we've recognized that the company is generally seen as liberal by policymakers." Like Facebook, Google proved remarkably reluctant to ban even Alex Jones. At Twitter, CEO Jack Dorsey consistently took the same tack, attempting to assuage Trump and his supporters while at the same time trying—and most often failing—to maintain some semblance of a commitment to civility and nonviolence. When Trump retweeted a video juxtaposing a speech by the Arab American congresswoman Ilhan Omar with footage of the 9/11 attacks on the

United States, sparking death threats against her, Dorsey, defending his decision to allow it to remain on the site, gave the excuse that the video had spread well beyond Twitter (though he did admit to Omar that Twitter "need[ed] to do a better job generally in removing hate and harassment from the site"). Asked if he would ban a tweet by the president that explicitly called on his followers to murder a journalist, he replied, "We'd certainly talk about it."[31]

Twitter did take a step in the right direction in October 2019, when it banned all political ads from its site. This was presumably to differentiate itself from Facebook and the latter's apparent openness to political lying. The Trump 2020 campaign, predictably, attacked the decision as "yet another attempt to silence conservatives." Trump's campaign manager, Brad Parscale, wanted to know if Twitter would "also be stopping ads from biased liberal media outlets." Many other pro-Trump sources joined in the attack. Even the Russian state television network RT evinced concern. The Russian network, identified by the US intelligence services as part of Vladimir Putin's efforts to try to undermine the integrity of the 2016 US election on behalf of the Trump campaign, was required by the US Justice Department to register as a foreign agent. After Dorsey's announcement, it sent out an "urgent" tweet attacking Twitter for "caving in to 'election meddling' fearmongers."[32]

The drumbeat continued. And no wonder. The tactic of constant complaint was a gift that kept on giving. Trump demanded a meeting with Dorsey in April 2019 to complain that he was losing followers, when in fact Twitter was merely eliminating phony accounts. Weeks later, he accused Google of seeking to "illegally subvert the 2020 election." In July 2019, Trump invited a large group of right-wing social media trolls to the White House to listen to him repeat his baseless complaints about the "tremendous dishonesty, bias, discrimination and suppression practiced by certain companies." Included on the guest list were a cartoonist whose work the Anti-Defamation League had called "blatantly anti-Semitic"; the criminal videographer who had infiltrated ACORN, James O'Keefe; and a reporter from Alex Jones's Infowars, among other fringe figures and malicious hate-mongers.[33] As Brian Rosenwald, author of *Talk Radio's America: How an Industry Took Over a Political Party That Took Over the United States*, observed of the gathering, "By inviting such extremist voices to the White House, Trump is signaling to his base that they are credible sources and worthy social media follows. This will exacerbate polarization, misinformation and gridlock by fueling the right's embrace of the worst—and least true—ideas about the political opposition."[34] It would also, at least implicitly, work to put social media companies on notice to be even more indulgent of the lies and baseless conspiracies regularly posted on the president's behalf.

Because Trump lied about virtually everything, virtually everyone who served under him understood that lying on his behalf would necessarily be a routine part of the job. White House senior policy adviser Stephen Miller, for example, proudly proclaimed his fealty to Trump's lies about voter fraud, saying, "I'm prepared to go on any show, anywhere, anytime…and say the president of the United States is correct one hundred percent." (To which Trump tweeted in reply, "Congratulations Stephen Miller- on representing me this morning on the various Sunday morning shows. Great job.")[35] Peter Navarro, the head of the White House National Trade Council, described this phenomenon quite candidly: "My function, really, as an economist," he said "is to try to provide the underlying analytics that confirm his [Trump's] intuition. And his intuition is always right in these matters."[36] Aides and advisers were sometimes called upon to lie about Trump's lying. When Lawrence Kudlow, the director of Trump's National Economic Council, was asked in July 2019 why Trump had said that he (Trump) had been asked to mediate the long-simmering dispute between India and Pakistan over Kashmir, which was news to the parties involved, Kudlow replied,

"The president doesn't make things up." He went on to scold the interviewer for having asked "a very rude question," before admitting that he had no idea whether what Trump had said was true.[37]

And yet, it was not only Trump's trolls on social media who believed whatever Trump said. Mainstream journalists also continued to take Trump's lies seriously. Kellyanne Conway may have made herself into a punch line in the early days of the administration, with her invention of the nonsensical notion of "alternative facts," but network and cable news stations remained more than willing to repeatedly bring her back, giving her opportunities to spout lie after lie in the defense of the liar she worked for.

As we saw in the previous chapter, Donald Trump had almost always made his living by lying before running for president. Remarkably, ascending to the most powerful position in the world—with millions of eyes observing his every move—did nothing to slow him down. Upon taking office, Trump retained full ownership of his myriad and tangled business interests, ignoring the advice of the government's independent ethics office and other ethics experts. Nine days before his inauguration, at a comically transparent news conference, Sheri A. Dillon, his tax lawyer, pointed to a large stack of papers that she said were compliance documents, proving the president's commitment to transparency. Alas, this commitment ended when the reporters present asked to actually examine the papers to make certain they were not, for instance, cut-up pages of the Washington, DC, Yellow Pages. No dice. Dillon insisted that "the president-elect will have no role in deciding whether the Trump Organization engages in any new deal," adding that Trump himself "will only know of a deal if he reads it in the paper or sees it on TV."[38] This statement was completely false. In truth, Trump placed his profits into an easily revocable trust, and he could draw funds from it whenever he felt like it without the public's knowledge.

Trump's businesses posed so many conflicts of interest that it soon became nearly impossible for any one person to keep track of them. To give just one of countless examples, Trump's companies reportedly received over $175 million annually from commercial tenants such as China's state-owned bank. Indeed, nobody knows how many such tenants his properties have, or how much money the Trump Organization took in from foreign governments, because the company refused to disclose that information. During just his first year in office, reporters uncovered at least three dozen known Trump tenants doing business with the federal government, including lobbying firms, contractors, and others subject to US government regulation. An analysis by the public-interest group Public Citizen found that between Trump's election and mid-2018, "more than 370 political candidates, foreign governments, businesses, corporate groups, religious groups, charities and other entities…held events" at Trump properties. Sixty of them were business groups, and twenty-eight were "foreign governments, officials or political groups." Sometimes these same foreign governments, US firms, and trade associations would book blocks of rooms in Trump hotels, pay in advance, and never bother to show up. Trump blew hot and cold on his trade war with China, but at the same time, his businesses benefited from the Chinese government granting his companies thirty-nine trademarks after he became president, after having specifically rejected granting the trademarks in the past. The president's daughter Ivanka Trump, who served as a White House adviser, was granted at least seven more.[39]

Trump and his family consistently ignored the emoluments clause of the US Constitution, which forbids a president from profiting from foreign governments or receiving any money from the US government except an annual salary. Trump used his office, for example, to funnel tens of millions, and possibly hundreds of millions, of US taxpayer funds—no one knows the exact figure—to Trump properties as the result of his frequent vacations, his children's business trips, his vice president's travels, and even redirected military exercises. One can find countless examples of what Gerry Connolly, a Democratic congressman from Virginia serving on the House Oversight Committee, called "near raw bribery." Trump reported an income of $486 million in 2017 and $461 million in 2018—a period during which the watchdog group Citizens for Responsibility and Ethics in Washington counted approximately two thousand conflicts of interest due to his business interests.[40]

Ivanka's husband, Jared Kushner, who also served as an adviser to the president, had similar difficulties telling the truth about his investments. Kushner was apparently so intent on hiding the various sources of his income from the American public that he found himself forced to revise his financial disclosure form over forty times. At the outset of the administration, ethics officials who had served in both the Bush and Obama administrations warned that if Kushner and Ivanka retained all their business holdings, they would face multiple conflicts of interest in advising the president.[41] Apparently, no one in the administration cared.

Trump's cabinet of millionaires and billionaires demonstrated a similarly relaxed attitude when it came to conflicts of interest and self-dealing—and lied repeatedly to cover up their wrongdoing. At least four Trump cabinet members were found to have made false claims in financial filings submitted during their Senate confirmation hearings. Billionaire Betsy DeVos, secretary of education, lied to the Senate during her confirmation hearings about the role she had played in helping to direct contributions made by a family foundation to anti-LGBT organizations. Elaine Chao, transportation secretary and wife to Senate Majority Leader Mitch McConnell, promised during her confirmation hearings to divest herself within a year of $400,000 worth of stock in a construction materials company contracted to the Transportation Department. Apparently, she forgot to do so, as she still retained the stock more than two years into the administration. Secretary of Commerce Wilbur Ross also lied to Congress, promising to divest from almost all his holdings as a condition of taking his job. He held onto his interest in myriad companies, including one co-owned by the Chinese government, and another closely tied to members of Vladimir Putin's inner circle. In an extremely unusual move, the Office of Government Ethics refused to certify Ross's financial disclosure because, the office said, it could not be trusted.[42] And these were only the ones who got caught.

It would be difficult to identify a single policy of the Trump White House that was not in some way based on a lie. Trump and his advisers lied about his policies on taxes,[43] trade,[44] the environment,[45] health care,[46] and national security and intelligence.[47] Trump even lied about the weather, using a Sharpie to try to cover up his lie, and then, true to form, he lied repeatedly about having lied about it.[48] But according to *Washington Post* fact-checkers, Trump told more falsehoods about immigration than any other topic.[49]

Trump's war on immigrants became the nexus of his racism, xenophobia, and political appeal; it also was at the center of what might fairly be termed his rendezvous with history. As we have seen repeatedly, much, if not most, of the lying presidents have done since the nation's founding has been driven by the need to placate Americans' racial anxieties, the nation's commitment to constant expansion, and its leaders' ever-elastic definition of "national security." The racist fears and animosities underlying American politics never fully disappeared from view, but they grew muted over time following the success of the 1960s civil rights movement. By the end of the twentieth century, the country had grown increasingly multicultural. One could find appeals to the old racial fears in isolated political races, but not, for the most part, in presidential contests. The election in 2008 of the first black president led many to hope, and some to believe, that the United States had finally "overcome" the legacy of its "original sin" of slavery and enforced racism. We now know the opposite to be true. Obama's presidency proved a catalyst to a renaissance of resentment toward all nonwhite minorities, especially blacks and Latinos.

Perhaps the most ludicrous lie Donald Trump has ever told was his claim that he was "the least racist person there is anywhere in the world." Trump's lifelong history of racism is documented beyond any reasonable doubt.[50] His rise to political prominence on the back of his "birther" lie about Barack Obama was a sadly predictable manifestation of that racism. It reflected his true feelings and helped explain his appeal to millions of Americans who shared his views.

What was new in Trump's formulation was the way he combined his peculiarly idiosyncratic brand of racism with a revival of old-fashioned American "isolationism" of the type that existed in the pre–World War II period. This was the origin of his "America First" slogan—originally, it was the slogan of the groups that opposed US entry into World War II. And in his formulation, America had two primary foes in the world: Chinese imports and foreign immigrants.

In the case of China, Trump had a point, though being Trump, he pursued it in a typically counterproductive fashion. Trump slapped significant tariffs on imports of Chinese goods and thereby drove up the costs of finished products as well as of the parts, raw materials, and components that US producers relied upon. China's retaliatory tariffs on US products hurt these same producers, and the two together threatened to destabilize the entire global economy. Faced with these real-world consequences, Trump did what came naturally: he lied. For instance, following a downturn in the stock market in late August 2019, caused by a breakdown in US-China trade talks, Trump reassured the country that China "called last night our top trade people and said 'let's get back to the table' so we will be getting back to the table and I think they want to do something." But Treasury Secretary Steve Mnuchin was soon forced to admit that there had been no call. Trump just made it up, in order to try to gin up the stock market. It was similar to what he had done earlier when, in business, he would make up stories about putative takeovers to make a quick, dishonest buck. Only this time, he was not just some stock scammer: he was the president of the United States, using his bully pulpit to manipulate markets, all to improve his image—or, as his anonymously quoted aides put it, "to project optimism."[51]

It was the second foe of America in Trump's eyes, immigration, however, that may have been the locus of Trump's most consequential lies. Here, he took the fear of Islamic terrorists—who, since 9/11, had replaced communists as Public Enemy #1—and infused it into the racist fears he shared with so many Americans about brown-skinned people in general. That especially included anyone seeking asylum from the violence, chaos, and poverty of their own countries of origin, whether they were in the Middle East, in Central and South America, or in Mexico. Stoking fears through his rhetoric almost nonstop, he alleged that those from the Middle East were potential terrorists, while anyone from south of the US border was intent on undermining our communities with drugs, rape, and murder. In pushing these arguments, Trump was aided by the prime-time hosts on Fox, especially Laura Ingraham and Tucker Carlson, whose shows provided a nightly cacophony of anti-immigrant rumor and rhetoric. In a poll carried out in the autumn of 2019, 78 percent of the Republicans who said they relied on Fox News as their primary news source said they believed that immigrants were "invading the country." Many other news organizations followed this lead, though those who chose other sources of news were much less likely to hold that belief (52 percent).[52]

Trump's policies dealing with the rights of nonwhite immigrants and the arguments he used to support them were, without exception, built on a foundation of racist lies. For instance, he frequently insisted that the number of undocumented immigrants was growing, when in fact it was declining—and more undocumented immigrants were returning to their home countries than were trying to enter. By 2017, net immigration, both legal and illegal, had fallen to its lowest level in forty-six years. Trump's constant harping on the criminality of immigrants was also misleading in general, and almost always false in its specifics. Study after study demonstrates that immigrants—especially the undocumented—commit far fewer violent crimes than native-born Americans do. But it was in his attempts to link immigrants to terrorism that Trump threw out some of his most destructive falsehoods. In July 2018, for instance, in an address before a joint session of Congress, he misrepresented data from the Department of Justice to claim that "the vast majority of individuals convicted of terrorism and terrorism-related offenses since 9/11 came here from outside of our country." The Justice Department found itself forced to admit that, in fact, it possessed no records to support that claim. The administration had rejected a report by the director of intelligence's National Counterterrorism Center showing that refugees seeking asylum in the United States posed almost no security threat. Instead, the Department of Homeland Security and the Department of Justice issued another report insisting that "three out of every four, or 402, individuals convicted of international terrorism-related charges in U.S. federal courts between September 11, 2001, and December 31, 2016 were foreign-born." Asked for records to support this contention, the departments came up empty yet again. In fact, according to reliable studies, attacks on Americans undertaken by Muslims have been all but nonexistent since 9/11. According to a 2019 report by the Anti-Defamation League, terrorist murders in the United States in between 2001 and 2018 were "overwhelmingly linked to right-wing extremists."[53]

The lies Trump told to exploit Americans' fear of terrorists were among his favorites, and they aided him in his effort to garner support for his inhumane policies directed toward refugees and asylum seekers, especially on the southern border. The pace of these lies intensified when Trump sought to stoke hysteria over a "caravan" of Central Americans making their way to the US border, just in time for the 2018 midterm election. Based on no verifiable evidence whatsoever, Trump and his supporters claimed that the asylum seekers included an unknown number of potential Islamic terrorists. As proof, the president cited unnamed and unverified sources quoted on right-wing news sites who claimed to have seen Muslim prayer rugs left at the border.[54] After the election, Trump continued to use dehumanizing rhetoric, complaining of an "infestation" by "rapists," "thugs," "monsters," and "animals," and warned of "murders, murders, murders. Killings, murders!" In just the first eight months of 2019, his reelection campaign took out over two thousand paid Facebook advertisements that repeated his warnings of the allegedly imminent immigrant "invasion."[55]

This phrase would prove central to the manifesto issued by Patrick Wood Crusius, a man who murdered twenty-two people and injured twenty-four others at an El Paso Walmart on August 3, 2019. Most of the victims had Latino names. It was also repeated endlessly by the hosts on Fox News and in other pro-Trump media, including such outlets as Sinclair Broadcast Group, Rush Limbaugh's radio program, the *Drudge Report*, Breitbart News, and Gateway Pundit.[56] In August 2019, ABC News identified "at least 36 criminal cases where Trump was invoked in direct connection with violent acts, threats of violence or allegations of assault." Specifically, the study found that "in nine cases, perpetrators hailed Trump in the midst or immediate aftermath of physically attacking innocent victims." In other cases, "perpetrators cheered or defended Trump while taunting or threatening others," or their lawyers cited Trump to "explain a defendant's violent or threatening behavior."[57]

Over time, many in the mainstream media and the political class reacted to Trump's incendiary rhetoric by trying to ignore its substance with the explanation that the president was just blowing off steam, stoking his base, flattering his followers, or repeating something he heard on Fox News and would soon forget. And so his hate-filled lies went unchecked. Many in the mainstream media had internalized the viewpoint of right-wing writer Salena Zito, who posited in a September 2016 *Atlantic* article that "the press takes [Trump] literally, but not seriously; his supporters take him seriously, but not literally."[58] In August 2019, the conservative pundit and former George W. Bush speechwriter David Frum, writing in the same magazine, argued that this sort of advice had been taken all too well: "Reactions to actions by Trump are always filtered through the prism of [an] ever more widely accepted view," he wrote: that he "is a reckless buffoon; a conspiratorial, racist moron, whose weird comments should be disregarded by sensible people." But, as Frum noted, ignoring Trump's statements would have been impossible. Because he was president, and because the media institutions felt compelled to report on whatever he said, Trump's words—no matter how ridiculous—were aired and re-aired, quoted and requoted, 24/7. They could not help but carry significant authority with millions of people.[59]

Trump's delusional views and his dishonesty presented a brand-new set of dangers for America and the world. It was true that Richard Nixon's lies about national-security-related matters were almost always colored by his racism. But unlike Nixon, Trump had no idea what he was doing—no understanding of the issues or the larger goals beyond his own ego, personal pique, and ignorant prejudices. Some of his distinctions made little sense. Why did Trump behave so belligerently toward Iran, for example, which had agreed to allow international inspection of its nuclear program, while simultaneously indulging North Korea, which did not? Trump lied frequently about both nations, but he lied to paint the former, a Muslim nation full of brown-skinned citizens, as threatening, and the latter as benign.

On May 8, 2018, Trump announced that he would withdraw the United States from the 159-page Joint Comprehensive Plan of Action that President Obama, the European Union, and the five permanent members of the UN Security Council had reached with Iran to restrict its nuclear weapons development. Trump repeatedly insisted that he did so because Iran was not complying with the terms of the agreement. Here, he was lying yet again. The chairmen of both the US Joint Chiefs of Staff and the International Atomic Energy Agency had confirmed Iran's strict compliance.[60] Shortly thereafter, Trump's handpicked director of national intelligence, Dan Coats, and his CIA director, Gina Haspel, presented the Senate Intelligence Committee with their annual Worldwide Threat Assessment. This, too, confirmed Iran's compliance. Rather than admit the truth, Trump sought to blame his intelligence chiefs, whom he called "naïve," telling them to "go back to school." He demanded that they recant. When they declined to do so, Trump asserted that Coats and Haspel had not said what all the news reports had confirmed they had said, and then called those reports "fake news."[61] Coats eventually resigned, and Trump chose an inexperienced, conspiracy-minded Republican, Congressman John Ratcliffe of Texas, to replace him. Ratcliffe, however, was forced to withdraw from consideration when, immediately after the announcement, he was found to have repeatedly lied on his official résumé.[62] Iran, meanwhile, without any incentive to heed the restrictions of the agreement, began to exceed the limits that it had imposed on its nuclear program.

At the same time, Trump indulged the brutal North Korean dictator Kim Jong-un to a degree that no other American president had ever considered, whether it was regarding Kim himself or his cruel and paranoid predecessors, who happened to be his father and grandfather. According to Trump, he "fell in love" with Kim after the dictator wrote him "beautiful letters." After giving Kim the high-profile presidential summit he sought in June 2018, without receiving any concessions in return, Trump tweeted, "There is no longer a Nuclear Threat from North Korea." But the claim evaporated almost immediately in the face of reality. Before the start of what were supposed to be detailed follow-up negotiations, the North Koreans looked at the US agenda and attacked its "unilateral and gangster-like demand[s]"; they did not even bother to show up. Even so, Trump continued to express his devotion, scoffing at complaints from US critics about the massive human rights abuses and official murders undertaken by Kim's regime ("It's rough in a lot of places"). According to a list compiled by the Carnegie Endowment for International Peace, Trump called Kim, among other things, "nice, funny, really smart, worthy, one in 10,000, [and] very talented" and insisted that he "loves his people." (When a second summit failed in February 2019, Trump's beloved friend reportedly had his top five negotiators executed.) For all Trump's boasting, the *Washington Post* reported in late December 2019 that US and East Asian officials had concluded that "North Korea has never halted its efforts to build powerful new weapons. Indeed, Kim's scientists appear to have used the lull to quietly improve and expand the country's arsenal." Trump had been told this many times by his own intelligence agencies, but he preferred to place his faith in the murderous, nuclear-armed mass murderer and lie to America and the world on his behalf. Barely a day before Trump authorized the killing of Maj. Gen. Qassim Suleimani, leader of the Quds Force of the Islamic Revolutionary Guards Corps, in a drone strike at Baghdad International Airport—thereby vastly expanding the degree of hostilities between the US and Iran, and which saw Vice President Pence begin lying about it almost immediately, with Trump doing so shortly thereafter—the president could be heard bragging at a New Year's Eve party in Miami that Kim, whom he termed "a man of his word," "likes me and I like him."[63]

From the standpoint of his own political survival, at least during the first three-and-a-half years of his presidency, Donald Trump's most successful lies were those told in the service of hiding his 2016 presidential campaign's exploitation of Russian interference on his behalf. These efforts also involved attempts to obstruct Special Counsel Robert Mueller's investigation of these matters. Mueller, a respected Republican litigator and former director of the FBI, was appointed by Trump's own Justice Department to take over an investigation that began when members of the FBI worried that Trump might actually be a Russian asset—or, as the *New York Times* put it more euphemistically, "whether Mr. Trump had acted at Russia's behest" (a theory that, based on Trump's behavior as president, remains to be disproved). They had discussed opening a counterintelligence investigation into his presidency, and possibly even suggesting his removal via the Twenty-fifth Amendment to the Constitution. Early in Trump's term, then FBI director James Comey refused Trump's entreaties to go easy on then assistant for national security Michael Flynn. This was after Flynn had been caught lying to FBI investigators about his efforts to undermine Barack Obama's policies toward Russia before the Trump team took office (Flynn would plead guilty to this charge in December 2017). Per usual, the Trump modus operandi in dealing with Mueller's investigation was to lie, and lie, and then lie some more. In going over Mueller's report, CNN found what it termed "77 specific instances where President Donald Trump's campaign staff, administration officials and family members, Republican backers and his associates lied or made false assertions (sometimes unintentionally) to the public."[64]

Despite criticism, Trump kept up a constant barrage of very public and unhinged attacks on Mueller and his staff. Apparently terrified, the president deemed "impeach" to be "a dirty, filthy, disgusting word," adding, "It had nothing to do with me." He called Mueller "highly conflicted" and insisted that the special counsel's staff was composed of "18 Angry Democrat Trump Haters" who were "some of the worst human beings on earth." He claimed they were conducting a "fundamentally illegal" investigation that he considered to be "the Greatest Witch Hunt in the History of our Country," as well as "an attempted overthrow of the United States government."[65]

The Mueller Report's release was initially confused by the fact that Trump's handpicked attorney general, William Barr, purposely misled the public about its contents before its publication. According to Barr's false assertions, the report exonerated Trump on virtually all matters. In fact, Mueller's report laid out at least ten instances in which Trump had attempted to obstruct justice and specified explicitly that it was not "exonerating" him of any of them.[66]

Barr, who appeared to view himself as Trump's personal attorney and protector rather than the nation's top law-enforcement official, also claimed that Trump and his advisers had "fully cooperated with the special counsel's investigation, providing unfettered access to campaign and White House documents, directing senior aides to testify freely, and asserting no privilege claims." This was all false as well. Trump, the report noted, "engaged in efforts" to "prevent the disclosure of evidence to [the special counsel], including through public and private contacts with potential witnesses." These efforts, according to the report, "materially impaired the investigation." Benjamin Wittes, a Senior Fellow in Governance Studies at the Brookings Institution and editor in chief of Lawfare, observed, writing in the *Atlantic*, that Trump had tried "to get witnesses not to cooperate—dangling pardons and seeming to threaten their families with investigation if they 'flipped.'" Trump had refused to be interviewed by Mueller, and when he responded to Mueller's questions in writing, he failed to "remember" the answers to key questions over thirty times. Moreover, he refused to address questions related to the issue of his attempts at obstruction. According to journalist Bob Woodward, Trump's lawyer John Dowd advised him against appearing before Mueller because Dowd judged Trump to be "not really capable" of responding truthfully to the questions in a face-to-face meeting. In order to keep the president from perjuring himself, Dowd, according to Woodward, felt he had "to dress it up as much as possible, to say, it's not your fault...He could not say what he knew was true: 'You're a fucking liar.'"[67]

Following Mueller's testimony to Congress, Trump's claim of "complete and total exoneration" turned into a series of complaints about the "Greatest Presidential Harassment in history."[68] But Mueller had identified at least ten instances in which Trump had attempted to obstruct justice. His investigation also led to indictments, convictions, or guilty pleas for thirty-four people and three companies, including the Trump campaign's onetime chairman Paul Manafort; Trump's close friend and confidant Roger Stone; his personal lawyer Michael Cohen; his adviser for national security Michael Flynn; and other campaign officials, together with at least thirteen Russian spies and hackers, including some close allies and confidants of Russian leader Vladimir Putin.

According to a CNN tally, Trump "spread at least 21 lies" about Mueller and his investigation immediately after May 29, 2019, when the special counsel made a public statement clarifying that his report did not exonerate Trump. And yet so inured were most members of the media by then to Trump's lies and likely criminality that the entire affair—including the hearings to follow in July, in which Mueller testified before the House Judiciary Committee—was presented as a disappointing denouement to what had become merely theatrical drama. Taking no side, once again, between truth and falsehood, front-page coverage in the *New York Times* explained the controversy as follows: "In an era of deep polarization, Mr. Mueller's 448-page report quickly became yet another case study in the disparate realities of American politics as each camp interpreted it through its own lens and sought to weaponize it against the other side." NBC News' Chuck Todd, host of *Meet the Press*, meanwhile, noted after the hearing that Mueller had basically endorsed the criminal case against the president in every detail—but Todd still thought it appropriate to cast the story in a similar "he said / she said" framework, in which the only criterion was the quality of the spectacle on offer. "On substance," he tweeted, "Democrats got what they wanted: that Mueller didn't charge Pres. Trump because of the OLC [Office of Legal Counsel] guidance, that he could be indicted after he leaves office, among other things. But on optics, this was a disaster."[69] Their disingenuous complaints of "fake news" notwithstanding, Trump and the Republicans could hardly have asked for a more sympathetic news frame for their campaign of lies.

At 8:30 p.m. Eastern Standard Time, December 18, 2019, Trump was finally, formally, impeached by the US House of Representatives. It was the third such vote in the nation's history and the second in twenty years. Unlike President Clinton, however, Donald Trump was not being impeached for lying. Rather, it was over his abuse of presidential power and purposeful obstruction of Congress. Trump, being Trump, defended himself with an exhausting barrage of wild charges characterized by unproven conspiracy theories, countless character assassinations, and of course lies. During the week leading up to the initial House vote merely to begin the proceedings, Trump, according to Daniel Dale's conservative count, made ninety-six false claims, including fifty-three on a single day.[70]

Considered out of context, the events that finally led Trump to the precipice of impeachment would strain credulity. On the basis of two separate conspiracy theories—both of which had already been disproved—Trump pressed a foreign leader, Ukrainian president Volodymyr Zelensky, to launch a high-profile investigation that Trump thought would serve his own domestic political interests. He intimated in a phone call with Zelensky that if the Ukrainian president wanted the $391 million in military aid that Congress had appropriated—which Ukraine desperately needed to defend itself against Russia—they had better come up with something.

The investigation that Trump demanded of Ukraine focused on a potential rival for the presidency in 2020, former vice president Joe

Biden. Trump wanted the Ukrainians to announce an investigation of Biden looking into whether Biden had intervened in Ukrainian affairs during the Obama administration in order to cover up the role of his son Hunter in allegedly corrupt business dealings there. In fact, Joe Biden did exert pressure on the Ukrainian government as vice president, but he did so in support of efforts to fight corruption, and there is no evidence that he did anything nefarious to help his son. Moreover, Hunter Biden did serve on the board of Burisma Holdings in Ukraine, a natural gas producer, and although he received a large amount of compensation for that role, no evidence has come to light anywhere that he acted in any way illegally according to either US or Ukrainian laws. Of course, none of this mattered to Trump. Throwing ordinary procedures out the window, the president undermined his diplomatic staff, replacing those who would not cooperate and sending a series of private individuals—most prominently his personal lawyer, Rudy Giuliani—to keep up the pressure on Zelensky to produce some dirt. It was when these initial tactics had failed, apparently, that Trump instructed his acting chief of staff, Mick Mulvaney, to withhold the military aid.[71]

The now-famous phone call took place on July 25, 2019, when Trump, speaking to Zelensky with some of his staff members listening in, uttered the words that became the subject of countless news shows, articles, and late-night comedy routines: "I would like you to do us a favor though."[72] He was asking not only for the Biden investigation but also for a second investigation. That one concerned an even more bizarre and convoluted conspiracy theory that had also already been "completely debunked," according to a top national security aide—who had told this to Trump personally. Trump's allies, including Giuliani, Sean Hannity, Steve Bannon, Breitbart News, and others, continued to push the theory, along with thousands of conspiracy aficionados who make up the Trump-supporting movement called "QAnon" (though Trump, incredibly, told his aides that he learned of the alleged plot because "Putin told me," which helps to explain his unshakable attachment to it). This second conspiracy theory was built on the nutty belief that CrowdStrike, a California-based cybersecurity company that the Democratic National Committee (DNC) used to investigate hacks against it in 2016, had somehow hidden a server in Ukraine to obscure the fact that the DNC had, in reality, hacked itself. If almost any other national politician or Western democratic leader had echoed a group of unbalanced conspiracy nuts to this degree, it would be worthy of concern, or even alarm. But when it came to Donald Trump, this practice had long ago been normalized. As the *New York Times* calculated in November 2019, after examining 11,000 Trump tweets, Trump had by then "retweeted at least 145 unverified accounts that have pushed conspiracy or fringe content, including more than two dozen that have since been suspended by Twitter." The *Times* added that "tinfoil-hat types and racists celebrate when Mr. Trump shares something they promote."[73]

The CrowdStrike theory attempted to exonerate the Russians of interference in the 2016 election while charging the Democrats— and possibly Hillary Clinton herself—with trying to frame them. Exposing this plot, the conspiracy theorists hoped, would demonstrate Trump's legitimacy as the honest victor of the 2016 election, by replacing the truth of Russian manipulation and interference with the lie that it was really Ukraine at work. It would, theoretically embarrass the Democrats—and possibly expose them to criminal prosecution. Since the very first month of his presidency, Trump had been attempting to discredit the well-established truth—endorsed by the entire US intelligence community and the Mueller Report—that the Russians had interfered on his behalf. By October 15, 2019, Trump had attempted to undermine Americans' understanding of these efforts in 1,400 separate tweets. But sadly, at least for Trump and his fellow conspiracy theorists, the story in question turned out to be entirely imaginary. Not only did CrowdStrike lack any Ukrainian connections whatsoever, but there wasn't even a "server" to be hidden, much less hidden somewhere in Ukraine.[74]

Even so, Trump would not let it go. He had been obsessed with this tale since he had first heard it. In June 2017, he tweeted, "Why did the DNC REFUSE to turn over its Server to the FBI, and still hasn't? It's all a big Dem scam and excuse for losing the election!" A month before his phone call with Zelensky, he had called into Sean Hannity's Fox News program and asked, "How come the FBI didn't take the server from the DNC? Just think about that one, Sean." In late October, in another phone call to Hannity's program, Trump added that he had "heard Clinton was involved," and he "would like the attorney general to find out what's going on. Because, you know what? We are investigating corruption."[75]

On July 25, however, he told the Ukrainian president, "I would like you to find out what happened with this whole situation with Ukraine, they say CrowdStrike...I guess you have one of your wealthy people...The server, they say Ukraine has it." Within ninety-one minutes of the end of the call, an official in the Office of Management and Budget sent a secret email to the Pentagon with instructions to "'please hold off on' distribution of the funds." Even without knowing this, however, Lieutenant Colonel Alexander Vindman, who was the National Security Council's director for European Affairs, and had been listening in on the call as part of his official duties, grew so alarmed after hearing Trump's threat that he went to see John Eisenberg, the White House lawyer responsible for the NSC's business. Eisenberg told Vindman not to tell anyone about the call—against all protocol, he suggested that a rough transcript of the call be hidden in a special computer system normally only used for highly sensitive documents.[76]

The apparent cover-up attempt failed, however, thanks to the bravery and patriotism of two anonymous whistleblowers who, like Vindman, were alarmed that their president had used the threat of losing congressionally mandated funds to shake down the head of a foreign nation for dirt on his political opponents. The first whistleblower submitted a detailed complaint on August 12, but Trump's acting director of national intelligence, Joseph Maguire, withheld it from Congress until he was compelled by subpoena to release it. It was made public on September 25, with transcripts appearing on multiple news websites the following day. (The second whistleblower's complaint remained classified throughout the House impeachment process.) When news of the call became public, the dam broke. Soliciting foreign help against one's opponents is a clear violation of US election law, and hence, Trump's impeachment became all but inevitable.[77]

On September 25, the president tried to save himself by releasing a rough transcript of the call—the same one his administration had previously hidden away on its secure computer system. Trump pretended that the transcript was, as he put it, an "exact word-for-word" and "comma-for-comma" re-creation of the conversation, and dubbed the phone call "perfect." Vice President Mike Pence asserted three times in an interview with PBS's Judy Woodruff that anyone reading the transcript "will see the president did nothing wrong."[78]

But anyone who did actually read the transcript of the call could see that it contained ellipses where crucial words were missing. A top White House official tried to explain away the ellipses by insisting that they did "not indicate missing words or phrases," but "a trailing off of a voice or pause." But as Vindman would later testify, the transcript did not match the call, especially in places where Trump brought up his nutty CrowdStrike conspiracy theory. Vindman had tried, he said, to get these sections rendered accurately on the transcript, but had been rebuffed without explanation.[79]

Over time, the excuses and explanations offered by Trump and his surrogates grew increasingly erratic and self-contradictory. Perhaps the oddest moment in the whole affair came when Trump, denying he had done anything wrong in asking a foreign government to funnel dirt to him about his political adversaries, chose to illustrate this point by doing it again, live on television. Asked about the matter on October 3 on the South Lawn of the White House, he told reporters that Ukraine should begin a "major investigation into the

Bidens." "I would certainly recommend that of Ukraine," he said, and then added, impromptu, that China, too, "should start an investigation into the Bidens." Two weeks later, on October 17, White House chief of staff Mick Mulvaney owned up to the charge in an attempt to shrug it off as no big deal. Asked by a reporter whether Trump's demand of Zelensky to announce an investigation before the military aid would be released constituted a "quid pro quo," Mulvaney replied, "We do that all the time with foreign policy.... And I have news for everybody: Get over it. There's going to be political influence in foreign policy." Within hours of having said this, he was denying that he had meant it.[80]

As members of the media debated the meaning of the Latin term "quid pro quo," and whether it constituted an impeachable act, Trump went off on one tantrum after another. He called the charges against him a "hoax," and he called the House impeachment investigation a "coup," a "lynching," "the Greatest Witch Hunt in the history of our country" (presumably surpassing the Mueller Report), and "THE GREATEST SCAM IN THE HISTORY OF AMERICAN POLITICS." Trump went after the "Do Nothing Democrats" for wasting "everyone's time and energy on bullshit" and demanded, apparently in all seriousness, that the congressman in charge of the inquiry, Democrat Adam Schiff of California, be charged with "treason." He warned the country of a "civil war like fracture." He even vaguely suggested that the whistleblower who started the whole thing should be executed, saying, at a private breakfast, that the whistleblower was a spy—and "you know what we used to do in the old days when we were smart? Right? The spies and treason, we used to handle it a little differently than we do now." In a furious, fact-challenged, single-spaced, six-page missive to House Speaker Nancy Pelosi, Trump called the impeachment process an "unprecedented and unconstitutional abuse of power by Democrat Lawmakers, unequaled in nearly two and a half centuries of American legislative history." He then accused her and her colleagues of "violating your oaths of office...breaking your allegiance to the Constitution, and...declaring open war on American Democracy," among many, many other alleged crimes he imagined had been committed against him, the country, and common decency. In this letter, in his rallies, in interviews, and on his Twitter feed, Trump told the country literally thousands of lies during the final months of 2019, averaging at one point more than forty "false or misleading claims" per day.[81] What's more, Trump also shut down all cooperation with the investigation and demanded that anyone connected to him, including those not employed by the government, refuse to honor congressional subpoenas, in yet another attempt to hide from Congress and the public the extent to which the defense of his actions had hitherto been built on lies.

Even as Trump appeared to be speaking from some fictional universe in which misinformation, disinformation, bald-faced lies, and purposeful "bullshit" combined into a narrative simultaneously malevolent and nonsensical, he could continue to count on the support of his base, especially those with media megaphones. Republican members of Congress still pretended to believe the crazy server story and demanded that the anonymous whistleblower be unmasked; one pair of right-wing operatives offered a $50,000 reward for "any information" about his identity. Senator John Kennedy, a Republican of Louisiana, went on both CNN and NBC's *Meet the Press* to argue, falsely, that it was "well documented...[that] the prime minister of Ukraine, the interior minister, the Ukrainian ambassador to the United States, the head of the Ukrainian Anti-Corruption League, all meddled in the election on social media and otherwise. They worked with a DNC operative." When *Meet the Press* host Chuck Todd replied, "Come on. You realize that the only other person selling this argument outside of the United States is Vladimir Putin," Kennedy stuck to his guns. A week later, Senator Ted Cruz, whom Trump had tortured during the 2016 campaign with cruel lies about his wife, as well as the lunatic accusation that Cruz's father had been involved in the assassination of President Kennedy, nevertheless took the same dishonest tack to protect the president and his party. Asked by Todd if he believed that Ukraine "meddled in the election of 2016," he replied "I do," and then added the falsehood, "And I think there's considerable evidence of that." He proceeded to change the subject to the alleged anti-Trump bias in the mainstream media. Not long after the show, and nearly three years after Kellyanne Conway personally explained her oxymoronic notion of "alternative facts" to Todd while trying to defend her boss's lies, Todd confessed to a reporter that it was fair to say that he had been "absurdly naive in hindsight," and that as it turned out, "the right has an incentive structure to utter the misinformation," whether it was on his program or elsewhere. Todd was promoting a special edition of the show to examine the "epidemic" of political disinformation that he and his colleagues had been so accommodating and "naive" in helping Trump, the Republican Party, and their allies to spread.[82]

Meanwhile, the days following these events demonstrated the cost to individuals in the Trump administration who had the necessary courage and patriotic concern to tell the truth in the face of the constant parade of lies told by the president, his advisers, and his supporters. Lawyers representing the (still anonymous) first whistleblower received death threats, even before Trump retweeted a link to his alleged identity, published by a conservative website. Lieutenant Colonel Vindman, a decorated veteran who had served in South Korea, Germany, and Iraq, and who received a Purple Heart following an encounter with an Iraqi roadside bomb, was subjected to a barrage of McCarthyite insinuation and veiled threats following his testimony. Fox News legal analyst John Yoo—who was previously best known for having authored legal arguments in support of the torture of terrorism suspects during the George W. Bush administration—wondered on air whether the whistleblower's actions might constitute "espionage." His host, Laura Ingraham, agreed that this was an "interesting angle." Rudy Giuliani, the president's personal lawyer and sometime spokesperson on Ukraine-related matters, had this to add: "How do we know he isn't a paranoid schizophrenic?" "How do we know he isn't an alcoholic?" At CNN, a recent hire, ex-Republican congressman Sean Duffy of Wisconsin, insisted that "it seems very clear that he is incredibly concerned about Ukrainian defense. I don't know that he's concerned about American policy." (Vindman, the son of a Jewish father and Christian mother, left Ukraine at age three.) When others on the network and elsewhere objected to this slander, network authorities referred back to the now perennially relevant excuse offered earlier that week by CNN president Jeff Zucker: "It is hard to find people who will come on and support the president's point of view."[83]

Trump and his allies also ramped up their smear campaign against the Bidens and other Democrats with a reported $10 million investment in political advertisements—timed, coincidentally, to Mark Zuckerberg's announcement that Facebook would allow political candidates to lie with impunity in Facebook ads. Amid this avalanche of lies by Trump and his supporters in Congress and the conservative media—lies that qualified as "bald-faced" in this case—key members of the mainstream media failed, repeatedly, to rise to the challenge they faced. Instead of standing up for what, by now, even remotely objective observers knew to be the truth of what had happened vis-à-vis Trump, Russia, and Ukraine, they took refuge in a particularly debased version of "both sides-ism" that treated truth as a matter of pure subjectivity—as if the evidence presented by the witnesses who came forward in the House impeachment proceedings was of no more value than the angry outbursts of Trump's supporters who objected to its public airing. In a number of cases, reporters simply asked the Biden campaign to respond, using a typical "he said / she said" framework that failed, anywhere, to indicate that one side was lying. As *New York Times* columnist Michelle Goldberg rightly observed, "Trump's weaponized disinformation" was proving "corrosive to democracy" regardless of its putative target, because it successfully "eroded the political salience of reality."[84]

Among the most egregious offenders in this category unfortunately was also likely to be the most influential: Goldberg's own *New York Times*. In a near-perfect example of false equivalence, its reporters failed to draw any distinction between one side's lies and the other's truth-telling. A page-one article, titled "The Breach Widens as Congress Nears a Partisan Impeachment," described what White House correspondent Michael D. Shear called "the different impeachment realities that the two parties are living in." Media scholar Jay Rosen noticed twelve separate instances in which this one account failed to distinguish between purposeful Republican falsehoods and what all sentient observers—including the entire US intelligence community—knew to be the truth. (The phrase "both sides" made four separate appearances in the piece.) Instead, the contest between truth and lies was posed as a war metaphor ("Both sides engaged in a kind of mutually assured destruction"), a childish spat ("They called each other liars and demagogues and accused each other of being desperate and unfair"), and the sad consequence of epistemological disagreement ("The two parties could not even agree on a basic set of facts in front of them"). *Times* readers were treated to bald-faced Republican lie after bald-faced Republican lie without any context provided by the author to indicate that their fictional narratives could not be trusted.

And regrettably, the article was no outlier in the paper's coverage. In another front-page analysis, *Times* White House correspondent Peter Baker described the drama of impeachment as playing out against "conspiracy theories," which he said were "everywhere," adding that "conspiracy theorists are in the White House and Congress," though he neglected to point to a single "conspiracy theory" that did not emanate from the Republican side of the aisle. This willingness to play patsy for purposeful misinformation had the effect of making America's most important and influential news source a willing participant in Trump's lies and his party's strategic decision to abandon all pretense of telling the truth. It disserved not only the paper's readers but also the paper's fundamental reason for being: holding the powerful—in this case the most powerful person on the planet—democratically accountable.[85]

Baker's article embraced yet another mainstream meme that under-girded the Republican playbook of deliberate dissimulation and ob-fuscation. Unlike Bill Clinton's December 1998 impeachment, which, he wrote, "felt like the ultimate drama, so intense that the rest of the world seemed to have stopped spinning on its axis," the Trump version twenty-one years later inspired "less suspense and an outcome seemingly foreordained."[86] Never mind that the stakes of selling out the national interest to a foreign power and demanding that another leader interfere in our democracy dwarf the significance of lying about a consensual sexual relationship. This embrace of the Republican strategy of claiming boredom, declining television ratings, and a lack of interest among "real Americans"—as if impeachment were just another reality-TV program, and in this case, one that was inferior in its entertainment value to the one Trump and Fox et al. were producing on their networks—was yet another trap that many journalists eagerly jumped into.

Writing for Reuters, Jeff Mason and Patricia Zengerle began their coverage of the House impeachment hearings with this lead para-graph: "Democratic lawmakers tried their hand at reality television with mixed results on Wednesday as they presented arguments to the American public for the impeachment of a former star of the genre, Donald Trump. Unlike the best reality TV shows—not to mention the Trump presidency itself—fireworks and explosive moments were scarce, however." They then proceeded to quote a tweet from none other than Eric Trump, who complained, "This is horribly boring..." NBC's Jonathan Allen also felt that the proper prism for the consti-tutional questions raised by the nation's third impeachment proceed-ings in its 230-year history was show business. He complained, "The first round felt more like the dress rehearsal for a serious one-act play than the opening night of a hit Broadway musical."[87]

Yet another significant weakness of the coverage of Trump's impeachment—and an ironic one, at that, given that the entire question of Trump's guilt turned on a "quid pro quo"—which was just a fancy way of saying "bribery"—was the willingness of most members of the media to ignore the acts of bribery that Trump deployed to get himself off the hook. Rarely, if anywhere, did one read or hear that, in preparation for his Senate trial, Trump was simultaneously showering cash contributions on the very same Republican senators who would constitute his jury. According to Richard Painter, formerly the chief White House ethics lawyer, under President George W. Bush, these contributions constituted "felony bribery" by the president. "Any other American who offered cash to the jury before a trial would go to prison," he tweeted, following up with "Any senator who accepts cash from @realDonaldTrump before the impeachment trial is guilty of accepting a bribe and should go to the slammer."[88]

Meanwhile, Trump never gave up his successful strategy of using the media attention he commanded to continue his never-ending campaign of lies. (He managed to make well more than 16,241 "false or misleading claims," according to the *Washington Post* fact-checking team's count during the first three years of his presidency, with a whopping average of just under thirty-four every single day during the combined months of October and November in both 2018 and 2019.) One tiny point of light appeared in the coverage of these lies, however, giving one a glimpse of what we might see if the president were held to even the most basic standard of truth-telling. During a September 25 press conference, as Trump was lying yet again about the Bidens—this time attacking accurate reporting in the *Washington Post* as a "fake article," inventing a threat allegedly made by Democratic senator Chris Murphy to Ukrainian officials, and pretending that Democrats had chosen to time their impeachment hearings to ruin his speech before the United Nations—something unprecedented in the history of American television news took place: "We hate to do this, really," MSNBC political analyst Nicolle Wallace said apologetically, as she stepped in front of what was suddenly a split screen. "But the president isn't telling the truth."[89]

Conclusion

SYSTEM OVERLOAD

In her 1967 essay "Truth and Politics," Hannah Arendt described "a consistent and total substitution of lies for factual truth" as the means by which dictators can undermine our ability to "take our bearings in the real world"—a necessary precondition for the replacement of a democratic system with a totalitarian one. This systematic use of lying as propaganda, as Arendt observed in her 1951 study of totalitarianism, would discourage people from even seeking truthfulness. "Under such conditions, one could make people believe the most fantastic statements one day, and trust that if the next day they were given irrefutable proof of their falsehood, they would take refuge in cynicism; instead of deserting the leaders who had lied to them, they would protest that they had known all along that the statement was a lie and would admire the leaders for their superior tactical cleverness."[1]

One can see the success of this approach in the attitudes of present-day Trump supporters. For instance, back in 2007, according to an Associated Press–Yahoo poll, 71 percent of Republicans felt that honesty was "extremely important" in presidential candidates. Seventy percent of Democrats and 66 percent of independents gave the same response. A *Washington Post* poll asking the same question eleven years later, about two years into the Trump administration, found no change in the percentage of Democrats or independents who answered similarly. Republicans, however, had become a great deal more relaxed about honesty. Fewer than half now thought that honesty in a candidate was "extremely important," and 41 percent were now fine with presidential lying, just so long as the lies were told "in order to do what's right for the country." This embrace of Trump's tactic of the bald-faced lie among contemporary Republicans is consistent with what Arendt argued are the necessary conditions for the creation of "the ideal subject of a totalitarian state"—that is, the person "for whom the distinction between fact and fiction (that is, the reality of experience) and the distinction between true and false (that is, the standards of thought) no longer exist."[2]

Arendt formulated her arguments after having witnessed the rise of the European fascist and communist movements of the early and mid-twentieth century. While it would be both ahistorical and alarmist to suggest that the circumstances that led to those movements are even remotely similar to contemporary conditions in the United States, it remains true that Trump and his movement share a number of similar attributes. An obvious one is their consistent exploitation and promotion of anti-Semitism, in which he (and his supporters) traffic in many of the same tropes that Nazi and other fascist leaders found (and still find) so effective when seeking to scapegoat their Jewish citizens. One can often hear echoes of fascist-style appeals, not only from Trump but also from his most devoted aides and political enforcers, who are signaling their unshakable devotion to their leader and simultaneously warning all who might refuse to go along with them of as-yet-unspeakable consequences. How else to interpret a comment like that of the architect of Trump's cruel and punitive immigration policies, Stephen Miller? "Our opponents, the media and the whole world will soon see as we begin to take further actions that the powers of the president to protect our country are very substantial and will not be questioned."[3] Many of Trump's other acolytes also mimic the behavior of the supporters of former fascist leaders.

In his 2018 book *How Fascism Works*, Jason Stanley identified a number of disturbing parallels between Trump's movement and those of Mussolini and Hitler. These include (and I paraphrase):

- The purposeful dehumanization of powerless minorities and the most vulnerable members of society
- A bottomless capacity for conspiratorial imaginings
- The willingness to exploit, and on occasion, encourage, anti-Semitic attacks and imagery
- The romanticizing of rural life over cosmopolitan life, together with an insistence on the moral superiority of the largely white, Christian inhabitants of rural areas[4]

Yet another frightening parallel between Trump's ascension to power and the ascent of twentieth-century German and Italian fascist leaders has been the unwillingness of conservatives to challenge him. Holocaust historian Christopher Browning noted that in the 1930s, "thinking that they could ultimately control Hitler while enjoying the benefits of his popular support, [German] conservatives were initially gratified by the fulfillment of their agenda: intensified rearmament, the outlawing of the Communist Party, the suspension first of freedom of speech, the press, and assembly and then of parliamentary government itself, a purge of the civil service, and the abolition of independent labor unions." Needless to say, the Nazis then proceeded far beyond whatever goals they may have initially shared with their conservative allies, who were by then powerless to hinder them. The Republican leadership in the United States signaled right from the beginning of Trump's term that they would offer little or no resistance to his demands. It even did him the transparently anti-Democratic favor of canceling 2020 caucuses and primary contests so as not to embarrass Trump by allowing any remaining Republican dissenters to vote for a potential opponent.[5]

This started even before his presidency began, when Trump made his ludicrous claim of having actually won the popular vote. Paul Ryan, the Republican Speaker of the House, was well aware that the claim was incendiary nonsense, yet when asked on CBS's *60 Minutes* whether he really believed Trump, Ryan could not bring himself to admit the truth out loud. The best he could do was: "I don't know. I'm not really focused on these things." Pressed on his cowardly response, Ryan demurred: "I have no way of backing that up. I have no knowledge of such things....It doesn't matter to me. He won the election." This was the same Paul Ryan who was present at a secret meeting in 2016 where Republican Kevin McCarthy of California, then House majority leader, said he thought Trump might have been in the pay of Vladimir Putin. When laughter followed, McCarthy added, "Swear to God." Ryan did not dispute McCarthy's assessment, but asked his colleagues to keep the meeting secret. That did not happen, however, as the press soon obtained a transcript of the taped remarks.[6]

The Senate, as well, soon became a kind of playpen for Trump's antics. Unlike the Nixon-era Republicans, who put their constitutionally mandated duties above their narrow political loyalties when it came time to hold Nixon accountable for his crimes, Trump's Republicans either cheered his lies, silently assented to them, or gave up and resigned. (Paul Ryan ended up doing all three.) As the authors of *How Democracies Die*, Steven Levitsky and Daniel Ziblatt, explained, "Unwilling to pay the political price of breaking with their own president, Republicans find themselves with little alternative but to constantly redefine what is and isn't tolerable. This will have terrible consequences for our democracy." And "the abdication of political responsibility by existing leaders," the authors noted, "often marks a nation's first step toward authoritarianism."[7]

Donald Trump knows, as all tyrants do, that without the accountability the media provide, almost anything can be justified. America's founders bequeathed the press its special status and protections under the First Amendment for exactly this reason—a democratic republic cannot function without it. Trump's insistent accusation that the media are the "Enemy of the American People" is intended to undermine confidence in the media and thereby its ability to fulfill its democratic function and hold his administration accountable for its actions. Trump began using the label during the early weeks of his presidency, in February 2017, specifically referring to the *New York Times*, CBS, NBC, ABC, and CNN, and repeated it frequently thereafter, using it in tweets sixteen times in 2018 and twenty-one in 2019. The phrase "enemy of the people" dates back to the Jacobin dictatorship in France during the Reign of Terror in the 1790s, the era of the French Revolution. In the mid-twentieth century it became common among mass-murdering dictators such as Stalin, Mao, and Hitler. It has remained popular with modern-day tyrants, including Venezuela's Hugo Chávez, Zimbabwe's Robert Mugabe, and the military junta that formerly ruled Myanmar.[8]

Trump started using it to attack any news organization that accurately reported on him in a way he disapproved of, which he called "fake news." By the time the deeply troubled Jarrod W. Ramos stormed the offices of the *Capital Gazette*, a daily newspaper in Annapolis, Maryland, and shot seven journalists, killing five of them, on June 28, 2018, Trump had already begun using the phrase regularly, including once just three days before. He continued to use it after an outspoken supporter in Florida, Cesar Sayoc Jr., sent bombs to CNN, as well as to the Clintons, Obama, George Soros, and other prominent Democrats, in October 2018. Trump, incredibly, appeared to side with Sayoc, sympathetically citing the "purposely false and inaccurate reporting of the Mainstream Media that I refer to as Fake News" as the basis for the "anger" that had inspired him.[9]

Trump has also repeatedly encouraged violence against journalists. At a campaign rally in Grand Rapids, Michigan, in December 2015, he pretended to reassure the crowd that even though he hated journalists, he "would never kill them." This was a relief, given that he frequently referred to reporters as "scum," "slime," "sick," and "lying, disgusting people," and often accused them of having committed "treason"—a crime punishable by death—when they criticized him. In May 2017, Greg Gianforte, then a Republican candidate for a US House seat in Montana, body-slammed a reporter who had asked a question about health care. Gianforte pled guilty to the charge of assault, but months later the president told a cheering crowd in Missoula, Montana, that "any guy who can do a body slam is my kind of guy." Trump also frequently riled up his supporters and taunted reporters with decidedly unfunny jokes about regimes that have murdered uncooperative journalists. In July 2017, he posted a short video to Twitter in which he was portrayed literally beating up someone whose head had been replaced by the CNN logo, as if to encourage his supporters to do the same in real life. (In October 2019, at a mass gathering of Trump supporters in Miami, the crowd cheered a video that pretended to show Trump literally murdering journalists with guns and knives, shooting and stabbing members of the media. This at least met with White House disapproval.)[10]

But it did not matter how frequently or how egregiously Trump and his administration lied to reporters, or how viciously they insulted their character, their professionalism, or even their ethnicity—these same reporters returned for more lies and more abuse. "We're not cheerleaders for the president nor are we the opposition," insisted *New York Times* White House correspondent Peter Baker, who added, "What we shouldn't do is let the noise overcome our journalistic values." But all too often, what was offered as a defense of old-fashioned journalistic commitments to "objectivity"—the need to provide "both sides" of any given controversy—devolved, in practice, to running interference for Trump's dishonesty.[11]

For instance, after covering Trump's presidency for over two years, Baker himself was well aware that Trump could not be trusted to tell the truth about anything. During an August 2019 summit meeting in Biarritz, France, he alerted *New York Times* readers to the fact that Trump had recently "seemed especially erratic, spinning out wild conspiracy theories, provoking racial and religious divisions and employing messianic language about himself." Two days later, he was allowing that, "like other presidents, and perhaps even more so, Mr. Trump tends to hear what he wants to hear at settings like this, either tuning out contrary voices or disregarding them." But Baker was describing a man who was nothing like other presidents. This was the president who had just tweeted an almost comically self-serving lie: "The question I was asked most today by fellow World Leaders, who think the USA is doing so well and is stronger than ever before, happens to be, 'Mr. President, why does the American media hate your Country so much? Why are they rooting for it to fail?'"[12]

In other words, the "journalistic values" that Baker was defending, when put into practice, had the effect of hiding the true extent of the president's transparent dishonesty from his readers. The values upon which this impulse was based may have worked well in the past, but they were forged in another time under radically different circumstances. "We're not at war. We're at work," was how *Washington Post* executive editor Martin Baron put it in October 2017.[13]

But that mantra was exactly wrong for the Trump era. As Trump continued his assaults on Baron, Baker, and their colleagues, it grew increasingly apparent that journalists and others representing the US media were making a mistake: they were so intent on insisting that they were not in a fight with the president that they were failing to inform the public of just how serious a threat he posed to its freedoms. Indeed, they were losing their ability to do so.

Joel Simon, the executive director of the Committee to Protect Journalists, which defends the rights—and sometimes lives—of journalists around the world, identified a pattern of behavior toward the press among all modern autocrats. Speaking to *New Yorker* editor David Remnick in 2018, Simon compared Trump to Venezuela's Hugo Chávez, Turkey's Recep Tayyip Erdoğan, Egypt's Abdel Fattah el-Sisi, and Zimbabwe's Robert Mugabe. These were all elected autocrats who attack the media in much the same way that Trump does, employing "deliberate and ominous intensity," he said, which in turn eventually leads the press to adopt a more oppositional tone and role. According to Simon, "That paves the way for the autocrat's next move....Popular support for the media dwindles and the leader starts instituting restrictions. It's an old strategy." Here again, Trump fit the model. Trump treats the press as illegitimate. By 2019, his press secretary ended the regular White House briefing and spoke only to Fox News and the equally sycophantic Sinclair Broadcast Group, while maintaining his constant campaign of vilification. In October 2017, he tweeted: "With all of the Fake News coming out of NBC and the Networks, at what point is it appropriate to challenge their License? Bad for country!" Trump said he found it "frankly disgusting the way the press is able to write whatever they want to write." In late 2018, Trump went so far as to suggest that criticism of him on the late-night comedy show *Saturday Night Live* was a form of "collusion" with his political opponents and should be "tested in courts." And again, remarkably, Trump's most devoted supporters proved happy to endorse such a crackdown. According to one 2018 poll, 43 percent of Republicans believed that Trump should be allowed to shut down media outlets that he disapproved of.[14]

Trump's contempt for the press and the First Amendment was just one component of his autocratic approach to the presidency. He also held himself to be above the law in refusing to recognize Congress's right to hold members of the executive branch accountable, seeking to evade or ignore its lawful subpoenas. He termed Article 1, Section 9, of the Constitution, its Foreign Emoluments Clause, to be somehow "phony" and therefore inapplicable to him and his businesses. He also claimed, without any justification in precedent or history, "I have an Article II where I have the right to do whatever I want as President." He has repeatedly threatened the country with extra-constitutional violence if he should be forced from office for any reason, up to and including a lost election. As a candidate, Trump repeatedly refused, when queried, to say that he would accept the results of the election if he lost. As president, he has threatened the country by explaining that, should he decide he needs them, "I have the support of the police, the support of the military, the support of the Bikers for Trump—I have the tough people, but they don't play it tough—until they go to a certain point, and then it would be very bad, very bad."[15]

Trump has already repeatedly shown himself to be willing to abuse his presidential power to punish those he deems to be adversaries, especially when it comes to the media and democratic accountability. Trump has twice deployed the power of the federal government to attack the financial interests of media organizations he doesn't like. The first time—when he instructed the Justice Department to block a merger between Time Warner—owner of CNN—with ATT, the order was carried out but blocked by the courts. The second, when he apparently ordered the Pentagon to deny a $10 billion cloud computing contract to Amazon because its owner, Jeff Bezos, also owned the *Washington Post*, succeeded. In neither case did anyone of significance in his government, his party, or the Trump movement at large raise their voice in protest of these obvious and egregious abuses of the office of the presidency.[16]

Yet even without these abuses, as well as his hints of coups and military takeovers, the presidency is already vested with enormous and often-unchecked powers under the Constitution. Even were Trump to respect the constitutional constraints on his office, he would still enjoy an awesome degree of potentially destructive power. Beginning with the birth of the atom bomb and the ever-expanding ideology of the "national security state," the prerogatives of the presidency have grown beyond anything the founders could have possibly imagined. With America's nuclear arsenal at his disposal, Trump could literally end all human life and destroy the planet should this notion somehow strike him as a good idea. Less dramatically, he could also decide to invoke any one of the emergency powers contained in the 123 statutory provisions that have been passed into law giving presidents near-dictatorial powers. Trump could, for instance, decide to shut down most forms of electronic communications within the United States. He could just as easily seize control of "any facility or station for wire communication," should he decide to proclaim "that there exists a state or threat of war involving the United States," and order it to broadcast only his voice and his orders.[17]

It may sound alarmist to some to suggest that a form of fascist totalitarianism is possible in the United States, the world's longest-surviving democratic republic. And the point is no doubt a contentious one. *New York Times* executive editor Dean Baquet is among those who feel that such concern is misplaced. "I get that people see the phenomenon of someone who says inflammatory statements as a new thing," he said. He went on to compare Trump to some of the more colorful politicians he had covered as a young reporter, offering, as one example, the corrupt Louisiana governor Edwin Edwards, famed for claiming that the only way he could lose an election was to be "caught in bed with either a dead girl or a live boy." But the experience of Trump's presidency so far demands that the institutions charged with protecting American democracy and civic life err on the side of vigilance rather than complacency. It was the complacency of both European and US elites in the 1920s and 1930s that allowed fascism to flourish. Coincidentally, this attitude was nowhere better illustrated than in the reporting of the *New York Times*, which reassured readers in 1922 that "several reliable, well-informed sources confirmed the idea that Hitler's anti-Semitism was not so genuine or violent as it sounded," and was just a political ploy "to catch masses of followers and keep them aroused, enthusiastic, and in line."[18] Again, Donald Trump is not Adolf Hitler, and the United States of the twenty-first century bears virtually no resemblance to the Germany of the 1930s and 1940s. Even so, history's warnings can be suggestive even when they do not arrive with precise instructions.

Reflecting on the corruption of his erstwhile friends and colleagues in the Trump administration, former FBI director James Comey explained, "It starts with your sitting silent while he lies, both in public and private, making you complicit by your silence." The silence is natural. "After all, what are you supposed to say? He's the president of the United States." The end result is that "you are lost. He has eaten your soul."[19] Comey's metaphor is a good one, but still the circle he drew was too narrow. Donald Trump's lies have not only eaten America's soul; they have undermined its values and threatened the future viability of its democratic republican form of government. His presidency is simultaneously a symptom and a cause of our descent into lying as way of life. And it is a warning. Trump, as we have seen, is as much a symbol of the problems America faces as he is the problem itself; he is the Frankenstein monster of a political system that has not merely tolerated lies from our leaders but has come to demand them. The weaknesses of the American political system that gave rise to Donald Trump will not disappear with his presidency. They must be confronted, head-on, while we still have a soul—and a republic—worth saving.

ACKNOWLEDGMENTS

First, a note: This book is the culmination of a project I originally began back in 1991 as a graduate student in history at Stanford University. My study of presidential lying back then resulted in, among other offshoots, my PhD dissertation on the impact of presidential lies told about Yalta and the Cuban Missile Crisis as well as my book *When Presidents Lie: A History of Deception and Its Consequences*, published by Viking in 2004. That work focused on Yalta, the missile crisis, the Second Gulf of Tonkin incident, and the Reagan administration's policies in Central America, with a short conclusion dealing with George W. Bush's then recently launched war in Iraq. Though all those topics are also examined in this one, readers with a particular interest in those topics may be interested in following up on them in the earlier work, where they are treated in far greater detail and with considerably more thorough documentary and bibliographic citation.

Writing and publishing books is an oddly lonesome process that simultaneously involves a great deal of collective effort by lots of people. I'm sure I don't know everyone at Basic Books I need to thank but I am deeply grateful to everyone who had or will have a hand

Acknowledgments

in it. I employed no researchers save Taia Handlin, who did a meticulous job of checking all the quotes in the final draft, and for that I give thanks. Earlier, inferior drafts were immeasurably improved by the expert readings I received from Michael Kazin, Danny Goldberg, Laura Hercher, and especially Kai Bird. My work also benefited from the interruptions and occasional mockery of the recent graduate of the University of Wisconsin Eve Rose Alterman. Having plans for graduate school, she would, I'm sure, be especially grateful if you actually purchased the copy you are currently reading.

My parents, Ruth and Carl Alterman, remain, at age eighty-five and (nearly) ninety, respectively, avid readers and commenters on my work, and for this I am also indebted, albeit in some ways more than others. I am more than happy, however, to once again lay the ultimate responsibility for whatever mistakes remain in this book on their strong shoulders.

ERA
New York City
January 3, 2020

NOTES

A Note on Definitions

1. Augustine, "On Lying," trans. M. S. Muldowney, 51–110, and "Against Lying," trans. H. B. Jaffee, 121–179, in R. J. Deferrari, ed., *Fathers of the Church*, vol. 16, *Treatises on Various Subjects* (Washington, DC: Catholic University of America Press, 1952), 55–56.

2. See Irfan Khawaja, "Not a Suicide Pact: The Constitution in a Time of National Emergency," *Dissent*, Spring 2007, 1–13.

Introduction: How Could Trump Happen?

1. Chris Hayes, "Chris Hayes Reviews Michiko Kakutani's Book About Our Post-Truth Era," review of *The Death of Truth: Notes on Falsehood in the Age of Trump* (New York: Tim Duggan Books, 2018), *New York Times Book Review*, July 29, 2018, 12.

2. Glenn Kessler, Salvador Rizzo, and Meg Kelly, "President Trump Has Made More Than 10,000 False or Misleading Claims," *Washington Post*, April 29, 2019, https://www.washingtonpost.com/politics/2019/04/29/president-trump-has-made-more-than-false-or-misleading-claims.

3. Genesis 27:12.

4. Exodus 1:20.

5. Deborah A. Kashy and Bella M. DePaulo, "Who Lies," *Journal of Personality and Social Psychology* 70, no. 5 (1998): 1037–1051.

6. For the San Blas Kuna and the Kalapalo, see J. A. Barnes, *A Pack of Lies: Toward a Sociology of Lying* (New York: Cambridge University Press, 1994), 65–69. For Hollywood and lies, see David Shaw, "Tinseltown Spins Yarns, Media

Takes Bait," *Los Angeles Times*, February 12, 2001, A12. For Henry Taylor, see John J. Mearsheimer, *Why Leaders Lie: The Truth About Lying in International Politics* (New York: Oxford University Press, 2011), 19. See also Hannah Arendt, "Truth and Politics," *New Yorker*, February 17, 1967, https://www.newyorker.com /magazine/1967/02/25/truth-and-politics.

7. See "Presidential Historians Survey 2017," C-Span, https://www.c-span.org /presidentsurvey2017; Frank Newport, "Americans Say Reagan Is the Greatest President," Gallup, February 8, 2011, https://news.gallup.com/poll/146183/Americans -Say-Reagan-Greatest-President.aspx.

8. Eric Alterman, *When Presidents Lie: A History of Official Deception and Its Consequences* (New York: Viking, 2004).

9. Hannah Arendt, "From an Interview," *New York Review of Books*, October 26, 1978, https://www.nybooks.com/articles/1978/10/26/hannah-arendt-from -an-interview.

10. Robert Dallek, *Franklin D. Roosevelt and American Foreign Policy: 1932–1945* (New York: Oxford University Press, 1995), 289.

11. William E. Leuchtenburg, *The American President: From Teddy Roosevelt to Bill Clinton* (New York: Oxford University Press, 2015), 9.

12. See Frederick Jackson Turner, "The Problem of the West," *Atlantic Monthly*, September 1896, https://www.theatlantic.com/magazine/archive/1896/09/the-problem -of-the-west/525699. See also Walter Nugent, *Habits of Empire: A History of American Expansion* (New York: Knopf, 2008), 236, 268; A. G. Hopkins, *American Empire: A Global History* (Princeton, NJ: Princeton University Press, 2018), 32.

13. These phrases are drawn from the Declaration of Independence, originally drafted by Thomas Jefferson in 1776, and are known to almost all American schoolchildren.

14. Harry S. Truman, "Address at Laramie, Wyoming," May 9, 1950, Harry S. Truman Library and Museum (HSTL hereafter), https://www.trumanlibrary.gov /library/public-papers/119/address-laramie-wyoming.

15. "United States Objectives and Programs for National Security," April 14, 1950, *Foreign Relations of the United States*, 1950, vol. 1, ed. Neal H. Petersen, John P. Glennon, David W. Mabon, Ralph R. Goodwin, and William Z. Slany (Washington, DC: Government Printing Office, 1977), 234–292.

16. There are no reliable figures for the number of deaths caused by the US wars in Vietnam and Cambodia. Three million is a midrange figure, but some estimates are below two million and some are over four million.

17. "President Delivers State of the Union Address," January 29, 2002, the White House, https://georgewbush-whitehouse.archives.gov/news/releases/2002/01 /20020129-11.html.

18. See Michael Kinsley, "Dead Wrong," *Slate*, April 6, 2001, www.slate.com /articles/news_and_politics/readme/2001/04/dead_wrong.html; Benjamin C. Bradlee, "Reflections on Lying," Press-Enterprise Lecture Series, Number 32, University of

California, Riverside, January 7, 1977, 12, reprinted in Ben Bradlee, "In His Own Words: Ben Bradlee on Liars," *Washington Post*, October 22, 2014, https://www.washington post.com/opinions/in-his-own-words-ben-bradlee-on-liars/2014/10/22/6236cadc -4a67-11e4-a046-120a8a855cca_story.html.

19. "The World Outside and the Pictures in Our Heads" is the title of the first chapter in Lippmann's 1925 masterwork, *Public Opinion*, and can be found at Monoskop, https://monoskop.org/images/b/bf/Lippman_Walter_Public_Opinion.pdf.

20. See Garry Wills, "The Triumph of the Hard Right," review of E. J. Dionne, *Why the Right Went Wrong: Conservatism—from Goldwater to the Tea Party and Beyond* (New York: Simon and Schuster, 2016), *New York Review of Books*, February 16, 2016, https://www.nybooks.com/articles/2016/02/11/ej-dionne-triumph-of-the-hard -right; Mike Lofgren, "Goodbye to All That: Reflections of a GOP Operative Who Left the Cult," Truthout, September 3, 2011, https://truthout.org/articles/goodbye-to -all-that-reflections-of-a-gop-operative-who-left-the-cult. See also Thomas Mann and Norman Ornstein, "Let's Just Say It: The Republicans Are the Problem," *Washington Post*, April 27, 2012, https://www.washingtonpost.com/opinions/lets-just-say-it-the -republicans-are-the-problem/2012/04/27/gIQAxCVUlT_story.html.

21. Eric Alterman, "How False Equivalence Is Distorting the 2016 Election Coverage," *The Nation*, June 2, 2019, https://www.thenation.com/article/how-false -equivalence-is-distorting-the-2016-election-coverage.

22. See Jürgen Habermas, *Theory of Communicative Action*, vol. 1, *Reason and Rationalization of Society* (Boston: Beacon Press, 1984); Thomas Carson, *Lying and Deception: Theory and Practice* (New York: Oxford University Press, 2010); Harry Frankfurt, *On Bullshit* (Princeton, NJ: Princeton University Press, 2005).

Chapter One: "The Serpent's Eye That Charms but to Destroy"

1. Gordon S. Wood, *Revolutionary Characters: What Made the Founders Different* (New York: Penguin, 2006), 43.

2. Ron Chernow, *Washington: A Life* (New York: Penguin, 2011), 636–664.

3. Mary V. Thompson, *The Only Unavoidable Subject of Regret: George Washington, Slavery, and the Enslaved Community at Mount Vernon* (Charlottesville: University of Virginia Press, 2019), 25.

4. Chernow, *Washington*, 334, 636–664, 802–803.

5. Joseph Ellis, *His Excellency: George Washington* (New York: Knopf, 2004), xiv; Eric Foner, "Tremendous in His Wrath," *London Review of Books* 41, no. 24 (December 2019): 13–15.

6. Dinitia Smith and Nicholas Wade, "DNA Tests Offer Evidence That Jefferson Fathered a Child with His Slave," *New York Times*, November 1, 1998, A1; Annette Gordon-Reed, "Sally Hemings, Thomas Jefferson and the Ways We Talk About Our Past," *New York Times Book Review*, August 24, 2017, 20.

7. James Thomson Callender, in the *Richmond Recorder*, September 1, 1802, quoted at "To Thomas Jefferson from John Barnes, dated August 31, 1802 (received

September 2, 1802)," Founders Online, https://founders.archives.gov/documents/Jefferson/01-38-02-0286; original reproduced in part at "Sally Hemings Accusation," September 1, 1802, PBS Archives, https://www.pbs.org/jefferson/archives/documents/ih195822z.htm.

8. Thomas Jefferson, *Memoirs, Correspondence, and Private Papers of Thomas Jefferson*, vol. 3 (London: Arkose Press, 2015 [1829]), 506.

9. James Parton, *Life of Thomas Jefferson* (Boston: James R. Osgood, 1874), 165.

10. Gordon S. Wood, *Friends Divided: John Adams and Thomas Jefferson* (New York: Penguin, 2017), 61.

11. John Adams to John Quincy Adams, January 3, 1794, quoted in Mark Silk, "Did John Adams Out Thomas Jefferson and Sally Hemings?," *Smithsonian Magazine*, November 2016, https://www.smithsonianmag.com/history/john-adams-out-thomas-jefferson-sally-hemings-180960789.

12. Arthur Schlesinger Jr., "Foreign Policy and the American Character," the Cyril Foster Lecture, in *The Cycles of American History* (New York: Oxford University Press, 1983), 51–68.

13. "Washington's Farewell Address 1796," Yale Law School, Lillian Goldman Law Library, Avalon Project, https://avalon.law.yale.edu/18th_century/washing.asp. For his first draft, see Patricia O'Toole, *The Moralist: Woodrow Wilson and the World He Made* (New York: Simon and Schuster, 2018), 211. See also "John Quincy Adams's Warning Against the Search for 'Monsters to Destroy,'" 1821, posted by Vincent Ferraro, Mount Holyoke, https://www.mtholyoke.edu/acad/intrel/jqadams.htm.

14. Walter Nugent, *Habits of Empire: A History of American Expansion* (New York: Knopf, 2008), xiii–xvi.

15. For Jefferson's views on the dangers of poverty and war, see Drew R. McCoy, *The Elusive Republic: Political Economy in Jeffersonian America* (Chapel Hill: University of North Carolina Press, 1980); Robert H. Wiebe, *The Opening of American Society: From the Adoption of the Constitution to the Era of Disunion* (New York: Knopf, 1984). For the "chosen people of God," see Thomas Jefferson, *Notes on the State of Virginia, 1781–85* (Boston: H. Sprague, 1802), 226. For the "empire of liberty," see Robert W. Tucker and David C. Hendrickson, *The Empire of Liberty: The Statecraft of Thomas Jefferson* (New York: Oxford University Press, 1990). For Jefferson's dream, see "Extract from Thomas Jefferson to James Monroe," November 24, 1801, Monticello, http://tjrs.monticello.org/letter/1743.

16. Nugent, *Habits of Empire*, 51.

17. "From Thomas Jefferson to Meriwether Lewis, 27 April 1803," Founders Online, https://founders.archives.gov/documents/Jefferson/01-40-02-0204.

18. For the treaty background, see Nugent, *Habits of Empire*, 125. For Madison's offer, see Michael Beschloss, *Presidents of War: The Epic Story, from 1807 to Modern Times* (New York: Crown, 2018), 57. For his blundering into war, see Walter LaFeber, *The American Age: United States Foreign Policy at Home and Abroad Since 1750* (New York: W. W. Norton, 1989), 50–51.

19. James Traub, *John Quincy Adams* (New York: Basic Books, 2016), 220–225.

20. Daniel Walker Howe, *What Hath God Wrought: The Transformation of America, 1815–1848* (New York: Oxford University Press, 2007), 348. For Forsyth, see Nugent, *Habits of Empire*, 227.

21. For O'Sullivan and Manifest Destiny, see LaFeber, *American Age*, 91–92; Beschloss, *Presidents of War*, 103. For Bennett, see Greg Grandin, *The End of the Myth: From the Frontier to the Border Wall in the Mind of America* (New York: Metropolitan Books, 2019), 91.

22. A. G. Hopkins, *American Empire: A Global History* (Princeton, NJ: Princeton University Press, 2018).

23. See ibid. For Walker, see Julius W. Pratt, "The Ideology of American Expansion," in *Essays in Honor of William E. Dodd*, ed. Avery Craven (Chicago: University of Chicago Press, 1935), 342.

24. For Polk's election, see LaFeber, *American Age*, 91–92; Beschloss, *Presidents of War*, 103. For the banner, see Beschloss, *Presidents of War*, 105.

25. Louis Fisher, "The Mexican War and Lincoln's Spot Resolutions," Law Library of Congress, August 18, 2009, https://www.loc.gov/law/help/usconlaw/pdf/Mexican.war.pdf.

26. For the Whigs and Polk, see Howe, *What Hath God Wrought*, 741. For Truman, see Beschloss, *Presidents of War*, 462.

27. Cong. Globe, 13th Cong., 1st sess., vol. 17 (1848), January 12, 1848, p. 156, https://books.google.com/books?id=9ZbhCyRXgjMC&dq.

28. "To William Herndon," February 15, 1848, in Abraham Lincoln, *Collected Works of Abraham Lincoln*, vol. 1, *1824–1848* (New Brunswick, NJ: Rutgers University Press, 1953), 452, online at University of Michigan Digital Library Production Services, https://quod.lib.umich.edu/l/lincoln/lincoln1.

29. "The Lincoln-Douglas Debates of 1858," Lincoln Home, National Historic Site, Illinois, National Park Service, https://www.nps.gov/liho/learn/historyculture/debates.htm; Beschloss, *Presidents of War*, 155.

30. James K. Polk, "Second Annual Message to Congress," December 8, 1846, Miller Center, University of Virginia, https://millercenter.org/the-presidency/presidential-speeches/december-8-1846-second-annual-message-congress.

31. Steven Hahn, *A Nation Without Borders, 1830–1910* (New York: Viking, 2016), 132.

32. Richard Shenkman, *Presidential Ambition: Gaining Power at Any Cost* (New York: HarperCollins, 2011), loc. 1761–1767, Kindle.

Chapter Two: "Yankeedoodledum"

1. Walt Whitman, *The Gathering of the Forces*, vol. 1 (New York, 1920), 32–33.

2. "Maddison Historical Statistics," University of Groningen, https://www.rug.nl/ggdc/historicaldevelopment/maddison.

Notes on Chapter Two

3. For the naval appropriations bill, see "Naval Appropriations Act for Fiscal Year 1891 (Battleship Act of 1890), June 30, 1890," General Records of the U.S. Government, National Archives and Records Administration, https://www.visitthecapitol.gov/exhibitions/artifact/naval-appropriations-act-fiscal-year-1891-battleship-act-1890-june-30-1890. For Mahan and Turner, see A. T. Mahan, *The Influence of Sea Power upon History, 1660–1783*, Gutenberg, www.gutenberg.org/files/13529/13529-h/13529-h.htm; Frederick Jackson Turner, "The Significance of the Frontier in American History, 1893," National Humanities Center, http://nationalhumanitiescenter.org/pds/gilded/empire/text1/turner.pdf; Frederick Jackson Turner, *The Frontier in American History* (New York: Henry Holt, 1921), available at Project Gutenberg, www.gutenberg.org/files/22994/22994-h/22994-h.htm.

4. Rudyard Kipling, "The White Man's Burden," originally published in *The Times* (London) on February 4, 1899, and in *McClure's Magazine* the same month in the United States.

5. Walter LaFeber, *The American Age: United States Foreign Policy at Home and Abroad Since 1750* (New York: W. W. Norton, 1989), 82.

6. Louis Fisher, "Destruction of the *Maine* (1898)," Law Library of Congress, August 4, 2009, https://www.loc.gov/law/help/usconlaw/pdf/Maine.1898.pdf.

7. General James Rusling, "Interview with President William McKinley," *Christian Advocate*, January 22, 1903, reprinted in Daniel Schirmer and Stephen Rosskamm Shalom, eds., *The Philippines Reader* (Boston: South End Press, 1987), 22–23, and available at History Matters, http://historymatters.gmu.edu/d/5575; "William McKinley," *New World Encyclopedia*, https://www.newworldencyclopedia.org/entry/William_McKinley.

8. James Ford Rhodes, *The McKinley and Roosevelt Administrations, 1897–1909* ([Australia]: Sagwan Press, 2018), 107.

9. John Lawrence Tone, *War and Genocide in Cuba, 1895–1898* (Chapel Hill: University of North Carolina Press, 2006), 246.

10. Daniel Immerwahr, *How to Hide an Empire: A History of the Greater United States* (New York: Farrar, Straus and Giroux, 2019), 103.

11. Ibid., 69.

12. William E. Leuchtenburg, *The American President: From Teddy Roosevelt to Bill Clinton* (New York: Oxford University Press, 2015), 42.

13. Walter LaFeber, *The Panama Canal* (New York: Oxford University Press, 1989), 35–36.

14. Ibid., 52–57.

15. Ibid.

16. See Walter LaFeber, *The Cambridge History of American Foreign Relations*, vol. 2, *The American Search for Opportunity, 1865–1913* (New York: Cambridge University Press, 1993), 194–195; Steven Hahn, *A Nation Without Borders: The United States and Its World in an Age of Civil War, 1830–1910* (New York: Viking, 2016), 499.

17. A. G. Hopkins, *American Empire: A Global History* (Princeton, NJ: Princeton University Press, 2018), 21.

18. C. J. Bullock, "The United States as a Creditor Nation," *Review of Economics and Statistics* 14, no. 4 (1932): 178–180.

19. Robert C. Hilderbrand, *Power and the People: Executive Management of Public Opinion in Foreign Affairs, 1897–1921* (Chapel Hill: University of North Carolina Press, 1981), 141.

20. Bruce D. Porter, *War and the Rise of the State* (New York: Free Press, 1994), 272–274.

21. Richard Polenberg, *Fighting Faiths: The Abrams Case, the Supreme Court, and Free Speech* (Ithaca, NY: Cornell University Press, 1998), 323; Adam Hochschild, "When America Tried to Deport Its Radicals," *New Yorker*, November 4, 2019, https://www.newyorker.com/magazine/2019/11/11/when-america-tried-to-deport -its-radicals.

22. Robert K. Murray, *Red Scare: A Study in National Hysteria, 1919–1920* (Minneapolis: University of Minnesota Press, 1955), 250–256.

23. For the CPI forgery, see Stephen Vaughn, *Holding Fast the Inner Lines: Democracy, Nationalism, and the Committee on Public Information* (Chapel Hill: University of North Carolina Press, 1980), 77. For CPI's nickname and overall record, see Thomas Fleming, *The Illusion of Victory: America in World War I* (New York: Basic Books, 2003), 119–120. For Lippmann, see Ronald Steel, *Walter Lippmann and the American Century* (Boston: Little, Brown, 1980), 147.

24. Richard Shenkman, *Presidential Ambition: Gaining Power at Any Cost* (New York: HarperCollins, 2011), loc. 4908–5055, Kindle.

25. John Milton Cooper Jr., *Woodrow Wilson* (New York: Knopf, 2009), 533; Richard P. Menger, Christopher M. Storey, Bharat Guthikonda, Symeon Missios, Anil Nanda, and John M. Cooper, "Woodrow Wilson's Hidden Stroke of 1919: The Impact of Patient-Physician Confidentiality on United States Foreign Policy," *Journal of Neurosurgery* 39 (July 2015), https://thejns.org/focus/view/journals /neurosurg-focus/39/1/article-pE6.xml?tab_body=pdf.

26. Kenneth S. Lynn, "The Agony of Woodrow Wilson," *Wilson Quarterly* (Winter 2004), http://archive.wilsonquarterly.com/essays/hidden-agony-woodrow -wilson; Kendrick A. Clements, *The Presidency of Woodrow Wilson* (Lawrence: University of Kansas Press, 1992), 198.

27. Patricia O'Toole, *The Moralist: Woodrow Wilson and the World He Made* (New York: Simon and Schuster, 2018), 431–432.

28. Cooper, *Wilson*, 546.

Chapter Three: Franklin D. Roosevelt: The "Juggler"

1. Walter LaFeber, *The American Age: United States Foreign Policy at Home and Abroad Since 1750* (New York: W. W. Norton, 1989), 382.

Notes on Chapter Three

2. For survey data, see Richard J. Barnet, *The Rockets' Red Glare: When America Goes to War. The Presidents and the People* (New York: Simon and Schuster, 1990), 197–198. For FDR on Jefferson, see Roger Daniels, *Franklin D. Roosevelt: The War Years* (Champaign: University of Illinois Press), 104–105, 152.

3. John A. Thompson, "The Exaggeration of American Vulnerability: The Anatomy of a Tradition," *Diplomatic History* 16, no. 1 (1992): 28.

4. For Roosevelt's "hope," see Daniels, *Franklin D. Roosevelt*, 33. For the secret talks, see *Churchill and Roosevelt: The Complete Correspondence*, ed. Warren Kimball, 3 vols. (Princeton, NJ: Princeton University Press, 1984), 227–231, "British War Cabinet Minutes, 19 August 1941, CAB6584(41)."

5. For Roosevelt's "push," see Robert Dallek, *Franklin Roosevelt: A Political Life* (New York: Viking, 2017), 422. For the rules of engagement, see William L. Langer and S. Everett Gleason, *The Undeclared War, 1940–1941* (New York: Harper and Brothers, 1953), 742–750. For FDR's description of "dupes," see LaFeber, *American Age*, 382.

6. For FDR's promise, see Barnet, *Rockets' Red Glare*, 211. For Luce, see Michael R. Beschloss, *Presidents of War: The Epic Story, from 1807 to Modern Times* (New York: Crown, 2018), 376.

7. Richard Breitman and Allan J. Lichtman, *FDR and the Jews* (Cambridge, MA: Harvard University Press, 2013), 319, 207.

8. Ibid., 319, 209; Beschloss, *Presidents of War*, 422.

9. Breitman and Lichtman, *FDR and the Jews*, 178.

10. "March 1, 1945 Address to Congress on Yalta," Miller Center, University of Virginia, https://millercenter.org/the-presidency/presidential-speeches/march-1-1945-address-congress-yalta.

11. For the false promise, see Edward Raczynski, *In Allied London* (London: Weidenfeld and Nicolson, 1962), 266. For "I know, Bill," see William D. Leahy, *I Was There* (New York: Whittlesey House, 1950), 315–316.

12. Joseph E. Davies Journal, April 23, 1945, Box 16, Joseph E. Davies Papers, Manuscript Division, Library of Congress, Washington, DC; Joseph E. Davies Diary, April 23, 1945, Box 16, Davies Papers.

13. "March 1, 1945 Address to Congress on Yalta."

14. For FDR's physician, see Ross T. McIntire, *White House Physician* (New York: G. P. Putnam's Sons, 1946), 204–205. For Duncan's prognosis, see Diane Shaver Clemens, *Yalta* (New York: Oxford University Press, 1970), 103–104. See also Dallek, *Franklin Roosevelt*, 578.

15. Raymond Swing, "What Really Happened at Yalta," *New York Times Magazine*, February 20, 1949, 10.

16. For Nixon's speech, see 95 *Congressional Record*, 81st Cong., 1st sess., 1949, Part 1, A1047–1048. For McCarthy, see Allen Weinstein, *Perjury: The Hiss-Chambers Case*, 2nd ed. (New York: Random House, 1997), 451.

Notes on Chapter Four

Chapter Four: Harry Truman Fights a "New Fanatic Faith"

1. Alden Whitman, "Harry S. Truman, Decisive President," *New York Times*, December 27, 1972, 46. See also B. Drummond Ayres, "Truman Buried in Presidential Library Courtyard," *New York Times*, December 29, 1972, A1.

2. James Hershberg, *James B. Conant: Harvard to Hiroshima and the Making of the Nuclear Age* (New York: Knopf, 1993), 222.

3. Estimates vary from 12,500 to 21,000 kilotons. Fifteen thousand is the figure according to the National Museum of the US Air Force, www.airforcemag.com /SiteCollectionDocuments/Enola%20Gay%20Archive/EG_bomb.pdf.

4. "August 9, 1945: Radio Report to the American People on the Potsdam Conference," Miller Center, University of Virginia, https://millercenter.org/the-presidency /presidential-speeches/august-9-1945-radio-report-american-people-potsdam -conference.

5. Ibid. For the debate over the bomb, see Barton J. Bernstein, "The Atomic Bombings Reconsidered," *Foreign Affairs*, January/February 1995, https://www .foreignaffairs.com/articles/asia/1995-01-01/atomic-bombings-reconsidered; Barton J. Bernstein, "Understanding the Atom Bomb and Japanese Surrender," *Diplomatic History* 19, no. 2 (1995): 227–274; Alex Wellenstein, "A 'Purely Military' Target? Truman's Changing Language About Hiroshima," Global Research, January 19, 2018, https://www.globalresearch.ca/a-purely-military-target-trumans-changing -language-about-hiroshima/5649821; Alex Wellenstein, "Nagasaki: The Last Bomb," *New Yorker*, August 7, 2015, https://www.newyorker.com/tech/elements/nagasaki -the-last-bomb; Sophie Pinkham, "The Chernobyl Syndrome," review of three books on Chernobyl, *New York Review of Books*, April 4, 2009, https://www.nybooks.com /articles/2019/04/04/chernobyl-syndrome. For the argument over the bomb's necessity, see Kai Bird and Lawrence Lifshultz, eds., *Hiroshima's Shadow: Writings on the Denial of History and the Smithsonian Controversy* (Stonybrook, CT: Pamphleteer's Press, 1988). See also Koto Ozasa, Eric J. Grant, and Kazunori Kodama, "Japanese Legacy Cohorts: The Life Span Study Atomic Bomb Survivor Cohort and Survivors' Offspring," *Journal of Epidemiology* 28, no. 4 (2018), https://www.ncbi.nlm.nih.gov /pmc/articles/PMC5865006.

6. Herbert Elliston, "Argentina Action: More Fear Than Strength," in *Report on San Francisco* (Washington, DC: Washington Post, 1945), 314–315; "Spain and Argentina," *New Republic*, April 30, 1945, 573; *Congressional Record*, 79th Cong., 1st sess., May 3, 1945, A2046.

7. Daniel Yergin, *Shattered Peace: The Origins of the Cold War and the National Security State* (Boston: Houghton Mifflin, 1977), 491.

8. See "Far East: Russian Desires," Harry L. Hopkins Papers, Sherwood Collection, Book 10: Yalta Conference, Group 24, Container 337, Folder 6, FDRL.

9. For Acheson's excuse, see "Memorandum of the Press and Radio News Conference," January 29, 1946, Byrnes Papers, Folder 556. See also "Secret of the

Notes on Chapter Four

Kuriles," *Time*, February 11, 1946, 20. For the Soviet response, see President to Harriman, August 23, 1945, transmitting text of message Stalin to Truman, August 22, 1945, Decimal File 740.0019 PW/8-2345, Record Group 59, US Department of State, Central Decimal Files, National Archives, Washington, DC.

10. For Truman's instructions, see drafts of this letter done for Clifford by Elsey in Box 63, folder 2, George M. Elsey Papers, HTSL. For the problems this created, see Arthur Krock, *Sixty Years on the Firing Line* (New York: Funk and Wagnalls, 1968), Appendix A, 421–482.

11. "George Kennan's 'Long Telegram,'" February 22, 1946, History and Public Policy Program Digital Archive, National Archives and Records Administration, Department of State Records (Record Group 59), Central Decimal File, 1945–1949, 861.00/2-2246, in "The Chargé in the Soviet Union (Kennan) to the Secretary of State," February 22, 1946, *Foreign Relations of the United States, 1946*, vol. 6, *Eastern Europe, The Soviet Union*, ed. Rogers P. Churchill and William Slany (Washington, DC: Government Printing Office, 1969), 696–709; Clark Clifford Oral History, April 19, 1971, HTSL, 180–184; George M. Elsey, "CMC Instructions," July 13, 1946, Box 63, Elsey Papers, HTSL; Elsey, handwritten notes, July 18 and 24, 1946, Elsey Papers, HTSL.

12. "United States Objectives and Programs for National Security," April 14, 1950, *Foreign Relations of the United States, 1950*, vol. 1, ed. Neal H. Petersen, John P. Glennon, David W. Mabon, Ralph R. Goodwin, and William Z. Slany (Washington, DC: Government Printing Office, 1977), 234–292.

13. See Henry Luce, "The American Century," *Life*, February 17, 1941; Alan Brinkley, "The Concept of an American Century," in *The American Century in Europe*, ed. R. Laurence Moore and Maurizio Vaudagna (Ithaca, NY: Cornell University Press, 2003), 7–10, 19; President John F. Kennedy, Inaugural Address, January 20, 1961.

14. "Report by the Policy Planning Staff: Review of Current Trends, U.S. Foreign Policy," PPS No. 23, February 24, 1948, *Foreign Relations of the United States, 1948*, vol. 1, part 2, *General; The United Nations*, ed. Neal H. Petersen, Ralph R. Goodwin, Marvin W. Kranz, and William Z. Slany (Washington, DC: Government Printing Office, 1976), 509–529.

15. Clark M. Clifford, Memorandum for the President, November 19, 1947, Clark M. Clifford Papers, HSTL.

16. "Jay Feldman's 'Manufacturing Hysteria,'" *Washington Post*, August 8, 2011, https://www.washingtonpost.com/entertainment/books/jay-feldmans-manufacturing -hysteria/2011/08/08/gIQAEF5aQJ_story.html.

17. For Clay, see Central Intelligence Agency, "The March Crisis and the Berlin Airlift," CIA Library, Center for the Study of Intelligence, https://www.cia.gov /library/center-for-the-study-of-intelligence/csi-publications/books-and-monographs /on-the-front-lines-of-the-cold-war-documents-on-the-intelligence-war-in-berlin -1946-to-1961/art-4.html. For the Joint Chiefs, see Frank Kofsky, *Harry S. Truman and the War Scare of 1948* (New York: St. Martin's Press, 1993), 133.

18. Athan Theoharis, "Roosevelt and Truman on Yalta: The Origins of the Cold War," *Political Science Quarterly* 87, no. 2 (1972): 210–241. See also Melvin Leffler, *A Preponderance of Power: National Security, the Truman Administration, and the Cold War* (Stanford, CA: Stanford University Press, 1992), xxviii. For the success of the strategy, see Kofsky, *Truman and the War Scare*, 133–137, 148–149.

19. Kofsky, *Truman and the War Scare*, 2.

20. John Davies Papers, Chronological File, Box 25, Diary Entry, March 12, 1947, Library of Congress. See also Theoharis, "Roosevelt and Truman on Yalta."

Chapter Five: Dwight Eisenhower's "Legacy of Ashes"

1. William I. Hitchcock, *The Age of Eisenhower* (New York: Simon and Schuster, 2018), 245, 278.

2. Eric Hobsbawm, *Interesting Times: A Twentieth-Century Life* (New York: Pantheon, 2002), 404.

3. Hitchcock, *Age of Eisenhower*, 81–82.

4. Ibid.

5. Greg Grandin, *The End of the Myth: From the Frontier to the Border Wall in the Mind of America* (New York: Metropolitan Books, 2019), 18.

6. Ervand Abrahamian, "The Enigma of Iranianism," review of Abbas Amanat, *The Enigma of Iranianism* (New Haven, CT: Yale University Press), *New York Review of Books*, June 7, 2018, https://www.nybooks.com/articles/2018/06/07 /enigma-of-iranianism. See also *Foreign Relations of the United States, 1952–1954, Iran, 1951–1954*, edited by James C. Van Hook (Washington, DC: Government Publishing Office, 2017).

7. See Ervand Abrahamian, "Now We Know What the State Department Was Hiding," History News Network, July 9, 2017, https://historynewsnetwork.org /article/166365.

8. For Kermit Roosevelt, see Bethany Allen-Ebrahimian, "64 Years Later, CIA Finally Releases Details of Iranian Coup," *Foreign Policy*, June 20, 2017, http:// foreignpolicy.com/2017/06/20/64-years-later-cia-finally-releases-details-of-iranian -coup-iran-tehran-oil; David S. Painter, "Overthrowing Mosaddeq," *Diplomatic History* 42, no. 3 (2018): 492–495. For the admissions (and lack thereof), see "CIA Admits Role in 1953 Iranian Coup," *The Guardian*, August 19, 2013, https://www .theguardian.com/world/2013/aug/19/cia-admits-role-1953-iranian-coup.

9. Hitchcock, *Age of Eisenhower*, 159–160.

10. For UFC's role, see Stephen Schlesinger and Stephen Kinzer, *Bitter Fruit: The Untold Story of the American Coup in Guatemala* (New York: Doubleday, 1982), 12. For Arbenz, see Stephen Kinzer, *Overthrow: America's Century of Regime Change from Hawaii to Iraq* (New York: Times Books, 2006), 132.

11. For UFC and the NYT, see Hitchcock, *Age of Eisenhower*, 162. For Bernays's role, see Kinzer, *Overthrow*, 135, 141.

12. For Gruson, see Tim Weiner, "Role of CIA in Guatemala Told in Files of Publisher," *New York Times*, June 7, 1997. See also "Relations of the United States and Guatemala, with Special Reference to the Concern of the United States over Communist Activity in Guatemala," *Foreign Relations of the United States*, 1952–1954, vol. 4, *The American Republics*, ed. N. Stephen Kane and William F. Sanford Jr. (Washington, DC: Government Printing Office, 1983).

13. Radio and television address, June 30, 1954, US Department of State, American Foreign Policy, 1950–1955, Basic Documents, 2 vols. (Washington, DC: Government Printing Office, 1957); Kinzer, *Overthrow*, 141–147.

14. Dwight D. Eisenhower, *Mandate for Change: The White House Years, 1953–1956* (Garden City, NY: Doubleday, 1963), 421–426.

15. Richard Sandomir, "Marcus Raskin, Co-Founder of Liberal Think Tank, Dies at 83," *New York Times*, December 28, 2017, A26.

16. Regarding the death squads, see Walter LaFeber, *Inevitable Revolutions: The United States in Central America*, 2nd ed. (New York: W. W. Norton, 1993), 126. For the Truth Commission, see "The Atrocity Findings: 'The Historic Facts Must Be Recognized,'" *New York Times*, February 26, 1999, A10.

17. James Mann, "CIA's Covert Indonesia Operation in the 1950s Acknowledged by U.S." *Los Angeles Times*, October 29, 1994, http://articles.latimes.com/1994-10-29/news/mn-56121_1_state-department.

18. Robert H. Johnson, who was assigned to take notes at the meeting in question, would later testify to Congress that he understood Eisenhower to be ordering the killing. At one point, when the coup finally took place, Eisenhower gave voice to his wish that Lumumba would "fall into a river of crocodiles." See Jim Newton, *Eisenhower: The White House Years* (New York: Doubleday, 2011), 327. See also Stephen Weissman, "Opening the Secret Files on Lumumba's Murder," *Washington Post*, July 21, 2001, B3.

19. Tim Weiner, *Legacy of Ashes: The History of the CIA* (New York: Anchor, 2007), 167.

20. Hitchcock, *Age of Eisenhower*, 277.

21. James Bamford, *Body of Secrets: Anatomy of the Ultra-Secret National Security Agency from the Cold War Through the Dawn of a New Century* (New York: Doubleday, 2001), 53.

22. Ibid., 54.

23. David Wise, *The Politics of Lying: Government Deception, Secrecy, and Power* (New York: Vintage, 1973).

24. Ibid., 35; Bamford, *Body of Secrets*, 59–60.

Chapter Six: John F. Kennedy and the "Right" to Lie

1. Hearings, House Foreign Operations and Government Information Subcommittee, 88th Cong., 1st sess., March 19, 1963, 15. See also Pierre Salinger, *With Kennedy* (Garden City: Doubleday, 1966), 299.

2. Richard Aldous, *Schlesinger: The Imperial Historian* (New York: W. W. Norton, 2017), 236.

3. Arnold L. Horelick and Myron Rush, "Deception in Soviet Strategic Missile Claims, 1957–1962," R-409-PR, Rand Corporation, May 1963; Peter J. Roman "Eisenhower and Ballistic Missiles Arms Control, 1957–1960: A Missed Opportunity?" *Journal of Strategic Studies* 19, no. 3 (1996), https://doi.org/10.1080/01402399608437644.

4. Seymour Hersh, *Reporter* (New York: Knopf, 2018), 284–285.

5. Robert Dallek, "The Medical Ordeals of JFK," *Atlantic*, December 2002, https://www.theatlantic.com/magazine/archive/2002/12/the-medical-ordeals-of-jfk/305572; "John Kennedy's Doctor Recalls Break-Ins Before '60 Convention," *New York Times*, May 3, 1973, 33, https://www.nytimes.com/1973/05/03/archives/john-kennedys-doctor-recalls-breaklns-before-60-convention.html.

6. Dallek, "Medical Ordeals of JFK."

7. Ibid.

8. Ibid.

9. John W. Dean, *Warren G. Harding* (New York: Henry Holt, 2004), Kindle; Arthur M. Schlesinger, "Historians Rate the U.S. Presidents," *Life*, November 1, 1948, 65–66, 68, 73–74.

10. See Robert Dallek, *An Unfinished Life: John F. Kennedy, 1917–1963* (New York: Little, Brown, 2003), 151, 475–476. According to Bobby Baker, a top aide to Lyndon Johnson when he was Senate Majority Leader, Rometsch was also intimate with the future president Gerald Ford. At the time, he was in the House of Representatives, representing Michigan, but already married. The affair allegedly gave J. Edgar Hoover an opening to blackmail him into secretly leaking material from the Warren Commission to him. Evan Thomas, *Robert Kennedy: His Life* (New York: Simon and Schuster, 2000), 255–256.

11. Thomas C. Reeves. *A Question of Character: A Life of John F. Kennedy* (New York: Free Press, 1991), 242–243.

12. Kitty Kelley, "The Dark Side of Camelot," *People*, February 29, 1988, http://people.com/archive/cover-story-the-dark-side-of-camelot-vol-29-no-8. Regarding the Castro assassination attempts, see Hersh, *Reporter*, 284–285. For Roselli and Giancana, see Nicholas Gage, "Mafia Said to Have Slain Rosselli Because of His Senate Testimony," *New York Times*, February 25, 1977, A1.

13. Reeves, *Question of Character*, 320.

14. Michael O'Brien, *John F. Kennedy: A Biography* (New York: Thomas Dunne, 2005), 687.

15. Kelley, "Dark Side of Camelot"; Hersh, *Reporter*, 284–285; Gage, "Mafia Said to Have Slain Rosselli."

16. For "top priority," see "Donald F. Chamberlain, CIA Inspector General, to Walt Elder," June 5, 1975, Rockefeller Commission Papers, Gerald R. Ford Library Materials, JFK Assassination Materials Project, National Archives, College Park, Maryland. For the Joint Chiefs' bizarre plans, see "Report by the Department of

Notes on Chapter Six

Defense and Joint Chiefs of Staff Representative on the Caribbean Survey Group to the Joint Chiefs of Staff on Cuba Project," March 9, 1962, in the papers of the Assassinations Records Review Board (ARRB), Annex to Appendix to Enclosure A, "Pretexts to Justify US Military Intervention in Cuba," 8–11. The CIA's "nutty schemes" are discussed in Robert G. Kaiser, "The Meddling American," review of Max Boot, *The Road Not Taken: Edward Lansdale and the American Tragedy in Vietnam* (New York: Liveright, 2018), *New York Review of Books*, June 7, 2018, 23–25. "More dynamic action" is demanded in "Memorandum of Mongoose Meeting Held on Thursday, 4 October 1962," item no. CC00520, NSA. On October 11 Action Proposals, see Mongoose, Top Secret, Memorandum, October 11, 1962, item no. CC02244, NSA. The Pentagon officials are quoted in "Why Cuba Isn't like Turkey," *Chicago Tribune*, October 24, 1962, 16.

17. "US Bases Abroad," *Time*, November 9, 1963, 17; Arthur Schlesinger Jr., *A Thousand Days: John F. Kennedy in the White House* (Boston: Houghton Mifflin, 1965), 827. Schlesinger in "Memorandum from Attorney General Kennedy to Secretary of State Rusk," October 30, 1962, in *Foreign Relations of the United States, 1961–1963*, vol. 11, *Cuban Missile Crisis and Aftermath*, ed. Edward C. Keefer, Charles S. Sampson, and Louis J. Smith (Washington, DC: Government Printing Office, 1996), 270–271; Arthur Schlesinger Jr., *Robert Kennedy and His Times* (Boston: Houghton Mifflin, 1978), 545.

18. For "I cut his balls...," see William Manchester, *One Brief Shining Moment: Remembering Kennedy* (Boston: Little, Brown, 1983), 215. See also *Newsweek*, November 5, 1962, 20; *Time*, November 2, 1962, 15; Walter Trohan, *Chicago Tribune*, October 27, 1962, 4.

19. Regarding the Turkish missiles, see Philip Nash, *The Other Missiles of October: Eisenhower, Kennedy, and the Jupiters, 1957–1963* (Chapel Hill: University of North Carolina Press, 1997), 153. See also C. L. Sulzberger, *The Last of the Giants* (New York: Macmillan, 1970), 928. For the accusation against Sulzberger, which the *New York Times* denied, see Carl Bernstein, "The CIA and the Media," *Rolling Stone*, October 20, 1977, www.carlbernstein.com/magazine_cia_and_media .php. For Bundy and Aron, see item no. CC02690, and [Summary of Dean Rusk's October 28, 5:00, Briefing of Latin American and OAS Ambassadors], Confidential, Cable State, October 28, 1962, item no. CC01509, NSA. For the nasty treatment of the Soviet diplomat, see Aleksandr Fursenko and Timothy Naftali, *One Hell of a Gamble: Khrushchev, Castro, and Kennedy, 1958–1964* (New York: W. W. Norton, 1997), 323. For the smearing of Stevenson in the *Saturday Evening Post* article, see Stewart Alsop to Hibbs, November 19 and 29, 1962, Joseph and Stewart Alsop Papers, Special Correspondence—Saturday Evening Post, October–December 1962, Box 31, Library of Congress; Kenneth O'Donnell Oral History, cited in Thomas, *Robert Kennedy*, 232.

20. Anatoly Dobrynin, *In Confidence: Moscow's Ambassador to America's Six Cold War Presidents (1962–1986)* (New York: Times Books, 1996), 98.

21. Kai Bird, *The Color of Truth: McGeorge and William Bundy, Brothers in Arms* (New York: Simon and Schuster, 1998), 249.

22. Charles E. Bohlen, *Witness to History, 1929–1960* (New York: W. W. Norton, 1973), 495–496.

23. James A. Nathan, "The Heyday of the New Strategy," in *The Cuban Missile Crisis Revisited*, ed. James A. Nathan (New York: St. Martin's Press, 1992), 1–39.

24. Cyrus Vance Oral History, March 9, 1970, Interview no. 3, p. 11, LBJ Presidential Library (LBJL hereafter).

25. "Notes of the Leadership Meeting," August 4, 1964, White House, in *Foreign Relations of the United States, 1964–1968*, vol. 1, *Vietnam, 1964*, ed. Edward C. Keefer and Charles S. Sampson (Washington, DC: Government Printing Office, 1992), 616.

26. Brian VanDeMark, *Into the Quagmire: Lyndon Johnson and the Escalation of the Vietnam War* (New York: Oxford University Press, 1995), 50.

Chapter Seven: Lyndon Johnson's "Credibility Gap"

1. The Gallup number can be found in John Mueller, *War, Presidents and Public Opinion* (New York: John Wiley and Sons, 1973), 113. For the Harris survey, see Ki Bird, *The Color of Truth: McGeorge and William Bundy, Brothers in Arms* (New York: Simon and Schuster, 2000), 297.

2. Francis Fukuyama, *Trust: Human Nature and the Reconstitution of Social Order* (New York: Free Press, 1995), 26.

3. For Lansdale, see Robert G. Kaiser, "The Meddling American," review of Max Boot, *The Road Not Taken: Edward Lansdale and the American Tragedy in Vietnam* (New York: Liveright, 2018), *New York Review of Books*, June 7, 2018, 23–25. For the Joint Chiefs' report, see "Letter to the Department of State from the International Security Agency, April 22, 1955," excerpted in Len Ackland, ed., *Credibility Gap: A Digest of the Pentagon Papers* (Philadelphia: American Friends Service Committee, 1972), 35. For Eisenhower's prediction, see Dwight D. Eisenhower, *Mandate for Change, 1953–1956: The White House Years* (Garden City, NY: Doubleday, 1963), 372. See also *The Pentagon Papers: The Defense Department History of Decisionmaking on Vietnam*, Senator Gravel edition, vol. 2 (Boston: Beacon, 1971–1972), 22. For Johnson's quote, Christian G. Appy, "What Was the Vietnam War About?" *New York Times*, March 26, 2018, https://www.nytimes.com/2018/03/26/opinion/what-was-the-vietnam-war-about.html.

4. George Packer, *Our Man: Richard Holbrooke and the End of the American Century* (New York: Knopf, 2019), loc. 7603, Kindle.

5. Michael R. Beschloss, *Taking Charge: The Johnson White House Tapes, 1963–1964* (New York: Simon and Schuster, 1997), 370–372.

6. Transcript, "Lyndon Johnson and Richard Russell on 27 May 1964," Miller Center, University of Virginia, Presidential Recordings Digital Edition, https://prde.upress.virginia.edu/conversations/9060283/notes_open. See also Marilyn B. Young

and Robert Buzzanco, *A Companion to the Vietnam War* (New York: John Wiley and Sons, 2008), 375; Robert D. Dean, *Imperial Brotherhood: Gender and the Making of Cold War Foreign Policy* (Amherst: University of Massachusetts Press, 2003), 218.

7. Jeffrey W. Helsing, *Johnson's War / Johnson's Great Society: The Guns and Butter Trap* (Westport, CT: Praeger, 2000), 37.

8. Hannah Arendt, "Lying in Politics: Reflections on the Pentagon Papers," in *Crises of the Republic* (New York: Harcourt Brace Jovanovich, 1972), 14.

9. H. R. McMaster, *Dereliction of Duty: Lyndon Johnson, Robert McNamara, the Joint Chiefs of Staff, and the Lies That Led to Vietnam* (New York: Harper-Collins, 1997), 133.

10. Bundy's comments were made on PBS, *MacNeil/Lehrer NewsHour*, April 17, 1995.

11. For a description of OPLAN 34-Alpha, see Edwin E. Moïse, *Tonkin Gulf and the Escalation of the Vietnam War* (Chapel Hill: University of North Carolina Press, 1996), 50–68. For Herrick's concerns, see Frank E. Vandiver, *Shadows of Vietnam: Lyndon Johnson's Wars* (College Station: Texas A&M University Press, 1977), 21; James Bamford, *Body of Secrets: Anatomy of the Ultra-Secret National Security Agency from the Cold War Through the Dawn of a New Century* (New York: Doubleday, 2001), 298.

12. Robert S. McNamara, *In Retrospect: The Tragedy and Lessons of Vietnam* (New York: Times Books, 1995), 120.

13. Michael Charlton and Anthony Moncrieff, *Many Reasons Why: The American Involvement in Vietnam* (New York: Hill and Wang, 1978), 108.

14. Daniel Ellsberg, *Secrets: A Memoir of Vietnam and the Pentagon Papers* (New York: Viking, 2002).

15. Saigon to State, July 27, 1964, Box 6, NSF VN LBJL.

16. For Herrick's request for review, see telegram in "Presidential Decisions—Gulf of Tonkin Attacks," vol. 1, Box 38, NSC History, NSF, Tab 13, LBJL. For "floating in the waters," see "Notes Taken at Leadership Meeting by Walter Jenkins," August 4, 1964, Johnson Papers, Meeting Notes File, Box 2, LBJL; Marshall Wright and Sven F. Kraemer, Vietnam Information Group, "Presidential Decisions: The Gulf of Tonkin Attacks of August 1964" (Draft), November 1, 1968, 10–11, NSC History, NSF, Gulf of Tonkin Attack, August 1964, Box 38, "Presidential Decisions—Gulf of Tonkin Attacks of Aug. 1964," Tabs 1–8, LBJL.

17. Moïse, *Tonkin Gulf*, 183, 220.

18. For Johnson's Syracuse speech, see President Lyndon B. Johnson, "Official Statements on the Gulf of Tonkin Attacks and on US Policy in Vietnam," "Presidential Decisions—Gulf of Tonkin Attacks," vol. 1, Box 38, NSC History, NSF, Tab 10, LBJL. For Khrushchev, see "Security Council Hears US Charge of North Vietnamese Attacks: Statement by Adlai E. Stevenson, US Representative in the Security Council, August 5, 1964," Department of State Bulletin, August 24, 1964,

272–274. For the State Department claim, see Outgoing Telegram, Department of State, Action Circular 248, August 7, 1964, "Presidential Decisions—Gulf of Tonkin Attacks," Box 38, NSC History, NSF, Tab 14, LBJL.

19. For McNamara's testimony, see "Briefing by Honorable Robert S. Mc-Namara, Secretary of Defense, 9:00AM, Wednesday 5 August 1964," and "Statement by Secretary of Defense Robert S. McNamara Before the Senate Foreign Relations and Armed Services Committees, August 6, 1964," "Presidential Decisions—Gulf of Tonkin Attacks," Box 38, NSC History, NSF, Tab 22, LBJL; US Senate, Foreign Relations Committee, Executive Sessions (Historical Series), vol. 16, 1064, 88th Cong., 2nd sess. (Washington, DC: Government Printing Office, 1988), 293. For the Vietnamese boat story, author's interview with Edwin Moise, June 9, 1994.

20. *Time*, August 14, 1964, 14; *Newsweek*, August 17, 1964, 20. For polling data, see John M. Blum, *Years of Discord: American Politics and Society, 1961–1974* (New York: W. W. Norton, 1991), 232.

21. Robert Dallek, *Lyndon B. Johnson: Portrait of a President* (New York: Oxford University Press, 2005), 179.

22. Fredrik Logevall, *Choosing War: The Lost Chance for Peace and the Escalation of War in Vietnam* (Berkeley: University of California Press, 1999), 218–221.

23. See Randall B. Woods, *LBJ: Architect of American Ambition* (New York: Free Press, 2006), 627–630; Robert Dallek, *Flawed Giant: Lyndon Johnson and His Times, 1961–73* (New York: Oxford University Press, 1998), 262–268; Lawrence Greenberg, "US Army Unilateral and Coalition Operations in the 1965 Dominican Republic Intervention," US Army Center of Military History, November 1986, https://history.army.mil/html/books/093/93-5-1/CMH_Pub_93-5.pdf; Alan L. McPherson, *Intimate Ties, Bitter Struggles: The United States and Latin America Since 1945* (Washington, DC: Potomac Books, 2006), 74.

24. Michael R. Beschloss, *Presidents of War: The Epic Story, from 1807 to Modern Times* (New York: Crown, 2018), 521.

25. "Statements Bearing on the Powers of the President Under the Gulf of Tonkin Resolution," "Presidential Decisions—Gulf of Tonkin Attacks," Box 39, NSC History, NSF, Tab 33, LBJL.

26. "Investigating Tonkin Gulf," *New York Times*, January 26, 1968, 36.

27. Randall Woods, *Fulbright: A Biography* (New York: Cambridge University Press, 1995), 407–408.

28. J. Norville Jones, "Robert McNamara's Bad Information," *Washington Post*, November 23, 1995, 22.

29. For Jack Cowles, see Anthony Austin, *The President's War* (New York: Lippincott, 1971), 165. For John White, see "Letters to the Editor," *New Haven Register*, December 6, 1967.

30. Woods, *Fulbright*, 472. See also Lloyd C. Gardner, *Pay Any Price: Lyndon Johnson and the Wars for Vietnam* (Chicago: Ivan R. Dee, 1995), 442.

31. See Louis Menand, "Lessons from the Election of 1968," *New Yorker,* January 8, 2008, https://www.newyorker.com/magazine/2018/01/08/lessons-from -the-election-of-1968.

32. Maurice Isserman and Michael Kazin, *America Divided: The Civil Wars of the Sixties* (New York: Oxford University Press, 1999), 189.

33. John F. Terzano, "It's Time to Normalize Relations with Vietnam: Begin with the Truth," *New York Times,* August 21, 1992, 26.

Chapter Eight: Richard Nixon: "It's a Win. See?"

1. See Robert Dallek, *Nixon and Kissinger: Partners in Power* (New York: HarperCollins, 2006), 93, 206, 250, 434.

2. For "President as Moral Leader," see Richard Reeves, *President Nixon: Alone in the White House* (New York: Simon and Schuster, 2001), 278. For "Grover Cleveland," see John A. Farrell, *Richard Nixon: The Life* (New York: Doubleday, 2017), 356. For "trivia," see Tim Weiner, *One Man Against the World: The Tragedy of Richard Nixon* (New York: Henry Holt, 2015), 110. Nietzsche's quote can be found in J. A. Barnes, *A Pack of Lies: Toward a Sociology of Lying* (New York: Cambridge University Press, 1994), 87.

3. Reeves, *President Nixon,* 285.

4. Ibid., 312; Seymour Hersh, *Reporter* (New York: Alfred A. Knopf, 2018), 202–203; Elon Green, "An Inquiry into Abuse," *Longreads,* August 2018, https:// longreads.com/2018/08/23/an-inquiry-into-abuse.

5. Reeves, *President Nixon,* 326.

6. For Dent's memo, see ibid., 244–245. For the cake, J. A. Barnes, *A Pack of Lies: Toward a Sociology of Lying* (New York: Cambridge University Press, 1994), 27.

7. Richard Nixon, "Remarks on Departure from the White House," August 9, 1974, American Presidency Project, University of California, Santa Barbara, www .presidency.ucsb.edu/ws/index.php?pid=4325.

8. For the Billy Graham conversation, see Debbie Lord, "Billy Graham– Richard Nixon Tapes: The One Time Graham's Image Was Tarnished," *Atlanta Journal-Constitution,* February 21, 2018, https://www.ajc.com/news/national/billy -graham-richard-nixon-tapes-the-one-time-graham-image-was-tarnished/DCj06g fORZJLYa30cLawWL. For the HUAC conversation, see Stephen J. Whitfield, "Nixon and the Jews," *Patterns of Prejudice* 44, no. 5 (2010): 432–453.

9. See Associated Press, "Haldeman Diary Shows Nixon Was Wary of Blacks and Jews," *New York Times,* May 18, 1994, A19; Tim Naftali, "Ronald Reagan's Long-Hidden Racist Conversation with Richard Nixon," *Atlantic,* July 30, 2019, https:// www.theatlantic.com/ideas/archive/2019/07/ronald-reagans-racist-conversation -richard-nixon/595102.

10. Farrell, *Richard Nixon,* 526.

11. Dallek, *Nixon and Kissinger,* 68–76.

12. John A. Farrell, "Nixon's Vietnam Treachery," *New York Times*, December 31, 2016, https://www.nytimes.com/2016/12/31/opinion/sunday/nixons-vietnam -treachery.html; Peter Baker, "Nixon Tried to Spoil Johnson's Vietnam Peace Talks in '68, Notes Show," *New York Times*, January 2, 2017, https://www.nytimes.com /2017/01/02/us/politics/nixon-tried-to-spoil-johnsons-vietnam-peace-talks-in-68 -notes-show.html; John A. Farrell, "When a Candidate Conspired with a Foreign Power to Win an Election," *Politico*, August 6, 2017, https://www.politico.com/magazine /story/2017/08/06/nixon-vietnam-candidate-conspired-with-foreign-power-win -election-215461.

13. Arnold Offner, *Hubert Humphrey: The Conscience of the Country* (New Haven, CT: Yale University Press, 2018), 315–336.

14. Farrell, "When a Candidate Conspired." See also William P. Bundy, *A Tangled Web: The Making of Foreign Policy in the Nixon Presidency* (New York: Hill and Wang, 1998).

15. For the details about Operation Linebacker, see David E. Hoffman, "Secret Archive Offers Fresh Insight into Nixon Presidency," *Washington Post*, October 11, 2015, https://www.washingtonpost.com/news/post-politics/wp/2015/10/11/secret -archive-offers-fresh-insight-into-nixon-presidency.

16. Fred Emery, *Watergate: The Corruption of American Politics and the Fall of Richard Nixon* (New York: Times Books, 1994), 71–73; Neil Sheehan: "TV: 'Vietnam Hindsight' on the Kennedy Years," *New York Times*, December 22, 1971, https:// www.nytimes.com/1971/12/22/archives/tv-vietnam-hindsight-on-the-kennedy -years.html.

17. Dallek, *Nixon and Kissinger*, 261; George Lardner Jr. and Michael Dobbs, "New Tapes Reveal Depth of Nixon's Anti-Semitism," *Washington Post*, October 6, 1999, A31.

18. See Dobrynin's "Memorandum of Conversation (USSR)," May 14, 1969, https://nsarchive2.gwu.edu/NSAEBB/NSAEBB233/5-14-69.pdf. See also Dallek, *Nixon and Kissinger*, 257, 415, 431.

19. Sunil Khilnani, "In 1971, a Genocide Took Place. Richard Nixon and Henry Kissinger Did Nothing. Intentionally," *New Republic*, November 9, 2013, https://newrepublic.com/article/115435/gary-basss-blood-telegram-reviewed-sunil -khilnani.

20. Most of the details of this story derive from Gary J. Bass, *The Blood Telegram: Nixon, Kissinger, and a Forgotten Genocide* (New York: Knopf, 2013), esp. 84, 154, 177, 301, and 319. See also Farrell, *Richard Nixon*, 455–457; Weiner, *One Man Against the World*, 142, for Nixon's and Kissinger's quotes. Additional information can be found in *Foreign Relations of the United States, 1969–1976*, vol. 11, *South Asia Crisis, 1971*, ed. Louis J. Smith (Washington, DC: Government Printing Office, 2005), as well as in documents collated in National Security Archive Electronic Briefing Book No. 79, Sajit Gandhi, ed., "The Tilt: The U.S. and

the South Asian Crisis of 1971," National Security Archive, December 16, 2002, https://nsarchive2.gwu.edu/NSAEBB/NSAEBB79, esp. docs. 14, 15, 30, 31, and 32.

21. John M. Orman, *Presidential Secrecy and Deception* (Westport, CT: Greenwood Press, 1980), 126–129.

22. Dallek, *Nixon and Kissinger*, 231.

23. Joe Renouard, *Human Rights in American Foreign Policy: From the 1960s to the Soviet Collapse* (Philadelphia: University of Pennsylvania Press, 2016), 91.

24. For Schneider's killing, see ibid., 91. For Kissinger's comments, see Sebastián Hurtado Torres, "The U.S. Press and Chile, 1964–1973: Ideology and U.S. Foreign Policy," *Revista de Historia Iberoamericana*, June 21, 2012.

25. For Kissinger's comments to Nixon, see David Briscoe, "CIA Admits Involvement in Chile," ABC News, January 6, 2006, http://abcnews.go.com/International/story?id=82588. The cable in question is available in "Public Library of US Diplomacy," WikiLeaks, https://wikileaks.org/plusd/cables/1973STATE182051_b.html. For the *Times* editorial, see Dallek, *Nixon and Kissinger*, 238.

26. Reuters in Santiago, "Victor Jara Murder: Ex-Military Officers Sentenced in Chile for 1973 Death," *The Guardian*, July 3, 2018, https://www.theguardian.com/world/2018/jul/03/victor-jara-ex-military-officers-sentenced-in-chile-for-1973-death.

27. For the reporting of the raids, see Weiner, *One Man Against the World*, 42. For Nixon's reaction to the report, see Dallek, *Nixon and Kissinger*, 121–124. For Hoover's role, see Reeves, *President Nixon*, 75; Farrell, *Richard Nixon*, 365.

28. For Kissinger's comments, see Farrell, *Richard Nixon*, 403. For Nixon's, see Weiner, *One Man Against the World*, 261.

29. For Nixon's reaction, see Farrell, *Richard Nixon*, 504. For Pappas, see 477–478, 504.

30. Reeves, *President Nixon*, 339; Weiner, *One Man*, 20. For Agnew's vice-presidential payoffs, see *The Rachel Maddow Show*, October 29, 2018, https://www.msnbc.com/bagman.

31. Reeves, *President Nixon*, 339.

32. Reeves, *President Nixon*, 506. For Nixon to Haldeman, see Emery, *Watergate*, 54, though this is according to Colson's recollection. Nixon's memoirs do not mention it. See also John Dean, *Blind Ambition: The End of the Story*, updated ed. (Palm Springs, CA: Polymedia, 2009), 512; Emery, *Watergate*, 209.

33. For Nixon to Ehrlichman, see Emery, *Watergate*, 54. For Dean, *Blind Ambition*, chap. 20.

34. "President Nixon's Resignation Speech," August 8, 1974, PBS, https://www.pbs.org/newshour/spc/character/links/nixon_speech.html. See also Tim Naftali, "The Secret Plan to Force Out Nixon," *Atlantic*, December 17, 2019, https://www.theatlantic.com/ideas/archive/2019/12/when-house-republican-leadership-wanted-oust-nixon/603706.

35. See Dallek, *Nixon and Kissinger*, 417. See also Scott Kaufman, *Ambition, Pragmatism, and Party: A Political Biography of Gerald R. Ford* (Lawrence:

University of Kansas Press, 2017), 171–172; Bob Woodward, *Shadow: Five Presidents and the Legacy of Watergate* (New York: Simon and Schuster, 1999), 7; Evan Thomas, "When the Center Held" *New York Times*, June 26, 2016, https://www.nytimes.com/2018/06/26/books/review/donald-rumsfeld-when-the-center-held.html.

Chapter Nine: Gerald Ford: A Time for More Lying

1. Bob Woodward, *Shadow: Five Presidents and the Legacy of Watergate* (New York: Simon and Schuster, 1999), 27, 33, 38.

2. John Prados, "The Navy's Biggest Betrayal," *Naval History* 24, no. 3 (2010): 36.

3. See Denise M. Bottsdorf, *The Presidency and the Rhetoric of Foreign Crisis* (Columbia: University of South Carolina Press, 1993), 123–143; Scott Kaufman, *Ambition, Pragmatism, and Party: A Political Biography of Gerald R. Ford* (Lawrence: University of Kansas Press, 2017), 243–251. For the press release, see "Gerald R. Ford Administration White House Press Releases," May 14, 1975–June 3, 1975, Gerald R. Ford Presidential Library and Museum (FPLM hereafter), https://www.fordlibrarymuseum.gov/library/document/0248/whpr19750515-013.pdf; "Charles T. Miller, Captain, SS Mayaguez: Telegrams, April–June 1975," FPLM, https://www.fordlibrarymuseum.gov/library/guides/findingaid/Miller,_Charles_T._-_Telegrams.asp.

4. "President Ford Informs Congress About Military Action in Cambodia," May 15, 1975, NBC Learn, https://archives.nbclearn.com/portal/site/k-12/flatview?cuecard=2921.

5. *Time* and *Newsweek* quoted in Bottsdorf, *The Presidency and the Rhetoric*, 123–143. See also Office of the White House Secretary, "Notice to the Press," May 16, 1975, FPLM, https://www.fordlibrarymuseum.gov/library/document/0248/whpr19750516-005.pdf. For Ford's comments, see "Public Papers of the Presidents of the United States: Gerald R. Ford, 1976–1977," April 23, 1976, 356.

6. Christopher J. Lamb, *The Mayaguez Crisis, Mission Command, and Civil-Military Relations* (Washington, DC: Joint History Office, Office of the Chairman of the Joint Chiefs of Staff, 2018), https://www.jcs.mil/Portals/36/28270_Mayaguez Crisis_web%20updated.pdf.

7. "Secretary's Meeting with Foreign Minister Chatichai of Thailand," Memorandum of Conversation, Department of State, November 26, 1975, National Security Archive, George Washington University, https://nsarchive2.gwu.edu//NSAEBB/NSAEBB193/HAK-11-26-75.pdf; Henry A. Kissinger, *Years of Renewal* (New York: Simon and Schuster, 2012), 575.

8. Nathaniel Davis, "The Angola Decision of 1975: A Personal Memoir," *Foreign Affairs*, Fall 1978, https://www.foreignaffairs.com/articles/angola/1978-09-01/angola-decision-1975-personal-memoir.

9. John Stockwell, *In Search of Enemies: A CIA Story* (New York: W. W. Norton, 1978), 214–218.

10. Senator Dick Clark, "Frustration," *New York Times*, January 29, 1976, 33.

11. See Harold Hongju Koh, *The National Security Constitution: Sharing Power After the Iran-Contra Affair* (New Haven, CT: Yale University Press, 1990), 52; Benjamin Beit-Hallahmi, *The Israeli Connection: Whom Israel Arms and Why* (New York: I. B. Tauris, 1988), 65.

12. Gerald Bender, "Kissinger in Angola: Anatomy of a Failure," in *American Policy in Southern Africa: The Stakes and the Stance*, ed. Rene Lemarchand (Washington, DC: University Press of America, 1978), 63–114.

13. Bernard Gwertzman, "Ford Denies Moscow Dominates East Europe," *New York Times*, October 7, 1976, A1; Amy Davidson Sorkin, "How to Create a Gerald Ford Moment: Five Steps," *New Yorker*, October 22, 2012, https://www.new yorker.com/news/amy-davidson/how-to-create-a-gerald-ford-moment-five-steps.

14. For Cheney, see Sorkin, "How to Create." For Kissinger, see Stuart Eisenstadt, *President Carter: The White House Years* (New York: Thomas Dunne, 2018), loc. 1128, Kindle.

Chapter Ten: Jimmy Carter "Will Never Lie to You"

1. The logic of the Cold War led Carter, for instance, to sign two presidential findings in July 1979 to secretly supply the insurgent forces in Afghanistan fighting against the Soviet-backed regime there. The purpose, according to those documents, was to "expose the Democratic Republic of Afghanistan and its leadership as despotic and subservient to the Soviet Union." It would have been ridiculous to pretend, then or now, that the rebels receiving American aid were Western liberals. In fact, they eventually mutated into the Taliban, with support from Osama bin Laden, who was one of the leading warlords receiving US support under the program. This program, which predated the December 25, 1979, Soviet invasion of Afghanistan, could not possibly have been revealed publicly, lest the cause of the rebels be tainted by association with the nation that so many of their Islamic allies considered to be "the Great Satan." It remained secret until the early 1990s. Jimmy Carter Presidential Library, Staff Offices, Counsel's Office (Cutler), Box 60, folder: "CIA Charter: 2/9-25/80."

2. James Deakin, *Straight Stuff: The Reporters, the White House and the Truth* (New York: William Morrow, 1984), 162.

3. Wendy Swanberg, "The Gossip Makes the News: Washington Reporting in the Carter Years" (master's thesis, University of Wisconsin–Madison, 2005), 25.

4. *Washington Post* editor Ben Bradlee also became an American icon as a result of Watergate and was portrayed no less heroically in *All the President's Men* by Jason Robards, and posthumously in 2017 by Tom Hanks (opposite Meryl Streep) in Steven Spielberg's *The Post*.

5. Swanberg, "The Gossip Makes the News," 93–94.

6. "Toasts of the President and the Shah at a Dinner Honoring the Shah," November 15, 1977 (the website is mistaken; the date was December 31, 1977),

American Presidency Project, University of California, Santa Barbara, www.presi
dency.ucsb.edu/ws/index.php?pid=6938.

7. As governor, Carter apparently organized an "American Fighting Men's
Day" for Calley, and according to some, he exhorted the citizens of Georgia to
turn their automobile headlights on to "honor the flag as 'Rusty' had done" (using Calley's nickname), though this quote has never been authenticated. During the
speech in question, Carter did say he thought Calley's superiors should be held accountable, however. And he later tried to explain what he meant: that it was "not
right to equate what Calley did with what other American servicemen were doing
in Vietnam"—although this is not even a remotely sensible interpretation of his
earlier remarks. Whatever Carter may have said—or meant—the offensiveness of
his comments at the time pales beside those of Richard Nixon, who said of Calley,
"Most people don't give a shit whether he killed them or not." Charles Mohr, "Carter Credibility Issue: Calley and Vietnam War," *New York Times*, May 21, 1976,
A1; Matthew Lippman, "War Crimes: The My Lai Massacre and the Vietnam War,"
San Diego Justice Journal, Summer 1993, http://teachers.colonelby.com/krichardson
/Grade%2012/Carleton%20-%20Int%20Law%20Course/Week%205/WarCrimes
.pdf; Greg Grandin, *The End of the Myth: From the Frontier to the Border Wall in
the Mind of America* (New York: Metropolitan Books, 2019), 210.

8. Swanberg, "Gossip Makes the News," 200–224.

9. Sally Quinn, "Peach Frost and Soft Talk of the President's Secretary,"
Washington Post, December 6, 1977, https://www.washingtonpost.com/archive
/lifestyle/1977/11/06/peach-frost-and-soft-talk-of-the-presidents-secretary/851c984b
-e779-45b4-b1d0-850166d4ddd2.

10. Ibid.; Wendall Rawls Jr., "Slur to Envoy's Wife Tied to Carter Aide," *New
York Times*, December 19, 1977, 7.

11. Hamilton Jordan, *Crisis: The Last Year of the Carter Presidency* (New
York: G. P. Putnam's Sons, 1982), 173.

12. Lilly Rothman, "The '70s Cocaine Scandal That Could Have Rocked the
White House," *Time*, September 3, 2014, http://time.com/3207118/studio-54-cocaine
-carter-white-house.

13. Woodward, *Shadow*, 41–53. See also "The Carter Devolution on the CIA:
A Chronology," prepared by the American Civil Liberties Union and the Center
for National Security Studies, March 4, 1977, https://library.ucsd.edu/dc/object
/bb18784386/_1.pdf.

14. Woodward, *Shadow*, 41–53. See also Bob Woodward, "CIA Paid Millions
to Jordan's King Hussein," *Washington Post*, February 18, 1977, A1.

15. Rosen did not define his term in print until 2011. I am applying it retroac-
tively to a place where I detect its origins. See Jay Rosen, "Why Political Coverage Is
Broken," *PressThink*, August 26, 2011, http://pressthink.org/2011/08/why-political
-coverage-is-broken.

Notes on Chapter Eleven

Chapter Eleven: Ronald Reagan: America's "Magic Totem"

1. For McCain, see Eric Alterman, "Where's the Rest of Him?" *The Nation*, March 9, 2000, https://www.thenation.com/article/wheres-rest-him. For Reagan's personal history, see Lou Cannon, "Actor, Governor, President, Icon," *Washington Post*, June 6, 2004, A1.

2. Marilyn Berger, "Reagan Dies at 93: Fostered Cold War Might and Curbs on Government," *New York Times*, June 6, 2004, A1.

3. For Trillin's line, see Robert G. Kaiser, "Reagan's America: An Intoxicating Myth for Our Times," *Washington Post*, October 14, 1984. For the false pope statement, see "Remarks at a Conference on Religious Liberty, April 16, 1985," Reagan Papers, 1985, Book 1, 437–440; Joanne Omang, "Democrats Draft Latin Aid Options," *Washington Post*, April 18, 1985; Sara Gilbert, "Vatican Disputes Reagan Statements," *Washington Post*, April 19, 1985. For the false South Africa statement, see Jane Mayer and Doyle McManus, *Landslide: The Unmaking of the President, 1984–1988* (Boston: Houghton Mifflin, 1988), 131. For the false statement on missile recall, see "On the Record: Reagan on Missiles," *New York Times*, October 17, 1984, A25. Regarding the disagreement over the death camp remarks, while Reagan's partisans have tried, unsuccessfully, to push back on this story, their objections remain unconvincing. See Charles Hill and Joan Didion, "The Lion King: An Exchange," *New York Review of Books*, March 5, 1998, www.nybooks.com /articles/1998/03/05/the-lion-king-an-exchange. For Conan and Gergen, see David Corn, "Reagan and the Media: A Love Story," *The Nation*, June 10, 2004, https:// www.thenation.com/article/reagan-and-media-love-story.

4. For "He makes things up," see Alterman, "Where's the Rest of Him?" On failing to recognize his son, see H. W. Brands, *Reagan: The Life* (New York: Doubleday, 2015), 197. For Ron Reagan, see Ron Reagan, *My Father at 100*, reprint ed. (New York: Plume, 2012), quoted in Eric Alterman, "Ronald Reagan, Superstar," *The Nation*, February 17, 2011, https://www.thenation.com/article/ronald-reagan -superstar. For the Poindexter testimony, see Michael Kinsley, "Lies, Damned Lies, and Impeachment," *Slate*, December 25, 1998, www.slate.com/articles/news_and _politics/readme/1998/12/lies_damned_lies_and_impeachment.html.

5. See Lance Morrow, Lawrence I. Barrett, and Barrett Seaman, "Yankee Doodle Magic: What Makes Reagan So Remarkably Popular a President," *Time*, July 7, 1986, http://content.time.com/time/magazine/article/0,9171,144460,00.html.

6. See Morton Kondracke, "The Myth and the Man," *Newsweek*, July 29, 1985; Morrow et al., "Yankee Doodle Magic"; Eric Boehlert, "Reagan Worship," *Salon*, June 12, 2004, https://www.salon.com/2004/06/11/media_263.

7. For Greider, see Mark Hertsgaard, *On Bended Knee: The Press and the Reagan Presidency* (New York: Farrar, Straus and Giroux, 1988), 101. For Bradlee, see Mark Hertsgaard, "Beloved by the Media," *The Nation*, June 28, 2004, https://www .thenation.com/article/beloved-media. Ironically, it would be Greider who would reveal one of the earliest and most egregious lies of the Reagan administration: the fact

that the economic program was known at the time he was selling it to Congress to be a scam. As David Stockman, his director of the Office of Management and Budget, who authored the plan, admitted to Greider after Congress agreed to pass the program, "None of us really understands what's going on with all these numbers." The president himself no doubt believed in the plan, which was called "supply-side economics," but the people writing the actual tax- and spending-cut program understood it as a smokescreen for the old-fashioned right-wing plan to reduce taxes on the rich through the discredited formula of trickle-down economics, while cutting social spending on the poor and the middle class into the bargain. "It's kind of hard to sell 'trickle down,'" Stockman admitted to Greider. "The supply-side formula was the only way to get a tax policy that was really 'trickle down.' Supply-side is 'trickle-down' theory." And so the rich got what they wanted and the poor suffered what they must. "The hogs were really feeding. The greed level, the level of opportunism, just got out of control," was the way Stockman put it, contra Reagan's claims and those of virtually everyone else in the administration at the time the tax cut and budget cuts were passed in Congress. After the article appeared, on November 12, 1981, the administration concocted a phony story in which Stockman was "taken to the woodshed" by Reagan—which Stockman, years later, revealed in his memoir to be a fiction from start to finish. Stockman wrote, "The press had made it into a roaring overnight scandal. The story line made for a red-hot melodrama: The President had been cynically betrayed. I was the Judas who had disavowed the President's economic program and undercut his presidency....His mettle was being tested....I was hanging by a thread....He was angry. That's what the news hounds in the White House press room were braying. And they were building it up by the hour. The reality inside the Oval Office was quite different." In fact, Reagan privately told Stockman, "You're a victim of sabotage by the press. They're trying to bring you down because of what you have helped us accomplish....Dave, I want you to stay on. I need your help." So Reagan, the actor, and Stockman, the wunderkind budget director, in the latter's words, "played out the script that the White House public relations men had designed. And the Atlantic scandal soon faded away." See William Greider, "The Education of David Stockman," *Atlantic*, December 1981, https://www.theatlantic.com/magazine/archive/1981/12/the-education-of-david-stockman/305760; David Stockman, "The Woodshed Revelation," *Washington Post*, April 30, 1986, https://www.washingtonpost.com/archive/lifestyle/1986/04/30/the-woodshed-revelation/975380bb-ab4c-4895-91ae-b6901db24d46.

8. See Eric Alterman, *What Liberal Media? The Truth About Bias and the News* (New York: Viking, 2004).

9. "Veterans of Foreign Wars Convention, Chicago, Illinois, PEACE: Restoring the Margin of Safety," August 18, 1980, Ronald Reagan Presidential Library, https://www.reaganlibrary.gov/sspeeches/8-18-80.

10. Steven R. Weissman, "President Appeals Before Congress for Aid to Latins," *New York Times*, April 28, 1983, A1.

11. For "We are helping the forces," see Corn, "Reagan and the Media." For the former "high-level intelligence official" admitting that the United States founded and financed the death squads, see Seymour Hersh, "The Coming Wars," *New Yorker*, January 24, 2005, https://www.newyorker.com/magazine/2005/01/24/the-coming-wars.

12. For the Maryknoll murders, see Lawyers Committee for International Human Rights, *A Report on the Investigation into the Killing of Four American Churchwomen in El Salvador*, September 1981, Appendix 1–4; Raymond Bonner, "America's Role in El Salvador's Deterioration," *Atlantic*, January 20, 2018, https://www.theatlantic.com/international/archive/2018/01/trump-and-el-salvador/550955. For Jeane Kirkpatrick and Alexander Haig, see US Congress, House Committee on Foreign Affairs, "Foreign Assistance Legislation for Fiscal Year 1982," Part 1, "Hearings," March 13, 18, 19, and 23, 97th Cong., 1st sess. (Washington, DC: Government Printing Office, 1981), 163. For Walter Stoessel, see David E. Anderson, "Washington News," United Press International, April 22, 1981. See also Stephen Kinzer, "US and Central America: Too Close for Comfort," *New York Times*, July 28, 2002, https://www.nytimes.com/2002/07/28/weekinreview/the-world-us-and-central-america-too-close-for-comfort.html.

13. For initial El Mazote reporting, see Alma Guillermoprieto, "Salvadoran Peasants Describe Mass Killing," *Washington Post*, January 27, 1982, A1; Raymond Bonner, "Massacre of Hundreds Reported in Salvadoran Village," *New York Times*, January 27, 1982, A1. For Enders, see Clifford Krauss, "How US Actions Helped Hide Salvador Human Rights Abuses," *New York Times*, March 21, 1993.

14. US Department of State, "US Condemns Salvadoran Death Squads," December 11, 1983, Current Policy, no. 533, Appendix A, 246.

15. United Nations Press Office, "Press Conference of Members of Guatemalan Historical Clarification Committee," March 1, 1999, https://www.un.org/press/en/1999/19990301.guate.brf.html.

16. *MacNeil/Lehrer Report*, Episode 8183, January 10, 1983, available at "The MacNeil/Lehrer Report; 8183; Sale of Guatemala Helicopter Spare Parts," American Archive of Public Broadcasting, https://americanarchive.org/catalog/cpb-aacip_507-mk6542k19c.

17. See Walter LaFeber, *Inevitable Revolutions: The United States in Central America* (New York: W. W. Norton, 1993), 322; Jon Schwarz, "Elliott Abrams, Trump's Pick to Bring 'Democracy' to Venezuela, Has Spent His Life Crushing Democracy," *The Intercept*, January 30, 2019, https://theintercept.com/2019/01/30/elliott-abrams-venezuela-coup. For Abrams and human rights organizations, see George Gedda, "Reagan Administration's Elliott Abrams: A Lightning Rod for Wrath," *Los Angeles Times*, July 31, 1988, https://www.latimes.com/archives/la-xpm-1988-07-31-mn-10724-story.html.

18. For Abrams, see Eric Alterman, "Elliott Abrams: The Teflon Assistant Secretary," *Washington Monthly*, May 1987, https://www.questia.com/read/1G1-4973377

/elliott-abrams-the-teflon-assistant-secretary; Eric Alterman, "An Actual American War Criminal May Become Our Second-Ranking Diplomat," *The Nation*, February 2, 2017, https://www.thenation.com/article/an-actual-american-war-criminal-may-become-our-second-ranking-diplomat; Isaac Stanley-Becker, "'Someone Is Not Being Honest': Elliott Abrams, Trump's Venezuela Envoy, Trailed by Mistrust," *Washington Post*, February 14, 2019; Eric Levitz, "Trump Nixes Plan to Appoint a War Criminal to the State Department," February 10, 2017, *New York*, http://nymag.com/intelligencer/2017/02/trump-nixes-plan-to-appoint-war-criminal-to-state-department.html. For Reagan, see Lou Cannon, Christopher Dickey, and Edward Cody, "Reagan Praises Guatemalan Military Leader," *Washington Post*, December 5, 1982, A1.

19. For "our sonofabitch," see Max Boot, *The Savage Wars of Peace: Small Wars and the Rise of American Power* (New York: Basic Books, 2002), 250. For the payments to the contras and Reagan's comments, see Gerald M. Boyd, "Reagan Terms Nicaraguan Rebels 'Moral Equivalent of Founding Fathers,'" *New York Times*, March 2, 1985, A1.

20. See Stephen Kinzer, "Nicaraguan Port Thought to Be Mined," *New York Times*, March 14, 1984; John F. Burns, "Moscow Holds US Responsible for Mines Off Nicaraguan Ports," *New York Times*, March 22, 1984, A1; William M. LeoGrande, *Our Own Backyard: The United States in Central America, 1977–1992* (Chapel Hill: University of North Carolina Press, 1998), 330.

21. See Mark Fazlollah, "NSC Bypassed Military with Covert Operations," *Miami Herald*, July 26, 1987; "CIA Employees Fought Nicaraguans," *Washington Post*, December 20, 1984; Doyle McManus, "U.S. Didn't Mine Ports: Weinberger," *Los Angeles Times*, April 9, 1984; LeoGrande, *Our Own Backyard*, 339.

22. For the history of the United States and Sandino, see Duncan White, *Cold Warriors: Writers Who Waged the Literary Cold War* (New York: HarperCollins, 2019), 606. For the debate, see "Transcript of the Reagan-Mondale Debate on Foreign Policy," *New York Times*, October 22, 1984, B4; Joel Brinkley, "CIA Chief Defends Manual for Nicaraguan Rebels," *New York Times*, November 2, 1984, A3.

23. LeoGrande, *Our Own Backyard*, 458–459.

24. "The President's News Conference, June 18, 1985," *Public Papers of President Ronald W. Reagan*, Ronald Reagan Presidential Library, www.reagan.utexas.edu/resource/speeches/1985/61885c.htm.

25. James M. Banner, ed., *Presidential Misconduct: From George Washington to Today* (New York: New Press, 2019), 405–418.

26. For a detailed discussion of these events, with a focus on the lies told and their consequences, see Eric Alterman, *When Presidents Lie: A History of Official Deception and Its Consequences* (New York: Viking, 2008), 238–293.

27. Christopher Lehman-Haupt, "Books of The Times: How Ronald Reagan Overcame Doubts and Became President," *New York Times*, November 5, 1990, C16.

Notes on Chapter Twelve

Chapter Twelve: George H.W. Bush: Don't Read His Lips

1. Douglass Kneeland, "Nominee for No. 2 Spot: George Herbert Walker Bush," *New York Times*, July 18, 1980, A1.

2. Walter Pincus, "Bush Out of the Loop on Iran-Contra?" *Washington Post*, September 24, 1992, https://www.washingtonpost.com/archive/politics/1992/09/24/bush-out-of-the-loop-on-iran-contra/4ee467ab-8531-46e5-8da5-ff7bd97a6609.

3. Michael Kinsley, "Lies, Damned Lies, and Impeachment," *Slate*, December 25, 1998, www.slate.com/articles/news_and_politics/readme/1998/12/lies_damned_lies_and_impeachment.html.

4. For Bush's diaries, see ibid.; Lawrence E. Walsh, *Final Report of the Independent Counsel for Iran/Contra Matters*, vol. 1, *Investigations and Prosecutions* (Washington, DC: Office of Independent Counsel, 1993), 473, xviii, https://books.google.com/books?id=6tYAMvPsPmkC&ppis.

5. Cecil V. Crabb and Kevin V. Mulcahy, "George Bush's Management Style and Operation Desert Storm," *Presidential Studies Quarterly* 25, no. 2 (1995): 251–265.

6. Shannon Poulsen and Dannagal G. Young, "A History of Fact-Checking in US Politics and Election Contests," in *Misinformation and Mass Audiences*, ed. Brian G. Southwell, Emily A. Thorson, and Laura Shelbe (Austin: University of Texas Press, 2018), 232–248.

7. "Text of the President's Speech on National Drug Control Strategy," *New York Times*, September 6, 1989, B6.

8. The teen arrested in the incident, Keith Jackson, was held without bail and eventually convicted on three counts of cocaine sales, even though the sale to Bush's agents was thrown out. He was sentenced to ten years in prison and served eight. Tracy Thompson, "D.C. Student Is Given 10 Years in Drug Case," *Washington Post*, November 1, 1990, https://www.washingtonpost.com/archive/local/1990/11/01/dc-student-is-given-10-years-in-drug-case/2384c4eb-8871-4d28-a4f0-a3919335c311; Corinne Purtill, "US Agents Lured a Teen Near the White House to Sell Drugs So George H.W. Bush Could Make a Point," *Quartz*, December 2, 2018, https://qz.com/1481809/george-h-w-bush-had-a-teen-set-up-to-sell-drugs-near-white-house.

9. For the Iran-Iraq War, see Williamson Murray and Kevin Woods, *The Iran-Iraq War: A Military and Strategic History* (New York: Cambridge University Press, 2014). For the specific details of US aid to Saddam's regime, see Shane Harris and Matthew M. Aid, "Exclusive: CIA Files Prove America Helped Saddam as He Gassed Iran," *Foreign Policy*, August 26, 2013, http://foreignpolicy.com/2013/08/26/exclusive-cia-files-prove-america-helped-saddam-as-he-gassed-iran; Seymour Hersh, *Reporter* (New York: Alfred A. Knopf, 2018), 163.

10. For the Reagan/Bush policy and the senators' visit to Saddam, see Harris and Aid, "Exclusive: CIA Files"; Hersh, *Reporter*, 163; Neil A. Lewis, "Washington at Work: Wyoming's Folksy Senate Orator, Sharp-Tongued Ally of the President," *New York Times*, October 24, 1990, https://www.nytimes.com/1990/10/24/us/washington-work-wyoming-s-folksy-senate-orator-sharp-tongued-ally-president

.html. For April Glaspie, see Jean Edward Smith, *George Bush's War* (New York: Henry Holt, 1992), 48, 56.

11. James Walcott, *Attack Poodles and Other Media Mutants* (New York: Miramax, 2004), 287.

12. "Transcript of the Comments by Bush on the Air Strikes Against the Iraqis," *New York Times*, January 17, 1991, https://www.nytimes.com/1991/01/17/us/war -gulf-president-transcript-comments-bush-air-strikes-against-iraqis.html.

13. Smith, *George Bush's War*, 135–140.

14. For the testimony, see ibid., 135–140. See also Douglas Jehl, "US General Says UN Move May Jolt Iraqis," *Los Angeles Times*, November 29, 1990, https://www.latimes.com/archives/la-xpm-1990-11-29-mn-7445-story.html.

15. Walter Cronkite, "What Is There to Hide," *Newsweek*, February 25, 1991, 43.

16. Thomas Frank, "Sins of the Father," *New Republic*, December 27, 2004; Neil A. Lewis, "Bar Association Splits on Fitness of Thomas for the Supreme Court," *New York Times*, August 28, 1991; https://www.nytimes.com/1991/08/28 /us/bar-association-splits-on-fitness-of-thomas-for-the-supreme-court.html.

17. For Thomas's ABA rating, see Robert L. Jackson, "Thomas Rated 'Qualified' by ABA," *Los Angeles Times*, August 28, 1991, https://www.latimes.com/ar chives/la-xpm-1991-08-28-mn-1149-story.html. See also Corey Robin, *The Enigma of Clarence Thomas* (New York: Metropolitan Books, 2019).

18. William Leuchtenberg, *The American President: From Teddy Roosevelt to Bill Clinton* (New York: Oxford University Press), 701–703.

Chapter Thirteen: Bill Clinton: Defiling the Temple of Justice

1. James Stewart, *Tangled Webs: How False Statements Are Undermining America. From Martha Stewart to Bernie Madoff* (New York: Penguin, 2011), xvi.

2. Ken Gormley, *The Death of American Virtue: Clinton vs. Starr* (New York: Crown, 2010), 309–314.

3. Joe Conason and Gene Lyons, *The Hunting of the President: The Ten-Year Campaign to Destroy Bill and Hillary Clinton* (New York: St. Martin's Press, 2001).

4. Here, as Congressman Bill McCollum of Florida pointed out on the floor of the House of Representatives, is where Clinton perjured himself to Starr's staff and the grand jury.

Clinton: "You are free to infer that my testimony is that I did not have sexual relations as I understood this term to be used."

Question: "Including touching her breasts, kissing her breasts, or touching her genitalia?"

Clinton: "That's correct."

This was a lie.

5. Joan Didion, "Clinton Agonistes," review of Office of Independent Counsel, *Referral to the United States House of Representatives Pursuant to Title 28, United States Code, §595(c) Submitted by the Office of the Independent Counsel, New York*

Review of Books, October 22, 1998, https://www.nybooks.com/articles/1998/10/22 /clinton-agonistes.

6. Eric Alterman, "The World as It Ought to Be," Center for American Progress, September 16, 2010, https://www.americanprogress.org/issues/general/news /2010/09/16/8372/think-again-the-world-as-it-ought-to-be; Eric Alterman, "Lies, Justice, and the Punditocracy's 'Place,'" Center for American Progress, July 5, 2007, https://www.americanprogress.org/issues/courts/news/2007/07/05/3345/think -again-lies-justice-and-the-punditocracys-place.

7. Michael Kelly, "The President's Past," *New York Times Magazine*, July 31, 1994, https://www.nytimes.com/1994/07/31/magazine/the-president-s-past.html.

8. Sally Quinn, "Not in Their Backyard: In Washington, That Letdown Feeling," *Washington Post*, November 2, 1998, https://www.washingtonpost.com /wp-srv/politics/special/clinton/stories/quinn110298.htm.

9. Kevin Merida, "It's Come to This: A Nickname That's Proven Hard to Slip," *Washington Post*, December 20, 1998, https://www.washingtonpost.com/wp-srv /politics/special/clinton/stories/slick122098.htm.

10. The December 1998 attacks were the second set of such attacks Clinton had ordered. The first took place in June 1993, when US intelligence services concluded that Saddam Hussein had attempted to have ex-president George H.W. Bush assassinated on a visit to Kuwait the previous April. See David Von Drehle and R. Jeffrey Smith, "U.S. Strikes Iraq for Plot to Kill Bush," *Washington Post*, June 27, 1993, A1; "Text of President Clinton's 1998 State of the Union Address," *Washington Post*, January 27, 1998, www.washingtonpost.com/wp-srv/politics/special /states/docs/sou98.htm; "Excerpts from the Discussion on Iraq at Ohio State University," *New York Times*, February 19, 1998, https://archive.nytimes.com/www .nytimes.com/library/world/021998iraq-text.html.

11. "Scott Ritter on the Untold Story of the Intelligence Conspiracy to Undermine the UN and Overthrow Saddam Hussein," *Democracy Now!*, October 21, 2005, https://www.democracynow.org/2005/10/21/scott_ritter_on_the_untold_story.

12. Marvin Kalb, *One Scandalous Story: Clinton, Lewinsky, and 13 Days That Tarnished American Journalism* (New York: Free Press, 2001), 193–194.

13. Ibid., 130, 146, 158–159, 193–194. See also Didion, "Clinton Agonistes."

14. For the political role of talk radio, see Brian Rosenwald, *Talk Radio's America: How an Industry Took Over a Political Party That Took Over the United States* (Cambridge, MA: Harvard University Press, 2019). For the increase of Fox's influence, see Neil Swidley, "How Democrats Would Be Better Off If Bill Clinton Had Never Been President," *Boston Globe*, July 10, 2018, https://www.boston globe.com/magazine/2018/07/10/bill-clinton-had-never-been-president-democrats -would-better-off-today/qsYmCo7ZEYpQr8fOZSkRLM/story.html.

15. David Brooks, "Let's Not Get Carried Away," *New York Times*, June 10, 2017, A26.

Notes on Chapter Thirteen

16. For Scaife, see "The Forbes 400: The Richest Americans," *Forbes*, September 13, 2002, www.forbes.com/2002/09/13/rich400land.html. For Brock's confession, see David Brock, *Blinded by the Right: The Conscience of an Ex-Conservative* (New York: Crown, 2001), 101. See also Jane Mayer, "True Confessions," review of David Brock, *Blinded by the Right: The Conscience of an Ex-Conservative*, *New York Review of Books*, June 27, 2002, www.nybooks.com/articles/15522.

17. Conason and Lyons, *Hunting of the President*. See also Robert G. Kaiser and Ira Chinoy, "How Scaife's Money Powered a Movement," *Washington Post*, May 2, 1999, A1.

18. Jeffrey Toobin, *A Vast Conspiracy: The Real Story of the Sex Scandal That Nearly Brought Down a President* (New York: Random House, 1999), xi–xv.

19. See David S. Broder, "The Livingston Challenge," *Washington Post*, December 20, 1998, C07. Note that according to L. H. Carter, the treasurer for Gingrich's congressional campaign, Gingrich divorced his first wife, eight years his senior, while she was hospitalized with cancer—because, he told Carter, "she's not young enough or pretty enough to be the wife of the President. And besides, she has cancer." She was forced to sue him for child support. This decision followed a campaign for Congress in which, after his female opponent explained that she would commute to Washington so that her husband might keep his job, and her children could remain in their schools, he distributed flyers reading: "When elected Newt will keep his family together." He later sheltered his $4 million book bonanza from his struggling, non-trophy ex-wife. Years later, in 2012, while Gingrich was running unsuccessfully for the Republican presidential nomination, he was asked during a debate about some of this history. In response, Gingrich "let loose" with what journalist McCay Coppins termed "one of the most remarkable—and effective—non sequiturs in the history of campaign rhetoric: 'I think the destructive, vicious, negative nature of much of the news media makes it harder to govern this country, harder to attract decent people to run for public office—and I am *appalled* that you would begin a presidential debate on a topic like that.'" Robert Scheer, "Gingrich Puts a Price on His Family Values," *Los Angeles Times*, December 25, 1994, http://articles.latimes.com/1994-12-25/opinion/op-12904_1_family-values; McCay Coppins, "The Man Who Broke Politics," *Atlantic*, November 2018, https://www.theatlantic.com/magazine/archive/2018/11/newt-gingrich-says-youre-welcome/570832.

20. For Hastert, see Associated Press, "Judge Bars Ex-Speaker Hastert from Being Alone with Minors," December 14, 2017, https://www.apnews.com/f0aca550dabc4e4c9c642e91f832d6ed. For DeLay, R. Jeffrey Smith, "Tom DeLay, Former U.S. House Leader, Sentenced to 3 Years in Prison," *Washington Post*, January 10, 2011, www.washingtonpost.com/wp-dyn/content/article/2011/01/10/AR2011011000557.html. For Starr, see Peter Sawson, "Report: Baylor Paid Art Briles and Ken Starr Millions After Sexual Assault Scandal," *Fort Worth Star-Telegram*, May 18, 2018, https://www.star-telegram.com/latest-news/article207544534.html.

21. For the details on Oreskes, see Paul Farhi, "NPR's Top Editor Placed on Leave After Accusations of Sexual Harassment," *Washington Post*, October 31, 2017, https://www.washingtonpost.com/lifestyle/style/nprs-top-editor-accused-of-sexual -harassment-by-two-women/2017/10/31/a2078bea-bdf7-11e7-959c-fe2b598d8c00_story .html. For Mark Halperin, see James Warren, "Mark Halperin Suspended from NBC amid Wave of Post-Weinstein Sexual Allegations," *Vanity Fair*, October 26, 2017, https:// www.vanityfair.com/news/2017/10/mark-halperin-out-at-nbc-amid-wave-of-post -weinstein-allegations. For Leon Wieseltier, see Sarah Wildman, "I Was Harassed at the New Republic. I Spoke Up. Nothing Happened," Vox, November 9, 2017, https:// www.vox.com/first-person/2017/11/9/16624588/new-republic-harassment.

22. For the Matt Lauer allegation and denial, see Bruce Haring, "Matt Lauer Rape Accuser Brooke Nevils Issues Statement on His Open Letter: 'A Case Study in Victim Shaming,'" *Deadline*, October 9, 2019, https://deadline.com/2019/10 /brooke-nevils-matt-lauer-statement-victim-shaming-1202756488. For the others at NBC and MSNBC (including David Corvo), see Analisa Quinn, "In 'Catch and Kill,' Ronan Farrow Offers a Damning Portrait of a Conflicted NBC," NPR, October 11, 2019, https://www.npr.org/2019/10/11/768346770/in-catch-and-kill-ronan-farrow -offers-a-damning-portrait-of-a-conflicted-nbc, which is drawn from Ronan Farrow, *Catch and Kill: Lies, Spies, and a Conspiracy to Protect Predators* (New York: Little, Brown, 2019). For Charlie Rose, see Irin Carman and Amy Brittain, "Eight Women Say Charlie Rose Sexually Harassed Them—with Nudity, Groping and Lewd Calls," *Washington Post*, November 20, 2017, https://www.washingtonpost.com /investigations/eight-women-say-charlie-rose-sexually-harassed-them—with-nudity -groping-and-lewd-calls/2017/11/20/9b168de8-caec-11e7-8321-481fd63f174d _story.html; Rea Bravo, "The Open Secret of Charlie Rose," *New York Review of Books*, May 4, 2018, https://www.nybooks.com/daily/2018/05/04/the-open-secret-of-charlie -rose. For Fager and Hewitt, see Rachel Abrams and John Koblin, "At '60 Minutes,' Independence Led to Trouble, Investigators Say," *New York Times*, December 6, 2018, A1. For Les Moonves, see Ronan Farrow, "Les Moonves and CBS Face Allegations of Sexual Misconduct," *New Yorker*, August 6, 2018, https://www.newyorker.com /magazine/2018/08/06/les-moonves-and-cbs-face-allegations-of-sexual-misconduct.

23. For Ailes's remarks at NBC, see Jill Lepore, "Bad News," *New Yorker*, January 12, 2014, https://www.newyorker.com/magazine/2014/01/20/bad-news-11. For a roundup of other Fox sexual harassment and abuse accusations, see Ryan Gajewski, "A Brief History of Fox's Sexual Harassment Scandals, from Roger Ailes to Charles Payne," *The Wrap*, July 7, 2017, https://www.thewrap.com/fox-sexual -harassment-jamie-horowitz-roger-ailes-bill-oreilly; Farrow, *Catch and Kill*.

24. Toobin, *Vast Conspiracy*, 320.

25. "Transcript: Former Sen. Dale Bumpers," CNN, January 21, 1999, www.cnn .com/ALLPOLITICS/stories/1999/01/21/transcripts/bumpers.html; "Jan. 21: Bumpers Defends the President," *Washington Post*, January 21, 1999, https://www.washington post.com/wp-srv/politics/special/clinton/stories/bumperstext012199.htm.

26. Toobin, *Vast Conspiracy*, 357; "Dec. 1 Afternoon Session: Nine Experts," *Washington Post*, December 1, 1998, https://www.washingtonpost.com/wp-srv /politics/special/clinton/stories/pmtext120198.htm.

27. "Poll: Clinton's Approval Rating Up in Wake of Impeachment," CNN, December 20, 1998, www.cnn.com/ALLPOLITICS/stories/1998/12/20/impeachment.poll.

28. Dinesh D'Souza, "How Obama Thinks," *Forbes*, September 9, 2010, https://www.forbes.com/forbes/2010/0927/politics-socialism-capitalism-private -enterprises-obama-business-problem.html#409e6d962217.

29. Julian E. Zelizer, *Burning Down the House: Newt Gingrich, the Takedown of a Speaker, and the Rise of the New Republican Party* (New York: Penguin, 2020), 297.

Chapter Fourteen: George W. Bush: "We're History's Actors"

1. Michael Kinsley, "Lying in Style: What You Can Learn About a President from How He Chooses to Deceive You," *Slate*, April 18, 2002, https://slate.com/news-and -politics/2002/04/what-you-can-learn-about-a-president-from-how-he-lies.html.

2. For the Bush argument, see Edward Walsh, "Harbury Loses Bid to Sue U.S. Officials: Rebel's Widow Alleged Deception," *Washington Post*, June 21, 2002, A09. For the Kennedy administration's, see John M. Orman, *Presidential Secrecy and Deception: Beyond the Power to Persuade* (Westport, CT: Greenwood Press, 1980), 46.

3. For the "Brooks Brothers riot," see John Lantiqua, "Miami's Rent-a-Riot," *Salon*, November 28, 2000, https://www.salon.com/2000/11/28/miami_8; Michael E. Miller, "'It's Insanity!' How the 'Brooks Brothers Riot' Killed the 2000 Recount in Miami," *Washington Post*, November 15, 2018, https://www.washingtonpost .com/history/2018/11/15/its-insanity-how-brooks-brothers-riot-killed-recount -miami. For a discussion of the vote count, and why Bush would likely have lost if it had been allowed to continue, see Eric Alterman, *What Liberal Media? The Truth About Bias and the News* (New York: Basic Books, 2003), 175–191.

4. For Bush's false deficit statement, see "President Works on Economic Recovery During NY Trip," White House, October 2001, www.whitehouse.gov /news/releases/2001/10/20011003-4.html; Jonathan Chait, "Red Handed," *New Republic*, May 13, 2002, www.tnr.com/doc.mhtml?i=20020513&s=chait051302. For Krugman's catch on the budget, see Paul Krugman, "The Memory Hole," *New York Times*, August 6, 2002, A17. For the "not a fact-checker" quote, see Dana Milbank and Dana Priest, "Warning in Iraq Report Unread," *Washington Post*, July 19, 2003, A01. For the quote on "history's actors," see Ron Suskind, "Faith, Certainty and the Presidency of George W. Bush," *New York Times Magazine*, October 7, 2004, https://www.nytimes .com/2004/10/17/magazine/faith-certainty-and-the-presidency-of-george-w-bush.html.

5. See Richard Bernstein, "Counterpoint to Unity: Dissent," *New York Times*, October 6, 2001, A13.

6. James Mann, *Rise of the Vulcans: The History of Bush's War Cabinet* (New York: Viking, 2004), 327. For Rumsfeld, see Ahsan I. Butt, "Why Did the United States Invade Iraq in 2003?" *Security Studies* 28, no. 2 (2019): 250–285.

7. For the report on ground zero, see Sierra Club, *Pollution and Deception at Ground Zero Revisited: Why It Could Happen Again*, September 2005; Suzanne Mattei, *Pollution and Deception at Ground Zero: How the Bush Administration's Reckless Disregard of 9/11 Toxic Hazards Poses Long-Term Threats for New York City and the Nation* (San Francisco: Sierra Club, 2004), https://www.gothamgazette.com/rebuilding_nyc/sierraclub_report.pdf. See also Eileen A.J. Connelly, "Former NYPD Detective and 9/11 First Responder Luis Alvarez Dead at 53," *New York Post*, June 29, 2019, https://nypost.com/2019/06/29/former-nypd-detective-and-9-11-first-responder-luis-alvarez-dies; Susan Edelman, "Nearly 10k People Have Gotten Cancer from Toxic 9/11 Dust," *New York Post*, August 11, 2018, https://nypost.com/2018/08/11/nearly-10k-people-have-gotten-cancer-from-toxic-9-11-dust; Thomas Tracy, "Facing a Grim New Year: Nearly 40 Die from 9/11 Illness in Last Four Months," *New York Daily News*, December 30, 2018, https://www.nydailynews.com/new-york/ny-metro-forty-people-dead-911-story.html.

8. For an overview, see Eric Alterman and Mark Green, *The Book on Bush: How George W. (Mis)leads America* (New York: Viking, 2004), 266–322. For Bush's statements, see US Congress, House of Representatives, Committee on Government Reform, "Iraq on the Record: The Bush Administration's Public Statements on Iraq," March 16, 2004, Homeland Security Digital Library, https://www.hsdl.org/?abstract&did=445160.

9. For the DIA report, see Robert Scheer, "Bad Iraq Data from Start to Finish," *The Nation*, June 11, 2003, https://www.thenation.com/article/bad-iraq-data-start-finish. For Tenet's comments, see Central Intelligence Agency, "DCI Remarks on Iraq's WMD Programs," February 5, 2004, https://www.cia.gov/news-information/speeches-testimony/2004/tenet_georgetownspeech_02052004.html. See also William Safire, "Prague Connection," *New York Times*, November 12, 2001, A19; James Risen, "Threats and Responses: The Czech Connection. No Evidence of Meeting with Iraqi," *New York Times*, June 17, 2004, A17, https://www.nytimes.com/2004/06/17/world/threats-and-responses-the-czech-connection-no-evidence-of-meeting-with-iraqi.html. For the five government officials (who were President George W. Bush, Vice President Richard Cheney, Defense Secretary Donald Rumsfeld, Secretary of State Colin Powell, and Assistant for National Security Condoleezza Rice), see US Congress, House of Representatives, "Iraq on the Record."

10. For Lindsey and Shinseki, see Eric Schmitt, "Pentagon Contradicts General on Iraq Occupation Force's Size," *New York Times*, February 28, 2003, https://www.nytimes.com/2003/02/28/us/threats-responses-military-spending-pentagon-contradicts-general-iraq-occupation.html; Thom Shanker, "New Strategy Vindicates Ex-Army Chief Shinseki," *New York Times*, January 12, 2007, https://www.nytimes.com/2007/01/12/washington/12shinseki.html. For Hardcastle, see Sidney Blumenthal, "There Was No Failure of Intelligence," *The Guardian*, February 5, 2004, www.guardian.co.uk/comment/story/0,3604,1141116,00.html.

Notes on Chapter Fourteen

11. Greg Miller, "Cheney Is Adamant on Iraq 'Evidence': Vice President Revives Assertions on Banned Weaponry and Links to Al Qaeda That Other Administration Officials Have Backed Away From," *Los Angeles Times*, January 23, 3004, A1.

12. See Thomas L. Friedman, "The Meaning of a Skull," *New York Times*, April 27, 2003, 13; "Keep Looking," *Washington Post*, June 25, 2003, A22, https://www .washingtonpost.com/archive/opinions/2003/06/25/keep-looking/115aa6b3-1708 -4d20-9aa4-fb9019b6d562. For Blair, see Rowena Mason, Anushka Asthana, and Heather Stewart, "Tony Blair: 'I Express More Sorrow, Regret and Apology Than You Can Ever Believe,'" *The Guardian*, July 6, 2016, https://www.theguardian.com /uk-news/2016/jul/06/tony-blair-deliberately-exaggerated-threat-from-iraq-chilcot -report-war-inquiry.

13. See "Reliable Sources," CNN, July 20, 2003, www.cnn.com/TRANSCRIPTS /0307/20/rs.00.html; Jay Rosen "Why Political Coverage Is Broken," *PressThink*, August 26, 2011, http://pressthink.org/2011/08/why-political-coverage-is-broken.

14. Jason Linkins, "River of No Return," *Baffler*, Spring 2018, https://thebaf fler.com/salvos/river-of-no-return-linkins.

15. For US and Iraqi casualties, see Philip Bump, "15 Years After the Iraq War Began, the Death Toll Is Still Murky," *Washington Post*, March 20, 2018, https:// www.washingtonpost.com/news/politics/wp/2018/03/20/15-years-after-it-began -the-death-toll-from-the-iraq-war-is-still-murky; Agence France Press, "Iraq Death Toll Reaches 500,000 Since Start of U.S.-Led Invasion, New Study Says," *Huffington Post*, September 15, 2013, https://www.huffingtonpost.com/2013/10/15 /iraq-death-toll_n_4102855.html. The financial cost of the war is taken from Joseph E. Stiglitz, *The Three Trillion Dollar War: The True Cost of the Iraq Conflict* (New York: W. W. Norton, 2008); Neta C. Crawford, "US Budgetary Costs of Wars Through 2016: $4.79 Trillion and Counting," Watson Institute of International and Public Affairs, Brown University, September 2016, https://watson .brown.edu/costsofwar/files/cow/imce/papers/2016/Costs%20of%20War%20 through%202016%20FINAL%20final%20v2.pdf. The source for the assessment of Iranian influence is the Pentagon's own two-volume study of the war, quoted in Jon Finer, "The Last War—and the Next? Learning the Wrong Lessons from Iraq," *Foreign Affairs*, May 28, 2019, https://www.foreignaffairs.com/reviews /review-essay/2019-05-28/last-war-and-next. For the success of Iran in turning the invasion to its geopolitical advantage and vastly increasing its influence in Iran, see Tim Arango, James Risen, Farnaz Fassihi, Ronen Bergman, and Murtaza Hussain, "The Iran Cables: Secret Documents Show How Tehran Wields Power in Iraq," *New York Times*, November 19, 2019; Mustafa Salim and Liz Sly, "Supporters of Iranian-Backed Militia End Siege of U.S. Embassy in Baghdad," *Washington Post*, January 1, 2020, https://www.washingtonpost.com/world/supporters-of-iranian -backed-militia-start-withdrawing-from-besieged-us-embassy-in-baghdad -following-militia-orders/2020/01/01/8280cb34-2c9e-11ea-9b60-817cc18cf173_story .html; Falih Hassan and Elizabeth Rubin, "Pro-Iranian Protesters End Siege of U.S.

Embassy in Baghdad," *New York Times*, January 1, 2010; Michael Crowley, Falih Hassan, and Eric Schmitt, "U.S. Strike in Iraq Kills Commander of Iranian Force," *New York Times*, January 3, 2020.

16. For the consistent lying about the progress of the US war in Afghanistan, see Craig Whitlock, "The Afghanistan Papers: A Secret History of the War. At War with the Truth: U.S. Officials Constantly Said They Were Making Progress. They Were Not, and They Knew It," *Washington Post*, December 9, 2019, A1, https://www.washingtonpost.com/graphics/2019/investigations/afghanistan-papers/afghanistan-war-confidential-documents; Craig Whitlock, "How the Post Unearthed the Afghanistan Papers," *Washington Post*, December 9, 2019, https://www.washingtonpost.com/investigations/how-the-post-unearthed-the-afghanistan-papers/2019/12/08/07ddb844-1847-11ea-a659-7d69641c6ff7_story.html.

Chapter Fifteen: Barack Obama vs. the "Propaganda Feedback Loop"

1. David Leonardt, Ian Prasad Philbrick, and Stuart A. Thompson, "Trump's Lies vs. Obama's," *New York Times*, December 14, 2017, https://www.nytimes.com/interactive/2017/12/14/opinion/sunday/trump-lies-obama-who-is-worse.html.

2. See Michael Cohen, "The Real Obama Scandal: Fighting Illegal Wars in Libya and Pakistan," *The Guardian*, May 15, 2013, https://www.theguardian.com/commentisfree/2013/may/15/irs-ap-benghanzi-not-real-scandals; Craig Whitlock, "The Afghanistan Papers: A Secret History of the War. At War with the Truth: U.S. Officials Constantly Said They Were Making Progress. They Were Not, and They Knew It," *Washington Post*, December 9, 2019, A1.

3. See Spencer Ackerman, "James Clapper: Obama Stands by Intelligence Chief as Criticism Mounts," *The Guardian*, June 12, 2013, https://www.theguardian.com/world/2013/jun/12/james-clapper-intelligence-chief-criticism. For the Espionage Act, see James Risen, "If Donald Trump Targets Journalists, Thank Obama," *New York Times*, December 30, 2016, https://www.nytimes.com/2016/12/30/opinion/sunday/if-donald-trump-targets-journalists-thank-obama.html.

4. Peter Drier, "The Right-Wing Firestorm That Rages On," *Dissent*, July 27, 2018, https://www.dissentmagazine.org/online_articles/acorn-firestorm-documentary-breitbart-vs-grassroots.

5. Eric Alterman, "The Liars' Network," *The Nation*, April 7, 2011, https://www.thenation.com/article/fox-liars-network.

6. See Walter Lippmann, "The Basic Problem of Democracy," *Atlantic Monthly*, November 1919, https://www.theatlantic.com/magazine/archive/1919/11/the-basic-problem-of-democracy/569095. For Sanchez, see Matt Grossman and David Hopkins, *Asymmetric Politics: Ideological Republicans and Group Interest Democrats* (New York: Oxford University Press, 2016). For the MIT Media Lab, see Yochai Benkler, Robert Faris, Hal Roberts, and Ethan Zuckerman, "Study: Breitbart-Led Right-Wing Media Ecosystem Altered Broader Media Agenda," *Columbia Journalism Review*, March 3, 2017, https://www.cjr.org/analysis/breitbart-media-trump-harvard-study

.php; Yochai Benkler, Robert Faris, and Hal Roberts, *Network Propaganda: Manipulation, Disinformation, and Radicalization in American Politics* (New York: Oxford University Press, 2018), 33.

7. Lauren McGan, "Bill Shine Covered Up Sexual Harassment at Fox News for Decades Until the Plot Blew Up in His Face," Vox, July 5, 2018, https://www.vox .com/2018/7/5/17538132/bill-shine-fox-donald-trump-communications-sexual -harassment.

8. For Nugent, see Elizabeth Goodman, "Ted Nugent Threatens to Kill Barack Obama, Hillary Clinton During Vicious Onstage Rant," *Rolling Stone*, August 24, 2007, https://www.rollingstone.com/music/music-news/ted-nugent-threatens-to-kill -barack-obama-and-hillary-clinton-during-vicious-onstage-rant-94687; E. J. Dionne, *Why the Right Went Wrong: Conservatism—From Goldwater to Trump and Beyond* (New York: Simon and Schuster, 2016), 303. For Beck's quotes, see Simon Maloy, "Self-Proclaimed Civil Rights Leader Glenn Beck's History of Racially Charged Rhetoric," *Media Matters*, August 25, 2010, https://www.mediamatters.org/research /2010/08/26/self-proclaimed-civil-rights-leader-glenn-becks/169797.

9. See Dorothy Rabinowitz, "The Alien in the White House," *Wall Street Journal*, June 9, 2010, https://www.wsj.com/articles/SB10001424052748703302604575294231631318728. For Charles Murray, see Jonah Goldberg, "Obama Ate Our Dog(ma)," July 27, 2012, https://www.nationalreview.com/g-file/obama-ate -our-dogma-jonah-goldberg. For Sununu and Heather Mac Donald, see Dionne, *Why the Right Went Wrong*, 371. For Gingrich and D'Souza, see Eric Alterman, *Kabuki Democracy: The System vs. Barack Obama* (New York: Nation Books, 2011), 100; Dinesh D'Souza, "Obama's Problem with Business," *Forbes*, September 27, 2010, https://www.forbes.com/global/2010/0927/issues-socialism-capitalism -obama-business-problem.html#26764ad87ff1.

10. For the multivariate study of Fox News viewers, see Sanford Schram and Richard Fording, "The Fox News–Fake News–Trump Nexus," Public Seminar, March 24, 2018, www.publicseminar.org/2018/03/the-fox-news-fake-news-trump -nexus. For the Democracy Corps study, see "The Very Separate World of Conservative Republicans," Democracy Corps, October 16, 2009, www.democracycorps .com/News/the-very-separate-world-of-conservative-republicans.

11. See Hendrik Hertzberg, "We Built It," *New Yorker*, August 28, 2012, https://www.newyorker.com/news/hendrik-hertzberg/we-built-it; "Remarks by the President at a Campaign Event in Roanoke, Virginia," White House, Office of the Press Secretary, July 13, 2012, https://obamawhitehouse.archives.gov/the-press -office/2012/07/13/remarks-president-campaign-event-roanoke-virginia; Aaron Blake, "Obama's 'You Didn't Build That' Problem," *Washington Post*, July 18, 2012, https://www.washingtonpost.com/blogs/the-fix/post/obamas-you-didnt-build-that -problem/2012/07/18/gJQAJxyotW_blog.html; "You Didn't Build That: A Theme Out of Context," CNN, September 1, 2012, https://www.cnn.com/2012/08/31 /politics/fact-check-built-this/index.html.

12. "GOP Announces Convention Theme 'We Built This' in Stadium Built with 62% Government Funds," *Daily Dolt*, August 30, 2012, https://politicalwire.com/ar chives/2012/08/22/gop_convention_held_in_stadium_built_with_public_funds.html.

13. For the *Post* and CNN, see Glenn Kessler, "An Unoriginal Obama Quote—Taken Out of Context," *Washington Post*, July 23, 2012, https://www .washingtonpost.com/blogs/fact-checker/post/an-unoriginal-obama-quote-taken -out-of-context/2012/07/20/gJQAdG7hyW_blog.html; "You Didn't Build That: A Theme Out of Context." See also "You Didn't Build That," *Wall Street Journal*, July 19, 2012, https://www.wsj.com/articles/SB10001424052702304388004577533 3300916053684; James Taranto, "You Didn't Sweat, He Did," *Wall Street Journal*, July 18, 2012, https://www.wsj.com/articles/SB10000872396390444873204577535053434972374. For the *Post* blogger, see Jennifer Rubin, "Obama Is Losing His Message Like Nobody's Business," *Washington Post*, July 24, 2012, https:// www.washingtonpost.com/blogs/right-turn/post/obama-is-losing-his-message-like -nobodys-business/2012/07/24/gJQAy1yK6W_blog.html.

14. See Blake, "Obama's 'You Didn't Build That' Problem." See also Rachael Larimore, "'You Didn't Build That' Isn't Going Away: It Doesn't Matter What Obama *Meant.* Here's Why," *Slate*, August 20, 2012, www.slate.com/articles /news_and_politics/politics/2012/08/_you_didn_t_build_that_it_doesn_t_matter _what_obama_meant_to_say_but_what_people_heard_.html; Roger Sollenberger, "Chris Cillizza, Milquetoast Hack and Enemy of Truth, Has Left the Washington Post. Good," *Paste Magazine*, March 29, 2017, https://www.pastemagazine.com /articles/2017/03/chris-cillizza-milquetoast-hack-and-enemy-of-truth.html.

15. Ben Smith, "I Helped Create Insider Political Journalism. Now It's Time for It to Go Away," BuzzFeed, August 30, 2018, https://www.buzzfeednews.com /article/bensmith/i-helped-create-insider-political-journalism-now-its-time.

16. Glenn Kessler, "The Truth? C'mon, This Is a Political Convention," *Washington Post*, September 12, 2012, https://www.washingtonpost.com/blogs/fact-checker /post/the-truth-cmon-this-is-a-political-convention/2012/08/31/88550120-f3c0 -11e1-892d-bc92fee603a7_blog.html.

17. Theda Skocpol and Vanessa Williamson, *The Tea Party and the Remaking of Republican Conservatism* (New York: Oxford University Press, 2016), 125–126.

18. Angie Drobnic Holan, "Lie of the Year: 'If You Like Your Health Care Plan, You Can Keep It,'" PolitiFact, December 12, 2013, www.politifact.com/truth-o-meter /article/2013/dec/12/lie-year-if-you-like-your-health-care-plan-keep-it.

19. Maggie Mahar, "Did President Obama 'Lie' When He Said 'If You Like the Policy You Have, You Can Keep It'? Context Is Everything," *Health Beat*, February 5, 2014, www.healthbeatblog.com/2014/02/did-president-obama-lie-when-he-said-if-you-like -the-policy-you-have-you-can-keep-it-context-is-everything.

20. Fredrika Schouten, "Exclusive: Secret Money Funds More Than 40 Percent of Outside Congressional Ads," *USA Today*, July 12, 2018, https://www.usatoday

.com/story/news/politics/2018/07/12/secret-money-funds-more-than-40-percent
-outside-congressional-tv-ads-midterm-elections/777536002.

21. Jill Lepore, *These Truths: A History of the United States* (New York: W. W. Norton, 2018), 240–241.

22. For the Koch network, see Matea Gold, "Koch-Backed Political Network, Built to Shield Donors, Raised $400 Million in 2012 Elections," *Washington Post*, January 5, 2014, A1; David Callahan, "American Elections Are a Battle of Billionaires. We Are Merely Spectators," *The Guardian*, July 5, 2018, https://www.theguardian.com/commentisfree/2018/jul/05/american-elections-battle-billionaires-civic-inequality; Steven Peoples, "'Koch Brothers' Rebrand Underway; Still a Conservative Force," Associated Press, July 29, 2018, https://apnews.com/05465050143f4ca699f8b79d7b681352. See also Stan Oklobdzija, "Dark Parties: Citizens United, Independent-Expenditure Networks and the Evolution of Political Parties," Political Networks Workshops and Conference 2018, June 3, 2018, https://ssrn.com/abstract=3189918.

23. "Scientific Consensus: Earth's Climate Is Warming," NASA, https://climate.nasa.gov/scientific-consensus.

24. See ibid.; John Cook, Sander van der Linden, Edward Maibach, and Stephen Lewandowski, "The Consensus Handbook: Why the Scientific Consensus on Climate Change Is Important," Climate Change Communication, George Mason University, March 2018, www.climatechangecommunication.org/all/consensus-handbook. For Whit Ayers, see Greg Price, "Climate Change a 'National Security Threat,' Republican-Led House Declares in Defense Bill Vote," *Newsweek*, July 14, 2017, https://www.newsweek.com/climate-change-national-security-republicans-637174. For the figure on Fox viewers, see Eric Wemple, "Fox News Botches Climate Coverage," *Washington Post*, April 7, 2014, https://www.washingtonpost.com/blogs/erik-wemple/wp/2014/04/07/study-fox-news-botches-climate-change-coverage.

25. Jane Mayer, "'Kochland' Examines the Koch Brothers' Early, Crucial Role in Climate Denial," *New Yorker*, August 13, 2019, https://www.newyorker.com/news/daily-comment/kochland-examines-how-the-koch-brothers-made-their-fortune-and-the-influence-it-bought. See also Christopher Leonard, *Kochland: The Secret History of Koch Industries and Corporate Power in America* (New York: Simon and Schuster, 2019), 392–497; Coral Davenport and Eric Lipton, "How G.O.P. Leaders Came to View Climate Change as Fake Science," *New York Times*, June 3, 2017, https://www.nytimes.com/2017/06/03/us/politics/republican-leaders-climate-change.html; Eric Alterman, "Lying About Climate Change Is What Makes a Good Republican," *The Nation*, June 15, 2017, https://www.thenation.com/article/lying-about-climate-change-is-what-makes-a-good-republican.

26. Bret Stephens, "Global Warming as Mass Neurosis," *Wall Street Journal*, July 1, 2008, https://www.wsj.com/articles/SB121486841811817591; Leonard, *Kochland*; Mayer, "'Kochland' Examines the Koch Brothers' Early, Crucial Role."

27. Frank James, "Political Scientist: Republicans Most Conservative They've Been in 100 Years," NPR, April 13, 2012, https://www.npr.org/sections/itsallpolitics /2012/04/10/150349438/gops-rightward-shift-higher-polarization-fills-political -scientist-with-dread.

28. See Scot Faulkner and Jonathan Riehl, "Republicans' Uncivil War," *Politico*, April 8, 2013, https://www.politico.com/story/2013/04/republicans-uncivil-war -089696?o=1; David Frum, "Don't Knock the Reform Conservatives," *Atlantic*, July 10, 2014, https://www.theatlantic.com/politics/archive/2014/07/dont-knock -the-reform-conservatives/374247; Ezra Klein, "John Boehner Just Confirmed Everything Liberals Suspected About the Republican Party," Vox, April 26, 2016, https://www.vox.com/2016/4/28/11526258/john-boehner-ted-cruz-republicans; Andy Kroll, "Ex-Republican Operative Steve Schmidt: 'The Party of Trump Must Be Obliterated. Annihilated. Destroyed,'" *Rolling Stone*, June 26, 2018, https:// www.rollingstone.com/politics/politics-features/ex-republican-operative-steve -schmidt-the-party-of-trump-must-be-obliterated-annihilated-destroyed-667008.

29. Trump's comments can be found in Julian E. Zelizer, "Policy Revolution Without a Political Transformation: The Presidency of Barack Obama," in *The Presidency of Barack Obama: A First Historical Assessment*, ed. Zelizer (Princeton, NJ: Princeton University Press, 2018), 24; Kevin Robellard, "Trump: Get Tougher on Obama 'Lies,'" *Politico*, July 16, 2012, https://www.politico.com /story/2012/07/trump-get-tougher-on-obama-lies-078545.

30. Inhofe and Shelby are quoted in Gabrial Winant, "The Birthers in Congress," *Salon*, July 28, 2009, http:// www.salon.com/2009/07/28/birther_enablers. For Palin, see Ben Smith, "Palin: Obama Birth Certificate 'a Fair Question,'" *Politico*, December 3, 2009, https://www.politico.com/blogs/ben-smith/2009/12/palin-obama -birth-certificate-a-fair-question-023233. For Deal, see Ben Smith, "Deal Wonders About That Birth Certificate," *Politico*, November 6, 2009, https://www.politico .com/blogs/ben-smith/2009/11/deal-wonders-about-that-birth-certificate-022649.

31. Josh Clinton and Cary Roush, "Poll: Persistent Partisan Divide over 'Birther' Question," NBC News, August 10, 2016, https://www.nbcnews.com/politics/2016 -election/poll-persistent-partisan-divide-over-birther-question-n627446.

32. George Zornick, "Boehner, Like Cantor, Refuses to Repudiate Birther Conspiracy Theories," ThinkProgress, February 13, 2011, https://thinkprogress.org/boehner -like-cantor-refuses-to-repudiate-birther-conspiracy-theories-51eb941619cf.

33. For overall Republican leadership, see ibid. For Cantor and for the views of Republican voters on the issue, see Clinton and Roush, "Poll: Persistent Partisan Divide."

34. "Trump Takes Credit for Obama Birth Certificate," CNN, April 27, 2011, http://politicalticker.blogs.cnn.com/2011/04/27/trump-takes-credit-for-obama -birth-certificate.

35. Ashley Parker and Steven Eder, "Inside the Six Weeks Donald Trump Was a Non-Stop Birther," *New York Times*, July 2, 2016.

36. Adam Tooze, "Is This the End of the American Century?" *London Review of Books* 41, no. 7 (April 4, 2019): 3–7, https://www.lrb.co.uk/v41/n07/adam-tooze /is-this-the-end-of-the-american-century.

Chapter Sixteen: Donald Trump's License to Lie

1. "Lie No. 10,000 Is Really a Whopper," *Washington Post*, April 29, 2019, https://www.washingtonpost.com/opinions/no-president-trump-your-family -separation-policy-is-not-remotely-humane/2019/04/29/63d189ce-6aae-11e9 -be3a-33217240a539_story.html.

2. In 2015, the Trump campaign released a letter from a Dr. Harold Bornstein declaring that Trump would be the "healthiest individual ever elected to the pres- idency." His strength and stamina were described as "extraordinary." His blood pressure was "astonishingly excellent." Alas, his cardiovascular status was only "excellent." Two years later, Bornstein admitted that the letter was a lie and had been dictated to him by Donald Trump. Bornstein also said his medical offices were "raided" by Trump's personal bodyguards and the original (and only) copies of the records were taken from him. Sarah Sanders said this was "standard procedure" for the White House Medical Unit—yet another lie. "Donald Trump Wrote Own Health Letter, Says Physician Harold Bornstein," BBC, May 2, 2018, https://www .bbc.com/news/world-us-canada-43970908.

3. As is well known, Trump's legal team, led by Michael Cohen, and his friend and publisher of the *National Enquirer*, David Pecker, repeatedly paid off a porn actress and others to try to protect Trump's lies about his relations with them, both sexual and financial. More about this below.

4. Cohen and others frequently insisted that Trump spoke disparagingly in private about people of color, often using racist epithets. Trump repeatedly lied about this as well. James Lartey, "Michael Cohen Claims Trump Said 'Black People Are Too Stupid' to Vote for Him," *The Guardian*, November 2, 2018, https://www.theguardian.com /us-news/2018/nov/02/donald-trump-michael-cohen-racist-language-vanity-fair.

5. David Leonhardt and Ian Prasad Philbrick, "Trump's Corruption: The Definitive List," *New York Times*, October 28, 2018, https://www.nytimes.com /2018/10/28/opinion/trump-administration-corruption-conflicts.html.

6. See Michael D. Shear and Emmarie Huetteman, "Trump Repeats Lie About Popular Vote in Meeting with Lawmakers," *New York Times*, January 23, 2017, A1 (note the exceptional use of the word "lie" in the headline).

7. David A. Graham, "What Trump Did Was Worse Than Lying," *Atlantic*, July 1, 2019, https://www.theatlantic.com/ideas/archive/2019/07/on-trumps-bullshit /593062.

8. For the December 6, 2019, "toilet" observation, see "Remarks by President Trump and Vice President Pence in a Roundtable on Small Business and Red Tape Reduction Accomplishments," White House, https://www.whitehouse.gov/briefings -statements/remarks-president-trump-vice-president-pence-roundtable-small

-business-red-tape-reduction-accomplishments. On Turning Point USA's mission, see Colleen Flaherty, "New College Professor 'Watchlist' Aims to Expose Professors Who 'Advance Leftist Propaganda,'" *Business Insider*, November 22, 2016, https://www .businessinsider.com/college-professor-watchlist-expose-professors-who-advance -leftist-propaganda-2016-11. For the purpose of Trump's December 22, 2019, remarks, see Charlie Kirk, quoted in Kim Lecapria, "'Professor Watchlist' Monitors 'Anti-American,' 'Leftist' Educators," Snopes, November 21, 2016, https:// www.snopes.com/news/2016/11/22/professor-watchlist-monitors-anti-american -leftist-educators. For Johnson's plagiarism, see Shane Hickey, "BuzzFeed Sacks Editor Benny Johnson over Plagiarism," *The Guardian*, July 26, 2014, https:// www.theguardian.com/media/2014/jul/26/buzzfeed-sacks-editor-benny-johnson -plagiarism. For Trump's thoughts on wind, see "Remarks by President Trump at Turning Point USA Student Action Summit, West Palm Beach, FL," White House, December 22, 2019, https://www.whitehouse.gov/briefings-statements/remarks -president-trump-turning-point-usa-student-action-summit-west-palm-beach-fl.

9. At a July 2018 campaign rally, Trump riled up the faithful by complaining that all the television cameras had been turned off. "CNN does not want its falling viewership to watch what I'm saying tonight," he said, to the great confusion of CNN viewers watching at home. His fans cheered and shouted epithets and threats to the journalists caged off behind them. This happened more than once. See Rob Tornoe, "Trump to Veterans: Don't Believe What You're Reading or Seeing," *Philadelphia Inquirer*, July 24, 2018, https://www.philly.com/philly/news/politics /presidential/donald-trump-vfw-speech-kansas-city-what-youre-seeing-reading-not -whats-happening-20180724.html.

10. Adam Tooze, "Democracy and Its Discontents," *New York Review of Books*, June 6, 2019, https://www.nybooks.com/articles/2019/06/06/democracy-and -its-discontents.

11. Quoted in Anne Applebaum, "The False Romance of Russia: American Conservatives Who Find Themselves Identifying with Putin's Regime Refuse to See the Country for What It Actually Is," *Atlantic*, December 12, 2019, https://www .theatlantic.com/ideas/archive/2019/12/false-romance-russia/603433.

12. About the anger issue, see Lilliana Mason, John V. Kane, and Julie Wronski, "Trump Support Is Not Normal Partisanship," Vox, June 21, 2019, https://www.vox .com/polyarchy/2019/6/21/18679314/trump-support-is-not-normal-partisanship. For the comparison to European parties, see Sahil Chinoy, "What Happened to America's Political Center of Gravity?" *New York Times*, June 26, 2019. See also Max Boot, "I Left the Republican Party, Now I Want Democrats to Take Over," *Washington Post*, July 4, 2018, https://www.washingtonpost.com/opinions/i-left -the-republican-party-now-i-want-democrats-to-take-over/2018/07/03/54a4007a -7e38-11e8-b0ef-fffcabeff946_story.html.

13. Charles Sykes, "Why Nobody Cares That the President Is Lying," *Jerusalem Post*, February 7, 2017, https://www.pressreader.com/israel/jerusalem

-post/20170207/282153586018647. See also Russell Muirhead and Nancy L. Rosenblum, *A Lot of People Are Saying: The New Conspiracism and the Assault on Democracy* (Princeton, NJ: Princeton University Press, 2019), 115.

14. See Karen Tumulty, "Carly Fiorina and the Underappreciated Art of Listening," *Washington Post*, September 17, 2015, https://www.washingtonpost.com/pol itics/carly-fiorina-and-the-underappreciated-art-of-listening/2015/09/17/1af4b92c -5d35-11e5-b38e-06883aacba64_story.html; Chris Cillizza, "Winners and Losers from the CNN Debate," *Washington Post*, September 16, 2015, https://www .washingtonpost.com/news/the-fix/wp/2015/09/16/winners-and-losers-from -the-cnn-debate.

15. See Eric Alterman, "How the Media Gave Carly Fiorina a Free Pass to Lie About Planned Parenthood," *The Nation*, September 29, 2015, https://www .thenation.com/article/how-the-media-gave-carly-fiorina-a-free-pass-to-lie-about -planned-parenthood.

16. I corrected many of the lies spoken that night in a column I wrote shortly thereafter. As I wrote then: "George W. Bush did not 'keep us safe,' and it was his administration, not Obama's, that ensured both the US exit from Iraq and the growth of ISIS. The Iran deal does not rest on self-inspection, and Iran did not invite Russia into Syria. Vaccinations do not cause autism. Climate change is not in doubt and attempting to address it would not 'destroy' the economy. Undocumented immigrants do not cost taxpayers $200 billion a year. Social Security is not going insolvent. Hillary Clinton is not being investigated because she 'destroyed government records.'" None of these falsehoods were corrected by the debate's moderators. See ibid.

17. Barbaro also mentioned the ongoing controversy over Clinton's use of her personal email while she was secretary of state. This alleged scandal would prove to be the single most covered "issue" of the election within the mainstream media, and virtually every mainstream media organization, including the *New York Times*, ran more articles about it than they did about all other issues in the campaign combined. Yet there was never any evidence that Clinton told any lies about this or that she engaged in any kind of cover-up. Indeed, she was cleared of all wrongdoing in 2019. See Michael Barbaro, "Candidates Stick to Script, if Not the Truth, in the 2016 Race," *New York Times*, November 7, 2015, A1; and Catie Edmondson, "State Dept. Inquiry into Clinton Emails Finds No Deliberate Mishandling of Classified Information," *New York Times*, October 18, 2019, A16; Ian Millhiser, "The Embarrassing Epilogue to the Media's Obsession with Hillary Clinton's Emails," Vox, October 22, 2019, https://www.vox .com/policy-and-politics/2019/10/22/20924795/hillary-clinton-emails-new-york -times-state-department.

18. Matt Yglesias, "Republicans Have a Huge Strategic Advantage in Shaping the News," Vox, October 23, 2018, https://www.vox.com/2018/10/23/18004478 /hack-gap-explained.

19. See, for instance, Eric Alterman, *What Liberal Media? The Truth About Bias and the News* (New York: Basic Books, 2003).

20. Note that Trump's term anticipates the oxymoronic coinage that Kellyanne Conway, counselor to the president, invented—"alternative facts"—to excuse his constant pattern of lying. Donald J. Trump, with Tony Schwartz, *Trump: The Art of the Deal* (New York: Random House, 1987), 56–58.

21. Jane Mayer, "Donald Trump's Ghostwriter Tells All," *New Yorker*, July 18, 2016, https://www.newyorker.com/magazine/2016/07/25/donald-trumps-ghostwriter-tells-all.

22. Maggie Haberman and Benjamin Weiser, "Trump Persuaded Struggling People to Invest in Scams, Lawsuit Says," *New York Times*, October 29, 2018, https://www.nytimes.com/2018/10/29/nyregion/trump-acn-lawsuit.html.

23. Russ Buettner and Susanne Craig, "Decade in the Red: Trump's Tax Figures Show over $1 Billion in Losses," *New York Times*, May 8, 2019, A1, https://www.nytimes.com/interactive/2019/05/07/us/politics/donald-trump-taxes.html.

24. Max Rosenthal, "The Trump File: The Shady Way Fred Trump Tried to Save His Son's Casino," *Mother Jones*, September 26, 2016, https://www.motherjones.com/politics/2016/09/trump-files-fred-trump-funneled-cash-donald-using-casino-chips.

25. For the vulgar comment about Ivanka, see Daniel Politi, "Trump Is OK with Calling Ivanka a 'Piece of Ass' and Other Horrible Things He Told Howard Stern," *Slate*, October 8, 2016, www.slate.com/blogs/the_slatest/2016/10/08/trump_to_howard_stern_you_can_call_ivanka_a_piece_of_ass.html. For Trump's children's charity theft, see Shane Goldmacher, "Trump Charity Agrees to End amid Lawsuit," *New York Times*, December 18, 2018, A1.

26. Michael Kruse, "Tales from the Tabloids," *Politico*, May/June 2016, https://www.politico.com/magazine/story/2016/04/tabloids-donald-trump-new-york-post-daily-news-gossip-1980s-1990s-213853.

27. See Michael Kranish and Marc Fisher, *Trump Revealed* (New York: Simon and Schuster, 2016), 213; Patrick Radden Keefe, "How Mark Burnett Resurrected Donald Trump as an Icon of American Success," *New Yorker*, January 3, 2019, https://www.newyorker.com/magazine/2019/01/07/how-mark-burnett-resurrected-donald-trump-as-an-icon-of-american-success. See also A. J. Catoline, "Editing Trump: The Making of a Reality TV Star Who Would Be President," *CineMontage*, October 12, 2016, http://cinemontage.org/editing-trump-reality-tv-star-who-would-be-president.

28. David Masciotra, "Vulgarians at the Gate: The Next 4 Years Could Be a Long, Slow, Messy Slide into Cultural Oblivion," *Salon*, January 21, 2017, https://www.salon.com/2017/01/21/vulgarians-at-the-gate-the-next-4-years-will-be-a-long-slow-messy-slide-into-cultural-oblivion.

29. For Zucker, see Jonathan Mahler, "CNN Had a Problem: Donald Trump Solved It," *New York Times Magazine*, April 4, 2017, https://www.nytimes.com/2017/04/04/magazine/cnn-had-a-problem-donald-trump-solved-it.html.For Kayleigh McEnany's quote, see Timothy Bella, "'I Don't Think This President Has Lied': Trump

Notes on Chapter Sixteen

Aide Denies He's Ever Misled the Public," *Washington Post*, August 29, 2019, https://www.washingtonpost.com/nation/2019/08/29/kayleigh-mcenany-trump-never-lies-chris-cuomo. For Lewandowski, see Zachary Basu, "Corey Lewandowski: 'I Have No Obligation to Be Honest with the Media,'" *Axios*, September 17, 2019, https://www.axios.com/corey-lewandowski-lying-media-house-judiciary-committee-2a24fcbc-f3dd-4b28-9b4b-2abfaaa44403.html; Andrew Rafferty and Ali Vitali, "Trump Defends Campaign Manager Corey Lewandowski After Battery Charge," NBC, March 29, 2016, https://www.nbcnews.com/politics/2016-election/trump-campaign-manager-charged-assaulting-reporter-n547306. Ironically, the woman Lewandowski allegedly assaulted worked for the pro-Trump site Breitbart.com, helmed at the time by Steve Bannon. For the sexual assault charge against him, see "Ex-Trump Campaign Manager Corey Lewandowski Accused of Sexual Assault," *The Guardian*, December 27, 2017, https://www.theguardian.com/us-news/2017/dec/27/ex-trump-campaign-manager-corey-lewandowski-accused-of-sexual-assault.

30. "A Compilation of Donald Trump's Campaign Lies, Misleading Statements, and Exaggerations," HubPages, June 9, 2018, https://hubpages.com/politics/American-Politics-A-Compilation-of-Donald-Trump-Lies-Misleading-Statements-and-Exagerations.

31. See Kalev Leetaru, "What Data-Mining TV's Political Coverage Tells Us," RealClearPolitics, August 10, 2017, https://www.realclearpolitics.com/articles/2017/08/10/what_data-mining_tvs_political_coverage_tells_us.html; Sarah Ellison, "CNN and Jeff Zucker Plot 2020 Election Coverage and Promise Things Will Be Different," *Washington Post*, July 30, 2019, https://www.washingtonpost.com/lifestyle/style/cnn-and-jeff-zucker-plot-2020-election-coverage-and-promise-things-will-be-different/2019/07/29/6d6f59a8-b21f-11e9-951e-de024209545d_story.html.

32. Eliza Collins, "Les Moonves: Trump's Run Is 'Damn Good for CBS,'" *Politico*, February 29, 2016, https://www.politico.com/blogs/on-media/2016/02/les-moonves-trump-cbs-220001.

33. See Matthew Yglesias, "The Hack Gap: How and Why Conservative Nonsense Dominates American Politics," Vox, October 23, 2018, https://www.vox.com/2018/10/23/18004478/hack-gap-explained. See also Jim Rutenberg and Ben Protess, "Tabloid Company, Aiding Trump Campaign, May Have Crossed Line into Politics," *New York Times*, July 22, 2018, A1; Michael Rothfeld, Joe Palazzolo, Lukas I. Alpert, and Rebecca Davis O'Brien, "National Enquirer's Yearslong Dealings with Trump Lawyer Fall Under Federal Scrutiny," *Wall Street Journal*, July 25, 2018, A1; Lucia Graves, "Meet Trump's Friend and Fixer: David Pecker, the Tabloid King," *The Guardian*, August 6, 2018, https://www.theguardian.com/media/2018/aug/06/david-pecker-donald-trump-national-enquirer-profile; David Graham, "The Other Way the *National Enquirer* Helped Elect Trump," *Atlantic*, December 14, 2018, https://www.theatlantic.com/politics/archive/2018/12/national-inquirer-helped-trump-attacking-clinton/578116; Ronan Farrow, "The National

Notes on Chapter Sixteen

Enquirer, a Trump Rumor, and Another Secret Payment to Buy Silence," *New Yorker*, April 12, 2018, https://www.newyorker.com/news/news-desk/the-national -enquirer-a-donald-trump-rumor-and-another-secret-payment-to-buy-silence-dino -sajudin-david-pecker.

34. Keegan Hankes, "Breitbart Under Bannon: How Breitbart Became a Favorite News Source for Neo-Nazis and White Nationalists," Southern Poverty Law Center, March 1, 2017, https://www.splcenter.org/hatewatch/2017/03/01/breitbart-under -bannon-how-breitbart-became-favorite-news-source-neo-nazis-and-white.

35. Yochai Benkler, Robert Faris, and Hal Roberts, *Network Propaganda: Manipulation, Disinformation, and Radicalization in American Politics* (New York: Oxford University Press, 2018), 54.

36. Ibid., 3; Associated Press, "Man Pleads Guilty to Setting Fire at 'Pizzagate' Restaurant," NBC, December 18, 2019, https://www.nbcnews.com/news/us-news /man-pleads-guilty-setting-fire-pizzagate-restaurant-d-c-n1103691; "Belief in Conspiracies Largely Depends on Political Identity," YouGov, December 27, 2016, https:// today.yougov.com/topics/politics/articles-reports/2016/12/27/belief-conspiracies -largely-depends-political-iden.

37. Regarding belief in the conspiracies, see Benkler et al., *Network Propaganda*, 3. For the tweets, see Michiko Katutani, *The Death of Truth* (New York: Tim Duggan Books, 2018), 123–124; Craig Timberg and Shane Harris, "Russian Operatives Blasted 18,000 Tweets Ahead of a Huge News Day During the 2016 Presidential Campaign. Did They Know What Was Coming?" *Washington Post*, July 20, 2018, https://www.washingtonpost.com/technology/2018/07/20/russian -operatives-blasted-tweets-ahead-huge-news-day-during-presidential-campaign -did-they-know-what-was-coming. See also April Glaser, "Twitter Admits There Were More Than 50,000 Russian Bots Trying to Confuse American Voters Before the Election," *Slate*, January 18, 2018, https://slate.com/technology/2018/01/twitter -admits-there-were-more-than-50-000-russian-bots-confusing-u-s-voters-in-2016 .html.

38. See Adam Fourney, Miklos Z. Racz, Gireeja Ranade, Markus Mobius, and Eric Horvitz, "Geographic and Temporal Trends in Fake News Consumption During the 2016 US Presidential Election," Microsoft Research, n.d., http://erichor vitz.com/CIKM2017_fake_news_study.pdf. See also Benkler et al., *Network Propaganda*, 54, 73. The phrase in question belongs to Richard Hofstadter.

39. For Trump and Alex Jones, see Zack Beauchamp, "Alex Jones, Pizzagate Booster and America's Most Famous Conspiracy Theorist, Explained," Vox, October 28, 2016, https://www.vox.com/policy-and-politics/2016/10/28/13424848/alex-jones -infowars-prisonplanet; Eric Hananoki, "A Guide to Donald Trump's Relationship with Alex Jones," Media Matters, May 3, 2017, https://www.mediamatters .org/research/2017/05/03/guide-donald-trump-s-relationship-alex-jones/216263. For Drudge, see Abby Ohlheiser, "No, John Podesta Didn't Drink Bodily Fluids at a Secret Satanist Dinner," *Washington Post*, November 4, 2016, https://

www.washingtonpost.com/news/the-intersect/wp/2016/11/04/no-john-podesta
-didnt-drink-bodily-fluids-at-a-secret-satanist-dinner.

40. Gregory J. Martin and Ali Yurukoglu, "Bias in Cable News: Persuasion and Polarization," NBER Working Paper No. 20798, National Bureau of Economic Research, June 2016, https://www.nber.org/papers/w20798.

41. Megyn Kelly's questions and Trump's responses were widely quoted. See, for example, Holly Yan, "Donald Trump's 'Blood' Comment About Megyn Kelly Draws Outrage," CNN, August 8, 2015, https://www.cnn.com/2015/08/08/politics /donald-trump-cnn-megyn-kelly-comment/index.html.

42. According to a detailed report in *Politico*, Ailes and Trump "spoke on the phone frequently during the campaign, sometimes several times a week." Whenever Trump went too far off the rails, according to an unnamed Fox host, Ailes would say, "Hey, Donald, settle the fuck down." Trump repeatedly expressed his admiration for Ailes on Twitter: "Roger Ailes just called. He is a great guy & assures me that 'Trump' will be treated fairly on @FoxNews. His word is always good!" Eventually Ailes was forced out of Fox owing to allegations of sexual blackmail toward his female underlings—though his departure was soothed by a $40 million pay-out coupled with a nondisclosure agreement. He immediately became an informal consultant to the Trump campaign. See Elaina Johnson, "How Trump Blew Up the Conservative Media," *Politico*, May/June 2017, https://www.politico.com/magazine /story/2017/04/21/trump-conservative-media-breitbart-fox-news-wall-street-journal -215035; Donald Trump, Twitter, August 10, 2015, 8:35 a.m., https://twitter.com /realdonaldtrump/status/630764447716540417. For Breitbart's rise, see Manuel Roig-Franzia and Paul Farhi, "Bannon Molded Breitbart into a Far-Right Sledgehammer. How Will It Be Wielded in the Trump Era?" *Washington Post*, February 19, 2017, https://www.washingtonpost.com/lifestyle/style/bannon-molded-breitbart-into-a-far -right-sledgehammer-how-it-will-be-wielded-in-the-trump-era/2017/02/19/422fbed2 -f704-11e6-be05-1a3817ac21a5_story.html. For Murdoch's surrender, see Gabriel Sherman, "Why Rupert Murdoch Decided to Back Donald Trump," *New York Magazine*, May 17, 2016, http://nymag.com/daily/intelligencer/2016/05/why-rupert -murdoch-decided-to-support-trump.html. For Fox's ratings, see Johnson, "How Trump Blew Up the Conservative Media"; Howard Polskin, "How Conservative Media Has Grown Under Trump," *Columbia Journalism Review*, August 19, 2019, https://www.cjr.org/analysis/conservative-media-grown.php; Jane Mayer, "The Making of the Fox News White House," *New Yorker*, March 4, 2019, https://www .newyorker.com/magazine/2019/03/11/the-making-of-the-fox-news-white-house.

Chapter Seventeen: The Trump Presidency: "What You're Seeing and What You're Reading Is Not What's Happening"

1. For the massive victory, see Margaret Sullivan, "What TV Journalists Did Wrong—and the New York Times Did Right—in Meeting with Trump," *Washington Post*, November 22, 2016, https://www.washingtonpost.com/lifestyle/style

/what-tv-journalists-did-wrong—and-the-new-york-times-did-right—in-meeting
-with-trump/2016/11/22/54fe17ba-b0d3-11e6-8616-52b15787add0_story.html.
For the polls, see Steven Levitsky and Daniel Ziblatt, *How Democracies Die*
(New York: Crown, 2018), 194; Eli Yokley, "Many Republicans Doubt Clinton
Won Popular Vote," *Morning Consult*, July 26, 2017, https://morningconsult
.com/2017/07/26/many-republicans-think-trump-won-2016-popular-vote-didnt.

2. See Tim Hill, "Bernhard Langer: Trump Apologized to Me over Voter
Fraud Story," *The Guardian*, February 9, 2017, https://www.theguardian.com
/sport/2017/feb/09/bernhard-langer-donald-trump-golf-voter-fraud; Donald Trump,
Twitter, November 28, 2016, 6:14 p.m., https://twitter.com/realdonaldtrump
/status/803421742815412224.

3. Adrianne LaFrance, "Calling Out a Presidential Lie," *Atlantic*, January 27,
2017, https://www.theatlantic.com/technology/archive/2017/01/calling-out-a-presi
dential-lie/514568.

4. Nearly three years later, in August 2019, Trump was still sticking to his
phony voter fraud story, this time tweeting that "Google manipulated from 2.6
million to 16 million votes for Hillary Clinton in 2016 Election!…My victory was
even bigger than thought!" And here again, the evidence did not even begin to
support this false claim. Daniel Dale, "Fact Check: Trump Falsely Claims Google
'Manipulated' Millions of 2016 Votes," CNN, August 20, 2019, https://www.cnn
.com/2019/08/19/politics/trump-google-manipulated-votes-claim/index.html.

5. For Baquet, see "Trump vs. New York Times: The Executive Editor's Perspective," World Congress Blog, International News Media Association, May 19, 2019,
https://www.inma.org/blogs/world-congress/post.cfm/trump-vs-new-york-times
-the-executive-editor-s-perspective. For Ruttenberg, see Mark Leibovich, "The Risky
Business of Speaking for President Trump," *New York Times Magazine*, May 23, 2008,
https://www.nytimes.com/2018/05/23/magazine/the-risky-business-of-speaking-for
-president-trump.html. For Baker, see Conor Friedersdorf, "The Wall Street Journal's Editor: Beware Calling Donald Trump a Liar," *Atlantic*, June 28, 2017, https://
www.theatlantic.com/politics/archive/2017/06/the-wall-street-journals-editor-beware
-calling-donald-trump-a-liar/532119. For the collection of euphemisms, I am indebted
to Reed Richardson, "The Pathological Refusal to Report the Simple Truth About the
President's Lying," Fairness and Accuracy in Reporting, November 16, 2017, http://fair
.org/home/the-pathological-refusal-to-report-the-simple-truth-about-presidential
-lying.

6. A Freedom of Information Act request by *The Guardian* revealed in September 2018 that Trump, with Spicer continually following up, had demanded
that the inspector general of the US Department of the Interior ensure that the
official photos from the inauguration be doctored to conform to Trump's lies. Jon
Swain, "Trump Inauguration Crowd Photos Were Edited After He Intervened," *The
Guardian*, September 6, 2018, https://www.theguardian.com/world/2018/sep/06

/donald-trump-inauguration-crowd-size-photos-edited. See also Philip Rucker, John Wagner, and Greg Miller, "Trump, in CIA Visit, Attacks Media for Coverage of His Inaugural Crowds," *Washington Post*, January 21, 2017, https://www.washington post.com/politics/trump-in-cia-visit-attacks-media-for-coverage-of-his-inaugural -crowds/2017/01/21/f4574dca-e019-11e6-ad42-f3375f271c9c_story.html.

7. See Rob Tornoe, "Trump to Veterans: Don't Believe What You're Reading or Seeing," *Philadelphia Inquirer*, updated July 24, 2018, https://www.inquirer.com /philly/news/politics/presidential/donald-trump-vfw-speech-kansas-city-what-youre -seeing-reading-not-whats-happening-20180724.html; Rebecca Sinderbrand, "How Kellyanne Conway Ushered in the Era of 'Alternative Facts,'" *Washington Post*, January 22, 2017, https://www.washingtonpost.com/news/the-fix/wp/2017/01/22 /how-kellyanne-conway-ushered-in-the-era-of-alternative-facts. For Hitler's use of "fake news," see Timothy Snyder, "How Hitler Pioneered 'Fake News,'" *New York Times*, October 16, 2019, https://www.nytimes.com/2019/10/16/opinion/hitler -speech-1919.html; Jon Schwarz, "Lesley Stahl: Donald Trump Said He Attacks the Media 'So When You Write Negative Stories About Me, No One Will Believe You,'" *The Intercept*, May 22, 2018, https://theintercept.com/2018/05/22/lesley -stahl-donald-trump-said-he-attacks-the-media-so-when-you-write-negative-stories -about-me-no-one-will-believe-you.

8. Eric Alterman, "Trump's Hiring of Fox's Bill Shine Illustrates Our De-based Politics," *The Nation*, July 10, 2018, https://www.thenation.com/article /trumps-hiring-foxs-bill-shine-illustrates-debased-politics.

9. Jeremy Barr, "'You're the Man': Fox News Emails with Trump Treasury Department Reveal Coziness," *Hollywood Reporter*, August 15, 2019, https:// www.hollywoodreporter.com/news/youre-man-fox-news-emails-trump-treasury -team-reveal-coziness-1231461.

10. See Alan Rappeport, "Columbia Inquiry Found Plagiarism in Monica Crowley's Dissertation," *New York Times*, December 21, 2019, B3. For her later adventures in plagiarism, see Timothy Noah, "Nixon's Monica Stonewalls About Plagiarism!" *Slate*, August 23, 1999, https://slate.com/news-and-politics/1999/08 /nixon-s-monica-stonewalls-about-plagiarism.html; Andrew Kaczynski, "Trump National Security Pick Monica Crowley Plagiarized Multiple Sources in 2012 Book," CNN Money, n.d., https://money.cnn.com/interactive/news/kfile-trump -monica-crowley-plagiarized-multiple-sources-2012-book/index.html.

11. See Michael D. Shear, Maggie Haberman, Nicholas Confessore, Karen Yourish, Larry Buchanan, and Keith Collins, "How Trump Reshaped the Presidency in Over 11,000 Tweets," *New York Times*, November 2, 2019, https://www .nytimes.com/interactive/2019/11/02/us/politics/trump-twitter-presidency.html.

12. Gabriel Sherman, "'Executives Are Very Worried *Fox & Friends* Will Be Next': After Taking over Fox, Lachlan Murdoch Is in a Trump Trap," *Vanity Fair*, May 2019, https://www.vanityfair.com/news/2019/04/fox-and-friends-will-be-next

-lachlan-murdoch-is-in-a-trump-trap; William Cummings, "Fox News Condemns Host Jeanine Pirro's Comments About Rep. Omar's Hijab," *USA Today*, March 10, 2019, https://www.usatoday.com/story/news/politics/onpolitics/2019/03/10/ilhan -omars-hijab-concerns-fox-news-host-jeanine-pirro/3124918002.

13. Terry Gross, "Journalist Sees 'Almost No Daylight' Between Fox News and White House Agendas," *Fresh Air*, July 12, 2018, https://www.npr .org/2018/07/12/628250994/journalist-sees-almost-no-daylight-between-fox -news-and-white-house-agendas; PRRI staff, "Fractured Nation: Widening Partisan Polarization and Key Issues in 2020 Presidential Election," Public Religion Research Institute, October 20, 2019, https://www.prri.org/research/fractured-nation -widening-partisan-polarization-and-key-issues-in-2020-presidential-elections.

14. Matthew Gertz, "I've Studied the Trump-Fox Feedback Loop for Months. It's Crazier Than You Think," *Politico*, January 5, 2018, https://www.politico.com /magazine/story/2018/01/05/trump-media-feedback-loop-216248.

15. See Shear et al., "How Trump Reshaped the Presidency"; Gertz, "I've Studied the Trump-Fox Feedback Loop."

16. Alvin Chang, "Sean Hannity Has Become the Media's Top Conspiracy Theorist," Vox, November 15, 2017, https://www.vox.com/2017/11/15/16649292 /hannity-conspiracy-theorist-transcript-data.

17. See Paul Farhi, "Fox News Personalities Continue to Stump for GOP Candidates," *Washington Post*, December 3, 2019, https://www.washington post.com/lifestyle/style/fox-news-personalities-continue-to-stump-for-gop -candidates/2019/12/03/7bbae48c-1525-11ea-9110-3b34ce1d92b1_story.html.

18. "Trump Speaks Out on 'Hannity' During Trip to Border," YouTube, posted by Fox News on January 10, 2019, https://www.youtube.com/watch?v=3h7OAlETfaY; "Yes, $1.7 Million Worth of Fentanyl Was Seized at the Port of Philadelphia," *Morning Call*, January 10, 2019, https://www.mcall.com/news/nationworld/pennsylvania /mc-nws-philadelphia-port-fentanyl-20190110-story.html.

19. See, for instance, Chuck Todd's disastrously indulgent interview with Trump on *Meet the Press* on June 23, 2019, where one lie after another went unchallenged and uncorrected. See "President Trump's Full, Unedited Interview with Meet the Press," YouTube, NBC News, June 23, 2019, https://www.youtube .com/watch?v=aBglxa6K8gc. See also Aaron Rupar, "Chuck Todd's Trump Interview, and the Backlash to It, Explained," Vox, June 24, 2019, https://www.vox .com/2019/6/24/18715361/trump-chuck-todd-meet-the-press-interview-explained; Chris Cillizza, Twitter, December 11, 2018, 9:24 a.m., https://twitter.com/Cillizza CNN/status/1072542712732270595.

20. Matt Gertz and Rob Savillo, "Study: Major Media Outlets' Twitter Accounts Amplify False Trump Claims on Average 19 Times a Day," Media Matters, May 3, 2019, https://www.mediamatters.org/blog/2019/05/03/study-major-media -outlets-twitter-accounts-amplify-false-trump-claims-average-19-times-day/223572.

21. Given that this is not something anyone is likely to be proud to admit to a pollster, the real number is probably much higher. See Maksym Gabielkov, Arthi Ramachandran, Augustin Chaintreau, and Arnaud Legout, "Social Clicks: What and Who Gets Read on Twitter?," ACM Sigimetrics / IFIP Performance 2016, June 2016, https://hal.inria.fr/hal-01281190/document. See also Derek Thompson, "Trump's Lies Are a Virus, and News Organizations Are the Host," *Atlantic*, November 19, 2018.

22. Daniel Dale, "It's Easy to Fact Check Trump's Lies. He Tells the Same Ones All the Time," *Washington Post*, November 16, 2018, https://www.washin gtonpost.com/outlook/its-easy-to-fact-check-trumps-lies-he-tells-the-same-ones -all-the-time/2018/11/15/5effb25c-e874-11e8-a939-9469f1166f9d_story.html; Daniel Dale, Twitter, October 28, 2019, 10:13 p.m., https://twitter.com/ddale8 /status/1189047477669978114.

23. See the figures in Pew Research Center, Project for Excellence in Journalism, "State of the News Media 2008: An Annual Report on American Journalism," http:// assets.pewresearch.org/wp-content/uploads/sites/13/2017/05/24141607/State-of -the-News-Media-Report-2008-FINAL.pdf; Pew Research Center, "The Changing Newsroom: What Is Being Gained and What Is Being Lost in America's Daily News-papers?," 2008, https://www.pewresearch.org/wp-content/uploads/sites/8/legacy/PEJ -The-Changing-Newspaper-Newsroom-FINAL-DRAFT-NOEMBARGO-PDF.pdf; Elizabeth Grieco, "U.S. Newsroom Employment Has Dropped by a Quarter Since 2008, with Greatest Decline at Newspapers," Pew Research Center, July 9, 2019, https://www.pewresearch.org/fact-tank/2019/07/09/u-s-newsroom-employment-has -dropped-by-a-quarter-since-2008.

24. For Bannon, see Maggie Haberman and Katie Rogers, "'Drama, Action, Emotional Power': As Exhausted Aides Eye the Exits, Trump Is Re-energized," *New York Times*, June 10, 2018, https://www.nytimes.com/2018/06/10/us/politics/trump -turnover.html. See also Alexandra Neason, "The Burnout Year," *Columbia Journal-ism Review*, Winter 2018, https://www.cjr.org/special_report/burnout-journalism.php.

25. Brian Stelter, Twitter, January 7, 2019, 11:24 a.m., https://twitter.com /brianstelter/status/1082357359962456065.

26. For information consumption figures, see Pew Research Center, "Social Media Outpaces Print Newspapers in the U.S. as a News Source," December 10, 2018, https://www.pewresearch.org/fact-tank/2018/12/10/social-media-outpaces-print -newspapers-in-the-u-s-as-a-news-source. For the Zuckerberg quote, see Lisa Marie Segura, "They're Not 'Intentionally Getting It Wrong.' Mark Zuckerberg Says He Won't Ban Holocaust Deniers," Yahoo! Finance, July 18, 2018, https://finance.ya hoo.com/news/apos-not-apos-intentionally-getting-193801754.html; Sarah Frier, "Facebook Axed 583 Million Fake Accounts, Enforcing Standards," Bloomberg, https://www.bloomberg.com/news/articles/2018-05-15/facebook-removed-583 -million-fake-accounts-enforcing-standards.

Notes on Chapter Seventeen

27. For Jones's threats, see Luke Darby, "Alex Jones Said He Would Shoot Robert Mueller and Facebook Still Won't Ban Him," *GQ*, July 24, 2018, https://www.gq.com/story/alex-jones-shoot-robert-mueller-facebook.

28. For Facebook's response, see Segura, "They're Not 'Intentionally Getting It Wrong"; Charlie Devereux, "Facebook Isn't Responsible for Policing the Internet, Clegg Says," Bloomberg, October 5, 2019, https://www.bloomberg.com/news/articles/2019-10-05/facebook-isn-t-responsible-for-policing-the-internet-clegg-says; "Facebook Has Loosened Standards for Political Information Ahead of 2020 Elections," MSNBC, October 5, 2019, https://www.msnbc.com/msnbc/watch/facebook-has-loosened-standards-for-political-information-ahead-of-2020-elections-70711365570. For the studies of false information disseminated, see Andrew Guess, Jonathan Nagler, and Joshua Tucker, "Less Than You Think: Prevalence and Predictors of Fake News Dissemination on Facebook," *Science Advances 5*, no. 1 (January 9, 2019), http://advances.sciencemag.org/content/5/1/eaau4586.full; Vidya Narayanan, Vlad Barash, John Kelly, Bence Kollanyi, Lisa-Marie Neudert, and Philip N. Howard, "Polarization, Partisanship and Junk News Consumption over Social Media in the US," Comprop Data Memo 2018.1, February 6, 2018, http://blogs.oii.ox.ac.uk/comprop/wp-content/uploads/sites/93/2018/02/Polarization-Partisanship-JunkNews.pdf. For Twitter, see Ronald J. Dilbert, "The Road to Digital Unfreedom: Three Painful Truths About Social Media," *Journal of Democracy*, January 2019, https://www.journalofdemocracy.org/article/road-digital-unfreedom-three-painful-truths-about-social-media. For Facebook statistics, see "Facebook by the Numbers: Stats, Demographics and Fun Facts," Omnicore, https://www.omnicoreagency.com/facebook-statistics (the site is regularly updated; these statistics are from December 2019); "Number of Active Advertisers on Facebook from 1st Quarter 2016 to 3rd Quarter 2019," Statistica, https://www.statista.com/statistics/778191/active-facebook-advertisers.

29. For Twitter, see Maya Kossoff, "Jack Dorsey Breathes Life into the Right's Favorite Twitter Conspiracy," *Vanity Fair*, August 20, 2018, https://www.vanityfair.com/jack-dorsey-breathes-life-into-the-rights-favorite-twitter. For Bolten, see Deepa Seetharaman, "Facebook's Lonely Conservative Takes on a Power Position," *Wall Street Journal*, December 23, 3018, https://www.wsj.com/articles/facebooks-lonely-conservative-takes-on-a-power-position-11545570000. For Kyl's study, see Jeff Amy, "Advocates Fault Facebook for Misleading Posts," Associated Press, September 30, 2019, https://www.chicagotribune.com/business/sns-bc-us—facebook-civil-rights-audit-20190926-story.html.

30. For Zuckerberg's conversations, see Arjun Kharpal, "Facebook's Mark Zuckerberg Met with Conservatives over the 'Trending' Bias Spat," CNBC, May 19, 2016, https://www.cnbc.com/2016/05/19/facebook-mark-zuckerberg-met-with-conservatives-over-the-trending-bias-spat.html. For the dinner meetings with conservatives, see Natasha Bertrand and Daniel Lippman, "Inside Mark Zuckerberg's Secret Meetings with Conservative Pundits," *Politico*, October 13, 2019, https://www.politico.com/amp/news/2019/10/14/facebook-zuckerberg-conservatives

-private-meetings-046663. For Thiel and Zuckerberg's relationship and dinner meeting with Trump, see Emily Glazer, Deepa Seetharaman, and Jeff Horwitz, "Peter Thiel at Center of Facebook's Internal Divisions on Politics," *Wall Street Journal*, December 17, 2019, https://www.wsj.com/articles/peter-thiel-at-center-of-facebooks-internal-divisions-on-politics-11576578601. For Thiel's overall political views, see Scott Rosenberg, "Peter Thiel, the Bridge Between Trump and Facebook," Axios, December 18, 2019, https://www.axios.com/peter-thiel-the-bridge-between-trump-and-facebook-78512519-4023-4b34-bb53-e781e536da0c.html. For the inclusion of Breitbart, see Charlie Warzel, "Why Will Breitbart Be Included in 'Facebook News'?" *New York Times*, October 26, 2019, https://www.nytimes.com/2019/10/25/opinion/mark-zuckerberg-facebook.html. For Facebook allowing political lies in advertisements, see Queenie Wong, "Facebook CEO Mark Zuckerberg Defends Decision to Let Politicians Lie in Ads," CNET, October 17, 2017, https://www.cnet.com/news/facebook-ceo-mark-zuckerberg-defends-decision-to-allow-politicians-to-lie-in-ads. For Trump's spending spree on Facebook, see Donie O'Sullivan and David Wright, "Trump Is Using Facebook to Run Thousands of Ads About Impeachment," CNN, September 30, 2019, https://www.cnn.com/2019/09/30/politics/facebook-trump-impeachment/index.html; Editorial Board, "Facebook Shouldn't Run Trump's Lie-Laden Ads," *Washington Post*, October 16, 2019, https://www.washingtonpost.com/opinions/facebook-shouldnt-run-trumps-lie-laden-ads/2019/10/16/3ab84136-f04b-11e9-b648-76bcf86eb67e_story.html. For Zuckerberg's admission that "lying is bad," see Emily Stewart, "Watch AOC Ask Mark Zuckerberg If She Can Run Fake Facebook Ads, Too," Vox, October 23, 2019, https://www.vox.com/policy-and-politics/2019/10/23/20929350/alexandria-ocasio-cortez-mark-zuckerberg-testimony-green-new-deal.

31. Alison Durkee, "Jack Dorsey Keeps Finding New Reasons to Defend Hate Speech on Twitter," *Vanity Fair*, April 26, 2019, https://www.vanityfair.com/news/2019/04/jack-dorsey-ilhan-omar-defend-hate-speech-twitter; Nitasha Tiku, "Leaked Audio Reveals Google's Efforts to Woo Conservatives," *Wired*, December 10, 2018, https://www.wired.com/story/leaked-audio-reveals-googles-efforts-woo-conservatives.

32. Makena Kelly, "Trump Campaign Says Twitter Ad Block Will 'Silence Conservatives,'" *The Verge*, October 30, 2019, https://www.theverge.com/2019/10/30/20940840/donald-trump-twitter-facebook-political-ads-ban-ron-wyden; Caroline Orr, Twitter, October 30, 2019, 5:43 p.m., https://twitter.com/RVAwonk/status/1189704364883107840. For RT as a foreign agent, see Mike Eckel, "U.S. Justice Department Says Intelligence Report Spurred FARA Requirement For RT," Radio Free Europe / Radio Liberty, December 17, 2017, https://www.rferl.org/a/russia-rt-fara-intelligence-report-us-justice-department/28931638.html.

33. The anti-Semitic cartoonist was disinvited after the list of invitees was made public, but the speech was attended by yet another conspiracy theorist, who blamed Jewish financiers for Central Americans wishing to immigrate to the

United States. Luke Barnes, "The List of People Attending the White House Social Media Summit Is Something Else," ThinkProgress, July 10, 2019, https://think progress.org/white-house-social-media-summit-far-right-ben-garrison-matt-gaetz -pro-trump-a20dc2725d82.

34. See Tony Romm, "Trump Met with Twitter CEO Jack Dorsey—and Complained About His Follower Count," *Washington Post*, April 23, 2019, https:// www.washingtonpost.com/technology/2019/04/23/trump-meets-with-twitter-ceo -jack-dorsey-white-house; Brian Rosenwald, "Trump Just Launched the Newest Phase of the GOP's Romance with Right-Wing Media," *Washington Post*, July 13, 2019, https://www.washingtonpost.com/outlook/2019/07/13/trump-just-launched -newest-phase-gops-romance-with-right-wing-media.

35. Cliff Sims, *Team of Vipers: My 500 Extraordinary Days in the Trump White House* (New York: St. Martin's Press, 2019), 168; Greg Evans, "Trump Advisor Stephen Miller Makes Contentious Sunday Morning Debut," Yahoo! Finance, February 12, 2017, https://finance.yahoo.com/news/trump-advisor-stephen-miller -makes-171001804.html; Donald Trump, Twitter, February 12, 2017, 7:41 a.m., https://twitter.com/realdonaldtrump/status/830804130692268032.

36. See Evan Osnos, "Only the Best People," *New Yorker*, May 21, 2018, https://www.newyorker.com/magazine/2018/05/21/trump-vs-the-deep-state. As an author of academic texts on economics, Navarro would, like Trump with his phony publicists, invent fictional characters and put words into their mouths, as if they were real, in order to bolster arguments that, apparently, could not be supported with actual, verifiable research. When confronted about this, he compared himself to Alfred Hitchcock. See Alan Rappeport, "Peter Navarro Invented an Expert for His Books, Based on Himself," *New York Times*, October 16, 2019, https://www .nytimes.com/2019/10/16/us/politics/peter-navarro-ron-vara.html.

37. The *Huffington Post* reported that "Indian government spokesman Raveesh Kumar dismissed Trump's claim less than an hour after the White House meeting, issuing a statement that 'no such request has been made.'" Jenna Amatulli, "Larry Kudlow Insists Trump 'Doesn't Make Things Up,' 'Very Rude' to Suggest He Does," *HuffPost*, July 23, 2019, https://www.huffpost.com/entry/larry -kudlow-trump-lies-kashmir_n_5d372b0fe4b004b6adb68fa6.

38. Karen Yourish, Troy Griggs, and Larry Buchanan, "Records Show Trump Is Still Tied to Empire," *New York Times*, January 20, 2017, A1.

39. See Alan Zibel, "Catering to Conflicts: Influence and Self-Dealing at Trump's Businesses," Public Citizen, November 11, 2019, https://www.citizen .org/article/catering-to-conflicts-influence-and-self-dealing-at-trumps-businesses. For the room bookings, see Anita Kumar, "A Trump Hotel Mystery: Giant Reservations Followed by Empty Rooms," *Politico*, October 2, 2019, https://www .politico.com/news/2019/10/02/trump-hotel-empty-rooms-016763. For the Chinese trademarks, see Robert Schlesinger, "Ka-Ching: Donald Trump Is Raking in the Big Bucks from Emoluments, Foreign and Domestic," *US News and World*

Report, March 5, 2018, https://www.usnews.com/opinion/articles/2018-03-05/how-is-donald-trump-profiting-from-the-presidency-let-us-count-the-ways.

40. Anita Kumar, "A Trump Hotel Mystery: Giant Reservations Followed by Empty Rooms," *Politico*, October 2, 2019, https://www.politico.com/news/2019/10/02/trump-hotel-empty-rooms-016763; "Trump's 2300 Conflicts of Interest and Counting," Citizens for Responsibility and Ethics in Washington, August 16, 2019, https://www.citizensforethics.org/2000-trump-conflicts-of-interest-counting; Karl Evers-Hillstrom, "Trump Has Reported Earning an Estimated $2.3 Billion Since Announcing Presidential Run," Open Secrets, May 16, 2019, https://www.opensecrets.org/news/2019/05/trump-reported-2-3-billion-in-income.

41. See Justin Elliott, "Whoops! Jared Kushner Made Even More Mistakes in His Federal Filings," ProPublica, May 3, 2018, https://www.propublica.org/article/whoops-jared-kushner-made-even-more-mistakes-in-his-federal-filings; Richard Painter, Norman Eisen, and Virginia Canter, "Ethics Laws Will Sideline Jared and Ivanka: Experts," *USA Today*, April 3, 2017, https://www.usatoday.com/story/opinion/2017/04/03/ethics-laws-will-sideline-jared-kushner-ivanka-trump-painter-eisen-canter-column/99955864; Jesse Drucker, Eric Lipton, and Maggie Haberman, "Ivanka Trump and Jared Kushner Still Benefiting from Business Empire, Filings Show," *New York Times*, March 31, 2017, A1.

42. See Eric Umansky and Marcelo Rochabrun, "5 Trump Cabinet Members Who've Made False Statements to Congress," ProPublica, March 2, 2017, https://www.propublica.org/article/five-trump-cabinet-members-made-false-statements-to-congress; Jeremy Scahill, "Trump Education Secretary Betsy DeVos Lied to the Senate," *The Intercept*, January 18, 2017, https://theintercept.com/2017/01/18/trump-education-nominee-betsy-devos-lied-to-the-senate; Ted Mann and Brody Mullins, "Transportation Secretary Still Owns Stock She Pledged to Divest," *Wall Street Journal*, May 28, 2019, https://www.wsj.com/articles/transportation-secretary-still-owns-stock-she-pledged-to-divest-11559035921; Dan Alexander, "Wilbur Ross Confirms He Made False Statement," *Forbes*, June 18, 2018, https://www.forbes.com/sites/danalexander/2018/06/18/following-forbes-report-wilbur-ross-confirms-filing-false-statement/#3199e0a91d0e; David A. Graham, "The Unchecked Corruption of Trump's Cabinet," *Atlantic*, May 20, 2019, https://www.theatlantic.com/ideas/archive/2019/05/watchdog-ben-carsons-table-spending-broke-law/589804.

43. "President Trump's Ten Biggest Falsehoods of 2018," NBC News, December 26, 2018, https://www.nbcnews.com/politics/politics-news/president-donald-trump-s-10-biggest-falsehoods-2018-n949121.

44. "AP Fact Check: Trump's Fog of Misinformation on Trade," PBS, May 11, 2019, https://www.pbs.org/newshour/economy/ap-fact-check-trumps-fog-of-misinformation-on-trade.

45. National Resources Defense Council, "Trump Lies," continually updated at https://www.nrdc.org/trump-lies.

46. Nicholas Bagley, "Some of Trump's Most Devious Lies Are About Health Care," *New York Times*, November 12, 2019, https://www.nytimes .com/2019/11/12/opinion/trump-healthcare.html?smid=nytcore-ios-share.

47. Rod Schoonover, "The White House Blocked My Report on Climate Change and National Security," *New York Times*, July 30, 2019, https://www.ny times.com/2019/07/30/opinion/trump-climate-change.html.

48. See Michael D. Shear and Zolan Kanno-Youngs, "Trump Insists He Was Right About Hurricane Dorian Heading for Alabama," *New York Times*, September 4, 2019, https://www.nytimes.com/2019/09/04/us/politics/trump-hurricane -alabama-sharpie.html; Daniel Dale and Brandon Miller, "Anatomy of a Fiasco: A Detailed Timeline of Trump's Alabama Map Meltdown," CNN, September 6, 2019, https://www.cnn.com/2019/09/06/politics/fact-check-timeline-of-trumps-alabama -dorian-map-fiasco/index.html.

49. Glenn Kessler, Salvador Rizzo, and Meg Kelly, "President Trump Made 8,158 False or Misleading Claims in His First Two Years," *Washington Post*, January 21, 2019, https://www.washingtonpost.com/politics/2019/01/21/president -trump-made-false-or-misleading-claims-his-first-two-years.

50. German Lopez, "Donald Trump's Long History of Racism, from the 1970s to 2019," Vox, July 19, 2019, https://www.vox.com/2016/7/25/12270880 /donald-trump-racist-racism-history.

51. Jordan Weissman, "It Is Very Bad That Our President Reportedly Lied About Trade Negotiations with China," *Slate*, August 30, 2019, https://slate.com /business/2019/08/trump-phone-call-china-trade.html.

52. See PRRI staff, "Fractured Nation."

53. For net immigration and crime figures, see Christopher Ingraham, "There's No Immigration Crisis, and These Charts Prove It," *Washington Post*, June 1, 2018, https:// www.washingtonpost.com/news/wonk/wp/2018/06/21/theres-no-immigration-crisis -and-these-charts-prove-it. For immigration's relationship to terrorism, see Veronique de Rugy, "The Facts About Immigration and Crime," American Institute for Economic Research, September 3, 2018, https://www.aier.org/article/facts-about-immigration -and-crime; "DOJ, DHS Report: Three out of Four Individuals Convicted of International Terrorism and Terrorism-Related Offenses Were Foreign-Born," January 16, 2018, US Department of Justice, Office of Public Affairs, https://www.justice.gov/opa /pr/doj-dhs-report-three-out-four-individuals-convicted-international-terrorism-and -terrorism. For the Justice Department's lack of records, see Benjamin Wittes, "The Justice Department Finds 'No Responsive Records' to Support a Trump Speech," Lawfare, July 31, 2018, https://www.lawfareblog.com/justice-department-finds-no-responsive -records-support-trump-speech. For the Trump administration's refusal to admit this, see Dan De Luce and Julia Ainsley, "Trump Admin Rejected Report Showing Refugees Did Not Pose Major Security Threat," NBC News, September 5, 2018, https://www .nbcnews.com/politics/immigration/trump-admin-rejected-report-showing-refugees -did-not-pose-major-n906681. And for accurate figures on who commits acts of

terrorism, see "Murder and Extremism in the United States in 2018," Anti-Defamation League, https://www.adl.org/murder-and-extremism-2018.

54. Linda Qui, "Trump's Baseless Claim About Prayer Rugs Found at the Border," *New York Times*, January 19, A13.

55. Thomas Kaplan, "How the Trump Campaign Used Facebook Ads to Amplify His 'Invasion' Claim," *New York Times*, August 5, 2019, A13.

56. Jeremy W. Peters, Michael M. Grynbaum, Keith Collins, Rich Harris, and Rumsey Taylor, "How the El Paso Killer Echoed the Incendiary Words of Conservative Media Stars," *New York Times*, August 11, 2019, A1.

57. Ike Levine, "'No Blame?' ABC News Finds 36 Cases Invoking 'Trump' in Connection with Violence, Threats, Alleged Assaults," ABC News, August 14, 2019, https://abcnews.go.com/Politics/blame-abc-news-finds-17-cases-invoking-trump/story?id=58912889.

58. Salena Zito, "Taking Trump Seriously, Not Literally," *Atlantic*, September 23, 2016, https://www.theatlantic.com/politics/archive/2016/09/trump-makes-his-case-in-pittsburgh/501335.

59. David Frum, "The Shame and Disgrace Will Linger," *Atlantic*, August 10, 2019, https://www.theatlantic.com/ideas/archive/2019/08/trumps-conspiracy-theory-about-clintons-and-epstein/595915.

60. Ben Rhodes, "Trump's Iran Policy Is Rooted in Lies—the Kind That Got Us into the Iraq War," *Washington Post*, May 16, 2019, https://www.washingtonpost.com/outlook/2019/05/16/trumps-iran-policy-is-rooted-lies-kind-that-got-us-into-iraq-war.

61. Matthew Choi, "Trump Claims His Intel Chiefs Were 'Misquoted' When They Publicly Broke with Him," *Politico*, January 31, 2019, https://www.politico.com/story/2019/01/31/trump-intelligence-leaders-haspel-coats-1140281.

62. Samantha Vinograd, "Why Trump's Ratcliffe Nomination Was Such a Disaster," CNN, August 4, 2019, https://www.cnn.com/2019/08/04/opinions/trump-ratcliffe-dni-national-security-failure-vinograd/index.html.

63. For Trump and Kim, see Jessica Tuchman Matthews, "Singapore Sham," Carnegie Endowment for International Peace, July 31, 2018, https://carnegieendowment.org/2018/07/31/singapore-sham-pub-76944, originally published in *New York Review of Books*, August 16, 2018, https://www.nybooks.com/articles/2018/08/16/singapore-sham; Donald Trump, Twitter, June 13, 2018, 2:56 a.m., https://twitter.com/realdonaldtrump/status/1006837823469735936. For the murders, see Shinhye Kang and Jinye Lee, "North Korea Executed Envoy over Trump-Kim Summit, Chosun Reports," Bloomberg, May 31, 2019, https://www.bloomberg.com/news/articles/2019-05-30/north-korea-envoy-executed-over-trump-kim-summit-chosun-reports. For North Korea's nuclear program, see Joby Warrick, "North Korea Never Halted Efforts to Build Powerful New Weapons, Experts Say," *Washington Post*, December 23, 2019, https://www.washingtonpost.com/national-security/north-korea-never-halted-efforts-to-build-powerful-new

-weapons-experts-say/2019/12/23/a820327e-259d-11ea-b2ca-2e72667c1741_
story.html. For the attack in Baghdad, see Michael Crowley, Falih Hassan, and
Eric Schmitt, "U.S. Strike in Iraq Kills Commander of Iranian Force," *New York
Times*, January 3, 2020, A1. For Pence's falsehood about Suleimani, see Maanvi
Singh, "Mike Pence Pushes 9/11 Conspiracy Theories to Justify Suleimani Killing,"
Guardian, January 3, 2020, https://www.theguardian.com/us-news/2020/jan/03
/mike-pence-iran-911-suleimani. For Trump's New Year's Eve party chitchat, see
Dominique Mosbergen, "Trump Shrugs Off Kim Jong Un's Nuclear Testing Threat:
'He Likes Me,'" *Huffington Post*, January 1, 2020, https://www.huffpost.com
/entry/trump-kim-jong-un-nuclear-testing-threat_n_5e0c5efec5b6b5a713b4dca4.

64. For the early FBI panic over Trump, see Sharon LaFraniere, "A Momentous
Week in May: Book Details Early Days of Russia Inquiry," *New York Times*, October
6, 2019, https://www.nytimes.com/2019/10/06/us/politics/russia-investigation-book
.html. See also Michael D. Shear and Adam Goldman, "Michael Flynn Pleads Guilty
to Lying to the F.B.I. and Will Cooperate with Russia Inquiry," *New York Times*, December 2, 2017, A1; Katelyn Polantz and Marshall Cohen, "The Mueller Report: A
Catalog of 77 Trump Team Lies and Falsehoods," CNN, April 30, 2019, https://www
.cnn.com/2019/04/30/politics/mueller-report-trump-team-lies-falsehoods/index.html.

65. See Jordan Fabian and Brett Samuels, "Trump Escalates Attacks on Mueller,"
The Hill, May 30, 2019, https://thehill.com/homenews/administration/446130-trump
-escalates-attacks-on-mueller; Steve Benen, "Trump Insists There Was 'an Attempted
Overthrow' of US Government," MSNBC, April 26, 2019, www.msnbc.com/rachel
-maddow-show/trump-insists-there-was-attempted-overthrow-us-government;
Donald Trump, Trump Twitter Archive, www.trumptwitterarchive.com/archive
/Witch%20Hunt.

66. "Full Transcript of Mueller's Statement on Russia Investigation," *New York
Times*, May 29, 2019, https://www.nytimes.com/2019/05/29/us/politics/mueller
-transcript.html.

67. See Benjamin Wittes, "The Catastrophic Performance of Bill Barr," *Atlantic*,
May 2, 2019, https://www.theatlantic.com/ideas/archive/2019/05/bill-barrs-perfor
mance-was-catastrophic/588574; George T. Conway III, "Unfit for Office," *Atlantic*,
September 2019, https://www.theatlantic.com/ideas/archive/2019/10/george-conway
-trump-unfit-office/599128. The quotes attributed to Dowd are Woodward's para-
phrasing as quoted in Conway's article.

68. Donald Trump, Twitter, May 30, 2019, 4:21 a.m., https://twitter.com/real
donaldtrump/status/1134057302821150722.

69. For the "21 lies," see Marshall Cohen, "Fact-Checking Trump's Flurry of
Falsehoods and Lies After Mueller Declined to Exonerate Him," CNN, May 31, 2019,
https://edition.cnn.com/2019/05/30/politics/fact-checking-trump-mueller-claims
/index.html. See also Peter Baker and Nicholas Fandos, "Reaction to Mueller Report Divides Along Partisan Lines," *New York Times*, April 19, 2019, A1; Chuck

Todd, Twitter, July 24, 2019, 9:16 a.m., https://twitter.com/chucktodd/status/1154062809338195968.

70. Daniel Dale and Tara Subramaniam, "Trump's Ukraine Dishonesty Barrage Continues. He Made 96 False Claims Last Week," CNN, October 30, 2019, https://www.cnn.com/2019/10/30/politics/fact-check-trump-96-false-claims-ukraine/index.html.

71. See Louis Jacobson, "Fact-Checking Joe Biden, Hunter Biden, and Ukraine," PolitiFact, May 7, 2019, https://www.politifact.com/truth-o-meter/statements/2019/may/07/viral-image/fact-checking-joe-biden-hunter-biden-and-ukraine; Michael D. Shear and Maggie Haberman, "'Do Us a Favor': Call Shows Trump's Interest in Using U.S. Power for His Gain," *New York Times*, September 25, 2019, https://www.nytimes.com/2019/09/25/us/politics/ukraine-transcript-trump.html.

72. "Memorandum of Telephone Conversation," "Subject: Telephone Conversation with President Zelenskyy of Ukraine," July 25, 2019, White House, https://www.whitehouse.gov/wp-content/uploads/2019/09/Unclassified09.2019.pdf.

73. Mike McIntyre, Karen Yourish, and Larry Buchanan, "In Trump's Twitter Feed: Conspiracy Mongers, Racists and Spies," *New York Times*, November 2, 2019, https://www.nytimes.com/interactive/2019/11/02/us/politics/trump-twitter-disinformation.html. For Trump's admission regarding Putin, see Shane Harris, Josh Dawsey, and Carol D. Leonnig, "Former White House Officials Say They Feared Putin Influenced the President's Views on Ukraine and 2016 Campaign," *Washington Post*, December 19, 2019, A1.

74. Shear et al., "How Trump Reshaped the Presidency"; Dave Alba, "Debunking 4 Viral Rumors About the Bidens and Ukraine," *New York Times*, October 29, 2019, https://www.nytimes.com/2019/10/29/business/media/fact-check-biden-ukraine-burisma-china-hunter.html.

75. See Donald Trump, Twitter, June 22, 2017, 7:08 a.m., https://twitter.com/realdonaldtrump/status/877891129194102785; Craig Timberg, Drew Harwell, and Ellen Nakashima, "In Call to Ukraine's President, Trump Revived a Favorite Conspiracy Theory About the DNC Hack," *Washington Post*, September 25, 2019, https://www.washingtonpost.com/technology/2019/09/25/trumps-mention-crowdstrike-call-with-ukraines-president-recalls-russian-hack-dnc; Liam Quinn, "Trump Tells 'Hannity' He Wants AG Barr to 'Find Out What Is Going On' with Potential Ties Between Hillary Clinton, Steele Dossier and Ukraine," Fox News, October 21, 2019, https://www.foxnews.com/media/trump-hannity-barr-ukraine-hillary-clinton-steele-dossier.

76. Carol D. Leonnig, Tom Hamburger, and Greg Miller, "White House Lawyer Moved Transcript of Trump Call to Classified Server After Ukraine Adviser Raised Alarms," *Washington Post*, October 30, 2019, https://www.washingtonpost.com/politics/white-house-lawyer-moved-transcript-of-trump-call-to-classified-server-after-ukraine-adviser-raised-alarms/2019/10/30/ba0fbdb6-fb4e-11e9-8190-6be4deb56e01_story.html; Natasha Bertrand, "Testimony: White House Lawyer

Told Vindman Not to Discuss Ukraine Call," *Politico*, November 1, 2019, https://www.politico.com/news/2019/11/01/white-house-vindman-ukraine-call-063892. The email to the Pentagon can be seen at "Liveblog: Digging into the #Ukrainedocs," Center for Public Integrity, December 21, 2019, https://publicintegrity.org/national-security/digging-ukrainedocs-omb-foia.

77. James Gordon Meek and Anne Flaherty, "2nd Whistleblower Comes Forward After Speaking with IG: Attorney," ABC News, October 6, 2019, https://abcnews.go.com/Politics/2nd-whistleblower-forward-speaking-ig-attorney/story?id=66092396; Eugene Kiely, Lori Robertson, and D'Angelo Gore, "The Whistleblower Complaint Timeline," FactCheck.org, https://www.factcheck.org/2019/09/the-whistleblower-complaint-timeline.

78. Carol Leonnig, Craig Timberg, and Drew Harwell, "Odd Markings, Ellipses Fuel Doubts About the 'Rough Transcript' of Trump's Ukraine Call," *Washington Post*, October 2, 2019, https://www.washingtonpost.com/technology/2019/10/03/odd-markings-ellipses-fuel-doubts-about-rough-transcript-trumps-ukraine-call; "Mike Pence Is Reliably, Relentlessly Wrong," *Washington Post*, October 29, 2019, https://www.washingtonpost.com/opinions/global-opinions/mike-pence-spews-indefensible-falsehoods/2019/10/29/4943b28a-fa73-11e9-8906-ab6b60de9124_story.html.

79. See Leonnig et al., "Odd Markings"; Julian E. Barnes, Nicholas Fandos, and Danny Hakim, "White House Ukraine Expert Sought to Correct Transcript of Trump Call," *New York Times*, October 29, 2019, https://www.nytimes.com/2019/10/29/us/politics/alexander-vindman-trump-ukraine.html.

80. See Kevin Breuninger, "Trump Says China Should Investigate the Bidens, Doubles Down on Ukraine Probe," CNBC, October 3, 2019, https://www.cnbc.com/2019/10/03/trump-calls-for-ukraine-china-to-investigate-the-bidens.html; Aron Rupar, "Team Trump's Efforts to Spin Mulvaney's Quid Pro Quo Confession Are Not Going Well," Vox, October 21, 2019, https://www.vox.com/2019/10/21/20924687/mick-mulvaney-fox-news-sunday-ukraine-quid-pro-quo-mike-pompeo-this-week; "Mick Mulvaney Briefing Transcript: 'Get Over It' Regarding Ukraine Quid Pro Quo," Rev, October 17, 2019, https://www.rev.com/blog/mick-mulvaney-briefing-transcript-get-over-it-regarding-ukraine-quid-pro-quo.

81. Ben Gittleson and Elizabeth Thomas, "Trump Refuses to Explain What He Wanted Ukraine's President to Do About the Bidens," ABC News, October 2, 2019, https://abcnews.go.com/Politics/trump-coup-taking-place-democrats-push-forward-impeachment/story?id=66001006; Eli Stokols, "Listen: Audio of Trump Discussing Whistleblower at Private Event," *Los Angeles Times*, September 26, 2019, https://www.latimes.com/politics/story/2019-09-26/trump-at-private-breakfast-who-gave-the-whistle-blower-the-information-because-thats-almost-a-spy; "Letter from President Donald J. Trump to the Speaker of the House of Representatives," December 17, 2019, https://www.whitehouse.gov/briefings-statements/letter-president-donald-j-trump-speaker-house-representatives; Glenn Kessler, "Fact-Checking

President Trump's Impeachment Letter to Pelosi," *Washington Post*, December 18, 2019, https://www.washingtonpost.com/politics/2019/12/18/fact-checking-president-trumps-impeachment-letter-pelosi; Daniel Dale and Tara Subramaniam, "Fact Check: Trump's Wild Letter to Pelosi Is Filled with False and Misleading Claims," CNN, December 17, 2019, https://www.cnn.com/2019/12/17/politics/fact-check -trump-impeachment-letter-to-pelosi/index.html; "Read Trump's Letter to Pelosi Protesting Impeachment," *New York Times*, December 17, 2019, https://www.ny times.com/interactive/2019/12/17/us/politics/trump-pelosi-letter.html, among many other such fact-checks of this letter; as well as Glenn Kessler, Salvador Rizzo, and Meg Kelly, "President Trump Has Made 15,413 False or Misleading Claims over 1,055 Days," *Washington Post*, December 16, 2019, https://www.washingtonpost .com/politics/2019/12/16/president-trump-has-made-false-or-misleading-claims -over-days; Annie Karni and Maggie Haberman, "Trump Has a Habit of Quoting His Allies on Twitter Saying Things They Never Said," *New York Times*, December 20, 2019, A19.

82. For Kennedy, see *Meet the Press*, NBC News, December 1, 2019, https://www .nbcnews.com/meet-the-press/meet-press-december-1-2019-n1093781. For Cruz, see *Meet the Press*, NBC News, December 9, 2019, https://www.nbcnews.com/meet-the -press/meet-press-december-8-2019-n1097796. For Todd's confession, see Peter Wade, "How Disinformation Spreads, According to Chuck Todd," *Rolling Stone*, December 20, 2019, https://www.rollingstone.com/politics/politics-news/how-disinformation -spreads-according-to-chuck-todd-interview-929912.

83. Natasha Bertrand, "Trump's Attacks Fuel Alarm That Whistleblower Protections Fall Short," *Politico*, October 9, 2019, https://www.politico.com /news/2019/10/09/trump-ukraine-whistleblower-attacks-043567; Zachary Cohen, "Whistleblower's Legal Team Says They Have Received Death Threats," CNN, October 30, 2019, https://www.cnn.com/politics/live-news/impeachment-inquiry -10-30-2019/h_79f2a3bb9ff5eaedf5d6104aaa25f62b; Ryan Mac, "Trump Retweeted the Name of the Alleged Whistleblower," BuzzFeed, December 28, 2019, https:// www.buzzfeednews.com/article/ryanmac/trump-whistleblower-name-retweet; Olivia Nuzzi, "A Conversation with Rudy Giuliani over Bloody Marys at the Mark Hotel," *New York Magazine*, December 23, 2019, http://nymag.com /intelligencer/2019/12/a-conversation-with-rudy-giuliani-over-bloody-marys.html; Michael Calderone, "CNN Defends New Contributor Sean Duffy While Anchors Decry His 'Anti-Immigrant Bigotry,'" *Politico*, October 29, 2019, https://www .politico.com/news/2019/10/29/cnn-sean-duffy-anti-immigrant-bigotry-061434. For John Yoo and the torture memos, see Andrew Cohen, "The Torture Memos, 10 Years Later," *Atlantic*, February 6, 2012, https://www.theatlantic.com/national /archive/2012/02/the-torture-memos-10-years-later/252439.

84. Michelle Goldberg, "Trump's Claims About Biden Aren't 'Unsupported.' They're Lies," *New York Times*, September 30, 2019, https://www.nytimes.com /2019/09/30/opinion/trump-ukraine-republican.html.

85. Michael D. Shear, "The Breach Widens as Congress Nears a Partisan Impeachment," *New York Times*, December 13, 2019, A1; Peter Baker, "Clinton's Impeachment Was Suspenseful. Trump's Grip on G.O.P. Means His Won't Be," *New York Times*, December 15, 2019, A1.

86. Baker, "Clinton's Impeachment."

87. Jeff Mason and Patricia Zengerle, "Consequential, but Dull: Trump Impeachment Hearings Begin Without a Bang," Reuters, November 13, 2019, https://www.reuters.com/article/us-usa-trump-impeachment-response/consequential-but-dull-trump-impeachment-hearings-begin-without-a-bang-idUSKBN1XO059; Jonathan Allen, "Plenty of Substance but Little Drama on First Day of Impeachment Hearings," NBC News, November 13, 2019, https://www.nbcnews.com/politics/trump-impeachment-inquiry/plenty-substance-little-drama-first-day-impeachment-hearings-n1081926.

88. Alex Eisenstadt, "Trump Lures GOP Senators on Impeachment with Cold Cash," October 31, 2019, https://www.politico.com/news/2019/10/31/trump-impeachment-senators-donor-062084; Jason Lemon, "Trump Is Committing 'Felony Bribery' by Giving Fundraising Cash to GOP Senators Ahead of Impeachment Trial, Ex-Bush Ethics Lawyer," *Newsweek*, October 31, 2019, https://www.newsweek.com/trump-committing-felony-bribery-giving-fundraising-cash-gop-senators-ahead-impeachment-trial-1468946.

89. Glenn Kessler, Salvador Rizzo, and Meg Kelly, "President Trump has made 16,241 false or misleading claims in his first three years," *Washington Post*, January 20, 2020, https://www.washingtonpost.com/politics/2020/01/20/president-trump-made-16241-false-or-misleading-claims-his-first-three-years/; Michael M. Grynbaum, "Citing Falsehoods, Nicolle Wallace of MSNBC Cut Away from Trump's Remarks," *New York Times*, September 25, 2019, https://www.nytimes.com/2019/09/25/business/media/msnbc-nicolle-wallace-trump.html; "'We Hate to Do This, but Trump Isn't Telling the Truth': Watch Nicolle Wallace Cut Away from Trump Presser," MSNBC, September 25, 2019, https://www.msnbc.com/deadline-white-house/watch/watch-nicolle-wallace-cuts-away-from-trump-we-hate-to-do-this-but-trump-isn-t-telling-the-truth-69905989594?cid=sm_npd_ms_tw_ma.

Conclusion: System Overload

1. See Hannah Arendt, "Truth and Politics," *New Yorker*, February 25, 1967, https://www.newyorker.com/magazine/1967/02/25/truth-and-politics; Hannah Arendt, *The Origins of Totalitarianism* (New York: Harvest Books, 1973 [1951]), 382.

2. Glenn Kessler and Scott Clement, "Trump Routinely Says Things That Aren't True. Few Americans Believe Him," *Washington Post*, December 14, 2018, https://www.washingtonpost.com/graphics/2018/politics/political-knowledge-poll-trump-falsehoods; Arendt, *Origins*, 474; Hannah Arendt, "Preface," *The Origins of Totalitarianism*, 1953 ed., quoted in Paul Mason, "Reading Arendt Is Not

Notes on Conclusion

Enough," *New York Review of Books*, May 2, 2019, https://www.nybooks.com/daily/2019/05/02/reading-arendt-is-not-enough.

3. Regarding the exploitation of anti-Semitism, see, for instance, Mairav Zonszein, "How the Right Has Tried to Rebrand Anti-Semitism," *New York Review of Books*, September 4, 2019, https://www.nybooks.com/daily/2019/09/04/how-the-right-has-tried-to-rebrand-anti-semitism; Jennifer Rubin, "Trump's Anti-Semitic Attacks on American Jews Keep Coming," *Washington Post*, December 9, 2019, https://www.washingtonpost.com/opinions/2019/12/09/trumps-anti-semitic-attacks-american-jews-keep-coming; Eric Alterman, "Trump's Executive Order on Anti-Semitism Isn't About Protecting Jews," *The Nation*, December 19, 2019, https://www.thenation.com/article/executive-order-anti-semitism; Eric Alterman, "Trump's Comments on the 'Disloyalty' of Jews Have a Sordid History," *The Nation*, September 6, 2019, https://www.thenation.com/article/trump-jews-disloyalty; Eric Alterman, "Soros Slander Reveals Anti-Semitism at the Heart of the Far Right," *The Nation*, September 7, 2017, https://www.thenation.com/article/soros-slander-reveals-anti-semitism-at-the-heart-of-the-far-right. See also Cliff Sims, *Team of Vipers: My 500 Extraordinary Days in the Trump White House* (New York: Thomas Dunne, 2019), 168.

4. See Jason Stanley, *How Fascism Works: The Politics of Us and Them* (New York: Random House, 2018).

5. See Christopher R. Browning, "The Suffocation of Democracy," *New York Review of Books*, October 25, 2018, https://www.nybooks.com/articles/2018/10/25/suffocation-of-democracy. Regarding primaries and caucuses, see Perry Bacon Jr., "Trump Completed His Takeover of the GOP in 2019," FiveThirtyEight, December 23, 2019, https://fivethirtyeight.com/features/trump-completed-his-takeover-of-the-gop-in-2019.

6. "Read the Transcript of the Conversation Among GOP Leaders Obtained by the Post," *Washington Post*, n.d., https://apps.washingtonpost.com/g/documents/national/read-the-transcript-of-the-conversation-among-gop-leaders-obtained-by-the-post/2437.

7. Stephen Kotkin, "American Hustle," *Foreign Affairs*, May 2019, https://www.foreignaffairs.com/articles/2019-05-21/american-hustle; Steven Levitsky and Daniel Ziblatt, *How Democracies Die* (New York: Crown, 2018), 201.

8. William P. Davis, "'Enemy of the People': Trump Breaks Out This Phrase During Moments of Peak Criticism," *New York Times*, July 19, 2018, https://www.nytimes.com/2018/07/19/business/media/trump-media-enemy-of-the-people.html.

9. For the *Capital Gazette* attack, see Kathy Frankovic, "Most Americans Don't See the Media as the Enemy of the People," YouGov, August 13, 2018, https://today.yougov.com/topics/politics/articles-reports/2018/08/13/most-americans-dont-see-media-enemy-people. See also Timothy Bella, "Trump Blasts CNN in 3 a.m. Tweet for 'Blaming Me' for Bombs," *Washington Post*, October 26, 2018, https://www.washingtonpost.com/nation/2018/10/26/trump-blasts-cnn-am-tweet-blaming-me-bombings; Donald Trump, Twitter, October 25, 2018, 4:18 a.m., https://twitter

383

.com/realdonaldtrump/status/1055418269270716418. For the 2018 and 2019 Twitter statistics, see Michael M. Grynbaum, "After Another Year of Trump Attacks, 'Ominous Signs' for the American Press," *New York Times*, December 30, 2019, https://www.nytimes.com/2019/12/30/business/media/trump-media-2019.html.

10. David Remnick, "Trump and the Enemies of the People," *New Yorker*, August 15, 2018, https://www.newyorker.com/news/daily-comment/trump-and-the-enemies-of-the-people; Brent D. Griffiths, "Trump on Gianforte: 'Any Guy Who Can Do a Body Slam Is My Kind of Guy,'" *Politico*, https://www.politico.com/story/2018/10/18/trump-gianforte-body-slam-praise-915047; David Nakumura, "Trump Appears to Promote Violence Against CNN with Tweet," *Washington Post*, July 2, 2017, https://www.washingtonpost.com/news/post-politics/wp/2017/07/02/trump-appears-to-promote-violence-against-cnn-with-tweet. For the video, see Franco Ordonez, "White House Distances Itself from Violent Fake Video Targeting Media and Critics," NPR, October 14, 2019, https://www.npr.org/2019/10/14/770076816/white-house-distances-itself-from-violent-fake-video-targeting-media-and-critics.

11. For Baker's quotes, see Paul Fahri, "New York Times Demotes Editor After Twitter Controversy as Paper Takes Fire from Left, Right and Within," *Washington Post*, August 13, 2019, https://www.washingtonpost.com/lifestyle/style/new-york-times-demotes-editor-after-twitter-controversy-as-paper-takes-fire-from-left-right-and-within/2019/08/13/d0cb58fa-bde4-11e9-a5c6-1e74f7ec4a93_story.html.

12. Peter Baker, "A Gyrating Economy, and Trump's Volatile Approach to It, Raise Alarm," *New York Times*, August 23, 2019, https://www.nytimes.com/2019/08/23/us/politics/trump-economy-trade.html; Peter Baker, "Rule 1 at the G-7 Meeting? Don't Get You-Know-Who Mad," *New York Times*, August 25, 2019, https://www.nytimes.com/2019/08/25/world/europe/trump-g7-allies.html. For Trump's quote, see Nikki Schwab, "Trump Lashes Out at US Media amid Tense G-7 Summit," *New York Post*, August 25, 2019, https://nypost.com/2019/08/25/trump-lashes-out-at-us-media-amid-tense-g-7-summit.

13. For Marty Baron, see Nicole Corea, "Washington Post Editor Marty Baron Says Journalists Are at Work, Not at War," Aspen Institute, October 6, 2017, https://www.aspeninstitute.org/blog-posts/marty-baron-says-journalists-work-not-war.

14. See Remnick, "Trump and the Enemies of the People"; Sam Stein, "New Poll: 43 Percent of Republicans Want to Give Trump the Power to Shut Down Media," *Daily Beast*, August 7, 2018, https://www.thedailybeast.com/new-poll-43-of-republicans-want-to-give-trump-the-power-to-shut-down-media.

15. For Trump's quotes, see John Nichols, "Trump Thinks the Emoluments Clause Is Phony," *The Nation*, October 22, 2019, https://www.thenation.com/article/trump-impeachment-emoluments; Cristina Cabrera, "Trump Claims Article 2 Gives Him 'The Right to Do Whatever I Want as President,'" TPM, July 23, 2019, https://talkingpointsmemo.com/news/trump-claim-article-2-right-whatever-want-president; Thomas J. Edsall, "Will Trump Ever Leave the White House?" *New York Times*, October 2, 2019, https://www.nytimes.com/2019/10/02/opinion/trump

-leave-white-house.html. The constitutional clause in question reads: "No Person holding any Office of Profit or Trust under [the United States], shall, without the Consent of the Congress, accept of any present, Emolument, Office, or Title, of any kind whatever, from any King, Prince, or foreign State."

16. Jane Mayer, "The Making of the Fox News White House," *New Yorker*, March 4, 2019, https://www.newyorker.com/magazine/2019/03/11/the -making-of-the-fox-news-white-house; Jonathan Chait, "Trump's Attack on Amazon May Be His Most Egregious Abuse of Power Yet," *New York*, December 18, 2019, http://nymag.com/intelligencer/2019/12/donald-trumps-war-on-journalism -and-his-attack-on-amazon.html.

17. Elizabeth Goitein, "The Alarming Scope of the President's Emergency Powers," *Atlantic*, January/February 2019, https://www.theatlantic.com/magazine /archive/2019/01/presidential-emergency-powers/576418.

18. For Baquet, see Gabriel Snyder, "The Readers vs. the Masthead," *Columbia Journalism Review*, August 6, 2019, https://www.cjr.org/public_editor/nyt -headline-trump-mass-shootings.php. For the *Times* on Hitler, see Zack Beauchamp, "The New York Times' First Article About Hitler's Rise Is Absolutely Stunning," Vox, March 2016, https://www.vox.com/2015/2/11/8016017/ny-times-hitler. For Edwin Edwards, see Sean Sullivan, "The Greatest Quotes of Edwin Edwards," *Washington Post*, March 17, 2014, https://www.washingtonpost.com/news/the-fix /wp/2014/02/20/edwin-edwardss-greatest-hits-crooks-super-pacs-and-viagra.

19. James Comey, "How Trump Co-opts Leaders Like Bill Barr," *New York Times*, May 1, 2019, https://www.nytimes.com/2019/05/01/opinion/william-barr -testimony.html.

INDEX

Index

Index

Trump's abuse of executive power, 315–316

Trump's lies about his business holdings, 283–284

Trump's war on immigrants, 287

US involvement in Angola, 149–150

Conkling, Rosco, 234

Constitution, US, 21, 46–47, 234, 282–283

contras, Nicaraguan, 170–175, 178

Conway, George, 196

Conway, Kellyanne, 196, 264, 281, 302

cornpone syndrome, 154

corruption
  among members of Congress, 197–198
  British oil monopoly in Iran, 73–74
  Harding's administration, 93
  Iran-contra affair, 174, 178
  Nixon's impending indictment, 141–142
  Trump administration, 282–284, 317–318
  Trump's attack on Biden, 296

coups d'état, US involvement in, 74–83, 114–115, 133–138

Cowles, Jack, 117

Crane, Michael, 210

Creel, George, 43, 77

crime, Trump linking immigrants to, 286–287

Cronkite, Walter, 182–183

Crosby, Bing, 95–96

CrowdStrike company, 297–298, 299

Crowe, William, 182

Crowley, Monica, 265–266

Crusius, Patrick Wood, 288

Cruz, Ted, 301–302

C-Span survey, 3–4

Cuba, 33–34, 80, 87–88, 92, 97–103, 135, 167

Cuban Missile Crisis, 87–88, 92, 97–103

Curry, Betty, 188

cyberhacking, 297

Czolgosz, Leon, 36

Dale, Daniel, 271–272, 295

Dallek, Robert, 57, 90, 91, 92

Deakin, James, 153

Dean, John, 140–142

death squads, Salvadoran, 167–169

Debs, Eugene V., 42

decisionmaking process, the effect of chronic lying on, 4

DeLay, Tom, 198

democracy
  corporate interests threatening, 233–234
  lies undermining, 307–308
  Nixon's involvement in Chile's coup, 133–138
  parallels between Trump and European fascism, 308–311
  Trump's abuse of presidential power as threat to, 316–318
  Trump's lies as threat to, 244
  Trump's weaponized disinformation threatening, 303
  US and Britain undermining Iran's Mosaddegh, 74–75
  US coups in Indonesia and Africa, 81–83
  US overthrow of Guatemala's president, 76–80

Democratic Republic of the Congo (DRC), 81–82

desegregation and busing, Trump's ignorance of, 243

Dewey, George, 35

Diem, Ngo Dinh, 129–130

Dirksen, Everett, 127

disinformation, defining, 11–12

Dobrynin, Anatola, 101

Dole, Robert, 181

dollar diplomacy, 39–40

Dominican Republic, right-wing coup in, 114–115

Douglas, Stephen, 28–29

Dowd, John, 293–294

Dowd, Matthew, 230

Downie, Len, Jr., 156

Dreams from My Father (Obama), 222

drone strikes, 216, 219, 291

Index

Index

Index

Index

Nathan, James, 102
national interests and security
  Bush II lies justifying the war in Iraq,
    209–210
  Carter's lies about CIA covert
    operations, 158–159
  Clinton's lies in the name of, 191–193
  Cold War lies in the name of, 60–61
  Cuban Missile Crisis, 87–88
  Eisenhower's lies perpetuating the
    Cold War, 72–73
  as justification for presidential lies,
    7–9
  media scrutiny of Obama's honesty,
    219–220
  origins of and justification for the
    Cold War, 66–67
  the Panama Canal, 38
  Reagan's justification for Central
    American intervention, 166–167
  Trump's enormous presidential
    power, 316–317
  Trump's racism affecting views and
    foreign policy, 289–290
  US overthrow of Guatemala's
    president, 77–80
National Security Archive, 217
Native Americans, 23–24, 31–32
nativist policies, 49
Navarro, Peter, 280
Nicaragua, 170–171
Nixon, Richard, 59
  campaign against JFK, 89–90, 91
  Ford's succession, 143–144
  lies about genocide in East Pakistan,
    132–133
  media skepticism of presidential
    honesty, 153–154
  motives for presidential lies, 244–245
  obsession with public image,
    122–124
  personality and demeanor, 120–122
  racism and hatred, 124–126
  reputation for lying, 4, 7
  Sinatra's political support, 96
  US involvement in Chile's coup,
    134–138

war as a tool for reelection, 129–132
  Watergate scandal, 138–142
North, Oliver, 175
North Korea, 144–145, 289, 290–291
nuclear capability, 1
  Bush's dishonesty over the war in
    Iraq, 211–214
  Clinton's lies about Saddam's WMD,
    192–193
  Japanese surrender in World
    War II, 56
  racism influencing Trump's policies,
    289–291
  Reagan's muddle over, 164
  Truman's decisions on the Manhattan
    Project, 61–62
Nugent, Ted, 224
nuns, rape and murder of, in El
    Salvador, 167–168

Obama, Barack
  Affordable Care Act, 231–233
  corporate interests attacking, 233–237
  election campaign, 216
  increased political polarization during
    the 2016 campaign, 237–240
  Iran, 289–290
  media exclusion, 274
  media scrutiny of his honesty,
    218–220
  Monica Crowley's attacks on,
    265–266
  renaissance of racism after the
    election of, 284–285
  Republican National Convention
    misrepresentation, 226–230
  right-wing media attack on, 220–226,
    257
  Trump undermining Russian policy,
    292
  Trump's exploitation of social media,
    275
objectivity, journalistic, 9–11
Ocasio-Cortez, Alexandria, 278
oil industry, 74–75, 77, 80–81
O'Keefe, James, 221, 280
Oklobdzija, Stan, 235

398

Index

Index

Index

ERIC ALTERMAN is a CUNY Distinguished Professor of English at Brooklyn College and "The Liberal Media" columnist for *The Nation*. In the past, he has been a Senior Fellow of the Center for American Progress, the World Policy Institute, and the Nation Institute; a columnist for *Rolling Stone*, *Mother Jones*, *The Guardian*, *The Forward*, *Moment*, the *Daily Beast*, and the *Sunday Express* (London); and a contributor to the *New*  *Yorker* and the *Atlantic*, among other publications. He has also been named a Media Fellow at the Hoover Institution at Stanford University, a Schusterman Foundation Fellow at Brandeis University, a Fellow of the Society of American Historians, and a member of the Usage Panel of the *American Heritage Dictionary of the English Language*.

Alterman is the author of ten previous books, including the *New York Times* best seller *What Liberal Media? The Truth About Bias and the News*. He is a winner of the George Orwell Prize, the Stephen Crane Literary Award, and the Mirror Award for media criticism (twice). He holds a PhD in US history from Stanford, an MA in international relations from Yale, and a BA from Cornell. He lives in Manhattan. For more information, please go to ericalterman.com as well as @eric_alterman and https://www.facebook.com/alterman.eric.